MEYER BERGER'S NEW YORK

Meyer Berger's
NEW YORK

With an Introduction by Pete Hamill

Fordham University Press : New York

ISBN 0-8232-2327-2 (hardcover)
ISBN 0-8232-2328-0 (paperback)

Library of Congress Cataloging-in-Publication Data
is available from the Library of Congress

Printed in the United States of America
07 06 05 04 03 5 4 3 2 1

Fordham University Press edition, 2004
First published by Random House, 1960

One day, while discussing the selection of the columns for publication, Mike told me that the book's dedication was to read

"Once More for Mae"

I want to share this honor with his colleagues on the New York *Times,* his friends and his readers. They made many of the columns possible by asking questions, contributing ideas, and sending in unusual items that led to research and adventures "About New York."

Gratefully,
Mae Berger

Contents

Introduction

NOSTALGIA is the most pervasive of all New York emotions. There is ample, sometimes violent evidence in the vast city of human irritation, anger, fear, disappointment, even despair. But if you talk to New Yorkers in the quiet moments, you will hear recurring notes, almost musical, of this more common sentiment. Nostalgia comes to you in phrases that begin *"When I was a kid . . ."* or *"In the old days, we . . ."* Sometimes it doesn't come in words at all, but comes instead from an old song that brings tears to aging eyes. Some vagrant television image—a lost ballpark or a foreign countryside—causes a person on the couch to pause, breathe hard, and slip into reverie for a long moment. The country of nostalgia issues no passports, but it exists all the same.

This is explained in part by the nature of New York itself. From its beginnings almost four centuries ago, the city has been a place of immigrants. At the time of the Dutch, eighteen languages were spoken in the hamlet below Wall Street. Those early settlers made up the now-familiar assembly of idealists, adventurers, opportunists, religious and political refugees, scoundrels on the run from the law, or simple men and women whose own countries had failed or disappointed them and who hoped to begin anew in the great emptiness of North America. In the nineteenth century, as the hamlet grew into a metropolis, the flood of immigrants from Ireland, Italy, Germany, and Eastern Europe began their new lives in New York. They settled. They worked. They had American children.

But as immigrants, they also carried the permanent baggage of memory. They remembered what had driven them to America: starvation, bigotry, tyranny. They had few regrets about finding their various ways to a place where they no longer had to bend knee to a king or fear the midnight arrival of Cossacks. The streets, alas, were not paved with gold. But here, no count or baron could assert his feudal ownership of any young woman. Here, you could go on election day and choose your leaders, and none of them carried regal titles. Their children would know true royalty: Count Basie, Duke Ellington.

And yet, and yet . . . all those new Americans carried memories of what each group called the Old Country. Some remembered the way the sun gilded the hills above Palermo on spring mornings. Others gazed in memory upon sheets of rain washing across the fields of Mayo. Others remembered the dense, close life of the shtetls, with joyous weddings, family feasts, and laughter. In the Old Country, they learned to walk, to run, to play, to sing. But most immigrants, then as now, were young. And for millions of them, youth ended with the cheapest ticket for the hard Atlantic passage to the great port of New York. Memory did not end.

Their nostalgias were visible or audible when I was a boy growing up in Brooklyn after the Second World War. On long summer days, you could hear the many languages of immigrant New York from dozens of radios: sentimental Irish ballads (created for the immigrant market in Tin Pan Alley), Yiddish radio stations (there were at least five of them at their peak), opera from the Italian-language stations (until the invention of the phonograph—and then of radio—the Italian and Sicilian poor had never truly heard opera in the Old Country, because they had neither the money nor the clothes to enter the opera houses). Yiddish and Italian newspapers were on the stand of the candy store two doors from my house. Sometimes the root of nostalgia is language.

The other cause of our permanent New York nostalgia is the impermanence of the city itself. We grow up in certain neighborhoods, where we know most of the people and all of the buildings, including the institutions of saloon, church , synagogue, police station, school. We think they will last forever. Then, while we are not paying attention, they vanish. The Polo Grounds vanishes, and Ebbets Field, and Pennsylvania Station, and a lot of places with smaller claims to grandeur. On Saturday mornings, I used to venture from Brooklyn with my father to Radio Row on Cortlandt Street in Lower Manhattan, where he and hundreds of other New York men moved from stall to stall in search of the elusive tube that would make the radio work again. Later, my younger brothers went there with him in search of television components. Radio Row was a piece of all our interior maps. And then in the late 1960s, it was bulldozed away for the building of the World Trade Center—all its nineteenth-century buildings, its very sidewalks shoveled into the North River to serve as landfill for Battery Park City. Each day in this new century's New York, I take a long walk from my TriBeCa loft along the lovely promenade of Battery Park City, with the river to my right and the Statue of Liberty and Ellis Island off in the distance, and I always remember that deep beneath me are stones and concrete slabs upon which my father once walked, with his sons beside him. Sometimes I hear him singing about the green glens of Antrim.

In some mysterious, elusive ways this splendid collection of Meyer Berger's columns about New York is infused with a double portion of that same powerful nostalgia.

The first variety is Berger's personal, unstated nostalgia for the city of his own youth, inhabited by so many people born, as he was, in the nineteenth century (1898 to be exact). Mike Berger, as he was called by all who knew him, was a grammar-school dropout (aged 12) who served a traditional nineteenth-century apprenticeship: messenger boy, copy boy at the *New York World*, reporter. He found time at age 19 to join the United States army (after memorizing the eye chart to hide his poor eyesight). He went off to the Great War with the 106th Infantry, where he won a Purple Heart and a Silver Star, about which he seldom said anything later. One thing his writing tells us: He was an enlisted man forever. Almost certainly, he was fighting for that part of his country that he knew, where a boy who grew up in dreadful poverty could cross the

Brooklyn Bridge and arrive in Park Row, where all the great newspapers had their offices, and where he could dream of having an
honorable life. I like to think that when Woodrow Wilson talked
about making the world safe for democracy, Mike Berger capital-
ized "World."

In 1928, Berger found his permanent home at the *New York
Times,* where he swiftly became a star—a newspaperman who could
do anything, from breaking front-page news to deeper reporting.
He would stay at the *Times* for the rest of his life, with a year's
interruption as a writer for the *New Yorker* (many of those longer
magazine pieces can be found in his 1942 collection, *The Eight Million*). His basic lifetime subject was the city where he was born, the
place that, as he grew older, became his own Old Country. Like all
New Yorkers who had grown up with the violent hypocrisies of
Prohibition and the more quiet terrors of the Depression, he knew
about the city's various brutalities, its corruptions, its treacherous
secret agendas. He carried a press card, after all, and that compelled him to see what was in front of him. But that compulsion
included seeing the wider context too: the city's grandeur, a quality as invincible as the city's capacity for folly. Mike Berger seems
to have been a man capable of forgiving any sin except cruelty.

Most of his surviving work (many articles were published without bylines and are beyond tracking down) had an understated
grace, permeated by a special quality of lightness. I don't use that
word as a synonym for superficiality. In his 1985 essay on "lightness," the great Italian writer Italo Calvino places it in the context
of underlying myths: "With myths, one should not be in a hurry.
It is better to let them settle into the memory, to stop and dwell
on every detail, to reflect on them without losing touch with their
language of images. The lesson we learn from a myth lies in the
literal narrative, not in what we add to it from the outside."

In the spring of 1953, Berger resumed writing his "About New
York" column for the *Times.* An earlier version had been cancelled
with the advent of World War II because of paper rationing and
Berger's own unease about the column's appropriateness while so
many people were dying. During wars, the front page is everything. In 1953, when he turned his gaze upon the city, its overlap-
ping secrets, its details, Berger was full of honors. He had won a

Pulitzer Prize and, probably more important to him, the respect and affection of his fellow reporters. But the mature Berger of 1953 also embraced the underlying myth of New York, which was settled into his memory. For him, as for so many children of immigrants (including me), the city was still the Great Good Place, where everything was possible. In this city, if we worked hard and had even a minimum amount of luck, we could live full lives. And nobody could tell us what form those lives must take. This was America. Even more important, this was New York. And there were many ways to be New Yorkers.

Mike Berger looked at his mythical city, stopped and dwelled on every detail, reflected on those details, and did not lose touch with the city's various languages. Calvino, also a superb journalist, would have loved him. Berger had almost no interest in the doings of the rich and famous, except as evidence of human folly. As a newspaperman, he knew the difference between accomplishment and publicity. Instead, Berger brought to spotlight many of those New Yorkers who usually exist on the journalistic margins. They have neither fame nor notoriety. They never hit game-winning home runs and do not murder their spouses. They work. They do good deeds in quiet ways. They live private lives of considerable density. And they know things. Often, they know amazing things.

Such New Yorkers live on in these pieces. Without ever adding italics, Berger expresses his own feeling by the way he chooses the people and places that are departing. He has a recurring fondness for nuns who are kind to people in pain, from old men to little blind girls. He loves obsessives: bird fanciers (though he has no patience for the chatter of starlings), rock collectors, miniature gardeners, sellers of love potions. He loves the men who lay underground pipes that protect the city's functioning ganglia, even when such men are bedeviled by the predatory genius of a single termite. He feels kinship for the men who salvage things of value from old mansions—things overlooked by auctioneers, from old timbers to worn brick (such men's vocation resembles Berger's own). He cherishes one woman who has collected 500,000 wishbones from chickens, turkeys, and geese. He loves clock-makers, egg-jewelers, potters, the Ukranian women who clean office building late at night. They are not the subjects of page one. But they are valuable in their own special ways, part of a chorus of individuals.

These Berger columns are not exercises in verbal mush. We almost always learn something concrete. In one piece, dated July 25, 1956, he consults the men and women who keep track of the city's trees, and he learns from them which ones fare best in the big city ("pin, red and scarlet oaks; American and European elm, European ash, linden, Norway maple, honey locust, tulip and the gingko"). He also tells us which trees are not welcome in the city of welcome ("poplar, silver maple, box elder, black locust, horse chestnut, the Chinese mountain ash, beech, birch, sugar maple, the American plane, dogwood and hornbeam"). The problem with the latter group, Berger tells us, is "they go thirstily for under-pavement plumbing in their search for water." What Berger learns, we learn.

Like a Gothic novelist, Berger understands that every house has its own legend, its own secrets. When he visits the remains of Colonnade Row on Lafayette Street, he knows that Abraham Lincoln passed this way, and it's sad to know that Berger didn't live to see the street given renewed dash and vigor by Joseph Papp and the Public Theater in the building across the street (once the Astor Library). He visits the mansion of Andrew Carnegie on Fifth Avenue and 91st Street, and we are reminded that the greatest of all millionaires (he used his money to open 1,600 libraries, 65 of them in New York alone) was a very short man, and finicky about details. He goes to see the gutted shell of the Broome Street Tabernacle near the old Police Headquarters and discovers a glorious human story that I won't try to abbreviate. The date of the story is July 11, 1958. Read it, and know that it has a larger point: Human stories lie all around us, if only we will ask, and listen.

There are, of course, set pieces here too. Berger tours the town at Christmastime, dazzled by the lights and ornamentations, and he cheers the grand spectacle without worrying about whether a Jew should do such a thing. This is a gorgeous New York season, and Mike Berger is a genuine New Yorker. He loves learning something new each time about the celebrations of the Chinese New Year. He doesn't just describe the St. Patrick's Day parade; he gives us its history, and its beginnings under the British, of all people (an irony that clearly warms his heart). He loves returning to Trinity Church, whose walls expand and contract in heat or cold, whose history is in some ways the history of the city (this is the third Trinity), and whose graveyard reminds every visitor of the limits of fame and mortality.

In many ways, Berger's collected columns remind me of the great nineteenth-century diaries kept by George Templeton Strong and Phillip Hone. Those men were not journalists, of course; they were writing for themselves or for history, and so their millions of words are sprinkled with various bigotries of the time and too many rigid moral certainties. Berger wrote for a contemporary public, which could read him in the *New York Times*. And yet in one important sense, Strong, Hone, and Berger were doing similar things: They were freezing time to the rhythm of a daily clock. In a way, time is their basic subject. Each lamented the changes that were moving so inexorably through the city they loved. Each was capable of rue. Each, in different ways, was subject to bouts of nostalgia.

And that is why this collection from the late 1950s can create still another form of nostalgia. Berger's subjects often lament the lost New York of the late nineteenth century, or the years before the Great War, or even the Depression. But a reader my age can be moved to lament the lost years when Berger was writing these pieces for the next day's paper. I was young in the late 1950s, not yet a newspaperman, but I was reading everything, and I would find Berger's columns deep inside the *New York Times*. I knew they were special, but I didn't know why. The front pages and the sports pages absorbed me, along with the brilliant styles of writers such as Jimmy Cannon, Murray Kempton, and Red Smith. Reading Berger now, after living a life and learning to deal with time's erosions, I yearn for the peculiar innocence of the years in which these pieces were first published. He was writing about the present and the past. Up ahead lay the future, with its assassinations, its riots, its anger and rampant decay. New York was assaulted by a variety of plagues: heroin, crime, homelessness, the near bankruptcy of the government, and the endless wretched quarrels over race. It was impossible in those terrible years to avoid feelings of nostalgia for a time when the Dodgers were playing the Giants at

Ebbets Field and Machito was on stage at the Palladium, when every telephone exchange had a name and not a number (so that you could call Whitehall 4-9000 and get the city desk of the *New York Post*), and you went with someone you loved to Coney Island on the Sea Beach Express. The 1960s taught me what Mike Berger was all about.

Berger saw none of that great unraveling. In the last piece in this book, dated January 23, 1959, he tells a tale that could have come from Charles Dickens (one of his favorite writers). Again, don't depend on a summary. Read it with care, and then read the brief, graceful, understated coda, dated January 26. The story does what so much of his work always does: It makes us more human.

Less than two weeks after putting the story of Laurence Stroetz and his violin into the paper, Mike Berger was dead. Men and women in newspaper city rooms all over New York wept without shame. A lot of other people did too.

—Pete Hamill
September 20, 2003

Foreword

Aₗₜₕₒᵤ𝗀ₕ his name was Meyer Berger, he was Mike to his colleagues on the New York *Times* and to his many hundreds of friends. For a man who was so accessible to everyone, "Meyer" seems too formal. It lacks the quiet intimacy that his nickname expresses.

In his professional life he was a brilliant, tireless, probing reporter who assembled and wrote some of the most memorable stories the *Times* has published. In 1950 he won a Pulitzer Prize for one of his greatest. It was an inspired police reporter's chronicle of the shooting of thirteen persons by an insane war veteran in Camden, N.J. No one else could have collected and observed so closely all the facts and homely details of a multiple crime and then told them so swiftly in four thousand concise words that put a grisly news event into human perspective.

Since Mike was a great reporter, no one would have blamed him if he had been cocky, callous and omniscient. But nothing coarsened in any way the innate gentleness of a shy, kindly, humorous man whose sympathies reached out in all directions. Although he was not a formally religious man, he had the reverence for life that religious people cherish. He could not bear to see a moth killed; if it was in the house it had to be liberated through the window. Nothing alive was outside his range of sympathy.

He was born on September 1, 1898, on New York's Lower East

Side, one of eleven children; and he was raised in poverty in a slum in Brooklyn. He had to leave high school after the second term. Beginning as a messenger for the old *World* at $1.50 a week, he grew up in the newspaper business the hard way. He joined the staff of the *Times* in 1928 and flourished there. Since his knowledge of New York was more extensive than that of any other writer, *The New Yorker* felt that it needed him and persuaded him to join its staff in 1937. But Mike's heart belonged to the *Times*. After he had remained for one year in an alien pasture, his colleagues on the *Times* were delighted and g atified to receive him back, for it was not only pleasant but reassuring to have Mike in the city room.

Outside his home, over which his wife, Mrs. Mae Gamsu Berger, presided, his order of loyalties was, one, his country and, two, the *Times*. Although the army rejected him in 1917 because of defective eyesight, he managed to enlist, by memorizing the eye chart. As a combat soldier he served through the fighting in France. He won the Silver Star for carrying wounded men back to the American lines when their position was under enemy fire. He also won the Purple Heart.

In World War II he went to London as a war correspondent, but he was invalided home after two months because his health, already impaired by stomach ulcers, was shattered by the restricted food supply. Being emotionally involved in the ordeal of his country, he was devastated by his abortive experience as a war correspondent. In 1945, when the war was drawing to a conclusion, he managed to slip away on a tour of North Africa, Europe and other war areas, although this was only a consolation tour for a man who believed in sharing the worst aspects of the war with other Americans.

Whether his devotion to New York City was a third category in his order of loyalties or part of his loyalty to the *Times* is difficult to determine, both being so closely interrelated. He first began to write his column "About New York" in 1939, but it was discontinued in 1940 when the supply of newsprint was curtailed. The column was reinstated in 1953, and continued until he died, quite without warning, on February 8, 1959. Having already contracted to prepare this book, he had selected the columns he wanted to put into it.

The reader will discover for himself how intimately Mike knew even the most obscure places and people that constitute a huge, heedless cosmopolis. The reader will also discover for himself the pithiness of the writing. But the reader may not discover for himself something else that is obvious to Mike's friends: All the people interviewed and described have traits of Mike's character. They are modest, self-effacing and slightly wistful people with a romantic enjoyment of what they know or do. There is not a mean bone in any of them. Although Mike had a passion for objective writing, every line reflects his character. In the process of losing himself for the sake of his topic he found himself more triumphantly than he knew.

Brooks Atkinson

Our Town:
Open Letter to a Visitor

WHEN you come to New York, guide books will give you lists of places almost every visitor gets to see—the Statue of Liberty, the new Coliseum, the bridges, the cathedrals, Wall Street, Fifth Avenue, Times Square. The City Convention Bureau puts out seasonal calendars to let you know what's going on in town—in the museums, the libraries and the public parks; what the theatres are showing; what colorful fiestas are due; what's at the United Nations or at Rockefeller Center. Tourist guides will herd you through the foreign quarters, but those get thinner and thinner through the years. Assimilation works in its quiet, mysterious way, you know, and new generations tend to blend into the national weave.

But commercial tours only whisk you through the foreign-flavored places and the impressions are such as you might get from the window of a speeding express—fleeting and unsatisfactory. You don't stop long enough to really see, hear or know the people. Better to come back on your own time, after the dry run, to study mood and dimension. If you're curious about ethnological groups going through the American hopper, you'll find, in most places, that the people are warm and friendly—even eager—to explain things. They talk more easily if you come in kindly spirit and don't just push through, gaping and staring behind a raucous shepherd giving out a tired and monotonous spiel.

You ought to know a little about New York's millions that somehow doesn't reach the visitor through guide books and guided tours. They're not a special species. Around 98 per cent of them are simple folk living in curious provincialism in quiet flats and little houses 'way out beyond the glare and harshness of Times Square and the night-club belt. They pour into Manhattan Island from around 6 o'clock in the morning to around 9:30, to fill the skyscrapers, the factories, the department stores, and work at appointed tasks for eight hours, or more. At twilight the tide reverses and the subways, buses and ferries hurry them out again to Queens, to the Bronx, to Brooklyn, Staten Island.

They're not at their best in the morning and evening rush hours and you're not to judge them by their worried and harried look in those periods. If they push and crowd into the subways, it's because their jobs depend on their getting to them on time. If they huddle and jostle on the way out again, it's partly because suppers and families are waiting, or because there won't be too much time after shop or office closing to get home to change, eat, and keep a romantic date. Even courtship in a city of more than eight million often is hurried, except on week-ends.

You'll find, if you're in New York for more than a few days, that the mill-race way of living gets to be habit. You're a human chip in a fast-moving tide and by and by, without meaning to, you find you're accommodating your pace to the common tempo.

People who come from less crowded cities are shocked when they first find themselves in the race. Those who can, flee from it. Men and women have written bitterly about it; have applied the literary quirt to New York and to its people. Some of this is justified, but mainly it comes from hasty judgment. Back in their own homes city dwellers are normal folk, content with normal living. They follow humble, normal family routines. On the Sabbath, when the work-a-day pace lets up, they put on their Sunday best as people in small towns do, to wend their way to quiet devotions in over 3,000 city churches. If you go to a neighborhood church in one of the outlying districts, you'll get the peaceful feel of it.

If you wander into Greenwich Village and come across men and women who affect Bohemian dress and the Bohemian manner, don't go away with the impression that they alone represent New York. The visitor from Flatbush and from Hunt's Point in the Bronx find them as strange as you do. If you stroll on the East Side of town and marvel at the splendor of specialty shops and at penthouses, be-furred matrons, pampered dogs, chauffeur-driven limousines and expensive restaurants, you ought to know that the stenographer from Brooklyn's Bushwick district and the clerk from Staten Island's Tottenville find them as extraordinary as you do. If you enter higher-priced night clubs and recoil from menu prices you can safely figure that 99 per cent of the city's eight million would react the same way.

One other thing about the townsfolk that may not come to you right away is that thousands who crowd the subways, who work in Madison Avenue and in Wall Street, who populate Greenwich Village and linger in the richer night clubs, the more expensive bars and restaurants, who dwell in penthouses and duplexes in the sky's-the-limit zones, are not New York natives. They are men and women who have come into the city from smaller communities throughout the United States and have won to high place.

It would be a mistake to snatch a few glimpses of the city when you get here, and decide, "This is an ugly city." Parts of it are indeed unsightly. Tenement districts are unlovely, overcrowded, untidy, though the city fathers keep trying to substitute newer dwellings—you'll see cleaner, fresher housing with touches of green and with more air space that have gone up where dark rookeries stood not long ago. You must reflect, though, that there is a wrong side of the tracks in every town; that city governments never quite achieve perfect housing for the poor anywhere.

But turn from the areas of extreme poverty and you meet extraordinary beauty. You find no ancient monuments as you would abroad, for the city is less than 400 years old and keeps undergoing endless change. Instead of ivied castles and historic ruins, your eyes sweep magnificent, modern towers, and the huddled towers have a curious, airy quality. They are lovely studies in gray-white and soft gold at sunrise and at sundown. They are ghostly structures, seen through rain, snow or light fog. When evening lights come on, they are banked diamonds against night's black velvet. Washed with moonlight they wear majestic mystery, a dreamy dull silver.

It is not enough to see the skyline from the north, say, in midmorning, and to think you know it. Stand off from it in the bay. Study it at twilight from the back of a ferry bound for Staten Island, and you find it a sparkling, burning cluster bathed in shifting golden-red and haunting purple shadow. Then its hundreds of thousands of windows catch and give back sunset's fire.

It is different again, when you stand braced against Brooklyn Bridge railing with East River a broad path of molten beauty sweeping around it; harbor craft staining the skies with graceful, writhing smoke plumes. Few visitors ever see it from Fulton Ferry, on Brooklyn's shore, from the Palisades across the Hudson River, from the Queens mouth of Midtown Tunnel, on Staten Island, across the bay. Yet each viewpoint shows it altered, always in fresh loveliness.

There are breath-taking views from the high places—from planes rising out of, or dropping down to, La Guardia Airport; from the four corners of the R. C. A. Building and Empire State Building towers. It is not enough, remember, to snatch quick glimpses. You must linger awhile to study changes in the far horizons, to tune to the city's whisper and hum.

For New York's voice speaks mystery, too. It has a soft, weird music, a symphony of wind at high altitudes, of muted traffic in endless serpentine twisting over city hills and grades; of jet hiss and propeller thrum, of the hoarse call of tugs on many waters, of great liners standing in from the broad sea, or moving out. You hear another voice at 300 feet when you stand on Brooklyn Bridge early morning; the sigh of great smokestacks, the raspy breathing of string-towing tugs, the gull flocks, sighing wind in the bridge cables, the quivering complaint of the whole span under its moving freight.

You will not then hold that New York is all rush and clangor. You will come to know that it has many moods; that it knows long hours of peace and that it does relax. You must not go from it without journeying into marginal Manhattan, to Brooklyn, Queens or the Bronx after the great apartment houses have gone dark, and the millions have bedded down to a night's rest. For then those communities are like any sleeping village. Their streets are bare. Few footfalls are heard. Shadows huddle as they do in any Main Street. In the morning, as in your home town, milkmen will start the first echoes, morning newspapers will drop at apartment house doors, babies will wail, children will trudge off to school and to play.

The legend has grown that no street on earth is so sinister as New

York's Bowery. Some professional tourist guides have swelled the libel. Well, The Bowery was dark, but even in the shadow patterns that covered it before the last of the city's elevated railroad trestles came down, The Bowery derelict was never a public menace. He was a sagging human who scuttled out of the path of any woman who came by. He wreaked harm only to himself. The Bowery bum was— and is—a sad and seedy fellow drifting in alcoholic haze, but rarely a man of vicious criminal instinct. You may want to visit down that way, but it's not what it was. With the trestles gone, and the sun pouring in, The Bowery is just another broad city street fast losing its time-blackened houses. They're making way for bright new apartment buildings and modern shops.

New York is mostly brick, asphalt, concrete and steel and so far as visitors get to know it has little green space except the public parks. Yet within the city limits, if you will seek them out, are districts that are semi-rural. Cross the bay to Staten Island, now it is spring, and buses or your own car will take you into dusty country lanes, to tiny hamlets dozing in the sun, to spaces covered with great flower gardens and truck patches. You will hear birds piping in the trees, hear the chuckle of running streams; find families who think a trip to Wall Street or to Times Square as much of a holiday as you do.

On Staten Island, more than in any other part of New York, you will see relics of the City That Was. You will come upon the Stillwell-Perine House, a stone cottage with a sloped shingle roof, built 275 years ago; see ivy-covered Britton Cottage in New Dorp, that went up right after the American Revolution.

If you get the chance, take the subway up to Van Cortlandt Park. You can lose yourself there in quiet paths. Rabbits will scuttle out of your way, garter snakes will slither off at your approach. You will move through dense tree shadow and where you move city sounds and noises will come to you but faintly. You are in the city, still, but you are beyond the pavement, beyond the towers that reach for the sky.

Before you walk about New York you should know that a good bit of the city's history is written right into street signs. Visitors are seldom aware of that. The street called Wall, for example, actually had a wall. The Dutch ran it across the narrow part of Manhattan as protection against Indians. Broadway was, literally, The Broad Way. First it was an Indian path. The pioneers widened it for the carts they sent north, through the wall toward the upper island. In Maiden Lane almost 300 years ago, Dutch girls did the family wash in a stream that ran across the island there. At night they walked the lane with the village beaux who knew it as The Maidens' Path. A mill actually stood in Mill Street.

Up Marketfield Street (old Petticoat Lane) the Dutch women trudged to buy their cloth, meats, fish and vegetables from peddlers' carts. A canal once ran across Canal Street. Minetta Street follows the line of Minetta Brook. In Colonial times Cherry Street was a cherry orchard. Stone Street was New York's first paved street. The names of original farm owners on Manhattan Island crop up everywhere— Rutgers, Duane, Stuyvesant, Warren, Lispenard, Doyers, Pell. When you trace those names, you begin to get some hint of the early city and of the pioneers who built it. Your imagination can help you, then, to picture New York when it was pasture, orchard, meadow and dusty highway.

The place wasn't always concrete and it wasn't always crowded. It just grew faster than any city in history.

April 29, 1956

1 9 5 3

ANTHONY MAZZA's job is one of the weirdest assignments a man ever undertook in The City of Ten Thousand Anomalies, although he doesn't often think of it in that light. He is probably the most overworked game warden in the country—and his territory is effete Manhattan Island.

Mr. Mazza's official title is game protector for the State Conservation Department. He wears the same campaign hat and gray State Trooper rig that fellow wardens wear in the Adirondacks, the same Sam Brown belt and holster, the same regulation sidearms.

Where his associates tread soft pine needles and mountain paths, though, Mr. Mazza clumps along New York's crowded sidewalks or drives tortuously through its strangled traffic arteries. Other wardens work in the woods; Mr. Mazza uses express elevators.

He spot-checks the city's 1,800 (more or less) fur shops, takes a whirl now and then in department stores that sell feathered trout flies, drops quietly in on feather merchants, peeks into refrigeration plants, hits the downtown fish markets.

He patrols the great galleys in big hotels and fish-and-game-serving eating places, is a familiar figure in millinery shops that use feathers, and pays an occasional call on pet shops where forbidden wild things might possibly turn up.

In fur shops he examines trappers' tags on all kinds of pelts. In restaurant and hotel iceboxes he makes certain that the pheasant and venison came off commercial breeding farms, and not from the wild.

He has a keen eye for restricted plumage in the trout-fly factories, the milliners' and the feather merchants', and is a shark at spotting undersize lobsters and shellfish in waterfront markets.

Once a year he issues fishing and hunting licenses at the Sportsmen's Show in Grand Central Palace. He likes that because he gets a chance to talk to real outdoors men. Once he found a woman leading a baby deer on a leash in Central Park, but it was ranch-born. No violation.

He's never had to draw his service pistol in Manhattan to serve an offender—not once in the twelve years he's had the assignment. The only active predators he meets are Broadway wolves but they don't interest him. "No bounty," he says.

April 20, 1953

⁋ The Waldorf-Astoria has its wine cellars, if you can call them that, on the fifth floor. The hotel is built on steel and concrete stilts, as most Park Avenue structures are that tower over the New York Central tracks. A stabilizer keeps the wine from being rocked by passing trains and other traffic.

April 22, 1953

⁋ Modern fire laws don't permit recording companies such as Columbia and R. C. A. Victor to build wooden studios, which are best for making records, so company engineers in New York keep looking for existing structures that have mellow interiors they can adapt for the purpose.

The old Adams Memorial Presbyterian Church in Thirtieth Street east of the Third Avenue "El," put up in 1875, was Columbia Records' best find. Johnny Ray has wept in it, Rosemary Clooney and Marlene Dietrich have sung "Too Old to Cut the Mustard" in it and its ancient rafters have reverberated to the full Met cast doing "Cavalleria Rusticana" and to Charles Laughton in "Don Juan in Hell."

The other day the full cast of "John Brown's Body," with Tyrone Power, Raymond Massey, Judith Anderson and a chorus, toiled through the entire play in the old church. Resonant declamations and thick, rich snatches of "The Battle Hymn of the Republic" were put on recording tape with a minimum of fluffs and retakes.

Miss Anderson had to do one passage over because her chair creaked when she leaped from it on cue, and the tape took notice of it. William Bachman, a Columbia engineer, recalled that a few weeks ago Rudolph Serkin was all but finished with a flawless version of Beethoven's Third Piano Concerto when they pulled the stop light on him. The clinking of silver in his pocket got on the tape as obbligato when he bounced on the piano stool. An assistant held his change while he did the number over.

Mr. Bachman said he and his staff made extensive tests before they leased the old church. They figured they could remove the old stained glass windows, substitute concrete brick and kill the traffic and other street noises. Borings and intricate electronic tests established that Adams Memorial was built on solid rock and would not communicate the rumble of the "El." Thick cement banks on the church's outer walls gave double insurance.

The dimensions of the church were close to perfect for recordings —ninety-six feet long, sixty-five feet wide, forty-five feet high. Any dimension greater than 100 feet spawns echoes that double-track on sensitive tape, one reason why such places as Madison Square Garden won't serve. Carnegie Hall would be all right except that it is directly over a subway, and its lush carpeting, heavily upholstered seats and voluptuous drapery swallow reverberations that give recording depth and "human" dimension. "Like hearing a string orchestra on Flushing Meadow," Mr. Bachman explained.

Even with almost perfect conditions, though, it's the human element that tries engineers' sanity. When the Balinese were in town a while back they went to the church to do a record, but their four-foot gong wasn't registering on the tape with a satisfactory impact.

"Hit it hard as you can," the Balinese gong artist was told through an interpreter. He shook his head, gave long and fluent answer. The interpreter made appropriate palm gestures, shrugged, and told the engineers: "He says he won't do it. He has too much reverence for the instrument." They never got him to do it, either.

April 24, 1953

¶ Praying mantis eggs are paying for a Ph.D. for Sidney A. Schwartz, a Government biologist studying at New York University in his spare time. He runs a praying mantis farm on Long Island; sells the eggs to farmers and to gardeners. When the eggs hatch—that happens when the weather warms up as it did yesterday—the mantes break out and destroy insect pests like mad. The big, grotesque fellows are congenitally dedicated to it.

The farm is the only one of its kind, so far as Mr. Schwartz knows, though there have been others. Wayside Gardens in Brookville, L. I., ran one as a sideline but gave it up some years ago. Demand held up, but not enough to justify the work entailed.

The Schwartz farm is a sideline, too. Mr. Schwartz is a full-time biologist in Suffolk County on Long Island, operating out of Riverhead. He and Mrs. Schwartz, both B.A.'s and M.A.'s, met, as he puts it, in Invertebrate Zoology at N. Y. U. in 1949. She helps him collect and ship the mantis oöthecae, or egg cases. These look like walnuts, more or less, and each will hatch out 120 praying mantes, sometimes more.

Spying out mantis oöthecae is something of a trick until you've worked at it a while. When the Schwartzes first went afield for them four years ago, they were lucky to spot a few each hour. The cases are cunningly hung, usually in September, from bushes and from long grass blades. Sometimes they're just left in the grass but placement is always a masterpiece in concealment coloring.

The Schwartzes are modest folk and not ordinarily secretive but they don't tell where the farm is. The closest they come to it is to disclose that it's on a stretch of Long Island Rail Road embankment where conditions for mantis farming are ideal. If they gave the secret away raiders might clean the place out.

The stock on a mantis farm must be kept outdoors. If the cases are brought into a heated room the young mantes come tearing out in a few weeks looking for grub. If they don't find any, they go for one another and you're apt to wind up with one whopper of a mantis, which isn't nice, nor economical.

The oöthecae sell to schools for nature study and to farmers and gardeners all over the country. There are ample reorders but the Schwartzes get a little nervous in April. They've had complaints from the Post Office because late mailings have hatched out before they reached addresses.

A lima bean farmer near the mantis farm hasn't had a red spider or any other bean pest on his spring growth since the enterprise started and is a little puzzled about it. The Schwartzes don't feel they're in a position to tell him, either. He's just reaping benefits from their unmailable surplus each year.

The Schwartzes are full of praying mantis lore. They collect pitcher plants, too. The pitcher plant traps and devours insects, but the one they keep at home is on a raw meat diet. They sold a few of these to schools, which use them for primitive digestion study. They're harder to find than mantis oöthecae.

Some people are shocked when they hear that the mantes' social system is homicidally matriarchal. After the female mantis is sure of her oöthecae supply she eats her mate. When people ask, "Isn't that shocking?" Mr. Schwartz quietly tells them, "There's ample human precedent for it."

MARGINALIA: ¶ New York's City Hall is 150 years old this year, but it almost passed out of the city's hands on Oct. 13, 1858. It was put up at public auction by Robert W. Lowber, a Wall Street man, to satisfy a $228,000 judgment he held against the municipality. Mayor Daniel Tiemann was nervous until Richard Scott, his clerk, bid it in for $50,000. The Mayor resold it to New York. . . . ¶ No one literally gets a key to the city nowadays, but during the Civil War the Board of Aldermen bought real gold keys in real gold boxes for visiting celebrities. The keys and boxes cost $500 a crack.

May 6, 1953

¶ New York University acquired a sizable lump of local history when it added to its Washington Square holdings the other day. At the same time it inherited a pesky underground stream that has waterlogged that part of Manhattan Island for, probably, hundreds of thousands of years.

Most of the new properties look right over the Square itself. A good part of that was the old Brevoort Farm. Six and one-half of its better than nine acres were Potter's Field from 1797 to 1823, and 10,000 New Yorkers were buried in it, including Rose Butler, a thief, the last woman hanged on Washington Square gallows back in 1819. The city gravedigger had free rent in a shack on Thompson Street, on the south side of the Square.

Before (and for some time after) the graveyard filled with yellow fever victims late in the eighteenth century, the widespread marshes around Minetta Water—the pesky watercourse—were a favorite hunting ground for townies with a taste for wild fowl. Minetta, incidentally, comes above ground in the Holley Chambers Hotel, at 33 Washington Square West, as a tinkly lobby fountain. It runs underground from Fifth Avenue, across the Square, to the southwest corner of the old graveyard.

Contractors who dug foundations for the big new apartment house at 2 Fifth Avenue in 1951 got their boots wet in the stream in bedrock, forty feet down. The management thought it might be a sentimental touch to keep the brook on display for tenants and visitors, and hitched a pump to it. It boils up in a glass container in the lobby, most days, from 8 in the morning to midnight, just as it has for many years at Holley Chambers.

University geologists had the happy thought that they might put the stream to work for air-conditioning in some of the new buildings the N. Y. U. administration had in mind, but they had to give up that idea. Air-conditioning experts ran a few tests and told them that the stream was temperamental, not to be counted on in rainless periods.

A good many of the old houses taken over by N. Y. U. have figured in popular fiction. George William Curtis, Brander Matthews, Julian Ralph, William Dean Howells, Henry James, and F. Hopkinson Smith all wrote them into their novels. Hard by at 108 Waverly Place, Richard Harding Davis banged out a good part of his stuff. Waverly Place figured indirectly in fiction, too. The city gave it that name on earnest petition from an organized group of Sir Walter Scott's admirers, pluggers of the Waverley Novels. Somewhere along the way the second "e" was dropped.

The original N. Y. U. building on the east side of the Square contributed not only to local but to international history. Samuel F. B. Morse worked some of his telegraph experiments in it, and Sam Colt, the ingenious Yankee inventor of the six-shooter, put together there a somewhat less helpful contribution, the single-barrel pistol.

Not many are left around to remember, but the arch that is the northern portal to the Square was a kind of afterthought. William Rhinelander Stewart and a group of other rich neighbors paid for a temporary arch at that spot for the centennial of Washington's inauguration. It framed the green so nicely that a movement got under way to build the permanent marble monument that is there now.

MARGINALIA: ¶ Bellevue Hospital was "a place of entertainment," as local advertising put it, back in 1797. Eleven years before that it was offered for sale in The New York Daily Advertiser as "a beautiful Country Seat situated on the banks of the East River, about three miles from the City."

May 8, 1953

¶ Someone with a long memory got the idea, when the Impellitteri-Dewey ruckus developed over the Transit Authority the other day, that it might be romantic if someone could dig up the special subway car—only one of its kind in the system—that Interboro big shots used when New York's underground was new, around fifty years ago.

The special was called the Directors' Car, but was formally the Mineola. The Wason Manufacturing Company of Brightwood, Mass., turned her out in 1904, a lovely thing of Philippine mahogany with mulberry silk drapes, knee-deep carpeting, sliding leatherette curtains, a kitchenette with kerosene stove and old-fashioned icebox, special subway-pattern china and glassware, overstuffed reclining couch, swivel chair and roll-top desk.

After the Mineola got here from Wason's in August, 1904, over regular rail lines, more fancy fittings went into her. The total cost for just the one car was $11,429.40.

August Belmont, I. R. T.'s chairman of the board, gave dinner parties on her to distinguished guests. He had special plate glass fitted to the front and rear ends for easier observation and had twelve special leather chairs built in. He ran the car over the line whenever the mood came on him, frequently with ladies who ordinarily wouldn't have gone underground.

Theodore Shonts, I. R. T. president, and Frank Hedley, who came after him, carried on the Belmont tradition. They used the Mineola all through the Hudson-Fulton Celebration in 1909; rode rajahs, princes and assorted noblemen around in it and in May, 1919, gave the grand underground tour for Sgt. Alvin York, World War I's greatest hero, a Tennessee mountaineer who had never played plush mole before. The sergeant was awed. "Funniest town I've ever been in" was his reaction when he got up to pavement.

Of all the subway nabobs who rode in Old Mineola, only one is still around to remember her. Mr. Hedley, uncle of Sidney Bingham, the chairman of the Board of Transportation for New York, still lives in Brooklyn. He is close to 90 years old and must dream rosy dreams of her because no other subway car ever approached her in beauty or luxury. The only other special that could claim even remote relationship was the funeral trolley car that ran the Brooklyn rails years ago. Where she is now, no one seems to know.

Anyway, the idea of digging the Mineola out for the new Transit Authority members is a little late. Old Mineola lay under sheeting for years in the 148th Street subway yards, was shifted to the 239th Street yards and gathered dust there, unused, until July 25, 1946, when she was bought in by the Schiavone and Bonomo Corporation, dealers in junk and scrap. They had Gerosa Brothers, a trucking firm, haul her away on a trailer across George Washington Bridge and out to Flemington, N. J.

There Old Mineola is now, stripped of her subway wheels and snugged in concrete. Richard Bonomo has converted her into a hunting lodge in the woods on his Flemington estate and throws great hunting parties in her, come fall. General Casey and his fellow Authority members will never know her mellow underground grace.

MARGINALIA: ¶ New York's subway cars and subway stations use left-hand threads in their electric-light bases. This discourages bulb snatchers from going after them for home use.

May 11, 1953

¶ New York's costliest fires, local historians will tell you, lighted all downtown in 1835 and in 1845. Between them they burned out 995 buildings and all that was in them for a total loss of $26,000,000.

Nowadays the major lower-city banks burn billions of dollars of matured bonds each year and, though the smoke curls up before New Yorkers' eyes, few are aware that fortunes are undergoing cremation.

Chase National Bank maintains a crematory at 11 Broad Street, run by a gentleman quaintly named Frank Ife. The man who was in the job before him, Samuel K. Pearson, was Chase cremator for twenty-six years.

Big banks have cremations on an average of twice a week. A single burning may see a single bond issue of, say, $200,000,000 go into a sub-basement gas furnace in a single day. Some banks have put as much as $750,000,000 worth through within a twelvemonth. "Two hundred million dollars in $1,000 bonds can make a lot of smoke," Mr. Pearson conservatively tells you.

Bank executives have strict cremation procedure for preparing a redeemed bond issue for the fire. Printed cremation orders are made out, followed by formal notice that the orders have been executed: "We have burned to ashes bonds . . ." followed by a complete list of items destroyed.

Though great corporations are traditionally pictured as heartless and without sentiment, they frequently ask that the No. 1 bond of an important issue be saved from the burning. Banks will hear such an appeal, but always demand a receipt.

Coupons that go into bank furnaces are listed one by one before cremation, just as bonds are, and it is tradition to have official witnesses at burnings. Unused stockholders' checks are destroyed by fire, too, and embarrassing estate records.

Cremation staffs find their work comfortable most of the time, but on blistering summer days, stripped to the waist, they look like undersized, dripping Vulcans. If fires are still burning at the end of a working day the furnace doors are locked.

Special chimneys that carry off the smoke and charred ends of the bond and coupon burning are covered with wire, but there have been cases where bonds only slightly charred have worked through, lifted by heat, and have been offered for payment by people who found them.

Bank customers who know about the crematories sometimes ask—and get—permission to burn diaries or other possessions in them. Chase even burned a whole batch of custom shirt bands once for a rich patron who didn't want them to get into circulation after he died.

May 18, 1953

❡ New York is a brittle city, but the weakness doesn't show up until a big parade is scheduled. The Army's atomic cannon was ruled off Fifth Avenue because its eighty tons would have snapped sub-pavement ganglia—the eight water mains that run abreast only four feet under street surface, and the sewer mains that lie another nine feet down. Fifth Avenue is weakest in dead center. The water mains are of cast iron eighty to ninety years old, and couldn't take the big cannon's weight. Consolidated Edison's gas mains, though set in close to the curbs, would probably have cracked, too.

The Police Department's chief engineer calls all Army, municipal and utility experts into a huddle before a big parade is staged in the city. These men get out their maps and figure the route to be taken by the heavy equipment. They know how much each street can bear. They make sure, for example, that no vehicle's load distribution will put more than 400 pounds to the

inch on Fifth Avenue's pavement. Park Avenue could never have an Army parade because its asphalt crust over the New York Central tracks at Fifty-ninth Street is only four inches thick, thinnest in all Gotham.

Getting big pieces of Army equipment into the city is another worry. Army's radar Skysweeper, originally routed through one of the vehicular tunnels, had to rumble over George Washington Bridge instead. The tunnels have only 13 feet 2 inches clearance; the bridge has 13 feet 2½ inches. At that, the radar machine had to let some air out of its tires to make it.

Parades are a menace to manholes on any city route. When the Eighty-second Airborne moved up Fifth Avenue at war's end, its equipment cracked Fifth Avenue's manhole covers as if they were so many plastic tiddlywinks buttons. Now Army orders detour tanks and cannon around the covers.

Engineers always see to it that a few cross streets are kept traffic-clear for fire apparatus. They work out a careful parade dispersal plan, too—fix things so that marching units drain off at different blocks without jamming post-parade traffic.

❡ Discounting a few decorative sundials around town, the oldest type of time-telling device in New York is the time ball above the ship's bridge on the Seamen's Church Institute tower in South Street. Old tugboat men and skippers on other harbor craft still set their chronometers by it, because they haven't quite come around to putting their faith in radio time signals.

The time ball is a memorial to the officers and crew of the Titanic. J. P. Morgan, who lost many friends when that ship went down, was treasurer for the memorial fund.

The ball, fourteen feet across, is a bronze-skeletoned sphere covered with black canvas. It is hand-cranked to the top of its mast each day, but is touched off by a time signal telegraphed from Washington to fall in the split second that spells noon. Sometimes, in severe winters, it freezes, and that always starts telephones ringing. Downtown skyscraper workers who set their watches by it call in by the dozens.

There's one other time ball in town, set high in the ceiling on the main floor at the Maritime Exchange at 80 Broad Street. It once served to clear the floor for the midday meal break, but it hasn't been used for years; just quietly gathers harbor dust.

❡ This is a piece about a girl in a large Government office in town who followed a weird path to marriage some months ago. It seems she got to brooding one day about the sizable amount of cash she had put up, through the years, for gifts and parties for other girls in the office who had got themselves engaged, and here she was with still no prospect in sight. In a heady moment she demurely let on that she had found herself a man, though she actually hadn't, and boldly announced a tentative wedding date.

She went to Florida on the purse her co-workers put up, but down there panic overtook her and she went on a desperate man hunt. It took all of her three weeks, but she bagged a weak-willed male and brought him back to the shop one day, certificate and all.

The story is being told around town by a woman to whom the girl confided it, and a Federal official known for his veracity says it's true. Working out all right, too.

May 25, 1953

❡ When indigenes say of the Brooklyn Bridge, which hit three score and ten yesterday, "There's life in the old girl yet," it's literally so. Fourteen bustling industrial concerns pay the city an average of around $27,000 a year for work space and storage space inside the span's landside arches.

The arches' interiors are damp, gloomy vaults and are weirdly medieval in general appearance, especially the abandoned wine cellars behind the studded heavy steel doors set in the arch at North William Street, just off the rear of the old World Building.

Current rentals are small compared to what the city got for the space in the delirious Nineteen Twenties; the charges then came to around $73,000. One of the oldest leaseholders was the Brooklyn Bridge Cold Storage and Freezing Company, which kept the Fulton Fish Market's surplus from going stale. It moved to a new plant two years ago.

Right now the principal tenants

are outfits that use the arches for the sale of rubber heels, for storing wire and cable and for stocking canned foods from Holland. Trucks and drays rumble up to and away from the arches all day; there's a lot of hoarse shouting.

The arches and the crooked little streets that bend and twist around them give that part of town something of the look of medieval Prague. When you get down into the wine cellars and away from the sound you're in a "Cask of Amontillado" setting. The damp drips, walls glitter, footfalls echo, shadows distort on ancient vaults.

Peeling whitewash has faded most of the painted legends on the wet brick down under the bridge, but you make one out here and there, with a bit of strain: "Who Loveth Not Wine, Women and Song, He Remaineth a Fool His Whole Life Long"; "The Best Wine Goeth Down Sweetly Causing the Lips of Those Who Are Asleep to Speak"; "Their Flavors Are as a Brook of Many Voices."

Theodore Mombelly, resident engineer for the Brooklyn Bridge, a scholarly gentleman whose chief hobby is the study of triremes, has a special fondness for the old wine cellars. He likes to tell the legend of "The Mystery of the Blue Madonna" in one melancholy corner of the echoing sub-span caverns.

In one high-vaulted corner of the wine caves, where the walls are a peeling sky blue, you notice an empty niche. Mr. Mombelly says this held a blue-robed Madonna in stone or marble. Who put her there, or why, he never heard.

The engineer clicked off his hand flashlight. Phosphorescent glow breathed and pulsed in rotted old wine-cask saddles.

Mr. Mombelly said: "The Blue Madonna had that phosphorescence, too, from this damp and all. If you stood here in the dark she'd seem to move out of her niche and kind of float in mid-air."

He thinks someone stole the Blue Madonna around 1942, even hints that he has some idea of who may have it now, but won't be pressed on it.

He just says: "It's a fair guess that whoever took the Madonna will handle her with tender care. No one would have done it for the statue's intrinsic value." He seems to prefer to drop it there.

There's a brief history of the bridge wine cellars on one of the deep inner walls. It's patchy and flaked, with painted vine trellises all around it crawling up the wet walls. It says, as close as you can make out:

"Legend of Oechs Cellars: These cellars were built in 1876, about seven years prior to the official opening of Brooklyn Bridge in 1883. From their inception they housed the choicest wines in New York City. . . . First occupied by Luyties Brothers & Racky's wine establishment until the Eighteenth Amendment was enacted in 1918. They became in 1933 upon repeal of Prohibition the home of Anthony Oechs & Co., a firm engaged in the wine and spirits business since 1846."

There's no such firm in the local phone book now.

MARGINALIA: ¶ The Manhattan pier of the Brooklyn Bridge covers the site of America's first White House at 1-3 Cherry Street. George Washington lived there when he was inaugurated. The street took its name from a cherry orchard cultivated there by Mayor Thomas Delavall in the seventeenth century.

May 27, 1953

¶ Until word got out that Kremlin doctors had used leeches in a last-minute attempt to save Joseph Stalin, most moderns thought that leechcraft was pretty much an obsolete practice and no part of the Atom Age.

It isn't, though Salvatore Anatriello, one of the last two importers of medicinal leeches (Hirudo medicinalis) in New York, thinks the end is almost in sight. Mr. Anatriello, snow-thatched and philosophic, has grown old in the trade and he ought to know.

When he worked into it, more than three decades back, there were sixteen importers in the city, and more than fifty drugstores in Manhattan alone handled the creatures to meet the big demand. Now only a half-dozen shops here sell them, and there's been a corresponding drop in major cities all over the United States.

Mr. Anatriello gets his specimens in shipments of 2,000 to 3,000 by air from hirudiniculturists who breed them in fresh-water lagoons on Portugal's coast. Three-inchers, the best size, fetch 75 cents apiece nowadays, three times the pre-war quotation, with demand steadily falling.

Mr. Anatriello attributes leech-use decline in the United States to two things—tighter immigration laws and the passing of second and third generation immigrants. Their offspring incline to newer things in medicine, and the importer isn't sure but that they think soundly.

Still, drug journals take Mr. Anatriello's ads, and orders keep coming. He goes out regularly to meet his cargoes at Idlewild, and gently takes them to his midtown storage place, where he transfers them with paternal care from metal containers into big tubs, native lagoon mud and all.

The importer rebukes druggists who keep their leeches too near hot electric lamps or steam pipes. He says: "They dislike warmth. They are happiest at from 38 to 60 degrees." He thinks they ail if they live in the same sleeping chamber as human beings, but can't prove that scientifically.

The soft-voiced leech importer speaks of the little creatures with peculiar affection. He thinks that in an animal kingdom gone mad they might be the only friendly species left. He says: "They harm no one, nor do they harm one another. To utter a word against the Hirudinea is libel." And he means it.

When Mr. Anatriello got into the business back in the Twenties it was flourishing. Foreign quarters in New York, Boston, Detroit, Chicago—almost everywhere except in the Deep South and Far West—couldn't get a sufficient supply.

Gray's Drug Store in Times Square handled them for the black-eye trade. They do a quick job on a discolored lamp.

Cutthroat methods came to pass, business was so good. Rivals sabotaged one another's cargoes. In those days miners used thousands of the Hirudinea for occupational injuries, and after a Saturday night exchange of compliments with discontented spouses, when the beer flowed fast.

Even during World War II, the Army and Navy had secret uses for leeches. Mr. Anatriello once politely asked the Navy why it wanted the things, but desisted when he got a vague, and somewhat frigid, reply. Actually, he's not the prying type. He just wanted the information for a treatise on leeches that he's worked on for years but that never seems to end.

June 1, 1953

¶ Pennsylvania Station, which next month will observe the fiftieth anniversary of the start of its construction, carries no sign indoors or out to show that it is the New York stop. Near-sighted persons and misdirected strangers heading for the station not infrequently wind up, instead, in the Post Office across the way in Eighth Avenue and get on stamp lines for their railroad tickets.

New York, incidentally, is only a way stop on the Pennsylvania Railroad. The station is open at both ends, with tunnels under the Hudson and the East River, so that trains from the West can get up to Boston.

This explains what seems to puzzle some city folk: Why does the Pennsylvania call its edifice a station when the New York Central calls its place in town Grand Central Terminal? The Central actually terminates at Forty-second Street. There's extra trackage south of that point, but it's only for turnarounds.

One daily train that whisks through Penn Station is so long that it can't stop there without blocking both ends; it's the American Express out of Sunnyside at 1 A.M. carrying mail and freight to Washington. The Congressional Limited, with eighteen cars and a locomotive, overlaps, too, but only at one end.

All but one of the Pennsylvania's through trains carry only a New Jersey liquor license, and drinks can't be served on them until the string has passed the center of the Hudson River going west. The only train on the line that carries liquor licenses for both New York and New Jersey is the Broadway Limited. No one seems to know why; the New York license allows only a couple of minutes extra drinking time under the river.

MARGINALIA: ¶ Brooklyn Bridge aerial workers never disturb birds' nests up in the towers if the nests hold eggs. Craft superstition says destruction of eggs means ill fortune. . . .

June 8, 1953

¶ Hardly any New Yorker who hears the twenty-four-hour-cycle sound-effects background for the Museum of Natural History's current "Man of the Montaña" show could guess what time and anguish went into the recording.

There are two minutes of sound for each hour of the cycle. Some of it was recorded in the Montaña high in the Peruvian Andes by P. P. Kellogg and A. A. Allen, Cornell University ornithologists. They got the rainstorm in the jungle, among other major sounds.

Much of it, though, had to be dubbed in to fit the actual hours when Montaña monkeys, birds, toads, frogs, cicadas and crickets are most vocal. Dr. T. C. Schneirla, head of the animal behavior department, and Dr. Harry Tschopik, assistant curator of anthropology (he's in Peru with sound tape right now, incidentally) firmly insisted on authentic background.

Moses Asch, son of Sholem Asch, the writer, got the assignment. He produces sound-effects records for educational institutions and ethnic recordings, too, partly on a Wenner-Gren Foundation research grant.

For months, Mr. Asch was literally up before the birds to record the macaws, wattled bellbirds, jays, toucans and parrots at the Bronx Zoo. They're noisiest before breakfast there.

Three mornings running, Mr. Asch and the zoo ornithologists set up their recorders but got no sound from a macaw. They played a lady-parrot tape to him and evoked a few squawks before he caught on, ruffed his feathers and clammed up again.

Then Mr. Asch played the macaw's own squawks back at him, and got him to bawl himself out long enough to satisfy the museum folk.

Bufo marinus, a giant jungle toad, was even more difficult. Mr. Asch heard of one in the Dallas Zoo but the curator there said he'd never heard the thing make a noise.

The crickets in the Montaña recording were taken on an eighteen-hour field trip in Connecticut. Mr. Asch was careful to get day and night sounds. He had been warned that crickets' stridulation picks up after sundown.

Mr. Asch thought no one would ever guess he had anything but a Peruvian jungle cricket on the record, but he was wrong. First time the thing was played a museum visitor told a man beside him, "That's a Yankee cricket they've got in there." Turned out he'd made a life study of crickets everywhere and could spot an accent. Mr. Asch was days getting over the shock, but the Yankee cricket's still in the recording.

June 15, 1953

¶ The Sanitation Department's sweep against "litterbugs" the other day aroused the reflection that the town hasn't changed much in 300 years.

"It has been found," the City Fathers announced on Feb. 20,

1657, "that within the City of Amsterdam in New Netherland many burghers and inhabitants throw their rubbish, filth, ashes, dead animals and such like things into the public streets to the great inconvenience of the community."

They passed an ordinance that day calling on the populace to deposit trash near the gallows, or near the City Hall, or near Hendrik the Baker's, or to suffer fines of three florins ($1.20)—a lot of money in those days—for a first offense, twice that for a second, and "arbitrary punishment" for a third. Human nature being what it is, the warning had to be repeated endlessly to keep the townsfolk aware of their untidiness, and it still has to be.

June 17, 1953

❡ The Scovill Manufacturing Company, one of three companies that won a bid yesterday to make transit tokens for New York, has been turning out that sort of thing for the last 151 years. Started with brass coat buttons back in 1802 up on Mad River at Waterbury in Connecticut, where the Scovill mill still stands. Lamson Scovill, fourth generation button man, has offices here in the Chrysler Tower.

Scovills turned out brass buttons for the United States Army and for the Navy in the War of 1812. They did their fanciest button job for the Marquis de Lafayette when he came avisiting in New York in 1825 —a set of gold buttons decorated with the image of his former Commander in Chief, Gen. George Washington.

The Scovills popularized the campaign button. They pressed the Log Cabin and Hard Cider items for William Henry Harrison's campaign. They made Gen. Zachary Taylor's buttons when he ran for President eight years later, in 1848. They still do quite a business in buttons; they equip the United States Air Force, among other military units.

Scovill records show they did business in New York in 1812. When war came in that year, they got the military button order, but learned with dismay that there was a wool shortage, so there were not enough uniforms to sew their buttons to.

The original Scovill got around that. He came to town, learned that a sharp young fellow here had sheep ready for the shears, rode back to Mad River with wool for uniforms. The sharp young fellow who owned the sheep got to be bigger than the Scovills. He was John Jacob Astor.

❡ The general notion around this city of concrete seems to be that New York is well off the tornado path, but it's not. Ninety-nine years ago, on April 27, 1854, a tornado out of the West ripped roofs off New York houses, smashed frame cottages in the rural area around 133d Street, lifted the covers off both the Baptist and Presbyterian Churches in that area, and left eight Thirty-first Street tenement houses open to the pounding rains. The same twister sank Capt. John Ericsson's experimental caloric ship in the Hudson. It was raised on May 12 that year.

A tornado that sank boats carrying twenty-nine men and women out for Sabbath sailing in New York Bay on July 1, 1792, came out of the West, too. Broadsides written about this one sold in the streets. Woodcuts of twenty coffins decorated the upper border above the heading, "A True and Particular Narrative of the Late Tremendous Tornado, or Hurricane, at Philadelphia and New York." This penny bit warned home folk: "Tell this not in Massachusetts, publish it not in the streets of Connecticut, lest their sober-minded young men and maidens should bitterly reproach thee in the Day of Thy Calamity."

June 19, 1953

¶ It's more than three months since the city asked the Federal Communications Commission for permission to use a WNYC beep for radio-controlled street lighting, but no word's come through on it.

The City Fathers, though, are no more anxious about it than engineers for the Broadway Maintenance Corporation, private contractors who not only take care of street lamps but do such odd jobs as maintaining the Eternal Light at Madison Square, the illumination around the Mayor's house, Gracie Mansion, and the rigging of the City Hall Christmas tree in season.

The maintenance company's men have radio lighting working perfectly now. They installed test outfits around their Long Island

City plant and in Times Square between Forty-third and Forty-fifth Streets, and are able to light them or turn them off in a split second with a barely audible beep from the municipal broadcasting station. The sound is similar to the Arlington time signal.

Lights are turned off now, and have been for years, by so-called astronomical clocks built into lightpost bases, but the engineers sneer at these as unfit for the Atomic Age. They're out of true astronomical step by at least fifteen minutes, can't compensate for late dawns or early twilights, and are forever being snatched by mischievous small fry who find no actual use for them.

The company tried electric-eye relays before it adopted radio, but these went mad along Broadway, affected by blinking signs, motor car headlights, and dust accumulation. They were all right in parks when trees were bare, but didn't function at the bidding of sun or darkness when foliage screened them.

The radio unit the company came up with after months of lab experiment seems just right. It is barely the size of a small orange-juice can, carries its own antenna, would be set at light-pole top away from moppets' hands, and could be completely discarded at the first sign of failure, without expensive loss.

Each of these units, the company says, is in effect a radio receiver. Its aerial picks up the beep and actuates a relay, or trip, to turn the light off or on. The engineers think New York should save around

$500,000 on its lighting bill if the F. C. C. comes through. Actual installation wouldn't take three months.

The maintenance men don't want to push things, but they've experimented quite a bit recently with fluorescent street lighting and think it's only a question of time before New York will adopt it, come—if ever—days of budgetary balance. They've experimented with such lighting in Glen Cove. It works fine there.

The same men, incidentally, clean city street signs with five specially designed rotary brushes and a detergent backed by live steam. The toughest assignment they took on was cleaning traffic light lenses. These hadn't been touched in ten years. It took acid to get them anywhere near original brightness.

June 22, 1953

❡ In all New York there are only a few who paint churches with light as Charles Thomas Henry does. It is a delicate art.

Right now Mr. Henry—"closing on seventy," as he puts it—is converting the St. Patrick's Cathedral lighting system from direct to alternating current. When he has done with it, the cathedral's soft illumination, indoors and out, will be controlled by ten silent push buttons instead of the clattery battery of eighty switches used now behind the altar.

"The old set sounds like a snare drum," Mr. Henry says.

The aim in church lighting, it appears, is to cause the light to seem to come out of the altar, from a crucifix, from a painting. Sacred objects, Mr. Henry says, must be made to give off spiritual glow. He accomplishes this with low-wattage lamps. He prefers 40-watters, never uses lights of more than 100 watts.

In churches and cathedrals where vaults soar high, Mr. Henry designs the lighting to fall short of the actual ceiling, or to barely reach it. That accentuates height, adds to the spiritual atmosphere. Cutout masks come into play in crucifix lighting; they project the light on the cross itself, but keep the source invisible.

Confessional lighting is difficult. It is usually minimum light, with enough illumination at the steps to guide the feet of strangers in a church. Enough spill light is let into the confessional itself so the priest may read his missal between confessions.

Sanctuary lighting, with lamps hidden behind pillars and other architectural screening, is particularly difficult, Mr. Henry finds. It must be designed so that, whatever position the priest must take during the service, no shadow falls upon the Book.

The requirement in sanctuary lighting is to maintain softness, yet provide enough glow for easy reading. "Men of the priesthood," Mr. Henry points out, "are apt to have poor eyesight, because they are devoted to study." He said sanctuary lighting was designed to reduce awkwardness of movement, too, such as might be caused by block shadow.

There are seventeen altars in St.

Patrick's. The lamps in these are balanced. If one goes out, the rest take over so that only Mr. Henry and his assistants notice a difference. Communicants never do. The cathedral lights burn an average of sixteen hours a day, which is hard usage. They are inspected daily.

Signal lights time responses between the grand organ loft on the Fifth Avenue side and the chancel organ of the cathedral. Otherwise, there would be a time lag in liturgical responses.

MARGINALIA: ⁋ Walking distance around Manhattan Island is twenty-nine miles.

⁋ Trinity Church, its rectors and vestrymen have probably given the city a larger number of street names than any other single institution. Church Street and Trinity Place were named after it; so was Rector. Vesey Street was named for the church's first rector, the Rev. William Vesey; Barclay for the second rector, the Rev. Henry Barclay; Moore Street for Bishop Benjamin J. Moore, sixth in Trinity's pulpit. Charlton, Chambers, Reade, Murray, Laight, Duane, Bleecker, Dominick and Barrow Streets were named after Trinity vestrymen, and Ann Street was named for Queen Anne, who granted the ground to the church. The "e" in Anne dropped off somewhere through the years.

June 24, 1953

⁋ Bee experts in New York were not astonished the other day when a swarm set up house in a neon sign over the Horn & Hardart shop on Lexington Avenue between Fifty-eighth and Fifty-ninth Streets. It seems bees frequently turn up in the city this time of year.

A physician at Wickersham Hospital who handles the 30,000 bees on the hospital roof, not far from the H. & H. shop, was able to testify that the sign squatters were not the hospital's swarm. The hospital keeps its queen bee's wings clipped, and bees won't swarm without a queen.

What probably happened, the doctor said, is that some bee community in Brooklyn, Queens or Long Island found its hive overcrowded and followed the queen in search of new housing. The doctor figured the neon sign was probably only a way stop.

Arthur L. Amundsen, assistant general manager for the American Society for the Prevention of Cruelty to Animals, didn't bother about the bees' move into Lexington Avenue for at least seventy-two hours. His outfit has had swarming bees in different parts of the city in other years in late spring, and it has been the bees' habit to move on to greener places within a few days.

Yesterday, Mr. Amundsen decided this swarm had overstayed a bit. He has a list of beekeepers in and around New York for just such emergencies. He got one to go over to the H. & H. shop and plant a fresh hive to tempt the squatters away. Last night it seemed to be working. A good part of the colony had moved in.

Mr. Amundsen carefully explained, though, that the society has no jurisdiction over visiting bees unless they become a menace to the public welfare, which they hadn't—or until someone reports some public act of cruelty to the bees, which no one had.

Incidentally, the bees on Wickersham Hospital roof were raised for bee therapy in arthritis cases. Bee venom seems to help in some forms of that ailment. In the last few years, though, the Wickersham swarm hasn't been used much. Doctors have found cortisone more effective than the venom.

The bee man who set the hive on the H. & H. sign yesterday was due back at 5:30 A.M. today to pick up the swarm. He chose that time on the sensible theory that if things went wrong fewer potential sufferers would be abroad in Lexington Avenue at that hour.

¶ All buildings used by diamond merchants in Forty-seventh Street between Fifth Avenue and the Avenue of the Americas are single-ended. Diamond men will not operate in a structure that might give thieves easy run-through from one street to another.

¶ Strangers in town are apt to get a little confused by the ancient gas-light street lamps in front of 106 West Fifty-fifth Street. They carry street signs that say "Bowery" and "Grand Street," which are 'way downtown. The lamps are relics set in front of the headquarters of the Grand Street Boys Association.

June 29, 1953

¶ In almost any community a mattress maker can be an important man, but along Mott and Mulberry Streets and in East Harlem and other large Italian colonies in New York, he's bound to be if he is expert in handling goat-hair and sheep's-wool mattresses—the kind that parents in some parts of Italy give to children in dowry.

These mattresses are heirlooms. They go down through generations with occasional additions of delicate fluffings and with carefully measured replacement when contents spill. Such operations are carried out under owners' eyes, in their own flats. That is tradition as much as it is precaution.

Successful immigrants who get more modern bed equipment usually ship their dower mattresses back to the towns or hamlets of their nativity, as this week did Louis (Luigi) Morino, who owns Sloppy Louis' seafood restaurant on the South Street waterfront opposite the main fishmongers' stalls at Fulton Dock.

When Louis left Recco, near Genoa, in Italy as a boy in 1905, to come to the United States, his mother split her ancient sheep's-wool mattress. She gave Louis half, and when his sister Teresa followed to New York in 1907 she proudly bore the other half. She was here only four years; she returned to Recco with her mattress in 1911.

Teresa's daughter Gina has a 9-year-old son, Giovanni Carlo Cartasegna in Voghera, near Milan, in Italy. In a recent letter Teresa timidly suggested it would make her happy if Giovanni might one day inherit Louis' mattress. Louis called in a Mulberry Street mattress man, had his half of the family pallet processed and crated; it was shipped home in the hold of the S. S. Eugene C., a vessel owned by a fellow Reccoan.

MARGINALIA: ¶ Mid-twentieth century New York still uses some brick sewers put down in the early nineteenth century. They're mostly below Canal Street. Parts of the Canal Street sewer carry their twentieth century load after 145 years. . . .

July 1, 1953

¶ Jake Bachtold was rewarded with a golden New York Central Railroad pass yesterday—for fifty years of clock watching, of all things. He mumbled his thanks and returned to his room to resume clock watching, which he had interrupted for the ceremony.

Mr. Bachtold is 76 years old, now. He was only 26 when the railroad hired him as electrician and stable foreman in its Fifty-first Street shop on Aug. 1, 1903. Six big draft horses were kept there. They turned freight cars around in the roundhouse.

When Mr. Bachtold came to the United States from Schaffhausen in Switzerland in 1900 he was a watchmaker, but after three years at the trade in Maiden Lane his eyes went weak. He sought work that might rest them—and landed in the stable.

Not for long. Because he was an electrician and because electric clocks were coming in apace, he was set to wiring Grand Central Terminal for six of the new-fangled units. One clock is much like another in essential works. He made the change.

He kept the original clocks in his dusty shop and from time to time used parts for other old railroad timepieces. The parts still work, one place or another, among the 1,000 railroad clocks now in Mr. Bachtold's charge.

The clock foreman—that's his official rating—isn't positive, but he thinks the oldest clocks in the system might be around 70, like the old Seth Thomas wallpiece in the office of Roland Gooch, assistant superintendent of power. That one came out of Wingdale station.

At current count, Jake figures, the road is using about 800 electric clocks, about 200 hand wound. The latter are all 50 years old, at least—Thomases, Howards and Ansonias, mostly.

The biggest hazard in country station clocks, Mr. Bachtold finds, is moths. They go after the felt under the dial rim and frequently gum up in the works. Phillipse Manor tower clock came to a dead stop three years ago. Mr. Bachtold found a live mouse in the works; he turned it loose.

Mr. Bachtold still lugs twenty-five-pound electric clocks up twenty-foot ladders, when need be; he still handles the sixty-pound marble dials on Grand Central Terminal's biggest time-tellers. It was his idea, too, to remove the glass faces from the information desk clocks. They reflected too much light and were hard to read.

The two big days in the clock foreman's life are the daylight-to-standard and standard-to-daylight change-overs. He had his crew start about three hours before the deadline to get all the pieces right. It's simple: The standard-time hands, which are black, are untouched. The red hour hand for daylight time, which fits snugly behind the black, is pulled out and set one hour ahead. It's tucked away again in September.

The golden pass Mr. Gooch gave Mr. Bachtold is good for any run on the New York Central. Mr. Gooch handed a pass with somewhat more restricted privileges to Snefrid, the clock foreman's wife. He said, "You must not sneak off, Jake, when you go on trips. You must take Mrs. Bachtold."

Jake's trembling fingers locked tightly behind his back and he nodded in all seriousness. Mr. Gooch put out his hand. He said, "God bless you, Jake," and Jake's fingers unlocked to take the grip. The office workers went back to their desks, and Jake trailed back to his dusty bin with Snefrid following him.

July 6, 1953

❡ Sami El Shawa the Amir El Kamanja was in town again recently after an upstate swing. Last Saturday he headed to Pawtucket, R. I., and on the 20th he will be heard in Binghamton, N. Y. A week later he will fly the modern magic carpet to California.

Sami El Shawa is an Egyptian violinist from Cairo. He is descended from a long line of immortal Arab violinists and his title Amir El Kamanja, Arabic for "Prince of the Violin," is gravely accepted by Americans of Arabic descent as it is in the Sahara, in Trans-Jordan, in Egypt, Tunis, Morocco, Iran, Iraq, Lebanon, Syria, Marrakesh and Istanbul.

This is the third visit Sami El Shawa has made to the United States. He came first in 1927, again in 1933, and flew in just before last Christmas for his current tour. He played in Brooklyn's Academy of Music last February to 1,400 Americans of Arabic descent, and his works have been heard, since, up and down the seaboard.

There are some 50,000 Americans of Middle East ancestry in and around New York City and a goodly number of them have thrilled to Sami El Shawa's music. He plays in their homes, at the Hotel St. George in Brooklyn, and in the public halls. His violin records are best sellers in Arab communities.

Some weeks ago the Amir El Kamanja was summoned to the Waldorf-Astoria suite of the Arabian Emir al-Saud to play for the emir and his retinue. He gave them improvisations from the "Takseem," ancient basic Arab tunes, which each Arab musician interprets in his own fashion.

Sami El Shawa speaks next to no English. He is a tense little man with the traditional collar-covering locks of his trade. His lively eyes protrude with emotionalism when he plays, or when excitement digs its fingers into him.

The Prince of the Violin swears he can make his instrument speak —literally, speak. He will ask your name, and he will make the violin say, "Hel-lo, Mis-ter Ne-Ja-Me," or whatever the name happens to be. The eyes creep from his lids as he demonstrates.

The Western ear may find Sami El Shawa's music strange; it usually does. But the artist explains: European music has fewer notes than Arabic music; it lacks certain quarter and three-quarter measures. He demonstrates that, too, with eye obbligato.

His greatest treasure is his Pharaonic violin. He says it was made of wood of the Cedars of Lebanon taken from ancient Egyptian tombs in The Valley of the Kings, and that the wood parts are 3,000 years old. The instrument head is an image of Queen Nefertiti.

The Prince of the Violin is a noted Arab composer. He cannot speak of his pieces, though, except through the violin. He tucks the mellowed wood under his chin, his dark head (astonishingly black for a man of sixty-four) snugs down and the strings take vibrant voice.

He plays the Music of the Koran, inspired by the "Azaan," the opening matutinal prayer, "Allahu Akbar" ("God Is All Powerful") and "Prayer in the Desert," a hauntingly melancholy piece that describes an Arab boy at prayer on the sands under the stars. Sahara's winds sigh from the strings. The chant is plaintive.

Traffic outside Sami El Shawa's window drowns some of it, but when the last notes die away into silence, the player earnestly tells you, "In the quiet of a sultan's palace even the lowest prayer notes would linger."

He should know. He has played for all the living sultans. He played for King Farouk and for the khedives before him in the royal palace in Cairo.

Only one great Arab ruler has not heard Sami El Shawa's music, and never will—King Ibn Saud of Saudi Arabia. He is of the Wahabi, or Arab Puritans, and will not profane the royal ears with worldly entertainment, Sami tells you.

Then the Prince of the Violin brings out a cedar chest filled with decorations from the great sultans to prove how they have applauded his works with high insignia, colorful orders. He would treasure the gold dagger or the white and gold aba that King Ibn Saud bestows, but knows he can never have it.

The interpreter tells you that Sami El Shawa's New York audience is predominantly Maronite Roman Catholic, with only a sprinkling of Moslems and Jews. Ninety per cent are Lebanese who worship in Maronite churches on West Street in Manhattan and on Clinton Street in Brooklyn.

Going down the hotel corridor you faintly hear the Pharaonic violin again, playing the last notes of an ancient Arab love song. "Id Maa Ahobak Lalan Minak"—"My Love Is So Deep That I Know Great Pain." The theme seems universally familiar.

July 8, 1953

¶ Hidden in blackened old Fletcher Street, a narrow lane off the waterfront at Manhattan Island's tip, is a curious little shop that sells obsolete ammunition. Philip Jay Medicus, a former Air Force man, darkhaired, grave, bespectacled, runs it. He began as a collector, turned his hobby into a business in 1946.

His little establishment is crowded with old, blackened shells, and with bright, new ones freshly manufactured for him to fit old weapons. He carries astonishing items—cartridges filled with rose, lilac, violet and lily of the valley "parfum," as his catalogue puts it. Germans fired the scented pieces from special pistols to sweeten air in confined quarters. The firing charge is extremely light.

Mr. Medicus has mock-duel cartridges, a French item. The cartridge heads are of wax and graphite; they look cruel as any bullet, but would barely sting a duelist at ten paces, or just enough to satisfy a man's honor. Mr. Medicus explains that the primer carries the charge. "No more kick to it than you'd get from a souped-up spitball," he says.

Museum items that Mr. Medicus will not sell include a rubber-cased cartridge that expands to seal the rifle breech, one in a leather case, one with the firing primer in its nose, one with the pin in its side. Mr. Medicus and his father make occasional trips to Europe to buy cartridge collections or large batches of usable cartridges. They have manufacturers turn out special ammunition in 100,000-piece lots for old guns still in use.

The Fletcher Street shop puts out a fat catalogue offering collectors and shooters ammunition for weapons turned out by craftsmen here and in Europe as far back as the American Revolution. They carry powder and shot for flintlocks, patches for muzzle loaders, bullet molds.

Mr. Medicus reports an increase in demand for derringer ammunition; he says peace officers in the West and in the Southwest are carrying derringers again for one-shot infighting with desperate quarries. Shooters—altogether a different breed, it seems, than collectors—are increasing their demand for ammo for liberated World War II weapons, German and Japanese, mostly.

The Police Department here sends its ballistics men down occasionally for old ammunition to test in weapons taken in assault and murder cases. They want the stuff to run comparative tests and to prove that a particular weapon, however ancient, could have been used in a crime. This precaution is standard because defense lawyers invariably argue that an obsolete weapon could not have been used in a crime.

Mr. Medicus was anxious to have it set down that he's a collector, not a shooter. No offer would tempt him to sell his most prized pieces.

July 13, 1953

¶ Thomas Street, between Broadway and Church Street, is owned by the Society of the Hospital of the City of New York. It holds fee title to the bed of the street because it paid for paving there in 1872. The society closes the street for twenty-four hours each Fourth of July. Trimble Place, hard by, belongs to the society, too.

Washington Mews, between Fifth Avenue and University Place, belongs to Sailors Snug Harbor Corporation. Sylvan Terrace, from St. Nicholas Avenue to Jumel Terrace between 160th and 162d Streets, paved under private contract, does not belong to the municipality.

The list is long—Patchin Place, Pomander Walk, Shinbone (Great Jones) Alley, Sniffen Court, Milligan Place, Macdougal Alley, Riverview Terrace, Franklin Place, Extra Place, Freeman Alley, Henderson Place, Broadway Alley, Bishop Lane, Depew Place, Washington Terrace, Vanderbilt Avenue from Forty-seventh Street to Forty-ninth, Lincoln Place, among others. They occur in greater numbers in sister boroughs within the city.

¶ Progress sometimes does sad things to poetic street names. It has, for example, changed "The Street That Leads to the Pie Woman's" to Nassau Street, "Windmill Lane" to Cortlandt Street, "Smell Street Lane" to Broad Street, "Tinpot Alley" to Edgar Street, "Sugarloaf Street" to Franklin Street. A country road that wound around the west end of what is now Times Square toward the river was Verdant Lane.

July 15, 1953

¶ The same Board of Transportation crews that refitted the city's 2,647 subway turnstiles when the subway fare went from 5 cents to 10 cents five years ago think they may better their time on the change-over for the 15-cent tokens next week.

Cameron A. Reed, board engineer of line equipment, set up an eight-hour work schedule for the 1948 switch, but his men were done with the job inside of four hours. He's drawn up the same eight-hour schedule for a week from Friday, but is fairly sure the maintainers won't take that long, or anywhere near it.

Turnstile change-over for the tokens actually started last November. The board's crews then began cutting tempered-steel drill rods into half-inch pins. These pins—hammered into the sides of one type of turnstile, screwed into the front of another type—will reduce coin slots one fifty-thousandth of an inch. The tokens are that much smaller than dimes.

Coin-box heads (top-castings to the trade) have been brought into the board's maintenance shops a few at a time since last November, have been drilled through to receive the slot-shrinking pins and have been hurried back to the turnstiles from which they came.

At 9 o'clock on Friday morning seventy-five of Mr. Reed's men will spread out to subway terminal points—Woodlawn, Pelham Bay, 242d Street and such places—to begin pegging the drilled holes with the pins. They'll do about four an hour, working their way downtown.

In each station crews will take alternate turnstiles, leaving the others free for customers. After midnight Friday they'll work back toward the terminals again, converting turnstiles they left free on the first tour.

Mr. Reed and Paul Anderson, supervisor of turnstiles, will direct the operation from the board's new maintenance headquarters on the Fourteenth Street (Seventh Avenue) station mezzanine. They have crews of trouble-shooters standing by to take over wherever change-over men run into difficulties.

Operation sheets read like wartime General Orders. Each maintenance man must call headquarters (command post) before he moves from one station to another. If he fails to call on scheduled time, Mr. Reed, Mr. Anderson or Tom Carroll, Mr. Anderson's assistant, will assume he is sick, or worse. Extra help will speed to the spot.

On Friday morning, the crews will work no farther south in midtown than Fifty-ninth Street. Most heavy-flow midtown stations will get concentrated attention before and after midnight on Friday, with lay-off for crowd traffic after the theatres close.

Turnstiles finished before the new-fare deadline will be roped off so that the moles don't damage their fingernails trying to jam dimes into them. As soon as the clocks show a minute after midnight, Saturday morning, agents will remove the rope barriers, and

the operation will have ended except for inspection.

Change-over on the system's 152 high turnstiles—the heavy prison-bar type at remote agentless stations—will be done more or less at leisure and should take three or four days. While crews work on these an agent will stand by to collect tokens or cash by hand.

This takes care of all but 400 other turnstiles—passimeters, they're called—along B. M. T. routes in Brooklyn that are controlled by boothed ticket agents with a pull-cord arrangement. They have no coin slots. The fare is passed under a grille to the agent.

The board, by way of incidental intelligence, pays $525 for each turnstile, another $75 to install each one. It has only thirty-five in reserve, because the things are long-lived. With routine overhaul every five or six years, lubrication and dusting every forty-five days and frequent sandpapering of electrical contacts, they could last almost forever.

July 20, 1953

❡ The New Yorker stumbling in and out of subway burrows is apt to be a bit blind to Nature's endless manifestations. Seldom does he become aware of them until he has driven past the city line, and then they seem to come swarming at his picnic lunch or at sensitive areas not covered by a bathing suit.

George I. Schwartz, biology teacher at Forest Hills High School and at New York University, thinks that almost any New York yard with a bit of shrubbery would yield close to 2,000 of God's smaller creatures.

For a recent TV "Back Yard Zoology" show, Mr. Schwartz got most of his specimens out of his own back yard on Fifty-ninth Avenue in Flushing in Queens. He came up with assorted beetles, cicadas, snails, slugs, butterflies, garter snakes, De Kay snakes, toads, mantises, moths, pill bugs, water bugs, caterpillars.

He did rather well, too, with gall-producing insects, which give a gouty appearance to whatever plant growths they choose to visit —blackberry bushes, oaks, pines. Mr. Schwartz said, in passing, that Dr. Alfred Kinsey, popular because of certain other studies, is a good gall man; he knows them well.

The biology instructor did not try for 2,000 species out of his back yard for his TV show, because countless small insects don't show too well even in special TV camera lenses. His largest show items were snakes—De Kays that measure up to six inches, garters up to eight and ten inches, a few fat bees off his back-yard roses.

There are a few tricks to backyard hunting. The little snakes are found under flat rubbish—boards, cast-off linoleum strips, old doors— and old tree stumps. They like the coolth, and flat cover attracts the things they feed upon. Mr. Schwartz knows a man who found 350 snakes within thirty square feet in Flushing.

July 22, 1953

¶ Chinese elders in New York cling to ancient beliefs and to ancient customs and traditions. Some still believe, for example, in ancient Chinese remedies—snake wine, wildcat soup and monkey soup.

Older Chinese laundrymen in town suffered in silence for years when rheumatics overtook them in damp back-of-the-shop sleeping quarters, because they found snakes and wildcats hard to come by in this city.

In 1935, though, Sou Chan, now a prosperous restaurant man, established contact with a snake dealer in Brownsville, Tex., and bought reptiles at 50 cents a pound, plus shipping charge. He got wildcats from the same dealer.

Rheumatic elders eagerly paid $1 to $1.50 for the snakes. They steeped them, alive, in rice wine mixed with special Chinese herbs and rubbed the resulting liniment on ailing parts. Many still use this specific, and wildcat soup, too.

American-born Chinese, though they respect their elders, have no truck with such remedies, but the ancients get their snakes and wildcats and monkeys now without difficulty. Most of them have standing accounts at Fulton Street pet shops, which supply their wants at pet-shop prices.

July 29, 1953

¶ New York's most difficult bulb-changing job, switching beacon lights on the Empire State Building TV tower, 1,472 feet above the pavement, is usually left to John Freehill, 51 years old, and to John Walsh, 43, two steeplejacks enrolled in Local 3 of the International Brotherhood of Electrical Workers A. F. L.

They make the climb two or three times a year. No matter how long the change-over takes they're good for a full day's wages and for an additional $5 an hour while they're at the TV tower stint. With the weather right they're usually finished inside two hours.

Mr. Walsh and Mr. Freehill use elevators and ladders to get them up to about the 105th floor. They climb the last seventy-five feet outside the tower, using safety belts, heavy gloves and a small map showing where they might come afoul of high-voltage TV lines.

Weather maps are consulted before the men go up, but even that doesn't always mean they get perfect conditions at 1,472 feet. Sometimes they start up to a clear sky and run into heavy mist, rain or snow that New Yorkers 'way down below don't have to share.

One day last winter, the pair stayed in the clear up to the last forty feet. Then they were caught in a sudden snowstorm. They hollered to one another above the wind's scream and philosophically decided they might as well continue on up. It would have been just as difficult to go down again.

Another thing about the job—rains and snows drive upward at 1,472 feet because of the peculiar midtown skyscraper updrafts. The climbers are used to that. So, now, are the lamps they change. They were specially developed in the General Electric lamp laboratories in Cleveland to withstand up-driving storms.

Red filters shield the lamps from side-blow, but the intense heat the lamps generate—they're special 620-watters that sell at $5.95 each —doesn't permit bottom closure. Until the G. E. researchers developed the new bulb cover, every storm, rain or snow caused damage.

The newer type 620-watters are good for around 3,000 hours now in almost any weather, but NBC-TV, which holds top position on the tower, has a mirror arrangement down at the base and a human monitor to watch it for lamp blowouts. The air beacons are important.

Tower beacons hold fourteen lamps, all 111-watters of special design, and twelve are fixed lights. The two topmost beacons are blinkers with 12,000 candlepower output between them. Mr. Walsh and Mr. Freehill carry the bulbs in canvas knapsacks, like mountain climbers.

Don Gibson, Empire State Building engineer, says the top lamps give *him* less concern than the thousands of others in use in the 'scraper. "No bulb-snatching problem," he explains.

August 5, 1953

¶ Quaintest spot in midtown, but little known to roisterers of that quarter, is Amster's Yard in Forty-ninth Street east of Third Avenue. You go through a thin-barred iron gate down a long flagged corridor till you're midway between the north side of Forty-ninth Street, but perhaps forty feet short of Fiftieth, and you're in a cool, ailanthus-shaded garden restored to look much as it was, say, 150 years ago.

White and gray cottages face each other across the court. The ground's neatly laid out in squares and oblongs that smell of rain and dew through lush fern growth and pachysandra. Lotus bowls and wrought-iron benches are cunningly placed in it and a wall sign reads "Boston Post Road, 1673."

The spot covers old Turtle Creek that ran down to the river through heavy swamp when George Holmes and Thomas Hall raised tobacco on it in 1639. They were, incidentally, the first Britons to settle on the island. A sawmill and a gristmill clattered away in almost primeval stillness in mid-seventeenth century.

Homicide and other violence became sadly routine in the neighborhood just before the United Nations group went up, hard by. The first recorded killing at Turtle Creek happened on Aug. 23, 1641. A Weckquesgeek brave used his tomahawk on Claes Cornelissen, a foolish wheelwright floundering through the great beeches there. The Union Flag Tavern stood just off Third Avenue in late seventeenth century. It was a place to change horses for the stage on the Eastern Post Road.

August 7, 1953

❡ New York's subways support 11,700 vending machines, a sub-asphalt copper mine that yields 1,167,000 pounds of pennies each year, the largest operation of its kind on earth. The combined railroad stations of the United States support fewer than 10,000 machines.

The American Chicle Company holds the New York subway vending contract, but assigns actual operation to the International News Company, which keeps 145 men underground all day, collecting, stocking and maintaining the units, a lively and rather complicated business.

Robert B. Kyle, sales promotion manager for American Chicle, figured the other day with George Booth and Charles Maloney, executives for the news company, that subway riders get about 2,500,000 pounds of merchandise each year for their copper, and for nickels and dimes put in larger machines.

The men who own the subway vending units are reluctant to discuss annual revenue. The closest they come is to tell you that thirty-four pounds of pennies comes to $50, and that their trucks take an average of 150 thirty-four-pound bags to the Federal Reserve Bank each day.

Vending machine executives are unhappy about the public view on pennies lost in their slot machines. They point out that when a machine sticks, the blockage costs them in sales eight to ten times the original 1-cent customer loss, not counting the repair job.

Around eight to ten persons of stern principle write in every day to complain of one-cent losses. It costs the company 8 cents to return the coin—reimbursement of the complainant's postage, their own stamp, and the cost of getting out the correspondence. They attach the returned coin to the letter with tape.

Chewing gum, the subway riders' favorite machine purchase, accounts for about 65 per cent of the total merchandise sold; 5-cent candy runs second, 1-cent chocolate third, 1-cent peanuts fourth. Weighing scales account for a good part of the remainder.

By union rules the men who fill the machines and collect coins from them never carry more than seventy-five pounds at a time, either in coin or in merchandise. They drop their coin in sacks at 100-odd mezzanine depots where they refill merchandise bags. They do minor repairs, but phone for troubleshooters on jobs they can't handle.

Few who drop tiddledywinks buttons, slugs, washers, paper clips, cardboard, hairpins—among other curious items—into vending machines are aware that they are violating a municipal law as well as Section 167 of the Federal Criminal Code.

Occasional gold-pieces turn up in the penny slots. International News recently returned a $2.50 gold coin; it has held another for years without a claimant. It keeps charts to show where rashes of distinctive types of slugs are showing up and catches the culprits sooner or later.

The company maintains a list of psychopaths who stuff machines with paper or cardboard, then fish out pennies put in by customers. One scholarly-looking old gentleman in his 60's and of good-blooded stock has been caught scores of times; so has a woman of about the same age. Their lawyers can't do anything with them.

One-cent machines cost the company around $100. Big units like the ice-cream venders run as high as $900. Repair cost is astonishing; shops at 11 Beach Street are always full. Two men there, Frank Kraft and Joe Dworkin, have been in the craft steadily the last forty-two years.

For a long time the company used a distinctive slug with the inscription "INCO" on it to make certain that its weighing-scale adjusters were making their proper rounds. The adjusters would put the INCO slugs in to test the machines. If the slugs didn't turn up it was plain the adjuster had skipped the unit.

It dawned on company executives one day that they were violating the Federal anti-slug law themselves by using the slugs. On their lawyers' advice they've dropped the practice.

August 10, 1953

❡ The melancholy dull-red brick schoolhouse on the south side of Thirteenth Street east of the Avenue of the Americas was hailed as "the perfection" of what a schoolhouse should be when it was opened in 1847 as Ward School 35.

Today it is the oldest of the city's 875 classroom structures, wheezy-staired, untidy, bulgy-walled and covered with sickly-green paint throughout, much like an old man whose skin is stretched almost to transparency. No sign of the old perfection.

The Board of Education owns older buildings. The orginal Erasmus Hall, used as a museum now and hidden by modern Erasmus Hall High School on Flatbush Avenue in Brooklyn, went up in 1787 but has had no classrooms for years.

The Thirteenth Street relic is an annex to the Food Trades Vocational High School. Few, if any, of the 400 students who sit under its dim lamps against a Dickensian background know its past. Pete Giannini, its custodian, got his job last November. Its story is a closed book to him, too.

But the place knew many boys who climbed to high place. The pale delicate youngster who gave the graduation speech in June, 1875, on the subject "Self Help," grew up to be Chief Justice Charles E. Hughes of the United States. Henry G. S. Noble, his classmate, became president of the New York Stock Exchange. Samuel Untermyer, the lawyer; Herman Ridder, the publisher; and Brevet Maj. Gen. Nelson H. Henry, former surveyor of the port, were other graduates of the school.

One of the school's principals, Thomas Hunter, founder of what is now Hunter College, made legend in Board of Education history.

Dr. Hunter came to the school as a drawing teacher in 1850. He was from Northern Ireland—a poor immigrant, less than 19 years old, hungry, almost starved. He had tramped the dusty city roads looking for anything, even common labor. He leaped at a three months' tryout.

He stayed on, became principal in 1857. He was the second head of Ward School 35. The first was John J. Doane, who with five other teachers to help, tried to beat the three R's into kids who yearned for the green spaces on Union Square and Central Park. Greenwich Village was still something of a real village then, and summons to study was by hand bell.

Dr. Hunter was a progressive. He liked to have his restless captives hear great men. One famous guest was Richard Cobden, the economist, stentorian advocate of Corn Law revision. Pete Giannini says he heard that Abraham Lincoln spoke in the building once, but records don't seem to prove it.

It was in Ward School 35 that bearded Dr. Hunter launched his movement to end the corporal punishment of pupils. The story is that he thwacked two pupils till they glowed like the back of a stove, then learned he had made a mistake. He is supposed to have said: "A blow struck can never be taken back. It is a barbaric relic." And he threw the rod away forever.

But there is not a single record left in old 35 to tell the story of its 106 years—not one. Pete Giannini searched from the dusty, blistered and blackened old basement to the wretched offices on the fourth floor. Nothing left. Old 35 is ready for the wreckers and, sentiment aside, the sooner the better.

August 12, 1953

¶ Generations of criminals and neighborhood topers have left whimsical or embittered thoughts in writing on the walls of long-abandoned, windowless cells in old East Thirty-fifth Street police station with outlaws' scorn for city property.

Some inscriptions date back to 1864, ten years after the East Thirty-fifth Street precinct house was opened. These are pretty much faded, and trying to read them by hand lamp is trying on the eyes. Among bawdier and more profane things, they say:

"Its Hell to be locked up like a wild beast." . . . "Kid Peppi. I cut up Bedinker." . . . "Pinched for Shooting a Dutchman. This happened on Friday the Thirteenth." . . . "William Scully, Co. B 69th Inf. AWOL 11 days, 9 months, 3 hours. 1918."

No one on duty in East Thirty-fifth now knows much of the station's history. Patrolman Thomas McNamara, with thirty-three years there, and Harry Osmund, with thirty-nine, remember a few dusty legends, but not many. Capt. Walter Clark got all his second hand, too.

East Thirty-fifth, on the street's south side just east of Third Avenue, is a pale-faced five-story relic with peeling metal ceilings. It used gaslight in the dark dormitories up to two years ago. The blackened cottage next door emphasizes its age.

Even back in the Eighties the building was listed as "fourth-rate," its quarters were described as "cramped" and the ugly old cells with cast-iron gratings were called "vile." One of the cells was for stray pups and still carries a faded sign with the word "Dogs," though it is no longer the local pound.

When the station house was built, a contemporary chronicler said of the precinct, "It runs to aristocracy on its western border and to squalor and petty crime as East River is approached." Almost 100 years later that line still fits, more or less.

The most wicked spot 100 years ago was Corcoran's Roost, a thieves' squatter colony cluttered with goats and porkers, at Fortieth Street and East River, where Tudor City is now. "The police here," set down the same chronicler, "have to deal with a ruffianly element . . . and a uniformed officer is fine game for the young thugs in the district."

Just before midnight on July 23, 1868, Patrolman John Smedick of East Thirty-fifth Street was shot dead in Third Avenue by John Real, a neighborhood buckaroo, for no obvious reason. Real was hanged in The Tombs yard on Aug. 5, 1870.

Time-decayed blotters in East Thirty-fifth show that the station house had its worst time during the Draft Riots in mid-July, 1863. Rioters looted homes on Murray Hill, wounded several policemen and murdered Col. H. J. O'Brien of the Eleventh New York volunteers in Third Avenue.

Among happier memories were precinct encounters with the Murray Hill gentry—with J. P. Morgan, who lived at 231 Madison; the Satterlees, the George Bakers of the banking family, the De Lamars, the Delanos, the Bacons, and with faded folk in the old Murray Hill Hotel and in the Belmont, where the Air Terminal is now.

It was nice, Patrolman McNamara remembers, to say good morning to blue bloods on their way to church of a Sabbath morning; it was something to talk about when you got home that night. The aristocrats were always generous at Christmas.

One favorite topic in the station house is Physick, the Morgan butler, who was a stiffish fellow with a rather high-pitched voice. They talk also about the tiger cat that drowses all day on the blotter desk.

The tiger is a direct link with J. P. Morgan. He is Mickey, one of a litter born in the Morgan mansion seventeen years ago. He looks at you through half-shut golden eyes with the same catlike contempt that he has for the tipsy, the wanton and the other human dregs that parade nightly across the creaking old station-house floor.

August 14, 1953

❡ One day in June sixty years ago Dr. William Hallock Park of the municipal Health Department's Bureau of Laboratories got a cablegram from Budapest. It said: "Start the horses. Antitoxin great success."

This cryptic key put the Health Department into the livestock field. Dr. Hermann M. Biggs, who had sent it from the International Medical Congress in Austria-Hungary, was the city's chief medical officer. He had just heard that antitoxin obtained from horses was a diphtheria preventive, and diphtheria was then a major killer.

Dr. Park got his first antitoxin samples from the New York College of Veterinary Surgeons at 154 East Fifty-seventh Street, where I. R. T. Substation No. 42 is now, just west of Third Avenue. They were ready by Jan. 1, 1894, and they worked.

In almost no time Dr. Park, his assistant, Dr. Anna Williams, and Dr. Biggs watched the diphtheria death chart go down close to the vanishing point. The improved serum earned Dr. Park and Dr. Williams the unofficial label "conquerors of diphtheria."

Today, the Health Department owns a 175-acre farm at Otisville in Orange County, forty-two miles north of the city, where fifty-nine horses, some of them retired police mounts, and a flock of fifty sheep produce $180,000 worth of biologicals each year.

On the farm, too, the Health Department maintains a more or less constant lively supply of around 600 guinea pigs, 2,000 white mice and 800 rabbits for laboratory experiments. It is probably the only municipal farm of its kind in the world.

In 1909, a year after the Health Department got its Otisville acreage, it brought Robert S. Lang, a Cavan man, from Ireland, to handle the horses. He's still on the job at 65, but by an odd twist works under his son, Walter.

Father and son came down in 1947 to take a Civil Service examination for the farm foremanship. Lang the Elder scanned the questions and threw in his pen. Young Lang breezed through it and came out top man. They work smoothly together.

The serum turned out at Otisville is processed at the Health Department's laboratories at the foot of East Fifteenth Street. It is distributed to 300 health stations and is available for physicians and clinics.

More than 500,000 doses of smallpox vaccine taken from Otisville sheep, are kept in refrigerated vaults. There is always enough diphtheria antitoxin in supply to inoculate the 150,000 children born each year in New York. And there is a surplus.

The original biologicals produced by Dr. Park and his assistants, first in New York and then at the farm, have spread over the globe, and the chances are their progeny will safeguard future generations against disease down to the end of time.

The valiants who started all this, and Otisville, have one by one gone to their hard-earned rest—Dr. Biggs in 1923, Dr. Park in 1939, most of their aides with them. Dr. Williams remains. She lives quietly at Meelan Lodge in Woodcliff Lake, N. J.

Still in practice, though, despite his 75 years, is Dr. Bela Schick of Mount Sinai Hospital, who worked with Dr. Park and in 1913 developed the Schick Test, a vital factor in diphtheria control.

August 19, 1953

❡ New York is a trembling city. It quivers most when subway, bus, elevated railroad and motor traffic picks up in morning and evening rush hours. Heavy milk trains make its rocky underpinning jig before dawn. Earthquakes clear across the world can titillate it.

One man in town, the Rev. J.

Joseph Lynch, has twelve eyes on the giant's tremors all the time; he has had these eyes for the last twenty-three years. Ten of his eyes are seismographs housed in concrete imbedded in solid rock below the Fordham University campus.

One of the ten machines is a Benioff that multiplies tremors 100,000 times, writes them with a fine light beam on photographic paper in the dark underground vault, as the others do. Between them they pick up local quivers and the most remote, each according to kind.

Father Lynch seldom takes his attention from the seismographs. If he is within telephone reach he calls every hour to ask if there's been anything lively on the recorders. If there has, he comes loping in for a reading and quick interpretation.

Last Sunday night he was downtown. When he called in just before midnight, his aides told him the newspapers were anxious to know if the explosion in the naval shipyard in Brooklyn had registered on his quiver gadgets. Father Lynch said he'd be right up.

The Third Avenue "El" does not operate on the Sabbath. Father Lynch caught a New York Central train to Fordham. He dived—all six lean feet of him—down the steep flight to the vault, walked cat-sure from one seismograph to another in the dark for quick reading.

He had a puzzle on his hands. There were two different readings —what looked like a local earthquake on the short-jolt seismograph, a second reading that indicated an earthquake about 2,000 miles away. Earth in spasm writes with distinctive mark; there is no mistaking a quake for an explosion reading.

It turned out, eventually, that the explosion in the Navy Yard had happened in the same split second as the faraway quake—at 11:33 P.M. The local reading, a kind of hammer-blow mark, had been recorded at 11:22. It took a bit of unraveling, but Father Lynch managed.

The explosion had left no mark. The local earthquake was merely one of earth's slight hiccups, just across the Hudson in Bergen County. Father Lynch gave that information, said it would take a while to pinpoint the tremor that came 2,000 miles. Then he prepared for bed.

He didn't make it just then. In town and all about, gay folk celebrating the Feast of St. Rocco were touching off a new type of carnival explosive that the trade jestingly calls Atom Bomb, because it's louder than old charges. Nervous people kept calling to ask Father Lynch if we weren't having a string of local earthquakes.

It was well past 3 A.M. before the last of these hysterical queries was answered. Mother Earth, a last check showed, was rid of her ague for the day. Father Lynch put out the last window light that showed on the lovely old campus; he fell off to deep, tremorless sleep.

August 21, 1953

❡ At noon 115 years ago yesterday some of the town's most distin-guished citizens followed to the Catholic Cemetery in East Eleventh Street, between what is now Avenue A and First Avenue, the body of Lorenzo da Ponte, who wrote the libretto for the Mozart opera "Don Giovanni."

The librettist, something of a spendthrift and eccentric, had been a grocer in town. He had been Columbia University's first Professor of Italian Literature, too, but death had come when he was an impoverished dodderer in his ninetieth year. The body was put in a vault while friends tried to raise funds for a monument.

They never got the money. The body was forgotten. When his native Ceneda, near Venice in Italy, asked for it years later, no one could locate it. His family, which had lived with him at 91 Spring Street, searched for it in vain; they finally gave up. Years later, even the cemetery vanished.

The most fantastic opera libretto could not match the mysterious evanishment of Lorenzo da Ponte —for this reason: Mozart, with whom he had worked in Vienna in the late eighteenth century on "Don Giovanni," "Figaro" and "Cosi Fan Tutte," had vanished in almost exactly the same way after his burial in December, 1791, in a Viennese graveyard.

August 24, 1953

❡ The nation's foremost Keeper of the Keys, W. E. Hough, a massive, fast-talking bachelor out of Ohio, has organized key control for the living and executive quarters in the new White House, for Rockefeller Center's 50,000 locks, for the 12,000 locks in Peter Cooper Village and in Stuyvesant Town, for Consolidated Edison and for great liners that put into the Port of New York.

The locks at Columbia University are controlled by the Hough system. So are the locks that guard the stores of narcotics, radium and valuable surgical equipment in most of the city's major medical institutions. The Navy, the Treasury, the Atomic Energy Commission, the Federal Bureau of Investigation and great warships and carriers assemble their keys pretty much as Mr. Hough dictates.

Mr. Hough took over the business from P. O. Moore, who founded it some time back in the Twenties and whose name it still bears. The heart of the system is key tagging and a cross reference key index equipped with safeguards against key loss and against key duplication. It provides for lock switch when keys do vanish.

The Hough system for larger institutions cunningly conceals the identity of what he calls the grand masters, masters and submasters. You can't tell a master key from any other in a tray or cabinet. Before he thought of making masters without distinctive markings, manufacturers labeled them for what they were, to crooks' delight. One grand master can open thousands of locks.

When John D. Rockefeller Jr. went to his private suite in Rockefeller Center after that building project was finished twenty years

ago, he was startled to find the place a roistering hangout for assorted artisans. Someone had duplicated any number of masters and grand masters from sets provided to contractors. Mr. Rockefeller's locks were changed—and so was the key-control system.

Nowadays most architects arrange for key control before a skyscraper goes up, to prevent key duplication, and sharp watch is kept on keys throughout the building period and after. This is especially true in large hotels, where masters are sacred and where maids', housekeepers', house detectives' and other employes' keys are designed for limited use. The average modern lock will take up to twelve differently cut keys.

You learn from Mr. Hough that each grinding in key duplication robs a key of approximately one two-thousandth of an inch, and that third generation keys, as Mr. Hough calls them, begin to harm locks and make them easier prey for a picklock. He frowns on over-duplication, thinks it's cheaper to get a new lock altogether.

When a man who runs a chain of laundromats in town grumbled the other day over the cost of a key-control set-up, the Keeper of the Keys got him to figure out how much had been stolen from the machines by collectors with duplicate keys. The man gave in.

Mr. Hough concedes he loses or forgets a key now and then. Only the other day he landed in Los Angeles without the key to his wardrobe trunk. He wired the key number to his housekeeper in New York and the trunk key came out in the next plane. Without the system, she wouldn't have known which it was.

Mr. Hough is working now on key control for the average home with the key-holding board fitted between the covers of a dummy book. He thinks it should meet with decorators' approval and have literary appeal.

August 26, 1953

¶ One of the city's quaintest subsurface institutions is the New York Reading Laboratory one floor below the street at 500 Fifth Avenue, across Forty-second Street from the New York Public Library.

In its dimly lighted, soundproofed space you see men and women, some up to 75 years of age, seated in deep concentration before mechanical gadgets designed to speed their reading rate, and it seems to work.

The laboratory is run by Kenneth P. Baldridge, an Ohioan. He finds that most persons without specialized training read around 250 to 300 words a minute of what he calls "popular material," roughly half that amount in expository works.

Most persons can double their reading speed in fourteen sessions of one and one-half hours each, and many do better. The most extraordinary client the laboratory has had is a young New York draftsman who pushed himself to 1,750 words a minute on popular material ("Don Quixote" and Sherlock Holmes stories were used in the tests) and to 1,095 a minute on factual material.

Mr. Baldridge finds that "motivation" is the key to quick success in the courses. The young draftsman was obsessed with the idea that he had to acquire great reading speed to get his electrical engineering degree. Executives take the course to speed them through their mail and company reports so they may have more time at golf duffering.

Men and women who read tremendous amounts of copy professionally, as magazine editors, have been through the courses, with benefit. The basic idea is to break beginners of the habit of pausing at syllables, or at the end of each word in reading and to get them to take in "clusters of words"—whole phrases, even whole paragraphs, at a glance. Can be done, and with comprehension.

Leaving the underground chamber the other day was one of New York's most eminent book reviewers. He figures if he can speed his reading he can cut his work hours, which now keep him indoors overlong. He wasn't embarrassed at having to go back to a subterranean school to make his job simpler.

The course worked so well for a retired executive that he complained to Mr. Baldridge. "Used to be, before I took the course," he wrote, "that I'd read a complete whodunit before I got to sleep. Now I read through two a night. Getting expensive."

¶ Seems a little odd that no one down in Greenwich Village has brought New York's first poet into the city's 300th anniversary doings.

He was Jacob Steendam, a stout fellow, with a somewhat sharper eye for material things than you've come to expect of poets. He owned acreage in Flatbush in 1652, a big house in Pearl Street on the Manhattan waterfront in 1653 and collected more real estate along Broadway and in Maspeth.

Mynheer Steendam's New World works had the Chamber of Commerce touch. He was forever touting Manhattan's charms and resources:

See, two streams my gardens bind
From the East and North they wind
Rivers pouring to the sea,
Rich in fish, beyond degree.
Milk and butter; fruits to eat
No one can enumerate.
Every vegetable known,
Grain the best that e'er was grown.

Goes on that way for pages.

October 5, 1953

¶ All day and through the night men and women volunteers on a high midtown rooftop follow aircraft flight over Manhattan's towers. They quietly call the point of approach, altitude and point of progress into a telephone connected with the White Plains filter center.

The center knows what planes are scheduled. Approach of unscheduled craft out of the sky would instantly alert interceptors and anti-aircraft snugged away beyond the city's margins. The rooftop watchers take up where radar leaves off.

A few nights ago when autumnal moon mellowed turret outlines, the Ground Observer Corps, at their high vigil, seemed quiet, friendly people. Up there, above the city, they were peculiarly invested with romantic aura.

Miriam Beatty, a pretty, dark-haired girl, wore the headset. She stood by the log sheet, face aglow in the light reflected from a gooseneck lamp bent over the work sheet. She caught motor hum somewhere above the little roof shack.

She called through the open door to the watchers outside, silhouetted against the spill of light from the street far below. She said, "Track that one." Heads had already pivoted to seek plane running lights among the stars.

Janet Livingston, a tall, slender girl who traces her American ancestry to Robert Livingston, Declaration of Independence planner, called back the plane's flight path.

She said, "One aircraft. Unknown. No delay. Southeast, three miles. Flying low to the northeast."

Miss Beatty relayed the information to White Plains, wrote it in the log. At night, when plane outlines are not visible, they are for filter purposes "unknown." "No delay" means the report is going through on the exact instant a plane is sighted.

Watchers said it is a little difficult at first to pick planes out of the stars but the knack comes pretty fast. You are taught by Air Force personnel to judge altitude, how to figure distance by skyline features.

A commercial plane navigator who frequently takes predawn watch can guess the number of motors in an approaching ship, just by ear. A long-lines operator who finishes her switchboard stint at midnight stands a 2 to 6 A.M trick, too.

Watchers said you get to know the city's wondrous night beauty from the high roof. You see the rivers running molten by moonlight; you get acquainted with the golden light pearls atop the Palisades, the Statue of Liberty in blurred white splendor far to the south.

Sometimes streams of shooting stars burn out over New York. You see mist and fog build up and catch Times Square glow on their undersides. Then you see the Square drop into sullen darkness, bit by bit, after 2 A.M.

Watchers come from everywhere. Some are lonely wives of G. I.'s on foreign duty. There are retired businessmen and retired Army officers, husband-and-wife teams, amateur astronomers, a Ford parts salesman, housewives on day tricks.

Elizabeth Haas, a girl flier, stands roof watch. Maria Yauger of the Metropolitan Opera Company chorus does a regular stretch. Anyone with normal sight and normal hearing can work at it. The corps takes volunteers between 18 and 65 years old.

Alfred P. Cloutier, a free-lance photographer, takes the 10 to 12 night trick on Mondays. He's chief observer. George Mueden, retired Army officer, is supervisor. One

man has put in 375 roof hours in the last two years. Most watchers have around 100 hours, accumulated at two each week.

Miss Livingston works as research statistician by day, puts in two hours each Monday night. She thinks it astonishing that in a city of 8,000,000, the corps has found it difficult to get more watchers. But Maj. Raymond T. Wendell, Air Force coordinator, standing with the group, said it's that way in most large cities. He can't understand it.

Volunteers are taken on at the West Thirtieth Street police station in Manhattan, at the West Eighth Street precinct in Brooklyn. After twenty hours they win silver wings, which they wear as lapel ornaments.

Just before midnight a man and woman climbed the stairs to the observation shack. The man stepped outside to scan the skies. He breathed deeply in the clear autumn night. The woman got into an Air Force parka and joined him.

Mr. Cloutier said, "They're Mr. and Mrs. Norman Yarmis, husband-and-wife team, like Mrs. Cloutier and me. They've been on this Monday midnight-to-2 A.M. trick the past seven months, now. She's a hospital technician. He's a C.P.A."

The 10-to-midnight crew took one last look around before it started down, called goodnight to the Yarmises and left them standing under the stars, bulky silhouettes in the moonlight, she with the coiled telephone extension cord for tether.

The last sound, before the door

shut, was of river craft hoarsely calling, as if to each other, from North
River to East, 'way off on Manhattan's margins.

October 7, 1953

❡ Meredith Wood, Book of the
Month Club president, and Ralph
Thompson, one of the club's editors, got into friendly controversy
the other day over pronunciation
of Greenwich Village's Houston
Street. Mr. Wood's Uncle Houston
has always called it "Hugh-ston," as
Houston, Tex., is. Mr. Thompson's
family had always called the street
"House-ton."

Quite a fellow for earnest research, Mr. Thompson got the New
York Historical Society to dig into
the question. They found a piece
in a 1936 copy of The Half Moon,
Holland Society publication, which
seemed to clinch things. It said the
Village street, deeded to the city in
1808 by the Bleecker family, appeared on early maps as "Houstoun
Street"; that this traced back to the
Dutch "Huijs Tuijn," which means
"House Garden." (There was a
time when the thoroughfare was
rich in house gardens.)

Anyway, Sam Houston was a lad
of only 15 when this city acquired
the street called Houstoun, so it
couldn't have been named for him.
It wasn't until twenty-eight years
later that he beat Santa Anna at
San Jacinto, which led to the city
in Texas being named in his honor.

Mr. Thompson won a dollar on
the wager. Mr. Wood said it was
worth it, to keep the record
straight.

October 9, 1953

❡ Not one passer-by in the Times
Square night tide looked a second
time at Annette Kellerman at the
Astor Hotel curb the other night,
but this same slender lady would
have jammed pedestrian traffic at
that spot if she had paused for even
a minute forty-three years ago.

She took the jostling without
murmur. You hoped some oldster
might step up and speak her name,
but young and old whisked by
in characteristic haste to nowhere.
Miss Kellerman wrapped a green
cloth coat around her thin shoulders and clutched at her black picture hat as it slatted in autumnal
gusts.

"It's busier," she commented.
"It's more crowded. It has millions
more lights than my Broadway.
But it's honky-tonk."

Her eyes strayed to the great
plaster nudes on each side of the
Bond sign's gray Niagara.

"The woman's vulgar. She may
represent progress in Times
Square, but she's horrid. She's as
thick at the ankles as she is at the
knees." Come to take a second look,
and she's right. You wondered why
you hadn't caught that yourself.

The woman whose perfect figure
had made the whole world gasp in
1910 looked around for something
more familiar. Gone, except a few,
like the faces she had known on
Broadway. She thought that the
Palace, where she had played,
looked hemmed in.

Rector's gone. Shanley's gone.
She spoke quietly of nights spent
in those legendary places with the

Dolly Sisters, with Billie Burke, Lillian Russell, Eva Tanguay. Her eyes grew a bit misty, though that may have come from cold wind, not sentiment.

Miss Kellerman remembered the night she rode through The Square —1909, she thought it was—on an open float after she had won a peach-colored Buick in a popularity contest. Toast of New York, then. Johnnies cheered and whooped at the curbs.

She smiled. "I was dressed as a mermaid with a long wig. Beastly cold. I shivered, but the johnnies didn't know that."

Reminiscence broke the flood gates. How the customers held their breath when she dived from the tight rope under the Hippodrome roof, a vision in silver scales, to join lesser mermaids in the glass tanks on the stage! What wonderful sets they had, with alligators, frogs, crocodiles placed along the green prop banks!

She walked east in Forty-fourth Street still unrecognized. Told how she's been married full forty-one years to J. R. Sullivan, who was her manager in 1912 when she was 24. They had a bridal suite at the Astor where she's staying now on her first visit in seventeen years.

The slender legs moved more quickly as she neared the Avenue of the Americas and the old Hippodrome site. She stared at the bone-white modern parking garage that has replaced the Hipp. She was silent a moment in the strong wind. Then she said, "Charlie Dillingham had my name in lights right there, two stories high." She

pointed at the corner opposite Stern's.

She remembered that she followed Anna Pavlowa into the Hipp some time during the First World War. She had worshiped Pavlowa. She recalled riding, one spring day, on a white horse in a Hipp parade led by John Philip Sousa's band.

She said: "His feet hurt from the pavement and he envied me on the horse. Poor Mr. Sousa. His feet always hurt."

Her greatest hour, she thought aloud, was when Dan Frohman staged a soldier benefit in the Metropolitan Opera House one night in 1917. She was on the same bill with Caruso, Scotti and Geraldine Farrar. They did "Butterfly," Kreisler played. Toscanini, dark-haired then, led a ninety-piece band.

"I did Pavlowa's 'Swan,'" Miss Kellerman said. "I'd always wanted to. Got a great hand with it."

Huddled in a doorway between a record shop and a dark-interiored bar-and-grill, she figured the drinking spot was where she had had so many after-theatre snacks—Jack Dunstan's, the restaurant with the flying wedge of waiters. A jukebox in the barroom blared each time the door swung.

She shut her wide dark eyes as if in pain. "It's all so raucous now," she sighed. It wasn't that way when she was billed across the street as "Daughter of the Gods."

She went back to the Astor, through the jostlers and the jostled, still a handsome figure, and you could believe that she still does pirouettes and high kicks. But this was not her Broadway. She tightened the green coat about her and vanished in the Astor's glistening chrome doors.

October 23, 1953

❡ Men and women who work in New York skyscrapers by day never meet the men and women cleaners who take over at night. They form independent tides that never rip or cross.

That's due to specialization. Few 'scraper owners use their own crews now for office and general building cleaning. They leave it to outside contractors who control large nocturnal armies.

Most skyscraper cleaners seem to be Slavs, recruited from the flow of Displaced Persons until immigration dried up. They keep at tasks more grimly and are honest. A few weeks ago a Slav charwoman found $28,000 in cash behind a teller's adding machine in a midtown bank. She turned it right in.

One of the largest cleaning contractors in town, the Handi-Man Company, gets better than $4,000,-000 a year for its work in the Lever, Crowell-Collier, General Motors, Cotton Exchange, Hudson Terminal and Cartier's buildings, among others. Its cleaners also operate in close to 200 banks and branches.

Relief cleaners on bank jobs face certain hazards. One was locking a bank door the other morning after a night's work when the cop on the beat, who had never seen him before, whanged his pate. Apologized, of course, but it hurt.

A major mail order house in town blamed night cleaners when stock losses showed up in inventory. So did the concern's chief guard. He insisted the cleaners must have been dropping stuff to confederates through warehouse windows.

Edward H. Hirst, who owns Handi-Man and swears by his help, hired two Burns operatives and put them in cleaners' rig. It took seven weeks before they caught on that stock was leaving the plant in false-bottom waste carts devised by the chief guard and unloaded outside by a friend of his who bought the waste.

Mr. Hirst thinks that some months ago his cleaners solved one of the city's great mysteries: Where do New York pigeons go to die? One of his crews found the answer in old Daly's Theatre in Sixty-third Street when they went to clean it after it had been closed for around ten years.

Mr. Hirst says there were dead birds in the orchestra almost to knee depth and also in the balcony and on stage. Took days to clear them out.

❡ Melancholy autumn almost always brings drifts of weird and macabre stories to town. One that's picking up fascinating detail right now is about a New Yorker, recently widowed, who moved a grand piano into a mausoleum in a local cemetery where his wife's body is entombed. The legend is that out of deep grieving he enters the tomb at irregular intervals and softly plays touching and romantic melodies that his wife had always loved.

The people who run the cemetery say it isn't true, but that stories in somewhat the same vein keep cropping up. The one most often told, but with no more basis than the pianist legend, is about the husband who holds sentimental feast in the crypt with an empty seat at table for his wife. No well-run cemetery, it seems, would permit that any more than it would mausoleum musicales. The only sound you hear at night in New York graveyards is the rustling of autumn leaves.

October 30, 1953

❡ Annie Appleseed, distaff counterpart of old Johnny Appleseed, operates from a quiet suite high in the Chrysler Tower. Chrysanthemum seed, from her supply, go out all over the world—to veterans' hospitals, to universities, city parks, garden clubs, housing projects and even to prisons when inmates ask for them.

"Annie" is Mrs. Albert D. Lasker, widow of the advertising pioneer and chairman of the United States Shipping Board after World War I. Her sister, Mrs. Allmon Fordyce, helps her at the task. They have been at it ten years, and the mailing list keeps growing. They delight in the work, because it is a memorial to their mother, Sara J. Woodard, who came to the United States as an immigrant girl in 1880 and was appalled at the drabness of cities. They were all gray asphalt and brick that shut out flowers and greenery.

The chrysanthemums now rich in bloom in Central, Riverside, Bryant, Bowling Green and Cadman Parks and in housing projects and veterans' hospitals were all Sara Woodard Memorial gifts from Annie Appleseed. The original seed stock for the plantings resulted from experiments conducted on the Lasker estate at Lake Forest, outside Chicago, back in the Thirties.

The plants were bred on the estate for extreme hardiness by Dr. E. J. Kraus of the Botany Department of Chicago University. He sent some of the experimental plants as far north as Alberta in Canada to test whether they could thrive there—and they did. Then they were ready for distribution, and Annie Appleseed arranged with Park Commissioner Robert Moses for the first mass plantings here.

The biggest displays in prime bloom now—they may last through Thanksgiving—are in Fifty-ninth Street Plaza, just south of Central Park; in Central Park just off Fifth Avenue at 106th Street, in Bryant Park and in Riverside Park. The next largest display, with shades running from soft white through copper and bronze to deep maroon, is in Cadman Park off Manhattan Bridge in Brooklyn.

Annie Appleseed's 'mums are blooming right now, too, in thirty parks in London. She sent the seed for those to the London County Council, which arranged the planting. They also are in London housing projects and even in window boxes there. The Park Department here collects the seed each winter after the last blooming, dries it and stores it. Mrs. Lasker and her sister begin shipping it out early in February for late March planting.

Sara Woodard's daughters intended the plants mainly for the underprivileged of great cities, but they were happy when they heard from an English friend that some fell into the hands of Queen Elizabeth and were thriving in Windsor Castle garden. They were touched, on the other hand, by a plea for seed from a woman inmate at Attica Prison upstate, though they don't know yet how she made out with it.

Maybe one day someone will write the full story of the woman who inspired these global plantings. The legend is that she may have been America's first woman fashion expert. She worked for Carson, Pirie & Scott in Chicago, brought some of the first Paris fashions to this country from great designers there and was a pioneer fighter against city smoke nuisance. She was 77 when she died in 1940.

November 16, 1953

¶ The nearest thing in this city to the old New England general store with cracker-barrel forum is the Quong Yuen Shing at 72 Mott Street in Chinatown. Neither its sober front nor dark interior has changed in seventy years.

Lee Toy Kin, who runs the place for a Chinese syndicate, is a smart-looking chap in banker's gray, descended from a long line of Lees who have owned the store since the Eighties. It sells Chinese herbs, dried oysters, water chestnuts, teas, spices, silks and laundry and restaurant supplies.

It also is a community post office. Chinese all over the world who know that one day they, or one of their kin, will stop in at the Quong Yuen Shing (Emporium, roughly speaking) use it as a mailing address. Letters are faithfully kept, sometimes for months or years, in a wire rack just inside the door.

Day and night, men and women wander in with ancient prescriptions that have been in their families for generations. The solemn little man behind the counter reaches into one of the many deep old wooden drawers stacked from floor to ceiling behind him and compounds the ingredients on a sheet of white paper.

A steady seller over the worn counter under golden bird-and-leaf framework is Six-Flower (Luk Mai) made up of dried almond, lotus nut, shaved lily bulb and the root Wai Shan. It's good for soup flavoring and supposed to be a cure for scratchy throat. The little man makes a few deft twists of the flat sheet of paper and converts it into an almost air tight envelope. He murmurs to the customer, then waits patiently for the next one.

The drawers, you learn from soft-voiced Lee Toy Kin, hold some 6,000 dried herbs, roots, berries, nuts. The syndicate has a fair supply in its warehouses, but nothing comes in now from the Red-controlled Chinese mainland. Unless the political picture changes and peace comes to Asia and the rest of the world, the Quong Yuen Shing may be up against it.

"This shop," says Mr. Lee, "is like Sleepy Hollow. You sit. You wait. Things maybe come out right. Things maybe come out wrong."

He wraps up a good part of gentle Chinese philosophy in that statement which preaches patience.

Sunday is the emporium's big day. Fellow-countrymen fly, drive, come by train from Boston, Washington, St. Louis and elsewhere for a bit of shopping, for an hour or two of chit-chat. They leave loaded with vegetables, roast duck, barbecued pig, or a bit of Nau Yeung-Fa (rhododendron blossom) for their asthma. That's when the ancient shop looks most like the cracker-barrel hangout.

The well-dressed elder behind a second counter rapidly flicks the pips on an old abacus, swiftly writes the results in Chinese characters with a fine brush. He keeps the emporium's books in the old brush marks but makes a summary later for books in English that may be needed for income-tax reckoning. He looks capable and wise. When he smiles it is just a wisp of a smile. Chinese do not go in for over-emphasis in facial expression.

November 20, 1953

❡ Some people live within a street or two of Pomander Walk, even pass it occasionally, and never know it exists. It is a development of twenty-seven English cottages, gardens and all, inspired by the stage setting for the play "Pomander Walk," which ran on Broadway in 1911.

Thomas Healy, the restaurant man, had an architect reproduce the cottages from the stage sets ten years later. He snugged them in a twenty-foot lane that runs from Ninety-fourth Street to Ninety-fifth in the block between Broadway and West End Avenue.

Actors and writers were the first tenants—Nancy Carroll, Madeleine Carroll, Louis Wolheim, Ward Morehouse, Herbert Stoddard, among others—but most of those moved out long ago. O. O. McIntyre loved the spot; often mentioned it in his column.

There's an old London-suburb watchman's box at the north end of the Walk, but it's locked and melancholy-looking now. The private bobby who used to sit in it passed long ago and was never replaced.

November 27, 1953

❡ Ancient dwellings with authentic ghosts are hard to find in mid-Twentieth Century New York City, but one still stanchly hangs on at 29 East Fourth Street, between the Bowery and Lafayette Street. It is The Old Merchant's House, which is open to the public from 11 A.M. to 5 P.M. on weekdays and from 1 o'clock to 5 on Sundays and holidays.

The house stood alone—with lovely gardens around it—when Seabury Tredwell, a hardware merchant, moved into it in 1835. The brick is weathered now and the house has the same complexion as the untidy warehouses and garages that crowd it, but its interior has been preserved.

Mr. Tredwell's mother was a descendant of John Alden and of Priscilla Mullins of the Mayflower. He was the last New Yorker to wear a queue—wore it until he died in 1865, when he was 85 years old. Of his five daughters and two sons, only one was born at No. 29—Gertrude Ellsworth Tredwell. Her name went into the family Bible (which is still in the house) on the day of her birth, Sept. 17, 1840.

Gertrude Tredwell never married. A tiny woman, she was 93, withered and snow-topped when she died in her great four-poster on the second floor in 1933 without so much as an obituary in the newspapers. She had outlived her generation and her surroundings. She had become something of a recluse—a gentle, well-bred one hemmed in by ugliness—and she had been forgotten.

You see today on all five floors the atmosphere in which Gertrude Tredwell spent her ninety-three years—the framed seashell-seaweed pictures, the great four-posters with their scarlet drapery, the ancient lamps and the gleaming old furniture made by Duncan Phyfe, a Tredwell neighbor.

You easily imagine her drifting from room to cavernous room over ancient carpet, through mahogany sliding doors, sometimes with candles, sometimes by gas light. Glassed closets still hold her ancient, but lovely, wardrobe—charming flowered straw bonnets, tightly bodiced gowns and summer dresses, slippers with paper-thin soles and lace-edged pantalettes.

You descend to the kitchen with its long-handle bread toaster, with the true Dutch oven, with the food warmer that showed an open back to the numerous fireplaces. The very books Miss Tredwell used, in faded bindings now, are in their place—"True Politeness," "Etiquette for Ladies" and originals of Irving's "Sketch Book." Also there are newspapers telling of the fall of Vicksburg and of Grant's taking of Richmond.

Miss Tredwell never became part of the world that grew up around her; she seldom moved out of the old house. She kept a maid in severe black with great, stiff white apron bows to greet the rare visitor that showed up. Small as she was, she would come down the stairs in the grand manner, always in her best, if long-outmoded, finery. The laces, veils and shawls she wore were beautiful, but they were museum pieces.

After Miss Tredwell died, distant kin and their friends formed the Historical Landmark Society to preserve the old house as she had left it, and that's the way it is. Her music is still on the ancient piano, her toilet kits are neatly spread and her delicate samplers and other handiwork are framed on the old walls, including the bedroom piece that says: "The Lord Is My Shepherd. I Shall Not Want."

Miss Florence Helm, a frail, gentle lady from up Ossining way, whose own home had pretty much the same type of furnishings as The Old Merchant's House, was brought in to care for the Tredwell place. It was a rather lonely assignment, especially at night after brawling cartmen and garage hands in the street had left off their hoarse outcry and heavy silence closed in. Miss Helm was never uneasy, though. She had had previous experiences with invisible folk and with weird night sounds up Truro way in New England. They had not frightened her.

One night, the silken tassel on the old lamp beside which Miss Helm sat reading in The Old Merchant's House stirred into swaying movement, though there was no breeze, no vibration. She watched it in quiet fascination. She thought it behaved as though an invisible, delicate hand had set it in motion. The tassel finally fell quietly back into place as if the hand had dropped it. It was a playful gesture, Miss Helm thought.

Harry Lundberg and his wife, who came to work about the house after Miss Helm did, heard the same sounds late at night that frequently had awakened Miss Helm. Distinct wall rappings; two, sometimes three; a few times as many as five. Miss Helm says, "It was not unlike telegraphic code, which I cannot read." They sounded, though, as though they might have been done by a gentle, womanly hand.

One morning about 3 o'clock, the rappings awakened Mrs. Lundberg, a sensible, well-balanced woman not easily scared. She left her bed and awakened her husband. He grunted sleepily; they changed beds. The knocks came again—in the dark under the soaring ceiling from the wall directly behind Mr. Lundberg's head.

"You get the hell out of here," he bellowed crossly.

The angry words echoed in the chamber. The rappings abruptly ended.

"That was five years ago," Mrs. Lundberg remembers. "We have not heard her since. Harry must have frightened the poor thing."

December 23, 1953

¶ Subway and bus advertisements of the Stephen Merritt Burial and Cremation Company these days show a picture of Grant's Tomb and carry the legend: "We conducted his funeral."

The proudest display in the stephen Merritt office at Twenty-second Street and Eighth Avenue supports this claim. It is a framed thirty-eight-star flag which, according to the label, covered General Grant's coffin.

Samuel L. Buckingham, now president of the company, likes to show the Grant funeral account. It has some astonishing items. It cost $150, for example, to bring General Grant's body to New York from Saratoga Springs in August, 1885. That was freight charge.

The coffin was what the trade calls "a state job"—silver handles, solid gold nameplate, royal purple silk velvet trim. Five hundred coaches for the funeral cost the company $10 each for one day's rental—$5,000.

Carrying the floral tributes from City Hall to Riverside Park was itemized at $30. Horse trappings for the truck that bore the catafalque cost $500—black nets, rosettes, leading cords. Scarves for twenty-seven pallbearers came to $243.

For years, Mr. Buckingham says, the company closely guarded one secret about the Grant funeral—the fact that the vehicle that bore the catafalque was an Ehrets Brewery truck pulled by twenty-four brewery horses. The truck was covered with crape so no one could recognize it, and it carried an invisible load of ten tons of pig iron.

"Had to do that," Mr. Buckingham explains, "or those horses would have run away with the funeral. They were used to big loads."

The total cost for the Grant burial came to $14,163.75; it was paid by the Government in two installments—one of $7,860, the other of $6,303.75.

¶ Not many spots on the Bowery today look at all as they did back in the Eighties, when that street rated as wicked, but one has changed hardly at all.

Diamond Dan O'Rourke's place at 156 Park Row, where Pearl Street crosses, has the same old mirrors, the same dusty old prizefighter paintings and framed jockey silks, the same old chandeliers with gas fixtures.

Beside the till behind the bar are Dan O'Rourke's heavily studded boyhood brogans, made by his daddy back in Mala in County Cork in the early Eighteen Seventies. Another exhibit is the blue policeman's helmet that was regulation in New York fifty years ago. The legend is that it once belonged to George Little, a customer who became a sergeant in the late Nineties —he left it there one night and never reclaimed it.

Jim Jeffries hung out in Diamond Dan's. So did Stanley Ketchel and Bob Fitzsimmons, Al Smith, John McGraw and Sheriff Tom Foley. Jeffries' portrait, done in 1903 for free beers and a meal by Charlie Rose, an itinerant artist, is the prize exhibit, almost life-size. Rose's tools were school chalks and burnt match heads.

Daniel Riggs O'Rourke, Diamond Dan's son, who manages the Bridge Cafe down at New Chambers Street and Park Row, remembers the boxful of diamonds his father kept in the saloon safe. Young Dan wore a four-carat job to school at P. S. 1 in Vandewater Street one day and startled the teacher.

The legendary Diamond Dan knew all the infamous Bowery characters of the Eighties and Nineties, including Hicks the Pirate, the way Young Dan tells it. He knew Carrie Nation, too, and it was his boast that she was so taken with his personality that the one Bowery saloon she always passed up on hatchet raids was Diamond Dan's.

Diamond Dan's daughter, Mrs. Irene Flynn, lives just up over the saloon and Charlie Deschon, her cousin, runs the bar now. It somehow retains vestiges of its old splendor, and would make an ideal setting for a motion picture or TV show that calls for a saloon background of the Eighties or Nineties.

December 25, 1953

¶ The other night, when The Town was bright with lighted trees and the air hummed with Christmas music, Father Jude of the Church of Our Lady Queen of Angels led his boy choristers down from one of the poorest and shabbiest parts of the city into the plush surroundings of the Savoy Plaza Hotel.

Most of his kids live either in 113th Street, where the church stands between Second and Third Avenues, or in blackened tenements you see from the church windows, to the north. They are kids who live in cold-water flats which, in many cases, have no furniture or next to no furniture. Some were children who almost from birth have known no bed but a pallet on a splintery floor.

Yet they looked healthy. It was sharp out in the Plaza and their cheeks glowed with cold's nip. Their eyes shone. Soft hotel lights slicked their freshly-wetted hair. Their jackets and their windbreakers were frayed and worn. Their shoes were scuffed, but had a kind of dull polish. They were boyishly noisy. Father Jude kept shushing them.

Brother Fidelis and Father Maynard, two soft-voiced young Capuchins, helped Father Jude ride herd on the troupe; stopped them from swinging their unwrapped red cassocks and white surplices. They filled two elevators on their way up to their dessing suite. They caught their breath and laughed at the sensation of swift ascent.

Something like awe was in their faces as they crossed the suite threshold on deep, green carpeting. Their eyes swept the salmon velvet furnishings, the soft lamplight, the delicate curtains that barely screened the view over the Plaza and the lights in Central Park.

One boy whispered, "Dig the crazy room," and the kids around him just murmured, "Hey." Edward McGill, their director, Brother Fidelis and Father Maynard helped them into their choir vestments; tied their scarlet silk bows. The director got them into their places, sounded a hoarse pitch pipe—and they were transformed.

The tough Harlem kids had vanished. The voices were the voices of angels. It made one's throat lump as they warmed up on "Noel" and on "Angels We Have Heard on High." Their music was tenderly sweet. It went through the open door and echoed in the hotel corridors.

There was a moment of mild panic. Counting heads, Father Jude found only twenty-two choristers where there should have been twenty-three, and the missing boy was Edgar Deutsch, a D. P. less than two years out of Germany. He was to have sung "Silent Night" as a solo.

There is no phone in Edgar's family flat. Brother Fidelis called the Capuchin monastery on the suite phone. Some minutes later an answering call relayed the word that Edgar was at home, crying. He had lost his surplice. He could not come in his threadbare jacket.

Brother Fidelis spoke urgently into the telephone. He said, "Get another surplice for Edgar. Put him in a cab right away. We'll pay for the cab when he gets here."

A few minutes later the director lined up his boys; adjured them to silence; got them to the lobby.

The director led them into the great Savoy Room under the sparkling chandeliers, singing "The First Noel." Men and women in rich evening attire left off their dining. The sound of clinking silver and crystal died away. The kids from Harlem assembled on the dais. The diners applauded.

The folk at the glittering tables did not know that the boys were poor Harlem kids. The kids had never seen such richly heaped tables, so much white linen, so many scarlet-coated waiters or such artfully calculated lighting and decoration.

Diners knew only that the hotel, two years ago, began the custom of having different church choirs sing at pre-Christmas dinners.

Father Jude's boys sang through the second carol before a pale-faced boy hurried in, head bowed to chest, and took his place at the extreme right in the front row. He had no carol book. He read from the pages held by the boy next to him.

Then Miss Herta Glaz of the Metropolitan Opera came to stand before the choristers to sing "Silent Night" in German, with the boys softly humming behind her. When applause patter washed away, the director nodded at Edgar. He stepped two paces forward and to soft accompaniment sang "Silent Night," also in German. The voice was like spun gold; true and with only a slight quaver. The room lay silent.

Then the kids moved out, two by two, between the rich tables, and the recessional was "O, Come All Ye Faithful." They left a wake of applause behind them. A little while later they went out, dressed like street kids again; cassocks and surplices under their arms, and headed back through the cold to bleak Harlem, beyond the other end of Central Park.

1 9 5 4

January 4, 1954

THE GOLDEN AGE for mineralogists in the city has passed but you still find in this delightful cult men who mined Manhattan's rich deposits before pavements, skyscrapers and soaring dwellings buried most of their quarrying grounds.

Gilman S. Stanton, for example, is 82 now and his memory is curtained by the years. He rarely gets to the New York Mineralogical Club meetings in Schermerhorn Hall on Columbia University campus the third Wednesday of each month from October through May.

But Mr. Stanton, probably the oldest living amateur mineralogist in the country, keeps wonderful dreams of the days through and after the Eighties when he and fellow cultists reaped rich harvest as New York subways, tunnels, skyscrapers, viaducts and apartment houses crept up the island.

Such delirious days will never come again for mineralogists on Manhattan. Every bite of the digging machines, every excavation blast released semiprecious stones and other geological specimens that Nature had locked away for hundreds of thousands of years.

New York City has yielded close to 200 mineral varieties of 100 or more distinct species, most of them originally laid down in pre-Cambrian sea. Before man covered Manhattan with stone and concrete it was a fabulous depository of glacial drift in endless formations and in incredibly beautiful colors.

Mr. Stanton likes to talk about the rich deposits of garnets he unearthed at Sixty-fifth Street and Broadway at the turn of the century. He loves to repeat the legend of the giant garnet (nine pounds, ten ounces) that came out of a sewer excavation at Broadway and Thirty-fifth Street.

These items are still on exhibit

on the fourth floor at the American Museum of Natural History, with other New York finds, and every member of the Mineralogical Club has a great store of others—rich blue, green, pink, yellow, purple, orange, white—that came from Manhattan, Staten Island, the Bronx and near-by territory.

Most of the men in the club get their thrill from hunting, identifying and building their finds into collections. Others, like Victor Pribil, a professional ironmonger who is club secretary, go a step beyond and turn lapidary. They make beautiful multi-faceted stones, set them in silver and in gold for wear.

The club keeps sharp tab on new developments in the city—the opening of new cuts, new building sites and other construction—but there has been no major hunting ground for the members since the Brooklyn-Battery Tunnel, which yielded the lovely fuchsite specimen now at the museum. There is something faintly amusing in the picture of these addicts trailing trucks to dumping grounds. Most of them are dignified professional men and women.

T. Orchard Lisle, head of Oil Forum, a grave gentleman; Dr. Frederick A. Stenbuck of Mount Vernon, a well-known allergy specialist who is president of the club; and a host of other amateur mineralogists and their spouses get into the country just outside the city, week-ends, to tap around with geologists' hammers. They pay tractor men to turn quarry piles over for them to get at unworked mounds.

This gentle group's chief adviser and foremost expert is Dr. Frederick H. Pough, former curator of minerals at the Museum of Natural History. He spends most of his time, though, flying or riding to distant places to test potential mines for major diamond and uranium syndicates. He has been a club member for years.

The outsider's eyes widen when he hears these men speak of newly created synthetic gems that might rudely nudge the diamond market if they did not meet with stern repression from those who control that market. They show you samples, set by their own membership, that are highly convincing.

You leave their meeting a little awed by the new-found knowledge that the greatest of cities towers above prehistoric depositories of garnet, beryl, tourmaline, jasper, muscovite, zircon, chrysoberyl, agate, malachite, opal, rose, smoky and milky quartz—even minute veins of gold and of silver.

It is a new slant on New York, the city that stands astride an ancient store of semiprecious stones of wondrous beauty, now doomed to remain forever unseen.

February 5, 1954

❡ When old mansions die Johnny Morgan and George Montanus take them over. They strip away likely fireplaces, expensive paneling, old lamps and chandeliers, lovely doorways, artistic fencing, good cabinetry or anything else they think a decorator or home-builder might want some day.

They cart some of the stuff to their dusty shop, which they call Locate Market. The heaviest pieces are stored in their Long Island City warehouse. In addition to what they remove from walls, from old staircases and from a mansion's exterior, they pick up what lies around loose.

Weird things turn up in abandoned mansions. But Johnny, who is half Cherokee, and George, a placid fellow anyway, have got to the point where nothing astonishes them. What other persons find thrilling and extraordinary leave this pair emotionally stable. Johnny says: "You get that way after thirty years in this racket."

The men denuded, among others, the Ogden Mills home, the Horace Harding dwelling, the Fahnestock mansion, part of the Grand Union Hotel in Saratoga, the Ritz Carlton Hotel, Eddie Cantor's place at Lake Success and the homes of J. P. Morgan partners. You think of a big name and the lads have had it, but they're not too good at remembering names.

In the old Hewitt Mansion at Lexington and Twenty-second Street a few years ago, the Locate boys took out the whole lovely ballroom and sold it dirt cheap to a decorator, who has made a tidy bit renting it for display to places like Bergdorf Goodman. Johnny says, "We didn't know, to be honest about it, what the room was worth."

In the same dwelling they picked up two blackened ends of thick copper cable. When they got the accumulation off the objects it was found they were Tiffany-certified lengths of the original Atlantic Cable, cut up for souvenirs. Each took one and each has it knocking "somewhere" around the house.

Locate did very well with the library and library doorways taken out of the old Juilliard mansion in West Fifty-seventh Street; sold almost every part. They couldn't handle the marble staircase, but they stripped it of some 200 bronze dolphins and sold them to a decorator in town.

The decorator used the dolphins for lamp bases. He made what Johnny calls a small fortune out of it and went back to England to live on the profits. The owners of Locate talk wistfully about profits others make out of their findings, but concede they could never have turned out the lamps.

The partners cannot recall the name of an inventor who had a handsome home in Thirty-second Street west of Madison Avenue. They took a lot of stuff out of the house. Just before they left, George picked up four of some hundreds of small envelopes that the wreckers were kicking around the floor.

He put them in his desk and it wasn't until four years later that he went to use one, and found in it a curious twist of gray human hair— at least that's what he thought it was. The other envelopes had strands of the same stuff. George lit one with a match and it glowed and went back to its original silver hue.

"That stuff," George still laments, "was pure platinum. We got $38 for that little bit. We and the other workers had kicked away a fortune."

After George F. Baker, the banker, died in his home at 258 Madison Avenue twenty-three years ago, George got the millionaire's overcoat and gave it to his landlord as a gift. "He used it when he shoveled snow," George remembers.

He and Johnny picked up two odd-looking stuffed cats, too. It developed these were no ordinary cats. They were a sacred Egyptian breed, thousands of years old. Clarence Low, a decorator, took them off their hands for a good price. A junky-looking fireplace that was in their dusty window for more than two years was grabbed by a decorator and is now in the Washington home of Senator Robert F. Kerr. They can't remember where they got it.

Their shop is haunted by decorators and small-pursed housewives looking for quaint glass and iron, odd lamps and odd bits of brass. They know virtually every male decorator in town, but confide that sometimes they wish they didn't. They find some difficult to handle.

They think their grimmest find was four bags of human bones in a sub-basement in the Old Tombs Prison. George recalls: "We worked hard to get 'em out thinkin' they might be historic; handled them really carefully and then—no market."

February 8, 1954

❡ Celestino Fontana is the St. Francis of East Forty-ninth Street. For some twelve years, now, the birds in the block between Third and Second Avenues have fed from his generous hands. He has healed the injured in neighborhood pigeon flocks, has reared their orphaned young.

Celestino is a bulky, gray-haired fellow. As a child in Crescentino near the Cottian Alps he tended wounded wild things, then freed them. At 12, he went into the world and much later, as maître d'hôtel on the Riviera, in London, in Boston and in New York, came to serve royalty.

Then he opened his little antique shop at 202 East Forty-ninth Street. He filled it with odds and ends from the homes of rich folk he had met. But the birds were really his prime interest. They run Celestino. They run the shop.

Each night before he locks the dusty little shop, Celestino goes outside and spreads whole-wheat bread crumbs close to the walls beside his place. He blankets Pop and Louie, his two hoary parrots, in their cages, then retires to the rear.

When morning light comes into Forty-ninth Street the pigeons fly down from Manny Wolf's roof across the street. They assail the shop's window. They peck at it with their beaks. Forty or fifty huddle expectantly in the stone doorway.

Then Celestino comes out and they cover him. One day, he remembers, some 400 swooped from near-by roofs and actually bore him to the flagstones. He feeds them four to six loaves of bread, hemp seed, prepared bird foods.

"Ho!" he trumpets. "Do they know Celestino? But watch them

one day. They embrace Celestino. They knock him down for love of him."

Rich customers bring sick birds to the shop. The stout shopkeeper makes splints for them with cigar-box wood and adhesive tape. He puts them in one of the five enormous cages. He says, "Pop and Louie, they would tear these other ones apart. They even scold the customers."

They do, too. They have free run of the shop, and a stranger is often startled by some acid comment from the top of a red plush screen or from the cornice of a gold-and-pink curio chest. Old Louie, gray-lidded, sleepily says, "Get out! Get 'em out!" It isn't good for trade, but somehow it delights Celestino.

When night comes in East Forty-ninth Celestino puts on a single, sickly yellow light, straps his big accordion to his shoulders and, with a cigar stump tight in his teeth, serenades Pop and Louie with ancient Italian folk tunes. The birds raucously sing them.

Passers-by who do not know Celestino's shop but come suddenly upon it are entranced by the night scene—the big accordionist, the swooping birds, the big cages, the dusty window, the neglected silver, glass and enamelware all cast in thin yellow light.

It is Dickens in low key in a New York side street.

February 19, 1954

❡ The staff at The New York School of Social Work, a Columbia Uni-versity affiliate that functions in the old Andrew Carnegie mansion on the southeast corner of Fifth Avenue and Ninety-first Street, is grateful for the space the structure affords, but sometimes wishes that the Laird had been a bigger man, physically.

Dr. Kenneth D. Johnson, the school dean, is more than six feet tall. He finds it a little difficult sometimes to get through doors built by Mr. Carnegie when the house went up in 1901. They were a fairly snug fit for the Laird, but he was only five feet, two inches in height. "Low Bridge" signs warn today's visitors to duck.

The steel man had forty-two servants to maintain his sixty-four-room dwelling. The school, with nowhere near his money, still spends about $50,000 a year to run the place, although it gets its rent free. It uses a ton of coal each winter day, and has a built-in narrow-gauge track on which to run a coal car to the furnace.

The legend is that Mr. Carnegie chose the Ninety-first Street site for his mansion because the view over the reservoir vaguely reminded him of his boyhood home in Dumfern-line, Scotland. The school staff still uses the high west catwalk on good days to get the park view, as his servants did.

The huge pipe organ that the Carnegies had installed, with piping to the third floor, has been left in place. Dean Johnson's staff plays it at Christmas parties for carol singing. At the same season they bring out the Carnegie Christmas tree base that plays "Holy Night" with its hidden music box.

In all the vast place with its magnificent carved woods, the old Carnegie study and library are probably the most fascinating rooms. They are richly adorned with quotations the Laird loved and the staff has traced the origin of all but four.

His favorite, in raised letters of dark wood, was:

"He that cannot reason is a fool,
"He that will not is a bigot,
"He that dares not, a slave."

That one paraphrases a passage in the Preface to Academical Questions written by Sir William Drummond in 1805.

Mr. Carnegie's Scottish-oak desk remains in the study. It was built there and the doorway is too small to allow its removal. His pencillings on drawer-edges—"balls," "odds and ends," "rubbish"—show where he stowed his different kinds of papers and documents.

The woman in charge says that the Laird signed away at that desk more than $375,000,000 in philanthropic bequests.

The staff likes to show newcomers the pumps that can suck water out of the deep artesian well, the air-cooling system put in the sub-basement fifty years ago and still operating, the wall safes for silverware, the great staircase and the old gymnasium.

The mansion's gardens are probably the richest on Fifth Avenue and the scent of the old wisteria carries above traffic fumes in the spring. Back of the main house is the forty-two-room home the Carnegies built for their daughter, Margaret, when she became Mrs. Roswell Miller Jr. It's empty now, and sometimes squirrels get into it.

You leave there with awe for a vanished age.

¶ One of the city's most extraordinary sights is the pre-dawn flight of the starlings from under the Riverside Drive viaduct at 125th Street. The birds go up with a great rush of wings and weird outcry, out of the dark into pale morning.

The return flight, when the flocks come back from Westchester at nightfall, is a bit more weird. It appears like a solid cloud, raucous and almost sinister, but it has some semblance of organization.

Homing, the starlings descend in a body for brief stop-off in Trinity Church Cemetery, 153d to 155th Street off Broadway. They weigh down bare-branched trees, cover the graves of such sleeping dead as the naturalist Audubon, the poet Clement C. Moore, who wrote "The Night Before Christmas," of Madame Jumel and of Col. John Jacob Astor.

Morning take-off and twilight homing should make remarkable shots for photographers.

February 24, 1954

¶ The New York Public Library is quietly celebrating this month the opening of the Astor Library in Lafayette Street below Astor Place 100 years ago. The vast plant that is the New York Library now had its origin in that humble unit.

When the Astor Library opened

its doors on Feb. 1, 1854, The New York Times ran a short piece about it that said: "No volumes can be taken from the building. No one is allowed to . . . remove a book from its place unless accompanied by an officer of the library. Smoking is particularly prohibited."

The same item said "the library will become a favorite resort," and it did, but not right off. In 1873, the record shows, "the daily average number of visitants is eighty-six, one-twentieth of them ladies."

In December last year, a season when scholars on holiday came from all over the country to do research, there were days when the number of visitants at the main library on Fifth Avenue at Forty-second Street went past 14,000. The figure for the month was around 250,000 visitors.

The first librarian, Joseph Green Cogswell, reported: "Readers read excellent books, except the small fry . . . [who read] the trashy Scott, Cooper, Dickens."

Mr. Cogswell's stacks didn't amount to much by current standards. He had more than 80,000 volumes. The main library now carries more than 3,500,000 works, has a sizable art gallery, a vast collection of prints and rare books and conducts concerts of recorded music from noon to 2 P.M.

The original library ran on a modest budget. Today the Forty-second Street Library spends around $4,000,000 annually, most of it privately subscribed. The branches use about as much again, all of it from the city budget.

Conservative folk, the library staff won't make outright claims; they just say they "think" they have the world's largest public library within the full meaning of that term.

The New York Public Library and its seventy-five branches and three mobile units is staffed by 2,000 men and women. The total running cost for all this comes to around $8,000,000 a year.

The largest single contribution the institution ever got was the $5,200,000 Andrew Carnegie put up in 1901 for the establishment of the first branches.

¶ The dusty and untidy pillared buildings on the east side of Lafayette Street just below Astor Place are among the oldest standing structures in the city.

When they went up 123 years ago, they were part of a much longer chain of dwellings that stretched southward and were considered rather hoity-toity for their period, as were the distinguished families who lived in them.

The structures were called the Colonnades, or Colonnade Row. The Stuyvesants, the Delanos, the Astors and the Langdons lived in the street. President Lincoln, a legend says, reviewed New York regiments from the balcony in 1864. The big ballroom at 432 Lafayette, now owned by Conte, the restaurant man, was used for the wedding of President Tyler and Miss Julia Gardiner on June 26, 1844.

Mr. Conte has had to paint over a good part of the original mahogany in the place and can't quite keep up with the dust that traffic keeps depositing in and on the Colonnades, but he loves to tell the Row's history.

A quaint touch in the old garden space back of Conte's now, is something the original tenants would probably never have understood—a long bocci court, a place for the Italian version of bowling.

February 26, 1954

¶ Residents in lower Fifth Avenue who tip a companionable cup now and then have been bothered by the notion that they have seen white rabbits hopping along the pavement, or down side streets.

Well, it wasn't just a notion, but it's nothing to be concerned about. White rabbits do appear in Fifth Avenue and sometimes in Eleventh Street, just west of the avenue. They belong to the nursery school of the staid First Presbyterian Church in the neighborhood.

A gentleman called this newspaper the other night to report that he had caught up with a white rabbit in the avenue near the church, learned that its hutch was on the church grounds and put it back inside the church fence.

Michael Kennedy, a sturdy fellow who works around the grounds, says there's just one rabbit in the hutch right now, an all-white one that is the pet of the kindergarten class. Someone—no one's ever found out who—left him on the lawn one night two years ago and the children adopted him. He has the run of the lawn sometimes and rarely strays.

Three weeks ago another unidentified benefactor left a second white rabbit on the lawn. Mr. Kennedy, after a talk with the kindergarten teacher, put him into the hutch with the first one.

They didn't get along, it seems, so Mr. Kennedy put the newcomer out on the lawn, and he's the one who keeps hopping through the fence to sample dangerous living. A Chinese laundryman brought him back after he'd gone almost as far as the Avenue of the Americas in Eleventh Street.

The other day he was gone again, but Mr. Kennedy didn't know where and didn't seem to care much. "That second one was too quarrelsome for a rabbit, if you ask me," was his comment.

¶ E. Joseph, Inc., game purveyors in Washington Market, sells ostrich eggs (laid on a Florida farm) to a Fifty-second Street night club where one egg, served for six persons, costs $75. He provides the same establishment with Mexican armadillo. A serving of that for four comes to $150.

March 3, 1954

¶ The area marked for the Bellevue housing project near the East River, notorious in recent years for its soot-fall, was once an idyllic spot. It's blackest day was Sept. 15, 1776, when there was no soot at all.

On that morning, five British men-o'-war stood out in Kips Bay to cover the landing of the invading force that was to take Manhattan Island. New England militia on shore fled under the bombardment and the invaders took the town in a breeze.

Gen. George Washington tried to stem the retreat. He lashed at the American officers and men with his cane, and in his despair and anger he almost got himself taken too. An aide turned his mount toward the Post Road (Third Avenue) and got him away.

The Bellevue housing site was part of Jacobus Hendricksen Kip's East River farm, and the Kip mansion, built in the cut that was to become East Thirty-fifth Street, was 200 years old when it was demolished in 1851, for street improvement.

Maj. John André, British spy, was wined and dined by fellow-officers in the Kip house the night before he went upriver to rendezvous with Benedict Arnold.

¶ Almost every morning, in flying weather, great planes from the earth's far corners bring T. V. W. O. V.'s to New York. The T. V. W. O. V.'s go in special buses to the Prince George Hotel, in East Twenty-eighth Street, between Fifth and Madison Avenues, with a McRoberts Detective Agency man aboard to see that none gets out along the way. The private eye carries a pistol but wears no uniform.

The hotel people figure they have handled around 2,600 Transient Visitors Without Visa—they refer to them merely as W. O. V.'s —since last July. They got the contract for the service then from the New York Air Facilitation Committee, in which the major overseas airlines are represented. They keep W. O. V.'s on the fifth floor.

The airlines pay for housing and feeding the W. O. V.'s at the hotel until the boarders get a ship or another plane to take them out of the United States. There's a McRoberts man in the fifth-floor corridor all the time to prevent fly-throughs from going out to explore the town, but it's all done with extreme politeness. Hotel help goes out of its way to see that no transients' feelings are bruised.

T. V. W. O. V.'s are persons on long journeys, who have permission to stop in the United States only long enough to make connections for their ultimate destinations. Sometimes they come through singly, sometimes in couples, sometimes in family groups or traveling troupes of one kind or another. Right now, the heaviest traffic is in native Jamaicans bound for Britain, where they have assured jobs as domestics.

The hotel had as many as 130 of these on one recent day. Another night, fifty-five flew in. It was just as well for them that they couldn't get onto New York's streets. They wore thin island garb and most of them were coatless and without hats. Like most other T. V. W. O. V.'s, all they saw of the city was the segment of skyscraper visible from a fifth-floor hotel window. Those with inside rooms didn't see even that much.

Ray Conboy, the hotel's assistant sales manager, who handles the W. O. V. operation, says he has run into no situation he couldn't handle. His general staff and his waiters have met every interpreting emergency and the chefs have studied what Chinese, Indians, Arabs and other transients expect in food. They know all the baby formulas, too. If, once in a while a boarder wants champagne or wines, and will pay, the hotel will serve him his choice.

Mr. Conboy says you get to meet some interesting W. O. V.'s—bullfighters, Italian auto racers, actresses, diplomats. Women in flight are apt to want nylons or fancy soaps. When they do, Mr. Conboy has a bellboy shop for them, or if the item is a little on the more intimate side, he recruits a distaff employe for the assignment. Prince George switchboard girls are sternly forbidden to allow the W. O. V.'s to make any calls within the United States, but will handle overseas messages.

Average wait-over runs from three to ten hours, but one man set a record of six days in a fifth-floor room because his ship was overdue. The W. O. V.'s, incidentally, do not register. Mr. Conboy just gets their names from the airlines people and checks them in and out. So does the McRoberts man. They haven't lost one yet. A few— mostly missioners—have been escorted to divine service on the Sabbath.

Mr. Conboy's toughest boarder was a French 7-year-old.

"Just a restless kid," he explained. "Kept opening his window and leaning 'way out to watch traffic. I finally nailed the window down."

March 5, 1954

¶ There were dramatic moments in the quest for the Constance Missal which the Pierpont Morgan Library acquired the other day.

Hans P. Kraus, the dealer in rare books who brought the missal from a Capuchin monastery in the medieval-walled city of Romont in Western Switzerland, was an agonizingly long time getting hands on it—and then almost lost it.

Months of scholarly research went into proving the missal's authenticity and into establishing beyond reasonable doubt that it was printed from type before the Gutenberg Bible came from the press. That phase had whodunnit flavor, but of the musty or academic kind, and was extraordinarily involved.

Mr. Kraus was aided in the task by Dr. Hellmut Lehmann-Haupt and Dr. Hans Nachod, his bibliographical consultants. Their knowledge of old books amounts almost to wizardry. They worked on photostats in the Kraus shop at 16 East Forty-sixth Street, the old Lehman Mansion into which the bookseller has fitted wall panelling from the old Union League Club.

A missal, in case you don't happen to know, is a work containing all that is said or sung at mass during the entire year. The missal Mr. Kraus fetched from Romont was printed for the Roman Catholic Diocese of Constance, Germany, which is near the Swiss border.

The Constance Missal is one of

three known existing copies printed in Mainz, Germany, about 1450, probably seven years before Johann Gutenberg turned out the first printed Bible. One copy is in the National Library in Munich and one is in the Library in Zurich.

Neither of them is for sale at any price. The copy held by the Capuchins in Romont was scuffed. The monastery cat had bedded down on it and the book had accumulated a little dust, but it was still one of the rarest volumes on earth. The monks were willing to dispose of it, they told Mr. Kraus, if the head of the order in Rome thought they should.

But time does not have the same breathless pace for a Capuchin that it does for a tensed-up bibliophile. Mr. Kraus waited in Zurich for three weeks, with no further word from the monks in old Romont, or from Rome.

Finally, he persuaded the calm-eyed Capuchins in Romont to telephone to Rome at his expense, though they saw no need for such haste. Rome decided to let Mr. Kraus have the missal for a good price. He nervously awaited delivery.

The Capuchins, though, wouldn't just turn the missal over, they gently explained to the bookman. They needed written confirmation of Rome's decision to sell. It came, slowly, by Capuchin courier while the book dealer's agitation increased.

One mild day in June, 1953, a slow-paced monk at last delivered the precious missal. It was wrapped in an old Swiss newspaper and had

been squeezed into an old cardboard box. Mr. Kraus fondled it, and when the monk had gone breathed a great sigh.

It was late afternoon. He could not insure it at that hour. He left the Hotel Eden with it for a celebration dinner at the Baur au Lac —caviar, vodka, a dish of meat, some pastry, and a liqueur. The meal relaxed him.

He started down street in happy post-prandial glow, headed for the hotel when behind him suddenly he heard a hoarse outcry and the pad of running feet. A waiter pounded up. "Sir," he panted in German, "have you not forgotten something?"

He held out the Constance Missal. Mr. Kraus' relaxed mood had exceeded proper bounds. He clutched at the 500-year-old treasure.

That night the dealer slept with the missal under his pillow at the Eden. Its wooden boards were hard on his neck, but he welcomed that, in a way; it kept him from further forgetfulness. Next morning he had it heavily insured. It is worth more than $100,000.

Mr. Kraus told the Swiss insurance man: "I will sleep on it on the plane, too, boards or no boards." But the insurance man said: "I'm afraid not, sir. We have insured you and the missal separately. To send both on one plane would be double risk. It will go on one plane, you on another."

It did, too. Mr. Kraus telephoned to Mrs. Kraus in New York. She met the missal at Idlewild Airport and took it directly to the store in East Forty-sixth Street. Her husband got in a day later. The missal then was turned over to Frederick B. Adams, director of the Morgan Library.

For eight months after that, Mr. Kraus, Dr. Lehmann-Haupt and Dr. Nachod kept utter silence about the delivery in the United States of one of the three known copies of the world's oldest typographical treasure. They left formal announcement to Mr. Adams.

March 8, 1954

❡ Room 300 in the Biltmore Hotel is a meditation chapel. The management thinks it is the only chapel ever built into a hotel. Guests and sometimes the hotel help go there to pray or to sit in mute contemplation.

The idea originated in 1923 with Joseph R. Wilson, attorney and engineer, a frequent guest from Philadelphia. Mr. Wilson had always advocated a chapel for every home and for every ship.

"There is no suggestion of God in your stately edifice," he wrote on March 3, 1923, to John McEntee Bowman, the Biltmore owner. "The haven of a little chapel in the hotel, with its doors ever invitingly open, would bring many a broken-hearted man or woman through the dark valley of hopelessness and desperation and give them new hope and a heart to forgive."

It took five years, but Mr. Bowman got Leonard Schultze, an architect, to set in the Gothic meditation room, done in light oak, fit

it with altar, stained glass, soft lighting, prie-dieux and dark red drapery. It is decorated every day with fresh white blossoms.

Hundreds of thousands of guests have used it since 1928. Six couples have been wed in it. Lulu Kennedy, a hotel maid who died a few weeks ago, always gave it her tenderest care. Its doors have never been locked.

They couldn't be. On Dec. 2, 1928, when the chapel opened, Mr. Bowman turned the key of Room 300 over to Mr. Wilson as guarantee that it would stay open as long as the hotel lasted.

March 10, 1954

❡ Perhaps few persons in the throngs previewing spring at the thirty-eighth annual international flower show in the Kingsbridge Armory ever heard of Grant Thorburn, but he was, in a way, the great-great-grandfather of flower shows in the United States.

Mr. Thorburn landed from a sailing vessel at the foot of Maiden Lane the morning of June 19, 1794. He had been a nailmaker in Dalkeith in Scotland and made by hand the first slate-roof nails ever used in this city. They went into slates atop the City Hotel in lower Broadway. Nail-making machinery came in right after that, so Mr. Thorburn turned grocer at 20 Nassau Street.

One day in 1799, though he knew little about flowers, he idly pinched the leaf of a plant he saw at another grocer's and was delighted with its scent. It was a rose geranium. He bought it for 50 cents, unpotted.

Mr. Thorburn put the plant in a flower pot that he painted green. A customer in his grocery store pinched a leaf, got the same delight from it that Mr. Thorburn had, and bought it for 75 cents. The grocer bought two more, potted them, and they sold right off.

That was the beginning of the florist business in the city. Mr. Thorburn, a canny fellow, knew a good thing when he had it. He laid in lots of pots and plants and branched out into selling seed, too. He prospered and soon afterward started a farm in Astoria.

The trade developed all sorts of angles. The florist made up bouquets for weddings and dinner parties and sold posies to the town's dandies. He got the contract for decorating tables at City Hall dinners. At the Independence Day dinner there on July 4, 1805, he supplied fifty dwarf orange trees and fifty dwarf lemon trees.

William Cobbett, an Englishman, set up shop near Thorburn's in 1818, but New Yorkers wouldn't support two florists. Mr. Cobbett had to give up. The dwarfed but pious and energetic Thorburn had no real competitors for decades.

He had some bad years, though. In 1816 he went in a bit over his head and landed in debtors' prison then on the site of the present City Hall Park, but eventually got out. In 1812 he printed the first seed catalogue in the United States,

"The Gentleman's and Garddeners' Kalendar for the Middle States of North America."

Anyone who thrills at a catalogue has that to thank Grant Thorburn for, too. The Scot left New York in 1855 and died eight years later at New Haven, Conn., in his ninetieth year.

March 15, 1954

¶ For more than two years Daniel De Koven, an artist who labors in a vast studio above the south end of Grand Central Terminal, has covered countless New York miles in spare-time quest for what he calls the Old Stone Face.

He noticed, just before he took up the task, that he had acquired a fairly common urban characteristic; he walked with eyes barely lifted above store-front level. In impulsive reform, he lifted his sights, so to speak.

Then his artist's eye began to take in things he had never noticed before. On the west side of town from the lower Seventies up into Harlem he saw quaint carvings on old brownstone fronts.

Mr. De Koven widened his field. He found Brooklyn Heights brownstones rich in the same crude art, and a lot more of it around Chelsea in the neighborhood of the General Theological Seminary at Ninth Avenue and Twenty-first Street.

He took photographs of the images and has run up a large collection. He hasn't had much luck identifying them. He did learn, though, that the brownstone era started in a large way around 1840 and lasted through the Eighties.

The foremost disciples of the brownstone school of architecture, near as Mr. De Koven could pin it down, were a Calvin Pollard, who did loads of brownstone fronts here from 1830 to 1850, and a Henry Hobson Richardson, who did brownstone Romanesques in the Seventies and Eighties.

Most of the facing material, which is Triassic sandstone stained by iron ore, was quarried at Portland in Middlesex County, Conn., and hauled to barges by oxen. It was excitedly bid for by contractors in New York Harbor. Much of the carving was done in Newark.

Italian, German, Scottish and Swedish immigrants who cut the images were just hard-working fellows with no great inspiration. They worked from sketches and in some cases from portraits. A few politicians around town had their own likenesses carved for their homes.

In the Eighteen Seventies the term "brownstone" was more or less interchangeable with "blueblood" in this city. A rich man was "a brownstone," flossy clubs had "brownstone membership" and the "brownstone vote" was the silkstocking vote right into early twentieth century.

Some brownstone was used before 1820 in New York, running second to brick and gray granite. The back of City Hall was covered with it 150 years ago because the town fathers didn't think that New York would grow much above that

point and that not many would see it.

Mr. De Koven kept running into people who have lived for twenty years, or more, in brownstones that have carved images on their facing, but had never noticed them until he began taking pictures.

MARGINALIA: ⸿ The bare little office in which Peter Cooper ran his affairs up to the time he died, aged 90, in 1883, still exists, pretty much as he left it. His old fireplace, wood box and stern-looking upholstered bench are still in the chamber. The room is on the second floor of the tired old brick relic at 181 Water Street, occupied now by Brewer & Co., a Massachusetts pharmaceutical house.

⸿ Sharp eyes can still make out the lines of the narrowest house in the city. It is part now of the American Banker building at 32 Stone Street, but in the early nineteenth century it was 32½ Stone Street, a snug bit of a structure built out of an alley between 32 and 34. The legend is that it was a resort for sailing men fresh in from sea, and had four bedrooms despite its bare width. It is only six feet five inches across.

March 17, 1954

⸿ Townsfolk who shake in cold Fifth Avenue blasts as they watch the St. Patrick's Day march each year must know that icy winds have been part of the parade tradition in this city for more than 100 years.

The first parade on record was

on March 17, 1779, when 400 "Volunteers of Ireland" tramped from Lower Broadway behind a British (Heaven forgive it) band to a restaurant on the Bowery for a St. Patrick's Day feast.

They were led by their colonel, Lord Rawdon, himself Irish-born, but then in the King's service, fighting Washington's men. He had enrolled the volunteers with the help of a Lieutenant Colonel Doyle, who had his recruiting station at 10 Wall Street.

After the parade, The New York Mercury noted, the Volunteers of Ireland sat down to "the enjoyment of a noble banquet . . . of 500 covers," but Lord Rawdon found later he had wasted the King's funds.

The Volunteers went over to General Washington in great numbers, which enraged his lordship. He offered ten guineas bounty for their heads; half that for any brought to him alive. He got no takers.

There were St. Patrick's Day breakfasts in the city before the parade tradition began. The earliest, held in 1756 at the Crown and Thistle that was conducted by Scotch Johnny Thompson in Whitehall Slip, was attended by Sir Charles Hardy, Governor of New York, with members of his Council and General Assembly.

In 1774, the breakfast was at Hull's Tavern in Lower Broadway, "attended by the principal gentlemen of this city," and the next year was held there again by the Friendly Brothers of St. Patrick. They continued through most of the British occupation.

Throughout the Revolution there lived, at 218 Pearl Street, a gentleman delightfully named Hercules Mulligan, who had come to New York in 1746, as a child. He was General Washington's secret agent in the city, a dangerous assignment.

Hercules had his reward after the last British soldier left Manhattan Island in November, 1783. The Commander in Chief, after reviewing his troops at Bowling Green, went to the Mulligans' house to dine.

It was not until the Eighteen Fifties that the St. Patrick's Day parades in New York assumed large proportions. By that time, immigration from Ireland was at flood and good-sized Irish county units were available. Marchers wore costumes that still smelled of native peat.

In 1851, when the parade formed in downtown Manhattan, icy winds cut at the assembled buckos and ice and sleet tore at their hats and jackets. But Col. Mike Phelan of the old Ninth Regiment, struck up the band and they fell in bravely behind him.

Again, in 1852, bitter winds knifed down and a blizzard swept the marchers' ranks as they assembled in Third Avenue at Eighth Street, but the pipers' shrill call and the boom of the drums got them stepping and they plodded full route through the storm.

The route in those days was up Third to Twenty-third, to Eighth Avenue, to Hudson Street, down to Canal, to West Broadway, to Chambers, to Broadway, to Park Row and then up to St. Patrick's Cathedral in Prince Street.

Mayor Ambrose C. Kingsland reviewed the 1852 parade and Archbishop Hughes celebrated High Mass at St. Patrick's. Eighty of the Friendly Sons of St. Patrick had dinner that night at Keefe's Racket Clubhouse in Broadway. Oratory and red grape flowed freely.

There were toasts to "Ireland, the Land of our Fathers," to "The Day, and to all who honor it," to "The Land of Our Adoption," to "The President of the United States," to "The Army and the Navy of the United States," to "The City of New York," to "The Harp of Innisfail"—and that was just a beginning.

Henry Raymond of The New York Times responded to a toast to "The Press," a scholarly response that brought the guests to their feet with applause. It was not a quiet evening.

There's one other thing worth mention this day. No man has ever proved to the true Son of Erin that Norsemen, Christopher Columbus, or any other Johnny-come-lately discovered this land of the free.

It was St. Brendan who found it, and it was named Irland et Mikla, or Greater Ireland. The voyage was made, so legend says, in nothing more than a craft whipped up of osiers and tanned hides, well greased to keep out the seas. The date of the landing was between 565 to 573 A.D.

That is the story come down through the ages, that it was St. Brendan of Tralee in Kerry who first set foot on America; St. Brendan, son of Finn Loga. Men of true faith will never agree that time has refuted the legend.

March 19, 1954

❡ It has taken the Park Department 100 years to get at the job of labeling its Central Park gates, or entrances, but it has a start on the project now. A little old gentleman has just finished the job at Fifth Avenue and Seventy-second Street, chiseling out "Inventors Gate."

There are twenty park gates altogether, but the money for having the stone cutters label the others hasn't come through and nobody seems to know if it ever will. The Inventors Gate job was done because it ties in with the opening of the new boathouse at Conservatory Lake.

The entrances include, on Fifth Avenue, the Scholars Gate at Sixtieth Street; Childrens Gate, Sixty-fourth; Miners Gate, Seventy-ninth; Engineers, Ninetieth; Woodmans, Ninety-sixth; Girls, 102d; Pioneers, 110th.

The northern park wall has the Farmers Gate at Lenox Avenue, the Warriors at Seventh Avenue, the Strangers at Eighth.

On the west side of the park there are the Boys Gate, 100th Street; Gate of All Saints, Ninety-sixth; Mariners, Eighty-fifth; Hunters, Eighty-first; Womans, Seventy-second.

The wide entry at Columbus Circle is the Merchants Gate and along the rest of the south wall, the Gate of the Artisans is at Seventh Avenue, and the Artists Gate at the Avenue of the Americas.

The gates got their names on April 2, 1861, after grave, drawn-out discussion by a nomenclature committee. There was some second-guessing even after that (Farmers Gate instead of Agriculturalists, for one instance) before the names won final approval. They showed on a Park Department map for the first time in 1865.

March 26, 1954

❡ A chap who likes to worm out origins of things got fussing among old records the other day to find out when New York had its first circus. He was inspired by a news note that Ringling's show would open in Madison Square Garden the end of this month.

The researcher couldn't quite pin down the date, but he thinks the first circus troupe rode into Manhattan around the close of the eighteenth century. It wasn't anything like the spectacles produced now, but it seemed wondrous to children of that day, for all its shortcomings.

The inquiring man said the first troupe set up its platform in the marshes above Collect Pond at Broome Street and Broadway. There was no admission charge because it was in the open, but a girl performer passed the tambourine, the troupe's only musical instrument.

John F. Watson, a chronicler of the period, saw the show as a boy. He remembered that coming home from school one day:

"We were struck dumb with amazement by the appearance of a band of splendidly clad horsemen, in the midst of whom rode a princess, as we supposed, gaily attired in habits of very unclean satin, bedizened with tinsel, a tiara of damaged plumes upon her head and her cheeks glowing with rouge of the most brilliant intensity.

"We had heard of the glories of circus-riding; suspicions of the delightful truth therefore flashed on our minds. This was soon heightened to certainty by the appearance of one of the horsemen, whose striped garments, fool's cap and antic maneuvers proclaimed him the clown of the company."

Mr. Watson said the youngsters gasped at the "leaps, tumbles, flip-flaps and somersets," and that their hearts went out to the clown because the ringmaster lashed him with a whip.

The town's first permanent circus was Pepe and Beschard's, a fenced-in affair that opened May 31, 1808, at Broadway and Worth Street. West's Circus replaced it at Canal and Broadway nine years later and ran through 1827, or longer.

❡ There's a more or less general notion that sidewalk superintendents —idling citizens who love to study building excavations—were officially recognized for the first time in the Thirties, when Rockefeller Center was building. The recognition is much older than that. John J. Downey, contractor, put up a bulletin in 1858 when he finished foundation construction at 52-56 Broadway, thanking spectators for their kind interest in the building's progress. "I regret," his notice concluded, "that I can no longer entertain you, and must bid you good day."

March 29, 1954

¶ Dean William B. Baer of New York University's College of Arts and Sciences cleared up for a lot of New Yorkers yesterday the origin of the quotation, "But Above All Things Truth Beareth Away the Victory," cut into the façade of the library at Fifth Avenue and Forty-second Street.

Dr. Baer traced it to the First Book of Esdras in the Apocrypha during his WCBS-TV show on Biblical literature. It seems three of King Darius' young bodyguards in Persia, some time around the fifth century, B.C., were asked to name for the King what they thought was the strongest influence on mankind.

One thought it must be wine. The second, a canny fellow, figured, "The King is the strongest." The winner somehow got over two entries. He first said, "Women." Then he added, "But above all things truth beareth away the victory." And so did he.

March 31, 1954

¶ Dwellers in thousands of New York City cold-water flats still use kerosine for room heating and for cooking. No other fuel is available in broad areas of Old Chelsea, farther up the West Side, in marginal slums along the East River and in the Greenpoint and Williams-burg districts of Brooklyn—among other places.

The men who produce the kerosine for this area and for Upstate New York, New England and New Jersey celebrated at the St. George Hotel in Brooklyn last night the 100th anniversary of the Sone & Fleming Refinery, a Socony-Vacuum unit on Newtown Creek's south shore.

Sone & Fleming, pioneers in kerosine production, started as a two-man operation in a crude little shack on the creek banks in 1854. They got the oil the hard way—wrested it from shale and from coal brought to the United States as ballast for sailing vessels out of Britain and Scotland.

Their product—they called it "astral oil"—was a wonder in its day. It pushed whale oil off the market. It was costly and something of a luxury; sold for $1.15 a gallon in the beginning. Right now, in the Atom Age, it is down to 15 cents. Certain types of industrial plants prefer it to other fuels.

Men at the dinner last night—Jim McGinley and the brothers Jim and Frank Barron—represent a third generation of kerosine producers on Newtown's banks and are filled with the history and legend of the place. No part of the original plant remains standing, but they have a good idea of where it was. They're a strangely loyal group with the high spirit of, say, sentimental collegiates.

Dr. W. L. Linton, a kindly West Virginian who came to Sone & Fleming almost thirty-five years ago, is head man now. He has absorbed all the plant legends and runs the refinery in the patriarchal manner. Like most of his workers he has become part of the community, and he has great pride in two Little League baseball teams, of which Sone & Fleming are sponsor.

Old plant hands have acquired odd bits of local lore. They tell you, for example, that Greenpoint, where they're located, got its name in the seventeenth century from bright green sea and river scum that patched the creek shores; that there still lies, under Central Park, a six-inch pipe that brought crude oil to Sone & Fleming after 1879. Crude oil provided the source for kerosine after the Drake Well came in in Pennsylvania in 1859.

Dr. Linton says most oil corporations, including Socony-Vacuum, prefer "kerosine" for spelling the name of their product. Cities Service Oil Company is the lone holdout. It sticks grimly to "kerosene."

¶ Union Square got its name in 1807 as the meeting place, or union, of Bowery Road and Broadway, then New York's main highways. General Washington's statue in the Square marks the area where he was met by the town's deliriously happy citizens on the November day in 1783 when the British pulled out of Manhattan.

April 2, 1954

¶ Bingler's bus trips for horseplayers dropped off yesterday with the start of the spring meeting at Jamaica Race Track, as the Bingler people knew they would. But the company ran two bus loads of sporting gentlemen down to Laurel in Maryland anyway and probably will again today.

The bus operators find that some horseplayers don't like bucking big throngs at New York tracks, that some follow certain horses and jockeys around, and that career horseplayers count pennies and prefer out-of-town tracks because admission prices, food and the state bite on pari-mutuels are lower.

The Bingler service for bettors, an astonishing institution, started in 1948. It provides transportation to and from Delaware, New Jersey and Maryland tracks, with track admission ticket included in what they call "the tour." It handles up to sixty-five bus loads, or around 2,600 customers, on summer Saturdays and a third that many on weekdays.

The racing fans assemble in the Consolidated Bus Terminal in Forty-first Street west of Seventh Avenue as early as 5:30 A.M. for long runs. The Bingler vehicles make the trip to Bowie and Laurel in about four and one-half hours on weekdays, but it takes five or six hours on Saturday when traffic thickens.

They can make the Garden State track at Camden in less than two hours, Delaware Park in about the same time and, by way of the New Jersey Turnpike, put the bettors in Atlantic City in about two and one-half hours. "You got to get them there for the daily double," the drivers say, "or they mark you." The line gets the same riders year in and year out. About 5 per cent are women.

Sandy Bain, a former advertising man who manages the service, is uncompromisingly stern about keeping it clean. He drove off a couple of three-card-monte teams that tried to ply their trade on long hauls. And he won't let his drivers carry bets or pay slips for customers. He finds his fares fascinating as social studies, but hasn't caught horse fever himself.

One rider, a wealthy gentleman, who spends around $25,000 each year on a safari in Africa, likes to pass around snapshots showing him with his feet on dead lions and other carnivora. An importer with a good credit rating uses the terminal each morning as his office. He dictates correspondence to a secretary who meets him there before bus take-off and catches him again at night with office memoranda. The main run of riders represents Guys and Dolls strains.

Mr. Bain has witnessed many minor tragedies. Charlie, a Chinese horseplayer, went broke after three years of middling good luck, and for weeks now has been washing Bingler buses at East Paterson, working up a fresh stake. One morning Mr. Bain tried to keep a woman from boarding a racetrack bus with an undersized boy. "I beg your parn, Mister," she told him frigidly. "He ain't no boy; he's a jockey."

You wouldn't expect, somehow, a horseplayer's bus service to have a poetic side, but the Bingler outfit has. It arranges one-day country tours for amateur archaeologists, painting classes for beginners, come-meet-spring rides, journeys into autumn foliage, trips to historic spots and mystery rides on which the drivers take their courses from sealed envelopes, opened one at a time.

¶ A Health Department statistician learned with some astonishment at a meeting of health statisticians in Washington last week that the greatest concentration of American Indians a square mile is in New York City, of all places. Most of the men are structural iron workers. The figure for the city is about 2,000 or about ninety a square mile. Most of them are Mohawks and live near Brooklyn's downtown waterfront. . . .

April 9, 1954

¶ The town's top theatre is twenty-five years old this year. Distinguished players have clumped its boards and have looked dreamily down upon the stone and concrete landscape from the city's highest dressing rooms, up among real stars.

The theatre is the Chanin Auditorium built by the brothers Irwin and Henry Chanin on the fiftieth floor of the Chanin Building at Forty-second Street and Lexington Avenue. Toscanini has conducted there, Lawrence Tibbett has sung there, Heifetz and Horowitz have played in the auditorium, so did Rachmaninoff and the Philharmonic and NBC orchestra groups.

That wasn't what the Chanins had in mind when they had their tower theatre included in the building plans. They thought it would be a nice place for sales talks for corporations that have space in the building and for meetings of boards of directors.

In the beginning the 192-seat auditorium was used mostly for such things, but little by little word got around that it was an ideal place for sneak previews and for plays by private companies. Excellent acoustics in this silver and black theatre in the clouds increased bookings.

Some of the shows in the skyscraper theatre have been put on at skyscraper prices. Seats for the Chatham Square Musical School benefit in 1939, which Mr. Toscanini conducted in a Prince Albert coat, red Ascot and spats, went at $100 each. Thirty standing room tickets fetched $1,500.

Lecture bureaus rent the place a lot. So do talent bureaus. They put on brief sketches for representatives of women's clubs in the metropolitan district as samplings of what they have to offer. Canada Dry and Pan American use it for stockholders' meetings. It has been taken for cram lectures for the New York bar and for some New York University summer sessions.

A portable box office is used when shows are on, and a large reception room just outside is for refreshments and lounging. WQXR and WHOM, incidentally, have their transmitters on the Chanin tower, and the place is still a tourist attraction. Between 15,000 and 20,000 persons each year pay a quarter to see the city from the parapets.

April 12, 1954

¶ A set of tiled arches on Grand Central Terminal's lower level, in front of the Oyster Bar, permits whispered conversations between persons facing diagonal corners under the arches.

The arches are above the transverse section, a compartment on a line with the Oyster Bar's front doors. Participants in the whispering trick, mostly college kids, get endless delight from it.

It works best with the lips almost touching the walls at the corners. In that position, no matter how much pedestrian traffic comes charging down the transverse or how loudly trains are called, each syllable is astonishingly distinct.

Most of the porters and the men at the lower level information desk know about the whispering arches. They say it's an acoustical freak. The trick doesn't seem to work under other arches near by.

April 14, 1954

¶ The Easter Parade tradition in New York isn't as old as many people seem to think. It started, in a small way, about 100 years ago, down around Old Trinity when the city had not begun to spread.

Ladies and gentlemen in spring finery usually strolled up Broadway toward Canal Street, or down to the Battery after church, and took the new sun with neighbors until it was time for the noonday meal. There was a great carriage turnout, too.

Newspapers in the Eighteen Fifties paid little attention to the strollers. There were short pieces about Easter Sunday sermons and masses; never a word about who wore what.

By 1869, though, the parade was pretty firmly established. It made the last page of some of the local dailies. The city line had surged northward quite a bit by then, but the larger churches were still down near the island's tip.

Easter Sunday, March 28, was balmy that year. The New York Times was delighted to report next morning: "The day being pleasant, the streets and parks were filled with pedestrians gladly enjoying the first airs of spring. The ladies were out in full force, looking doubly charming under the influence of those genial skies."

This was before the advent of the fashion reporter. Nothing was written, even then, about what women and their escorts wore at the Easter Sunday service.

It wasn't until the Eighteen Eighties that this note crept into newspaper reports about Easter Sunday. By that time the strolling area extended from around Madison Square into the Fifties on Fifth Avenue.

In that year The Times found the roadways lined with "elegant equipages at church doors, manned by pompous footmen." "The fashion parade," it said, "went on until the shades of night began to fall."

"The throng was almost exclusively composed of churchgoers," the reporter wrote. "Young men of the genus vulgarly yclept 'dude' were out in force in high hats and brilliant gloves." He noticed "a group of Italian immigrants in dirt and rags who were dazzled and awed by the splendor of the throng."

The writer decided that with all the "prancing horses, glittering harness, shining carriages thronging the thoroughfare" he could venture the statement that the show was "as splendid and beautiful a procession as could be found in the wide world."

In 1881 the Easter Sunday strollers made front page for the first time. Again the Avenue from Madison Square to Central Park looked from above like flowing flower beds.

Jay Gould, newsmen noticed, peeked at the passing show from his Fifth Avenue windows, and the Vanderbilts' houses farther uptown were decked with fresh greenery and blossoms. The tradition was fixed by then.

But the tradition has come full cycle. The after-church stroll is no longer an impromptu fashion display. Commercialism in the past few years overreached itself by sending professional models into the throng and even posed them on church steps.

That drove the gentry out of it. They have withdrawn from the day-long promenade, so the only significant display of the newest fashions by such folk is on opening night at the opera.

April 16, 1954

❡ Every school morning Sam picks up Veronica, Mary-Jo, Debbie, Davey, Jackie and Julio in a limousine owned by the Parochial Bus System, Inc. He drives Mary-Jo and Debbie to 59 East Fifty-seventh Street, between Second and Third Avenues. The others he puts down at Public School 135 on First Avenue at Fifty-first Street.

At 2:30 P.M. Sam calls for the children at the two schools and takes them home again. His boss, F. E. Arrigoni, has a contract with the Board of Education for the service. He runs limousines in other parts of Manhattan and in Brooklyn, the Bronx and Queens. The riders are youngsters with cerebral palsy, like Veronica, Davey, Julio and Jackie, or blind children, like Mary-Jo and Debbie.

The other day Sam called for his group at P. S. 135. The teachers dressed the children while they occupied their wheel chairs, which are their school seats, too. It is difficult to put coats and sweaters and hats on cerebral palsy sufferers, because their limbs and their heads keep convulsively pulling away all the time. But they laugh, like any other kids, and Big Sam and the teachers unlock their foot braces and lift them into the cars.

Curly-haired Veronica went in first to a corner back seat. Seven-year-old Jackie was put next to her, and dark-eyed Julio sat in his mother's lap. Davey got a jump seat. Sam looked them over to see that they were as comfortable as they can ever get to be and drove to the Fifty-seventh Street School. Two bright-faced little girls with sparkling eyes waited at the curb. You didn't know until they felt

their way into the front seat next to Sam that they were blind.

All the children had Easter baskets in brown paper bags. They had decorated them with crayons in all manner of scrawls and eccentric patterns, but the colors were cheerful and good to look upon. Mary-Jo stared straight ahead, unseeing, through the windshield, a pretty blonde thing in a light-blue leather jacket and dark-blue beret. She said, "Jackie, let me feel your Easter basket." Jackie fumbled for it, so Big Sam reached back for it and gave it to Mary-Jo.

Her fingers probed inside the bag, over the candy eggs and the rough sides of the basket. She passed it awkwardly back to Sam. "Jackie," she said, "that's the prettiest Easter basket I have ever seen." Jackie grunted and clutched his property again.

All the kids were quiet as the car pushed into Fifty-first Street, just below Ninth Avenue. A man came to the car, lifted Davey out, and carried him up a tenement stoop. The other youngsters shrilled goodby. Davey, limp in his father's arms, waved back and vanished in a dark hallway.

Sam drove down Ninth Avenue and into Twenty-fourth Street, eastward. A tired-looking woman came to help Debbie to the curb. The child turned sightless eyes on the group. She fingered her Braille wrist watch and said: "It's just exactly 3 o'clock, Sam. You're right on time." "Get going, Chatterbox," the good-natured driver told her. Debbie giggled. Her mother led her into a big apartment house.

Sam got onto the West Side Highway and headed for South Ferry. You wanted to tell the kids to see the big liner pulling out, and the gulls floating against spring's sky, but you remembered Mary-Jo and kept silent.

A gray-haired lady waited for Veronica at the Staten Island Ferry gate. It was difficult getting the little girl out and onto the ferry. Sam said: "That poor kid's got no more stand-up than a bag of pertaters." Veronica smiled. Her head pulled away, uncontrolled, but came right again, and a palsied little hand waved good-by.

Jackie's mother waited for him at the Alfred E. Smith Houses. He all but tumbled out, a wee thing. He caught the handles of a perambulator his mother pushed, got his sea legs, more or less, and hanging on, made slow progress up the walk.

Mary-Jo got off in crowded Elizabeth Street. Her mother, a young woman, was waiting for her with Francine, another blonde daughter, but younger, dressed in blue like Mary-Jo. Standing off a little from the limousine, eyes wide and clear gray, Mary-Jo said: "I go to the Lighthouse on Saturday, Sam. I dance with boys." Sam pretended gruffness. He said, gravel-voiced, "You got too many boy friends, Mary-Jo. You knock them dead," and the car parted a group of shrill children in the street. Mary-Jo and her sister waved after the car.

The extra rider cleared his throat. He said: "It's a heartbreaker, isn't it, Sam? Those poor kids."

"You didn't look right for the story, Mister," Sam suggested. "You got to look at those mothers' faces; that's the story."

April 19, 1954

¶ Guido Pagano is a hairdresser on Katonah Avenue in the Bronx. His hobby is amateur movies. Three years ago he returned to Avellino in the grape and olive country in the Apennines, where he was born, to visit his sister. He took his movie camera along, and used it.

He showed the pictures to some friends one night and was startled by a loud outcry from one of their neighbors. The neighbor had seen *his* sister in the film, one from whom he had been parted thirty-four years. The film was rerun for him.

In that moment, Guido the hairdresser got the idea for his Family Overseas Talking Picture Company. Last year he brought back on 16mm. film and on tape likenesses and voices of kin of 160 Italy-born New Yorkers who had not been back to their birthplaces for decades.

Guido had learned what to have his subjects say for the film—throbbing, emotional lines, with arms outstretched, and with familiar mountain or valley backgrounds, for which his clients had hungered. Sometimes his customers weep when a film is run.

Guido has an agent in Rome, now, to take mailed orders for 200-foot strips with tape, for which a client pays $100. Guido shows the film, when it gets here, at the customer's home; then he tells the customer where to rent a projector.

He said: "It goes well this year, too. I am thinking maybe one day I should have agents in France, in Ireland, in Germany, in all European countries." Right now his orders seem to cluster around southern Italy, around Naples, Sicily and Sardinia.

¶ No street in town maintains its melancholy charm so well as Pearl Street. Its dark cast, its weathered fronts, cobbled pavement and rather odd trades and industries keep it in nineteenth-century mood.

Not without reason. Many buildings along Pearl are from 100 to 150 years old. William F. Ransom, the tall, stately gentleman who owns L. E. Ransom Company, traders in dyestuffs at 279 Pearl, figures his place was built around 1810.

It looks very much like a neighboring four-story structure around the corner at 50 Cliff Street, and original building plans found on a beam in the cellar there are dated 1810. The two places are twins for outline, dustiness and somber mien.

Mr. Ransom's father, Lewis E. Ransom, came down from Fort Plain, in Niagara County, N. Y., to open a dyestuff plant at 47 Maiden Lane in 1864. He moved to Pearl Street forty years later. He was one of the original directors of the Chase National Bank.

William F. Ransom, taken into the dye firm as a boy, is 82 years old now, but unbent. He's kept the shop, with its narrow staircases, wrought-iron trimming and ancient furnishings, just as his father found them. He hangs on to the old pot-belly stove and long outmoded office equipment.

He has a lot of his father's old business cards listing annatto, annatto seed, cochineal, indigo and tumeric as being for sale in any quantity. He concedes that plastics and other synthetics have cut his market, but he still does well enough with the same wares that his father handled.

The office cat, the old stove, the gigantic roll-top desk, antique stencils and the pleasantly brooding nineteenth-century shadows that come early in Pearl Street seem perfect background for William Ransom.

A temperate man himself, and a kindly philosopher, Mr. Ransom likes to slip a certain bill under the eyes of any stray visitor not interested in madder and tumeric. His father made it out for a customer in 1867:

"One pint of old rye, and bottle, 35 cents." A bitter, wistful item for a thirsty man to look at now.

April 21, 1954

¶ City dwellers rarely see the crews that probe through asphalt and concrete for water leaks, a job crucially important when a water shortage threatens.

It's a difficult assignment. Divining rods won't find leaks through twenty inches of pavement. Aquaphones and geophones, on the other hand, are so sensitive that at Columbus Circle they can be used only at night or in early morning. They resemble stethoscopes, and work on the same general principle.

By day these listening devices are likely to confuse operators when they work in the downtown areas. The instruments pick up subway rumble, pedestrian pounding, the hiss of New York Steam Company conduits, the noise from Western Union and Consolidated Edison underground installations, the drone of refrigeration units and the considerable hubbub of motor traffic.

When the operators get above a leak on a quiet night, escaping water thunders in the earphones, especially if it is coming from a jagged crack in pipe bedded in solid concrete. Leaks are more difficult to hear when there's air space between them and the detectors.

Round or elliptical breaks give off less sound than jagged cracks and it takes a sharply practiced ear, like Bob Devinney's, to identify them for what they are. Muffling—water pooling and covering an opening—is even worse. That calls for experts, too.

Mr. Devinney is Manhattan borough engineer, a leak tracker from way back. The men who get into his crews—they include one truck driver, three laborers and a supervisor to each unit—are tested for hearing before they're sent out to hunt.

Leak-hunts follow an abitrary pattern. They start at control valves, which are mostly at street intersections, take the operators to fire hydrants, then along service pipes that carry water into homes, office buildings and factories.

Water at full normal flow sends up no sound, oddly enough, or a faint sound that is easily distinguished. Breaks are in constant uproar when heard through the geophone or aquaphone.

The trackers go out with maps and blueprints to guide them. They also carry the Velie maps that show the courses of suppressed underground streams, such as Minetta Brook in Greenwich Village, Collect Pond around the Civic Center and the streams that pour out of Central Park.

New York leaks rarely break through the city's hard crust, which makes the hunting more difficult. Searching for one in a skyscraper's subbasement is knotty business. On the waterfront, leaks are muffled at high-tide, and searchers must wait until the tide is out again.

Mr. Devinney's men average about one and one-half digs for each leak they locate, which they think is good going. If they have to break through, say, four or five places before they find one, they call the job a "golf course," figuring the openings as so many divots.

The toughest of the jobs that comes to Mr. Devinney's mind when he's asked about leak-hunting is the old Consumer's Brewery classic. This involved a leaking pipe at Fifty-fourth Street and Sutton Place. The pipe was covered with sand fill, and lying 'way down. The crew golfed that one like duffers gone berserk, but finally plugged it.

Leak-hunting is, in some ways, a thankless task, Mr. Devinney finds. Up in Riverdale, for example, a break left a pool in a householder's yard, so she used the pool for gold-fish. She was mean to the crew when it plugged the leak and drained her pool away.

If there's any doubt as to where water is coming from on a compli-cated hunt, samples go to the de-partment's laboratories at Mount Prospect in Brooklyn, for analysis. Experts there decide whether it is water from a main, a waste pipe, or from a brook. That's a vital link in the endless search for lost water.

April 23, 1954

❡ Hozen Seki, the Buddhist priest who dedicated the Japanese house in the garden of the Museum of Modern Art in West Fifty-fourth Street yesterday, founded the Ne Yu Yoku Buddhist Church here six-teen years ago.

It has its shrine now on the sec-ond floor of the brownstone and white-brick house at 171 West Ninety-fourth Street, once the quar-ters of Ross Williams' and Bill Mc-Keever's Democratic Club.

"Ne Yu Yoku" in the church's title is the Japanese version of "New York." "Hozen," the priest's first name, means, in rough trans-lation, "teacher of good." He is de-scended from a long line of priests reaching into antiquity.

Hozen Seki had served at Bud-dhist altars in Arizona and in Los Angeles before he was sent to New York in 1938 to set up the first and only temple for his sect in the East. Money to buy the old clubhouse in Ninety-fourth Street came from subscriptions.

The sect has flourished here and has 300 worshipers. In its building it has a lovely shrine, imported from Kyoto and done in traditional black enamel, gold and lacquer. In front of it are great golden lotus blossoms, enormous incense burn-ers and religious paintings. The lighting is extraordinarily subtle.

During the reading of the Sutra, or Scripture, the priests or their as-sistants lightly touch a great bronze gong, shaped like a jardinière. Sound swells up from it in grow-ing volume as mushrooming cloud swells from an atomic explosion. Then it dies a-lingering.

Buddha's high priest in New York has noble dreams. He intends one day to build a great shrine and a seminary for Buddhist instruc-tion. Japanese in the city have con-tributed generously, but another two or three years may go by be-fore the seminary can be started.

The high priest, meanwhile, seeks converts in Ne Yu Yoku. He has ten Caucasians in his flock now, most of them G.I.s who married Japanese girls. He turns out Bud-dhist literature in English to in-struct converts.

Most of this he gives away or has distributed. For the Buddha-Bha-sita-Amitayur Dhyana-Sutra, a book of meditations bound in hard scar-let covers, his group charges $1.25. It is an English translation from ancient Sanskrit, an introduction to basic tenets.

To attract folk to the Ninety-fourth Street shrine the priest and Satomi, his American-born wife, have arranged classes in flower ar-rangement, Japanese art and brush calligraphy. They give free Japanese language instruction.

Services are held in English and in Japanese. The English rites are at 11:30 A.M. on Sundays for Caucasians and Nisei and at 8 P.M. for Issei, or first-generation Japanese. There is Sunday school at 10:30 A.M. for Sansei, which is third generation.

The high priest arranges spring flower-arrangement exhibits, shows Japanese color motion pictures, has a committee to put on traditional Japanese dances and plays, and every few weeks offers a Japanese musicale.

The temple has a chorus of twenty mixed voices to chant the Gatha, or hymns. Its furnishings are a little on the poor side—only camp chairs for communicants—but one day there will be mats, as at home.

In some Japanese temples communicants leave their shoes, or clogs, at the door. The Sekis have had transients who insisted on following that custom—the last one a lad from Ceylon—but generally worshipers stay shod.

The great gong in the temple is very old—the Sekis haven't fixed its exact age yet, but are having its inscriptions studied—and of dreamlike tone. A Japanese butler got it from his employers, Mr. and Mrs. R. G. Packard of East Orange, N. J. They had owned it for decades.

The priests in Ne Yu Yoku Temple cannot buy their vestments and religious furnishings here, but get them by mail order from Kyoto. Their robes—scarlet for important ceremonies, white for weddings, black for informal occasions—come from Japan, too. So does their incense.

April 26, 1954

⁋ For weeks now Christian Buchheit has toiled in the basement in the Art Students League building at 215 West Fifty-seventh Street making a plaster Swan for a living Leda and a papier-mâché Bull for a living Europa. They will be borne on palanquins into the grand ballroom of the Plaza Hotel at midnight next Friday at the league's Dream Ball.

Chris, slight and gray, has put together many curious figures for the annual party in the fifty years he has been with the league as carpenter, handy man and superintendent. Nothing the artists dream up startles or dismays him, and he isn't too sure but that the first batch of artists he knew at the league were a bit more daring with designs than the new boys are.

He remembers that when he came to work for the league Fifty-seventh Street was a slower-paced neighborhood. The Goulds' stables were just west of the league studios. The family made brave show with its coach and four and with blooded mounts. Fifty-seventh Street was cobbled, poorly lighted by gas lamps.

Each year the league ball committee arbitrarily chooses the color scheme to be followed; it turns away any guest who departs from the scheme. Black and white are always included for people who come in formal dress. The bright colors are for livelier folk who come in costume to try for the $500 in prizes.

Because the annual romp is always a costume, or masked, ball, it is part of Chris' job to make certain there is a police permit for a masque. One year—around 1925—someone slipped up on this detail, and guests in masks, beards and facial make-up were not allowed onto the Astor dance floor—not until 2 A.M., when someone awakened the Police Commissioner at home and got permission to go ahead.

Pinkertons have become part of the show since a group of middle-aged but puckish business men hid in a balcony at the Waldorf a few years ago after a wild party of their own, and came down at midnight to paw league models. The league follows theatrical rules on nudity—participants must wear nothing less than would get by in a Billy Minsky show.

You learn that Lionel Barrymore was an etcher when he got out of the league studios in his youth and that some of his work still sells in Fifty-seventh Street art shops. Dan Beard, the Boy Scout founder in America, was a league man, too. He learned about the Scout movement while painting in Britain. Claudette Colbert got her start in realistic painting at the league.

May 3, 1954

❡ New York will give Brooklyn Bridge back to the populace today with $7,000,000 worth of new motor roadways and a new center promenade. For four years it has been restricted to one-way traffic.

Contractors' men and city workers spent the week-end hauling seven work sheds off the span, mechanically brooming up soot that had accumulated a quarter-inch in depth in the four years it has taken to make over the bridge, wiping off new traffic signs, polishing new lamps, testing new police phones and fire-signal wires, setting up stands for today's formal ceremony, running up ceremonial bunting.

The first pedestrian on the bridge was Howard Cook, an artist from Taos, N. M., in rather baggy tweeds and with a toothy grin under a broad red mustache. Because he's loved Brooklyn Bridge some thirty years or so, he got special permission to go out on the footwalk and paint before official opening. He was out there Friday in the warm sun, doing the new lamps and the new view.

Ted Mombelly, the city's Brooklyn Bridge engineer, was on the bridge, too, late Friday afternoon, critically watching last-minute tarring between concrete squares, picking up odds and ends left by technicians, passing his palm over new footwalk spruce, testing for warp.

He found everything just fine. The new salt-impregnated yellow pine planks on the pedestrian stairways seemed to his liking and he was proud of the fresh gray paint on railings and struts. Then he went briefly gloomy.

He said, "A week after opening, and the soot will have this paint ten shades darker." He shrugged that dark thought off, though, studied his overall handiwork, and seemed to find it good. The bridge shone clean and bright in the spring sun.

The only odds and ends left untouched by Mr. Mombelly and his crews were the pigeons' eggs on top of the great granite towers. His men think it's inviting bad luck to damage the eggs. He doesn't quite subscribe, but has learned it's best not to buck superstitions on the job.

Mr. Mombelly slapped the towers during his inspection and marveled at how they've defied weather, with no sign of wear in seventy years. He and other engineers seem even more amazed that the mortar that binds the granite blocks hasn't worn, either.

Mr. Mombelly said it was a natural mortar, used as it was taken from the earth, except that it was powdered. The bridge people have searched all the old records but haven't been able to learn just where the stuff came from. They'd like to lay their hands on some now.

Lamps that light the footbridge have been stepped up from 150-watt, the former strength, to 300-watt. Motor roadway lamps, curiously, will have lower wattage, but where there were thirty-seven of them before there are 260 now in the space between the towers. They're calculated not to throw shadow.

Mr. Mombelly's men and the contractors were mighty careful in their conversion job on the Old Lady. Before they laid down the new roadways and the new struts they marked the cables in the tower so they could easily spot slippage, the thing most feared in such construction.

Loads coming onto, and leaving, the span were carefully figured to maintain cable balance. The roadways were put down in exact balance, the same amount of steel and concrete going down either side of the towers at the same time. They used more caution the farther they got from the towers. "Balance got more critical with distance," Mr. Mombelly explained.

The new roadways are designed to carry heavy loads in an emergency, but ordinary trucking will be kept off them. Mail trucks, Army, Navy, Marine Corps and Air Force vehicles, ambulances and fire apparatus will be the exceptions.

The Post Office's pneumatic tubes that carried mail across the bridge between Brooklyn and Manhattan have been torn out, but the number of police and fire-alarm stations has been increased and so has the number of standpipes and fire-hose connections. The water pressure has been stepped up, too.

Fireboats that answer bridge alarms hook into hose connections on the towers just above river level. Land units hook in right from the roadways. Pumpers have to send the water up 136 feet, which is roadway height above the river. The new installations have been tested and have worked out all right.

Mr. Mombelly opened a new police signal box before he left the span last night. "This is Ted Mombelly, Lieutenant," he said into the box. "I'm the bridge engineer. Just want to see if this thing is working."

A piping voice assured him it was. Mr. Mombelly beamed, leaned on the bridge rail and stared dreamily westward to where the river, Staten Island and the Statue of Liberty were spread, throbbingly gilded with setting sun.

May 10, 1954

¶ Mary Elizabeth Banta can knock on any door in Chinatown and after the tenant's "Bing gaw lai?" ("Who comes?") gain swift entry with her soft answer, "Sing Sang Paw," which means "The Teacher Lady."

It has been that way for fifty years. Miss Banta, an Ohio Methodist minister's daughter, came to Chinatown as a missionary in 1904. Since that time she has grown into the community's warmest legend. No other outsider is so beloved.

She came as a tiny, pretty, blond young woman. Now she is almost white-haired. She wears rather old-fashioned little flowered hats, and time has engraved her face and her hands, but her eyes, behind spectacles, are wondrous blue.

Chinatown has changed a lot since Miss Banta came into it. Almost all the men, in the beginning, wore pigtails and the dark silken garb of their native country. She remembers how they padded and shuffled down the streets under the yellow gas lamps, hands folded and hidden in wide sleeves.

Her first pupils were young men anxious to learn English. She taught them in the old Methodist church in Forsyth Street that was swept away later for the Manhattan Bridge approach. One by one, as they became Westernized, they had their queues cut off and gave them to Sing Sang Paw. She has them in a trunk.

But Miss Banta's heart went out most to the few Chinese women and their young daughters. Fifty years ago they lived behind closed doors, went out only on rare occasions, and then only with their husbands or fathers. When Miss Banta wondered why, they told her: "China man too much long talk." They meant the men were gossips.

Sing Sang Paw did more than any other person in New York to free Chinatown's women. They were suspicious of her in the beginning. They could not understand why she handled their daughters so tenderly, why she gave long hours to teaching them English words.

Her first Chinese girl pupil was Te Ye Ho, who was 11, a pretty thing. Miss Banta taught her to say "apple," "book," "table," "hand," "fingers," "five fingers," "two hands." She knew little Chinese herself, then; she taught by touching or holding up objects.

Te Ye Ho's mother, whose feet were tiny, and bound, said to Sing Sang Paw, "Why do you love Te Ye Ho?" And the little missionary said, "I want her to know my Savior." It took time, but the Chinese woman finally understood. She came to join her daughter in a quaint version of Methodist hymns.

Sing Sang Paw's pure faith won through. Shavey Lee, the Mayor of

Chinatown today and an extraordinarily heavy man, used to sit on the little missionary's knee when he was a baby. A hundred Chinese merchants remember her kindnesses. A thousand Chinese mothers worship her because she emancipated them.

Miss Banta, through the years, adopted seven Chinese boys and girls. She paid their way through college. One of her grandsons through adoption played in "The King and I." She has gone to countless family parties in Chinatown, often as the most honored guest.

In the past twenty years Miss Banta has worked in the True Light Lutheran Church, first in Canal Street, now at Worth and Mulberry. Through all those years she has had one or more orphans as adopted children in her home, feeding, clothing and sheltering them at her own expense.

Yesterday morning she was crowned "Mother of Chinatown" during the service at the church, and later a service of commemoration was held there for her. In the evening Chinatown had her as dinner guest at the Port Arthur.

She recalled how, at first, it had been her tendency to shrink from the Chinatown assignment, and how, finally, she thought: "I must not refuse. I promised God I would enter any door He held open. So I came, and I have stayed."

May 14, 1954

❡ New York's effects on the human nerve system is explained to some extent by a Western Union report that 150,000 heavy sleepers use the company's Wake-up Service each year. Ralph D. Saylor, Western Union's general manager in the metropolitan area, thinks townsfolk sleep harder because they work and play harder, but that's only his guess.

Doctors, nurses, school teachers, airline pilots, business men and theatrical people use the wake-up service most. One teacher signed up for it after she had reached a point where four alarm clocks set in a washpan for extra clatter-effect couldn't pull her out of Morpheus' grip. An extraordinary subscriber was a nervous lady about to be married. On the wedding morning she had the service call the prospective bridegroom to say, "Wake up, dear. This is our wedding day. Remember?" She paid the usual fee.

The service has handled other unusual calls—one from a 10-year-old boy who wanted to get up at 3 A.M. to see the circus unload at Mott Haven Yards; one from a harried lady nursing several members of her family bedded down with influenza, and each with a different dosage schedule; one from a chick-hatchery man expecting a big run of peepers in a row of mornings.

Better than 75 per cent of the customers are persons who keep late hours but must be up before 7 A.M. After that hour, the calls sort of string out. The business picks up after Daylight Time starts, because some tightly rigged New Yorkers can't adjust to the change-over. The big increase comes with the first cold snap. It seems people snugged under warm blankets can't work up enough will power to get out on their own when icy blasts stand between them and an open window.

May 26, 1954

¶ August Belmont 3d climbed into the dank tomb of John Slidell in the churchyard at St. Marks-in-the-Bouwerie one afternoon a few weeks ago and cleared up, after almost a century, the mystery of the last resting place of Commodore Matthew Calbraith Perry.

The commodore was a Belmont kinsman through marriage. He died at 2 A.M. March 4, 1858, in his home at 28 West Thirty-second Street, four years after he had opened Japan to American commerce. The New York Times told of his burial in the churchyard a few days later. Some of his own Marines fired a farewell volley. City flags were placed at half-staff.

Last year, when Japanese representatives in the United States wanted to honor the Commodore on the 100th anniversary of his visit to Yedo, they came up against the mystery. There were two gravestones with the Commodore's name —one in Island Cemetery at Newport, R. I., and one in St. Marks.

The Health Department records here showed the burial in the Slidell vault, which seemed proper. The Slidells, too, were Perry kin. Then the Health Department dug out an order dated March 21, 1866, for transfer of the body from New York to Newport. C. L. Carpenter, probably an undertaker, got the order.

With two Perry tombstones, though, there was no proof that the Commodore's remains actually had been borne north in 1866. Miss Jeanne Tiffany of Newport, a Perry descendant, and the Belmonts in New York thought it high time to fix the Commodore's resting place. Mr. Belmont, the Rev. Richard E. McEvoy of St. Marks and Senley Monroe, an undertaker, repaired to the churchyard.

Workmen dug down 3 or 4 feet after removing the flat horizontal marker on which was inscribed: "Vault No. 95, John Slidell's Vault, 1834; Commodore Matthew Calbraith Perry 1794-1858." The diggers uncovered a sectional vault door fitted into brick channels. They took out the top section.

Mr. Monroe crawled through backwards with an unshielded electric light. Mr. Belmont went in the same way. Church records indicated there must be nine coffins, including the Commodore's and his daughter Anna's. They found only seven—some (the oldest) against the far brick wall, the more recent against the blocked door. The last burial had been in 1889. City traffic had shaken the oldest coffins into dust.

Mr. Belmont figured that the Commodore's body, and that of his daughter's, must have rested in the empty vault space between the earliest and the more recent groups. He looked about for the Commodore's gear, but saw no epaulettes, no sword, none of the Navy paraphernalia with which the Commodore had been borne to the tomb. That seemed to settle it. Mr. Belmont, a Navy man himself, came out into sunlight again.

In a letter to other members of his family he reported: "I am satisfied that the remains of Commodore Matthew C. Perry are not in the vault, and that they were in all probability moved to Newport."

The brothers, Commodore M. C. Perry and Commodore Oliver Hazard Perry ("We have met the enemy, and they are ours."), were probably the only pair to win, independently of each other, New York's gift of freedom of the city. Oliver got it Oct. 4, 1813, during the war of 1812. Matthew received it on July 12, 1848, for his Mexican War exploits.

May 28, 1954

❡ The Fifth Avenue bus line, through a $5,000,000 deal worked out the other day, was restored as a purely local institution, which it was when it started in 1885 with horse-drawn vehicles. The deal freed it from a Chicago affiliation.

The Fifth Avenue line, just short of seventy years old, is the oldest of its kind in the country. There were other Fifth Avenue omnibuses before 1885—one as far back as 1856 —but they just faded out of existence after brief operations.

The first line, run by Simeon M. Andrews, had twenty-eight two-horse omnibuses that ran from Fifth Avenue and Forty-second Street to the Fulton Ferry. They used Fifth Avenue only from Thirteenth Street to Forty-second. So did later lines.

The Fifth Avenue Transportation Company, Ltd., was started in 1885 to forestall the placing of trolley tracks in that plushy thoroughfare. It used London-type omnibuses, as did the Fifth Avenue Coach Company that succeeded it in 1896.

In the beginning the buses ran only to Eighty-ninth Street. They crept up the Avenue bit by bit as the Street developed, branching to Fort George, Fort Tryon and to Jackson Heights in Queens.

Two-horse and three-horse hitches were used until July 30, 1907, when buses with French engines and London chassis displaced the forty horse-vehicles and the stable of 400 horses that pulled them.

Electric buses were tried in 1900, but they were slow and generally inefficient. They were not much better than the horse-drawn jobs, which needed an auxiliary hitch of two horses to get them up the hill from Thirty-fourth to Thirty-eighth Streets.

All through the earlier years the Fifth Avenue Coach Company not only copied the London-type buses, but even hired a Colonel Green of the London Transportation Company, Ltd., to run them. He took on as general manager in 1910 and held the job a long time.

The double-decked open-air buses, used from 1907 to 1936, were favored by spooners, who flocked to them for the twenty-two-mile run from Washington Square to 168th Street and back for only 20 cents. But vinegary ladies crusaded against the open-air type as instruments of evil.

The late John A. Ritchie, who was head of the Fifth Avenue Coach Company in the Nineteen

Twenties, took pen in hand to meet the acidy complaints. His letter on open-deck spooning is a company classic, carefully preserved in the files. He had a literary bent and did another piece on whistling bus conductors.

Frederic T. Wood, a coach company officer now 80 years old, recalls his first ride on a horse-drawn Fifth Avenue bus in 1896 when he came down from Williams College on a fraternity bender. He has seen the company use modern double-deckers, or so-called Queen Mary's, which succeeded the open-air models, and the current models. The Queen Mary's were taken off Fifth Avenue in April, 1953.

John A. Moreland, vice president in charge of maintenance, remembers that as a boy in midtown he would join other neighborhood kids with whoop and holler when the extra team was hitched on at Thirty-fourth Street for the four-block uphill pull.

The line now uses a maximum of 285 buses in morning and evening rush hours, the most in its history. Executives concede that the open-decker, so stanchly defended by Mr. Ritchie, was abandoned not on moral grounds, but because spooners never got off, which lowered company revenues.

May 31, 1954

❡ Teddy May has walked and crawled through Manhattan's 560 miles of sewers for fifty-one years, but tomorrow he must be done with them forever.

There will be a little party for him in the Sewer Department office, and they will make him honorary Sewer Commissioner. Teddy will fidget, blush, scrub at his white thatch and go quietly into retirement—only because, at 80, the city says he must.

Borough engineers who have known him will be sad when he goes, because for all their formal knowledge and schooling, they know less about the system, in some ways, than he does. Teddy has had a minimum of schooling but loves sewers as other men love warmer and more easily understood creations.

Teddy, christened Edward Patrick May after he was born on West Forty-seventh Street down by the river on May 5, 1874, made the first comprehensive Manhattan sewer survey for Chief Engineer Harris Loomis in 1903. His affection for the system started then.

He is a small man, and he could get into small pipe. He got to know every foot of the sewer network, even the amazing brick sewers put down before 1850 that now carry skyscraper waste though they were designed for one- and two-story buildings.

Mr. May knows some fifty underground streams—where they are trapped into the sewers and where they trickle and course around them, stubbornly burbling on under countless tons of asphalt and concrete, in approximately the same beds they followed when the island was lush green.

Teddy has testified on sewers in the high courts for more than forty years, and his evidence has always held up. He has recovered murder weapons and robbery loot from catch basins. He has cleared the system of a rash of alligators. Dropped in by harassed parents when the reptiles were tiny pets, they grew amazingly.

The job has called for shrewd detective work. So many years ago that Teddy forgets the date completely, General Grant's daughter, a guest at the King's Hotel in Forty-third Street west of Fifth Avenue, lost in the plumbing a ring presented by the Japanese Emperor when she was married in the White House.

Lloyd's had the trinket insured. The hotel superintendent swore he had searched plumbing traps but hadn't found it. Mr. May had Lloyd's make an inexpensive duplicate of the ring and, in the presence of detectives and a Lloyd's man, proved it could not be flushed away.

The police got the ring back from the superintendent.

One October Saturday three years ago Teddy saw his men collapsing, one by one, in the Liberty Street sewer as if felled by an invisible hand. One of the men died. Teddy traced the cause of death to a cleaning establishment. It had used an odorless acid to clean its vats, and the acid fog from it was lethal.

Those are things to talk about now—those and countless others. And Teddy May will talk about them as he does of his boyhood when Times Square was a dark spot, when pigs, steers and mus-tangs were herded from barges down Eleventh Avenue.

If the city thinks, though, that it can break Teddy May of the sewer-walking habit after more than fifty years, it could be wrong. Teddy says, "You don't need keys to get into a sewer."

June 2, 1954

❡ In spring and summer birds pipe in the thick ivy and the white ramblers on the old stone house that stands high off the north side of East Sixty-first Street west of York Avenue. Industrial plants cruelly nudge it.

Few natives happen by, strangers almost never. Some who do pass the house wonder if there's a story behind the rough-stone and red brick dwelling, set in lovely gardens. The lawns start eight steps up from the sidewalk, behind tall hedges.

There is a story. One hundred and seventy-eight years ago Sir Edmund Andros, the Crown's head man in town, gave that part of the city, then a farm 'way out in wilderness, to Jacobus Fabricius, a Dutch gentleman.

Other Hollanders owned it after that—William Wouterse, Mangel Roll, Johannes Van Zandt, Peter Praa Van Zandt. It was a hilly spot, which explains the house being high above the present street level. It gave on sweeping views.

On March 25, 1795, the Van Zandts sold the farm to Col. William Stephens Smith, Princeton 1774, a young attorney who had been General Washington's military aide. The colonel had married President John Adams' daughter, Abigail, in 1786, three years after the Revolution's end. He had mapped the plan for British withdrawal from New York after the truce.

When the colonel took over he started to build a handsome mansion patterned on the lines of Mount Vernon, his old Commander's place. It went up west and north of the old stone house that still stands. That house was to have been the stable.

Bad luck interfered with the colonel's plans. He went broke— some say through gambling—before his Mount Vernon in New York was finished; before Abby Adams ever got to entertain in its thirty-three-foot living room. In 1798 he mortgaged it for $10,000, and the whole town came to call it Smith's Folly.

The main house had a succession of owners before it burned down, all except the chimneys, on March 26, 1826. The stable, with a loft to take three tons of hay, stalls for six horses and space for two coaches, became a fashionable inn deep in the country.

The gentry came to it by stage, by the river, or on horseback. It had a race course where meets were held in the spring and in the fall. Later it reverted to a private residence, but after 1880, when the Misses Isabella and Mary Jane Towle sold it to the Standard Gas Light Company, it went into decline.

Gas tanks went up east and north of it. Laborers became its tenants. In 1924 the Salvation Army used it as a soup kitchen. But in September that year the Colonial Dames of America rescued it. They restored the gardens and made the house their headquarters.

It is kept now as an old Colonial house. It is filled with Colonial relics, a few of them Abby Adams'. It has a lovely set of crystal chandeliers that glint and sparkle, old portraits, an old crib, eighteenth-century costumes, and a pretty four-poster of that period.

The Colonial Dames meet in it once a month and when the weather is chill, light one of the six fireplaces. The ladies who run the office use auxiliary heaters because there is no cellar, no central heating. Peter Cahill, the gardener, has the top floor with his family.

Sometimes men come from the Botanical Gardens in the Bronx to help Peter with the iris and with the ancient ivy and creeping roses. Mostly, though, the place is a lonely fragment of the past, echoing with dimensional silence. There is nothing else quite like it in the city.

¶ A piece of the wrought-iron railing from the balcony of old Federal Hall, where George Washington uttered the first Inaugural Address, is now part of Bellevue Hospital's main portico.

¶ Built into Joan of Arc's pedestal on Riverside Drive at Ninety-third Street are stones from old Rouen Tower, from which she went to her burning, and fragments from old

Reims Cathedral, where the king she enthroned took his crown.

June 7, 1954

MARGINALIA: ¶ The oldest structural elements in any building in the city are the pillars in the old Merchant Marine House at Beaver and South William Street. They were brought from Italy in 1840 by Lorenzo Delmonico to ornament the outside of the family restaurant. They are from the ruins of Pompeii. . . .

¶ "Columbia Triumphant," the lady driving three seahorses hitched to her seashell chariot, on Maine Memorial in Columbus Circle, was cast from cannon brought up from the sunken battleship Maine.

June 9, 1954

¶ Fifty years ago this mid-month the three-decked white paddlewheeler General Slocum moved upriver from its East Third Street pier in glaring sunlight, belching smoke in thick dusky folds from twin stacks.

She carried more than 2,000 picnickers, mostly women and children. The boat was bound for Locust Grove on the Sound with the Rev. George Haas' flock from St. Marks German Lutheran Church at 328 East Sixth Street.

Almost all the passengers lived between Houston and Twenty-third Streets, from the East River to Fourth Avenue, in the neat and sober area then called Little Germany—a kaffeeklatsch and turnver-

ein belt. The picnic was a neighborhood tradition.

The Slocum left the pier a little after 9 o'clock the morning of June 15, 1904. Less than an hour later she was a charred wreck against the beach wall at North Brothers Island opposite 145th Street, and 1,021 of Pastor Haas' flock, including his wife and his daughter, were dead or dying.

Albert F. Frese, white-haired now, treasurer of Funk & Wagnalls, publishers, had that day off. He was sixteen years old and had been with the company two years, sorting mail. His family lived in Fifteenth Street between First Avenue and Avenue A. His sister, Anna, and his mother boarded the Slocum with him.

So did Charlie Kuentsner, Charlie Cordes and Tony Schwartz, his closest friends. And there were Katie Klem, Clara Helmke, Grace Bruening and Elsie Eller. Albert Frese was a little soft on Elsie, as they used to put it in those days.

The other day Mr. Frese stared misty-eyed into middle distance through the Funk & Wagnall windows in East Twenty-fourth Street. He remembered the kids' shrill laughter that June morning in 1904. He recalled George Maurer's band playing the Luther hymn, "A Mighty Fortress Is Our God." He remembered the fat picnic lunch baskets.

Mr. Frese tries to shut out the horrors now, but he remembers too vividly the flame gout that leaped from the Slocum's forward deck. "No one screamed," he said. "No one cried out. Not at first. No one went haywire. Faces just froze." Then Capt. William Van Schaick began to push the Slocum.

Mr. Frese thinks that was a mistake. The ship vibrated as the skipper made for North Brothers Island under forced draft. The decks and the railings trembled. The breeze picked up with the Slocum's speed. The fire crackled and spread under its impetus. A white-faced man hurried by young Frese.

"He said 'Don't go down there. It's a furnace down there.' He meant the deck below. I never saw the fella again."

Tugs tried to catch up with the Slocum, but couldn't. Young Frese saw people on Blackwell's Island, racing beachward in carts and wagons. Some had planks on barrels. They wanted the Slocum to head in there, but the boat thundered upriver, tearing her iron heart to pieces.

Albert Frese went over the stern in a soldier dive—feet together, feet first, hands tight to the sides. Elsie Eller couldn't move. "I went straight down. It was so quiet down there. So awful quiet. I was a long time coming up again—my shoes and my clothes and all."

When he came up, there was no Elsie, no Clara Helmke, none of his gang. He remembered that Clara had walked forward toward the flames. She was saying, as someone in a dream might say it, "I must find Mama. I must look for Mama." He never saw Clara or Elsie again.

Tugboat men fished young Frese out of the river. They got Charlie Kuentsner, too. He was burned. When the boys got back to the neighborhood they walked into strange stillness. Little Germany was stunned. Even the itinerant strawberry vendors were hushed.

It is still difficult to go into the details. Albert Frese's mother was saved. She died seven years ago, aged 92. Sister Anna died in the flames with her friends.

Captain Van Schaick died in 1927, aged 90, in a Masonic home in Utica. He had spent a few years in Sing Sing Prison.

Mr. Maurer died with his children. Of his band, only his clarinetist, Julius Woll, survived. Jake Schrumpf, the neighborhood cop, lost all his kids. Mr. Frese says, "He grieved until he died of it."

Every year since, the Organization of the General Slocum Survivors meets at the graves in Lutheran Cemetery in Middle Village, Queens. In the beginning there were hundreds. Now there are only about twenty. The white-haired men and women, who were flaxen-haired boys and girls on a glaring white boat deck a half century ago, bow their heads and murmur prayers. They sit on cemetery benches—and remember.

June 11, 1954

¶ People who stop to wonder about such things sometimes ask if the modern-looking stone blocks over the Fifth Avenue façade of the Metropolitan Museum of Art are not a little out of keeping with the fancier ornamentation that surrounds them—and they are.

There are four huge blocks supported by four pairs of columns.

Richard Morris Hunt, the architect, originally figured in the Eighteen Nineties that the blocks would be carved to represent four great art periods—Egyptian, Greek, Roman and modern. He wanted them done in white, stained to simulate natural aging.

Mr. Hunt, a distinguished artist, had done a number of notable— and expensive—designs, including the Pavilion de Bibliotheque in France for Emperor Napoleon III, but the museum building committee didn't have the money to complete the façade as he wanted it. They were panting to get enough to finish the museum's interior before opening date, Dec. 23, 1902.

The architect died without seeing his blocks cut, and so did his son, Richard Howland Hunt. The estimates for the sculpture just frightened one museum board after another. Finally, Thomas Hastings, another famous architect, suggested the blocks be left rough, and they were.

MARGINALIA: ¶ The Mercantile Library at 17 East Forty-seventh Street was founded 134 years ago at 49 Fulton Street "to discourage young merchants' clerks from spending their evenings lounging on street corners or frequenting questionable places of amusement."

June 14, 1954

¶ Not many in town seem to know that the city had a Revolutionary War heroine as famous in her day (1776) as Mary McCauley Hays, who served her husband's cannon at the Battle of Monmouth in 1778 and came to be known as "Molly Pitcher" because she was voluntary water girl, too.

The New York version was "Captain Molly" Corbin, born Margaret Cochran in Franklin County, Pa., in 1751. She was with her husband, a gunner in the First Company of Pennsylvania Artillery, when he died on a height at Fort Tryon under Hessian attack on Nov. 16, 1776, almost two years before Molly Pitcher made legend.

John Corbin was killed at his gun. His wife took over until Hessian grape dropped her, too.

A marker in Holyrood Church at Fort Washington Avenue and 179th Street tells her story. She lies in the military cemetery at West Point.

June 21, 1954

¶ There was speculation around town last Tuesday when workmen took down the old railing at Federal Hall, at Wall and Nassau Streets, if that wasn't the oldest wrought-iron fence in the city. It was put up in 1842.

The wrought-iron fence around tiny Bowling Green Park is older by seventy-one years; it was brought from England in 1771. The high wrought-iron fence that runs the width of St. Peter's Protestant Episcopal Church in West Twentieth Street, between Eighth and Ninth Avenues in Old Chelsea, went up before the Federal Hall job, too.

It was originally in front of Trinity Church, downtown; probably it was put up between 1788 and 1790, when the second Trinity edifice was built. When the third Trinity was built, between 1830 and 1840, its old fence and gate were sent out into the country as a gift to St. Peter's in Chelsea.

Puerto Rican children play around the old St. Peter's Gate now and probably don't know that a long time ago the old gate had swung to the touch of George Washington, Alexander Hamilton, Robert Fulton and Capt. James Lawrence. It shows no sign of wear.

June 30, 1954

¶ It is probably not general knowledge even to natives that some New York walls and sidewalks breathe, but the high stone wall back of Trinity Church graveyard inhales and exhales from seven-tenths to eight-tenths of an inch, much like the rise and fall of a human's chest. The action is caused by temperature changes.

In the winter the soil in which the wall is based freezes and the whole structure seems to breathe in. In spring thaw the soil goes soft again and the wall throws its chest out toward Trinity Place. Both movements are carefully watched and measured to make sure the wall isn't going to drop on someone.

In a city where temperatures can vary from subzero to 100-plus degrees, the same breathing takes place in sidewalks, except that the action there is up and down instead of lateral. It is so gradual that pedestrians never are aware of it.

Trinity's breathing wall, incidentally, is checked in season by knowledgeable fellows from the offices of Spencer, White & Prentis, the engineering firm that underpinned the west end of the church when it sagged and cracked over twenty-five years ago.

The weakness developed through more than a century of blastings for new subways and skyscraper foundations around the edifice. The engineers dug through ancient vaults to do the job and turned over to living kin of the ancient dead such relics as came up under the laborers' spades and other digging machinery.

July 2, 1954

¶ Townsfolk who scatter to the hills and down to the sea on Independence Day in the mid-twentieth century ought to know that when the nation and the holiday were new New Yorkers celebrated the Fourth, broadly speaking, in soberer ways.

President George Washington, who lived in the Executive Mansion at 39 Broadway in 1790, for example, wrote in his diary on July 4, that year that:

"The members of the Senate, House of Representatives, public Officers, Foreign Characters, etc. [then all resident in New York] came with the compliments of the day to me. About 1 o'clock a sensible oration was delivered in St. Paul's Chapel by Mr. Brockholst Livingston on the occasion of the day, the tendency of which was to show the different situation we are now in, under an excellent government of our own choice, and how much we ought to cherish the blessings which are within our reach, and to cultivate the seeds of harmony and unanimity in all our public councils." The entry also noted that: "In the afternoon many Gentlemen and Ladies visited Mrs. Washington."

Senator William Maclay of Pennsylvania gave another slant on what went on in town that same day. He found "all the town . . . in arms; grenadiers, light infantry and artillery . . . firing of cannon and small arms, with beating of drums." Later: "All of us repaired to the President's. We got some wine, punch and cakes. From hence we went to St. Paul's. . . ." Senator Maclay, a sturdy fellow, was proud that his pew was next to General Washington's.

Thirty-one years later, on July 4, 1821, John Pintard Esq., an extraordinarily civic-minded merchant of the town set down that when he turned out at 10 A.M. his old eyes were delighted by enormous throngs, so thick between the Battery and City Hall Common, that a man literally could have walked that span, as he put it, "on the heads of the sovereign people." The sight brought to his mind the change that had come over the city since July 4, 1784, "the year after peace, when about a dozen of us called for a bowl of punch to drink prosperity to the United States at the old Coffee House." There was something sad in this entry. Good Citizen Pintard could see the brave sight, but could not hear the uproar —he had been deafened by a

Fourth of July explosion many years before.

July 21, 1954

❡ The men who nurse the city's 2,820,000 trees are in a sweat over the second year of drought in New York. Trees are dying in greater numbers than they have ever known, and there is not too much they can do about it.

Under stern city regulations the tree men are bound by the same drought-period restrictions as private tree owners. They can use their tank trucks for watering only between 7 P.M. and midnight.

That doesn't give them nearly enough time to get to all the trees in all the boroughs. In Queens alone, for example, the Park Department looks after 940,000 in its parks, another 28,000 in the streets.

Manhattan has 12,000 street trees, 170,000 in its parks. Brooklyn has 130,000 in parks, 105,000 on its streets, though people somehow have been misled by the book title "A Tree Grows in Brooklyn" into thinking it has only a few.

The Bronx has 330,000 park trees, mainly in the zoo area and in Van Cortlandt Park, and 45,000 on its streets. Richmond, across the bay, has 68,000 on its streets, 201,000 in its parks.

The Park Department census of street and park trees by no means covers the whole of the city's arboreal treasure. Ailanthus trees, the so-called trees of heaven, seem to flourish even in drought and grow in countless numbers in back yards.

They even grow in a half-inch of dust on some city ledges.

Trees that do best in New York's sidewalks are the pin, red and scarlet oaks; American and European elm, European ash, linden, Norway maple, honey locust, oriental plane, tulip and the ginkgo. The ginkgo, incidentally, rates as a fossil growth. It has gone unchanged for millions of years, is exactly like specimens found in Paleozoic, Triassic, Jurassic and Tertiary formations. The most famous ginkgo in town is the one sent by Li Hung-chang, Chinese statesman, for planting beside General Grant's Tomb in 1897.

Lots of trees thrive on New York sidewalks but are ruled out as undesirable because they have soft or brittle limbs and come down easily in storms. Some get thumbs down because they thirstily go for under-pavement plumbing in their search for water.

In this group the Park Department lists poplar, silver maple, box elder, black locust, horse chestnut, the Chinese elm, mountain ash, beech, birch, sugar maple, the American plane, dogwood and hornbeam. Several of these are highly susceptible to tree pests of one kind or another.

Curiously, the city has more street and park trees today than it had, say, twenty-five or thirty years ago. Replacements are always ready in the city's rich nursery built on a garbage dump on Rikers Island in the East River. Around 120,000 trees are in varying stages of growth there all the time.

The city's oldest trees are the great weeping beech in Weeping Beach Park in Flushing, some tulip trees in Fort Tryon Park and in Central Park. No one rightly knows how old these are but several are centenarians, or better. The weeper in Flushing stands 140 feet high, spreads eighty-five feet. It was planted in 1830.

This beech and a cedar of Lebanon at Thirty-second Avenue and 184th Street in Flushing date back to the eighteenth-century William Prince Nurseries in that community, which had George Washington, Lord Howe and Henry Clay among its customers.

July 23, 1954

❡ A Wall Street secret that has kept for eighteen years came out yesterday over talk about the new skyscraper that is to go up at 20-24 Broad Street. Its lower floors will be used as an addition to the New York Stock Exchange building next door.

Henry A. Erdmann, vice president of the century-old Vermilyea-Brown Company, builders, disclosed that the eleven figures in the pediment over the Stock Exchange's Broad Street portico were switched by his concern in 1936 when they became a public hazard.

The work was done on screened scaffolding. The original sculptured figures, done by J. Q. A. Ward and Paul W. Bartlett, were quietly destroyed by Vermilyea-Brown artisans and faithful reproductions in lead-coated copper were substituted.

The Ward originals, with the eleven figures representing commerce and industry and an eighteen-foot statue of Integrity as a center piece, were carved out of French limestone. The stone could not endure New York's extremes of temperature and in 1910, seven years after the figures went up, they started to flake.

By 1936, the city's weather had reduced the limestone to a really dangerous condition. Some of the tremendous statue heads—all the figures are of heroic proportions—leaned over the sidewalk, so the Stock Exchange called in experts.

Mr. Erdmann, an architect for Vermilyea-Brown, drew the assignment. He had photographers take pictures of the figures throughout a daylight cycle with the idea of having the substitute figures look exactly like the Ward originals, even to their weathering.

The photographs were taken from the J. P. Morgan offices across the way. Then, behind tight screening, artisans made perfect casts of all the detail in the figures and in the implements, or objects, they handled or carried.

From the casts, two complete sets of reproductions were made, one to be duplicated in lead-coated copper in a Long Island City plant, one to go in storage in Jersey City. The idea behind this was that if one should be destroyed by fire or otherwise a second would be available.

Then with sledge and hammer the originals were reduced to fragments, the large heads and torsos lowered to the sidewalk in covered slings. Still working behind screening, the Vermilyea-Brown men pieced together the hollow lead-coated copper stand-ins.

All the figures were covered with weather-resistant paint to simulate the original French limestone. Lampblack was used to darken spots that had weathered in the originals. A man with the photographs taken before the restoration, sat in the Morgan offices at a special phone and called for additional spots where they were needed.

To this day a bare handful of New Yorkers—Stock Exchange officials and employes, mostly, and the men who worked the switch— were the only ones who knew the switch had taken place. The copper figures, Mr. Erdmann thinks, could last forever with no chance that Integrity's massive head might one day fall and crush Broad Street pedestrians.

July 28, 1954

¶ Come Saturday, most of the farriers who shoe race horses at Belmont, Aqueduct, Jamaica and other Eastern courses will toss their equipment into trunk compartments in their cars to head for the last stand of summer at Saratoga.

The twenty-six men in the New York track area are members of Local 8, International Union of Journeymen Horseshoers of the United States and Canada, an A. F. L. unit that started under another name just after the Civil War.

They're brawny fellows, mostly, just like Longfellow's Village Blacksmith, but, curiously, they seem a little touchy about that designation.

"Blacksmith," they tell you, has come to mean the arty fellows who work wrought-iron ornament. The two groups don't mix—socially.

The race-track shops of the horse-shoers—some brick, some still of wood—haven't changed much since Longfellow's time. Anvil, forge and appurtenances look pretty much the same, but the forge bellows are automatic electrical contraptions and all but a few track farriers use an electric trip hammer instead of the traditional sledge.

You don't get the tang of burning hoof as much as you used to because more than half the shoes used now are aluminum and go on cold. Steel shoes are worn by race horses only between races. The idea behind the switch is that the animals feel the change in weight and run faster in aluminum.

Any belief that the farrier breed is falling off could not be further from truth. The race-track breed, at least, has all the men it needs—about 265, all told, in seventeen union locals throughout this country and Canada. Individual earnings run to comfortable figures; somewhere around $250 a week.

A set of shoes generally runs about $14.50, and $10 of that is for labor. A good man easily turns out seven, eight, or even more sets in a single day, if need be. The average seems to be four to five sets. An old hand can take care of a stable of 100 mounts, and some men do.

Shoeing fees are paid by horse owners and each track has its own farrier staff in addition to smiths who work only for certain stables.

Trainers are likely to be fussy about shoeing. Max Hirsch, for example, examines each set put on his charges and frequently calls for changes.

Among top farriers in Local 8 is Larry Goettishiem, who pushes around in a Cadillac and who has trained his son in the trade. The job, incidentally, calls for three years' apprenticeship and then examination before a farriers' board that is pretty stern in its judging.

The apprentice, ready for a master journeyman ticket, has to do his shoeing from scratch before no more than three examiners from his own local and before at least two men from any other local, or locals. Horse owners often shy from new journeymen until they've shoed a big winner.

One of the oldest track farriers is Pat Smith who got his start seventy years ago, when he was 15, in a stable in West Fifty-fourth Street. Nowadays he mostly examines mounts to describe their shoes on the board for bettors. He turns his hand to the forge only once in a great while.

Some of the farriers are descended from a long line of smiths. George Doyle at Aqueduct, for example, is the son of Jimmy Doyle, who was famous at track farrieries, and the strain reaches into remote time.

The horseshoers are sure of one thing—wrong shoeing can ruin a race horse. They tell about one owner who sneered at paying for specially built-up shoes for a famous racer and insisted on stock stuff. "That horse," the farriers will tell you sepulchrally, "had to be shot inside a couple of months."

August 6, 1954

¶ Joe A. Munang, a Dusun tribesman from British North Borneo, runs a little barber shop in Amsterdam Avenue opposite St. John's Cathedral. He shaves vicars and prebendaries and, except in summer, has good trade from college undergraduates and faculty.

There's something slightly odd about this because Joe is descended from North Borneo head hunters. He remembers grisly relics high in the smoky rafters in the community long houses there. He doesn't think there would be many left now. The missionaries made his folks burn them.

Joe is neat, bright-faced and extremely deft with razor and scissors, which isn't astonishing after you've learned his background. He really has a way with a head. His touch is gentle and reassuring if you can keep your mind off his ancestors.

He is one of seven North Borneo Dusans among New York's eight million, so that they run to somewhat fewer than one in a million. Two Dusuns whom Joe knows winter in town but raise vegetables in Wurtsboro in the Catskills in summer.

Another works in a TV factory in Brooklyn, one is a cook in a Monticello, N. Y., resort, one is a salad man in a Manhattan cafeteria and the seventh works in the galley on the liner Constitution and lives here between trips.

Joe is doing his bit for cultural progress. For the last seven months he has helped Dr. John L. Landgraf of Tappan, N. Y., a New York University social anthropologist, brush up on Murut, a Malay dialect that the barber speaks fluently.

Joe is 38 years old, but looks around 20. He is one of many sons of a Dusun rice farmer who died when Joe was a baby. Joe owns a 1949 Pontiac and has a TV set in his Forest Hills apartment, likes ball games, but spends almost all his spare time reading tractor catalogues.

He has his eye on a $6,000 red-painted job. In another two years, he figures, he may get to own it, with all its accessories. If he does, he'll put it aboard a freighter for the two-month journey home and set up in business there.

Joe has dreams of revolutionizing rice growing in and around Ranau, where his brother Leo runs ancestral acres.

Joe learned haircutting on tramp freighters along the China coast and did a lot of barbering on American LST's and LSD's in World War II. He was on an LSD in the Normandy invasion and wound up his Navy career as a Machinist Third Class.

He gets home news in eight days by airmail out of Penambang, mostly from his brother. He says the letters make him a little homesick.

When that mood comes over him he dreams of the peacocks, elephants, gibbons, orangutans, honey bears and flying foxes back home;

even about the rubber trees and the twenty-five-foot pythons.

The letters show Joe's family is uneasy over what life on Amsterdam Avenue may have done to him. One that came in only two days ago told the Dusun barber, "Mother was shading tears when I read to her your letter." Though you wouldn't expect emotionalism in a fellow whose ancestors had odd rafter-decorating habits, Joe was deeply moved by that line.

August 9, 1954

❡ Part of an old six-story building on the south side of Forty-second Street between Third and Lexington Avenues, the only structure left standing on the block-square site for the forty-two-story Socony-Vacuum skyscraper, is to be entombed in the new construction.

Legalistic hokey-pokey has something to do with it. The Transit Authority has easement rights under the building because its subway escalators have been there since 1907. So have the escalator machinery and the building's heating plant.

The easement takes in the corridor leading from Forty-second Street to the escalators, too.

Engineers for the Turner Construction Company, which is putting up the Socony-Vacuum Building, originally figured they would leave the lower east, west and south walls around the corridor and build around them, bridging over the corridor.

Now, though, they have worked things out so that those walls will come down, leaving only a mid-corridor partition standing. The escalator will be in use all the while they pile the forty-two stories around and over it.

❡ Mr. C. H. Bradner, a gentleman who lives at the New York Athletic Club, finds extreme delight in what he calls the Kansas Garden on the lip of Central Park Reservoir at about Eighty-sixth Street, a block or so in from Fifth Avenue.

The crew that works in the ninety-year-old reservoir pumping and chlorinating station at that spot has coaxed up a double row of sunflowers, ten feet high, in a garden just below the station steps.

Fat city bees have been making a good thing of the enormous sunflower heads, and lovely butterflies flutter around them.

A neat sign in the vegetable patch behind the sunflowers proclaims the spot "The Farm What Am." An old-fashioned flower garden across the walk from the sunflower-vegetable beds is called "Nature's Row." It's alive with portulaca, zinnias and petunias.

The pump-house hands cut tomatoes, lettuce and sweet fennel in their vegetable garden; they dig fresh scullions, cucumbers, too, to go with their lunches. When they take a fancy to little girls who come by with their mothers or their nurses—which is often—they cut little bunches of posies for them.

August 11, 1954

❡ Some of the town's oldest gentlewomen were dismayed yesterday by the news that the old Fifth Avenue Bank at the northwest corner of Forty-fourth Street is to be torn down.

No other bank in the city caters to so many dowagers, ladies who were Avenue belles sixty and seventy years ago. No other bank building has retained so warmly the social and physical flavor of the Eighties and Nineties.

The institution is remarkable for the number of employes who have been there close to fifty years or more, men and women trained in handling personal accounts for old New York families.

The men in the vaults know better than to lift an eyebrow when some quivery-fingered lady paws over her wig collection in the safe deposit chamber. They show no astonishment when an inventory after an aristocrat's death discloses that he has kept three empty whisky bottles in his box for many years at $45 a year, for reasons only Heaven knows.

The older men remember the elderly woman client in Westbury, L. I., who asked the bank to send her a man with a pistol. One of her stable of hunters had broken a leg. The bank sent George Schmolze, a bookkeeper, who is in his 80's now and lives in retirement in Jersey City.

No request seems too odd. One sweet old dowager had her butler call by telephone one day. Would the bank send someone to her mansion in the eighties, off Fifth Avenue, to wheel her downtown to visit her vault? The bank did, and saw to it that the man observed traffic light changes all the way back.

There has been a legend at the bank for years that on a damp day you still get a ghostly ammoniac whiff from the western end of the building where John Black Cornell, whose mansion it was in the Eighteen Sixties, had his stables.

The Cornell carriage house has been a gold-brocaded banking room for lady clients since 1880 and its teakwood tables hold now, as they did then, copies of the British journals Punch and The Tatler.

The upper floors of the Cornell mansion part of the bank are hollow sounding to footfalls now, because much of the clerical work that was done there in the institution's early history has been transferred downtown to the Bank of New York, with which the Fifth Avenue was merged in 1948.

The skylights have grown a bit dusty with Fifth Avenue grit and traffic film, the old fireplaces look sad and neglected and there is a strain of hurt in the voices of the older employes when they take you through the building and tell you for what each room was used in Mr. Cornell's day.

The committee that raises funds for the Metropolitan Opera House has had one of the upper mansion floors rent free for years. Mrs. August Belmont has a separate desk on that floor, but doesn't use it very often.

Donald McKay, William Walker and Dick Bunke, who went to work at the bank in 1906-7, recall wistfully the cotillions at Sherry's in Forty-fourth Street opposite the bank. They'd hear the waltzes and the laughter of women when there was late work in the bank.

F. L. Hokanson, like many others still in the place, has delightful stories about Hetty Green, called the Witch of Wall Street, and about Mr. and Mrs. Russell Sage, Mrs. Andrew Carnegie, Mrs. Robert Goelet, Anna Gould de Talleyrand, Enrico Caruso, Mme. Frances Alda, John Golden and Aimee Crocker Gouraud, the Princess Galitzene.

Mr. McKay thinks he can still close his eyes and revive the strong scent of mystic powders burned by the Princess in her Madison Avenue mansion. He had to go there often as a bank messenger and her personal incensed temple always awed him.

Lots of persons in the bank remember Barbara Hutton as a cute little girl, always showing up with her uncle, Edward F. Hutton, a bank customer. Mr. Hokanson recalls that one of the first Rolls Royces in New York had a specially high body to accommodate the tall silk hat worn by another client, the Honorable R. Horace Gallatin.

A very special customer is a dear old lady, now about 90, who shows up only on rainy days. "I find the buses aren't nearly so crowded when it rains," she confided to the staff.

Nothing, though, puts across the warmth and affection some of the old family customers have for the Fifth Avenue Bank as much as a large handmade Christmas card gathering dust on an upstairs wall. It was sent in December, 1945.

Colored cartoons show a Santa Claus tiptoeing up to a row of six cribs, one for the bank president, five for the vice presidents. It says, in part:

"Dear Bank:

"I just got your calendar, and I just got to thinking. I'll bet nobody ever sends you a Christmas card, personal like. Thanks for being a nice, gracious bank with good taste."

It was signed by a Miss Inza Stephens Pratt, a client of long standing.

August 16, 1954

MARGINALIA: ❡ A lovely New York spot that tourists as well as local hicks rarely ever get to see is old Fort Schuyler at Throgs Neck. Its medieval-looking moat, walls and quadrangle, the gingerbread lighthouse just outside it, the ancient trees and 1860 houses make it a tripper's or photographer's dream, color or black-and-white.

August 23, 1954

❡ Classicists will be delighted to learn that the original green and red guide lines in the subway shuttle system, which are being superseded by fluorescent directionals, stemmed directly from the legend of Theseus' slaying of the Minotaur in the labyrinth in Crete. The story has never been publicly told before.

When technicians started putting in the new guide lines last Monday and the story made the newspapers, Robert M. Derby of

Brookside Farm at Sweet's Corners in Williamstown, Mass., remembered what happened the day the shuttle first opened on Aug. 1, 1918. Without guide lines, New York's subway moles became confused, then frightened, and mauled one another in attempts to fight their way to the street.

Charles Bulkley Hubbell, a district chairman of the New York Public Service Commission, was agitated and upset by the rioting that day. It had caused immediate shutdown of the shuttle.

"Mr. Hubbell was my father-in-law. I was an engineer at the time," Mr. Derby remembers. "At dinner that night he said he was at wits' end over the problem of properly directing shuttle passengers. Frank Hedley, general manager of the I. R. T., wanted some solution by next day."

Everyone at table mulled over the problem, but all solutions that were offered were too complicated and impractical. Young Mr. Derby, not long out of college, suddenly remembered the Minotaur legend —how Theseus of Athens slew the Minotaur, then made his way out of labyrinthine darkness to the light by following the skein of linen thread that Ariadne had told him to unravel as he wandered through the caverns to the monster's lair.

Mr. Hubbell leaped on the idea. He put it up to Mr. Hedley next day, and Mr. Hedley glowed. It was the simplest and easiest solution. The green and red lines guided countless millions underground between Times Square and Grand

Central Station for thirty-six years, and the latest fluorescent version will carry on the Theseus legend for only the Lord knows how much longer.

August 30, 1954

¶ The report last week that artisans were putting up an all-stained-glass façade at Steinberg House, 50 East Eighty-seventh Street, led some people to wonder where stained-glass workers were to be found in mid-twentieth-century New York.

Well, the classified telephone directory shows almost a full column of them still at the 1,000-year-old art, right here in town, and thriving in it. Only one phase of it has almost completely died—stained glass in private homes. There's been virtually none of that since the depression.

The man who is handling the Eighty-seventh Street job, Otto W. Heinigke, has been at it since 1890. He took over from his father, a Bavarian, who landed here in 1851 and started an artists' colony on the old Ovington Farm in Brooklyn's Bay Ridge district around that time.

The Heinigkes have a most impressive number of works to their credit—Library of Congress, New York Stock Exchange, Cathedral of St. John the Divine (odd panels, including one now in work), Metropolitan Museum, the Cloisters and scores of others all over the United States.

They've done a lot of clubs— Harvard, University, Engineers, Crescent Athletic, Chi Psi at Amherst and at Yale, Downey House at Wesleyan are only a few on their list—and scores of great churches, including Trinity, Riverside, St. Mark's-in-the-Bouwerie, St. Thomas, Ascension.

They did the homes of Andrew Carnegie, J. B. Duke, Myron C. Taylor, Jules S. Bache, Marshall Field, Daniel Guggenheim, Mrs. Whitelaw Reid, William K. Vanderbilt, J. P. Morgan, Harry Payne Whitney, Thomas F. Ryan, Samuel Insull, and those represent probably a tenth of their private contracts.

Mr. Heinigke and his crew, at work over sketches and glass on the fifth floor of the dark-interiored loft building at 26 East Thirteenth Street, look like dim characters in a Dickensian play. The concern took the floor when the building first went up in 1896, and hasn't budged from it. It's delightfully dusty, cluttered and angly, a TV man's dream for color.

Mr. Heinigke, small, gray, bespectacled, but extraordinarily spry, says stained-glass technique hasn't altered, basically, in the last seven or eight centuries, except that modern artisans buy their colored glass ready-made from Germany, France and Italy, at so much a square foot, instead of making their own. They buy their lead in channeled strips, too.

An interesting relic in the shop is a twelfth-century window from Chartres, gift to Heinigke the Elder from the owner of a stained-glass shop two blocks from Chartres Cathedral. Old Mr. Heinigke picked it up there in 1901 when he dropped in for a professional chat. The Chartres man had just finished a restoration at the great edifice.

A curled and yellowed sketch tacked to an ancient wall in the Heinigke office has a rather happy story the stained-glass man likes to tell. It was for a window for Andrew Carnegie's library, ordered by Mrs. Carnegie. It pictured a wave breaking on a lonely shore.

Old Mr. Heinigke, who did the job, fixed out of sheer artistic impulse a golden crescent in the design to sort of balance it off. He had nothing special in mind.

When the Laird saw the window in place, he snorted. "What's that gold slice in there?" he wanted to know.

Mr. Heinigke was quick. "That?" he said. "That's a honeymoon, sir."

Mr. Carnegie liked that. "Nice sentiment," he said. Mrs. Carnegie beamed. She thought it was poetic, too.

¶ A clowder of some sixty to seventy semi-wild cats, mostly tiger-topped and white-bellied, prowls the yards and fences back of the chip-faced brownstones on the north side of Fifty-first Street between Eighth and Ninth Avenues. The block legend is that the cluster never leaves the yards, that it has lived there sixty years or so.

The odd thing is, or so the neighbors say, that all the cats have six claws on each paw. That's true, anyway, of the two or three cats that have been domesticated. Tenants feed the whole dout, or destruction, twice a day. Assembled under a window, then, with tommy-come-latelies dropping off fences and from lilac and ailanthus branches, they bring to mind Kipling's jungle tales of the mass meetings of beasts.

The cats come at call, but new-generation males scatter nimbly to fences and walls when The Boss, a muscle-rippling Tom with tiger-ish jowls, slithers into sight on a high cat walkway. The Boss has sired countless kindles of kittens and has run the clowder with stern paw the last eight to nine years. Weird, primitive thing to run into so near Times Square.

October 4, 1954

❡ When a City Commission—Gouverneur Morris, Simeon De Witt and John Rutherford—laid out the city's gridiron street plan in 1807 it figured on straight-sided and right-angled dwellings as cheapest to build and live in.

Merry-andrews of the period thought the whole plan, which the commission worked on for four years, was a little silly, and the gentlemen felt compelled to defend it.

They said: "It may be a subject of merriment that the Commissioners have provided space for a greater population than is collected at any spot this side of China. They have in this respect been governed by the shape of the ground. . . . It is not improbable that considerable numbers may be collected at Harlem before the high hills to the south of it shall be built upon as a city; and it is improbable that for centuries to come the grounds north of Harlem Flat will be covered with houses. To have gone farther might have furnished materials for the pernicious spirit of speculation." You wonder what the gentlemen must think now, if their spirits ever come to wander through Harlem and the Bronx.

October 6, 1954

❡ The Bronx has had its own Johnny Appleseed for fifty-four years. He has planted fig trees, peach trees, finochio, hot peppers, sweet peppers, miniature tomatoes, eggplant, beets, corn, lettuce, long squash, round squash, garlic (much garlic), onions, string beans, carrots, basil, Swiss chard.

He has sown seed of his own drying all these years. He has grafted apples onto pears, pears onto apples. He has preserved enough each fall to feed himself, his wife, his two sons, his daughters and sons-and-daughters-in-law and their five children. He has kept his neighbors in fruits and vegetables.

Each year, come late October, he buys many crates of upstate grapes to make red wine and white wine. He has reduced his food costs, except for the price of an occasional roast, to what he pays for olive oil and for spaghetti. He toils from sunup to sundown. He is a contented man.

His first name, curiously, is Johnny, just as John (Appleseed) Chapman's was when he spread his orchards down the Ohio Valley and through Indiana 150 years ago. He has never heard of Johnny Appleseed, though, because he had no formal schooling, neither in the rural hamlet outside Naples where he was born, nor here.

He was christened Giovanni Mazzelo. From barefoot childhood he labored in the crumbly furrows with his father, and from his father he learned love of the good earth and the good God who created it. He cannot see an empty lot but that he must plow and hoe it, plant it with seed that will bear fruits.

Giovanni is straight and tall and leathery. His eyes are blue. He says: "God gave the earth. It is a sin not to plant in it." He cannot recall how many lots he has cleared of rubble in the last fifty-four years, but they add to hundreds.

Giovanni does not ask who owns the lots he converts to gardens and orchards. He thinks the city owns some. The biggest one he works now—at Westchester and Havemeyer Avenues, east of the Pelham subway trestle—may be the property of a rich junk dealer—maybe. Giovanni isn't sure, doesn't care.

When he started working it about thirty-four years ago, he planted many acres. Other men envied his fall harvest. They said, wistfully, "Giovanni, give us a piece" and Giovanni gave pieces, cheerfully and without question, so long as they were worked and made to bear as the Lord meant them to, even in big cities.

Giovanni has a tar-paper shack on the Westchester Avenue farm. He keeps his hoe and his forks in it. His fruits are tied to blackened lumber. His gate looks a hundred years old. His well, which saved his tomatoes when other plants died all about him, has a barrel for a well head. He dug it fifteen feet deep with his own hands.

He has a weathered, ancient handmade bench outside the shack to rest on when the sun is hot. Sometimes he wanders to the shade of the towering old wild chestnut just east of the subway trestle and smokes sparingly of cigarettes. He hears the squirrels harvesting the wild nuts. He says, "This tree so old he must once see George Washington, I betcha."

Giovanni became a laborer on the New York subways when he came here at the age of 17 from his father's farm outside of Naples. He worked on Manhattan Bridge foundations, on the grading of Riverside Drive and the Grand Concourse. Even in his youth—he is 71 now— he planted seed in Bronx lots, nursed trees and berry bushes.

He took the visitor to a lot at Castle Hill Avenue and St. Raymond's Avenue, unlocked another ancient wooden gate to a fertile lot. He plucked a warm fig from one of five fig trees. It was rich and ripe. He said his peach trees had yielded many bushels this year. The tree tops were covered with wire mesh against blackbirds.

Giovanni said, "Blackbirds is t'ieves," but he said it without rancor.

Giovanni's only cash now comes from Social Security. It began to come after he had retired from street labor five years ago. With it he pays $40 a year taxes on the farm overseas on which he was born and which yields about $200 a year to a kinsman who works it. There is no return from it for Giovanni, but he cannot bear to let it go.

He says: "My roots are there. You do not tear good roots."

The Bronx harvest this year will be good. All the growth is fat and green, but no garlic until next June. The garlic shows now as thin sprouts. It shakes when the Pelham trains rumble by. So does the rich compost heap beside it. Giovanni starts his new seed in compost every spring.

"Makes a seed jump up," he says. He lifts his skinny arms to demonstrate.

Only on the Sabbath does Giovanni Appleseed rest from his earthy labor. Then he shucks his soil-covered jeans and sweated shirt, gets stiffly into clean linen and a dark suit and goes with his Teresa and their children and grandchildren to Santa Maria Church near their home at 1601 Parker Street.

If they pass an empty lot, Giovanni stops dead and his eyes come alight. He always says: "There is a sin." But his sons and his daughters gently keep him moving. Else he would drop to bony knees and begin to dress the ground for seed.

October 29, 1954

¶ One of the curious places in town is the curb on The Bowery just below Canal Street, facing the Manhattan Bridge approach. It has been called, for years, Poor Man's Market, or, by some unkindly guides, the Thieves' Market.

It is most lively on Sundays, before noon. The men who trade in it are mostly middle-aged, or in the sere. They openly peddle all manner of strange second-hand wares— watches, worn coats, worn shoes, worn trousers, old hats, re-strung artificial pearls and plated jewelry.

They are not thieves. They are men who have scrabbled for a living at other things and have failed. Many are as seedy and as untidy as the beer-sodden derelicts who drift drunkenly through their ranks as they haggle.

One man may wear as many as ten second-hand wrist watches on his two wrists. When he jerks his cuffs back, he is open for business. Others dangle their wares before one another, or feebly bid for transient trade.

Some cash changes hands, but not much. There is lively barter. Men and women come down from Harlem or up from other tenement districts to buy their wardrobe there. They try trousers, for example, by holding them against the body, right on the sidewalk.

Sometimes you see a customer pull on his new pants and walk off with them. Sometimes he kneels and turns over gaping-soled shoes for a pair only slightly better. Or you see a customer trying spectacles by squinting through them at the bridge.

The barterers argue a great deal. A man offers a brassy-looking watch, and the customer warily wants to know, "What's it worth in hock?" The would-be seller jerks it back in pretended bitterness and anger. He says, "I don't go by no hock. Go ask Tiffany."

The prowl car rolls up. The policeman leans out, red-faced. He bellows, "Break it up" and the Poor Man's Market reluctantly dissolves with flapping old pants and other arm-borne wares, only to reassemble after the prowl car is lost in the El shadows.

November 3, 1954

¶ Since newspapers reported about ten days ago that a little girl in Flushing, Queens, had been nipped by a black widow spider she had picked up with a stone, the Health Department in town has been getting quite a collection of live black widows.

More than thirty have been turned in to Clinton A. Garvin, chief for the Department's Bureau of Sanitary Inspection since the last week in October. Mainly they came in milk bottles, fruit jars, peanut butter containers, all grimly stoppered.

The bulk of Mr. Garvin's collection was rounded up in Kew Gardens and in Flushing in Queens, and in Canarsie, Fort Green, Bay Ridge and the Ericsson Beach districts in Brooklyn. They're jet black with red or orange abdominal markings.

The one that bit Deborah Dell Isola in Flushing is now at the American Museum of Natural History. Mr. Garvin sent that one and a few other specimens there. He dispatched the rest to a black widow research team working for the Army at 90 Church Street. He thinks he can keep both in good supply.

Dr. Willis J. Gertsch, entomologist at the museum, says there's nothing in the common notion that black widows came to New York in vessels from foreign ports, nor in the story that they reached Canarsie in surplus Army barracks returned to this country from the South Pacific.

New York has always had black widows, and Mr. Gertsch has documentary proof that they've lived quietly here since at least the mid-eighteenth century. He's equally certain that they're indigenous and that they must have been here before the Indians.

The black widows are night creatures, Dr. Gertsch says. They hide in the dark—under stones, in cellars, in dumps, in storage places. They never attack. You can tell their webs from other species; they're rough and linty-looking, without a pattern like that woven by the more common spiders here.

Dr. Gertsch pooh-poohs the notion that black widows have increased in number because of recent mild winters. He said they survive frost, and there's nothing to justify the belief that their tribe has increased. He says they are venomous, but wishes the newspapers would, as he puts it, "de-emphasize" black widow stories.

He says people ought to know, though, that the black widow will not initiate an assault, that it succumbs to the same sprays that kill most other insects and that it's a good idea to get to know them on sight and to teach children to recognize them.

¶ You come across odd collections in town, but you're not apt to match Miss Delphine Binger's 500,-000 chicken, turkey and goose wishbones—twenty years' accumulation. She has room for only a few thousand in her two-room flat at 145 West Ninety-sixth Street. Her aunts and other kin store the rest for her in trunks.

Miss Binger is a warm, bubbling personality. She kind of streams lush sentiment, mostly about wishbones and what they can do to make people happy. She sent her first one, a wee white thing out of a Friday dinner, two decades ago, to a friend bowed by misfortune.

She says: "It was just sheer inspiration. There was the clean, white, cute little bone with luck in it. I dressed it up, wrote a message from my heart on it and before I knew it word got around and friends and neighbors were asking for wishbone messages."

Wishbones in quantity were a little difficult to get at first, but a curator at the Smithsonian Institution put Miss Binger in touch with a poultrymen's convention, and the bones flooded in. The poultrymen wouldn't take the two cents apiece she offered for them, said they didn't want to barter away their luck.

The history after that is fascinating, but a little overlong. Miss Binger kept getting more and more wishbones—from Sherry's, the Waldorf and other big caterers until she had no room left for anything else. She couldn't catch up on her processing, either—the boiling, perfuming, polishing. It left her breathless.

Miss Binger found herself in the wishbone business before she quite realized it. New ideas for dressing them boiled over all the time. Now she dresses them in imported silks and laces, smothers them in imported flowerets, dangles gold-plated symbols from them—things like boxing gloves, golf sticks, baseballs, all in miniature, of course.

She makes them up in bridal sets (with matching place cards), does wedding-anniversary and baby-arrival models, get-well wishbones, bon-voyage wishbones, Easter sets, Valentines, Christmas and New Year novelties. She has had a few fat convention banquet orders. She does all the messages by hand on the bones with special ink, bending over a rickety bridge table.

A generous soul, Miss Binger avidly follows the papers and sends free wishbones to celebrities who are ill. She sends them to Presidents, too. The Roosevelts, the Trumans and the Eisenhowers have all acknowledged her unusual gifts and their tender sentiments. Her biggest job was a turkey wishbone with Greek inscription, ordered for the Duchess of Kent.

The Wishbone Lady—that's the name she likes best—hasn't been able to trace the beginning of the wishbone superstition. Smithsonian's curator had nothing on it, she reports, and Webster was a little confusing. It said a wishbone is a furculum, or merry-thought, but she's not a scholar or grind type, and she gave up the quest right there.

November 12, 1954

❡ No New York tower clock could seize a clock winder in its gears and do him to death as the old Royal Courts of Justice clock did with poor Tommy Manners in Fleet Street, London, a few days ago.

Rudolph Lamm and his crew, at Howard Clock Sales and Service in West Broadway, service most of this city's high chronometers—among others, Trinity's, St. Paul's, old St. Patrick's and City Hall as well as Stuff and Guff (bronze bell strikers) in Herald Square. Not one of those has homicidal works.

Mr. Lamm hasn't seen the inside of the Royal Courts of Justice job, but he figures it must operate on some long-outmoded belt system to be able to grasp a man and wring him. New York's giant clocks have all manner of safeguards against that sort of thing.

There was a time, up to about twenty-five years ago, when the clock gears in Trinity tower and in St. Paul's got an intruder pigeon or two almost every year. Now the winders and repairmen have all great clocks screened against local and migratory flocks, and few birds break the barrier.

Actually, Mr. Lamm says, the birds were a greater menace to the tower clocks than the clocks were to them, or to mortals. One night in 1929 he and his crew took between 200 and 300 pigeons out of

Trinity belfry—all alive—and their nests with them. The men got half as many out of St. Paul's, too. They sold the birds to a rooftop pigeon fancier.

The screen job saved money for the churches. Pigeons, Mr. Lamm explained, seem to be a little near-sighted. They're likely to scrounge glass marbles that kids use for shooters. They used to carry them to the tower clock nests, probably because they thought they were eggs. Some of the marbles dropped in the gears.

The clock man has kept the marbles he has found in tower clocks through his thirty-five years in the business. New York hasn't yielded many, but he has samples from Texas, Mississippi, Montana, Florida and Wyoming. The one that puzzles him is a black aggie.

"How blind can a bird be to pick on a black marble for an egg?" he wonders.

The Lamm crew does most of the New York church clocks and City Hall clock once each week, a few only four times a year. They can get at them from inside, through ports, to regulate the hands for Daylight and Standard time switchovers. At that time they work for two days, all punning aside, 'round the clock.

All New York tower clocks have hands of weathered Georgia pine treated with oil and surfaced with smalt, a silicate compound that keeps off rain and snow without adding much weight. Wooden hands replaced bronze and other metal long ago. Metal hands were too great a hazard in a crowded city.

The most complicated clock mechanism in town is the Minerva, the Stuff and Guff job in Herald Square. New York University acquired it from the James Gordon Bennett estate, but has lent it to the city virtually forever. It cost $26,000 to get it off the old Herald Building and into shape again after a nineteen-year lay-up on uptown N. Y. U. campus.

In Howard Clock's 112 years in New York, Mr. Lamm says probably no job quite matched the repair work on Minerva. Undergraduates had stolen her owls, her spear, and Stuff's and Guff's hands. All those pieces had to be dug out of dorms and frat houses. Owl eyes were missing, but Howard had built the clock originally and had some in stock. They still have a few spares.

The Lamm crew handles roughly 42,000 clocks of one kind or another all over the country, 1,000 of them in and around New York City. The men fly, or drive to a job. Most of the crew are comparatively young, now. Two seniors, G. A. Lindblad, 89, and W. R. Admus, 79, died within the last two years. Apprentices are few and too restless these days for tower training.

The West Broadway shop, heaped with massive bells, works, gears, hammers and gently ticking antiques, is astonishingly neat. One of the showpieces is a stately centenarian, a wall clock back of Mr. Lamm's desk. It is more or less retired now. It hung for forty years in the office of James F. White, a textile man, at an annual rental of $80. Not a piece in it has needed replacement in 112 years.

Mr. Lamm thinks it could go on forever.

November 15, 1954

¶ There's a historic green-lichened cave on Hoboken shore just below Castle Stevens that didn't quite come in for its share of public notice last Wednesday when the castle's one hundredth anniversary was formally celebrated.

Famous New Yorkers had homes along the Hoboken strip early in the nineteenth century when the ground about the castle site was a kind of Coney Island—for the carriage trade. It was called the Elysian Fields, a picnic ground for velvet-clad gentry.

John Jacob Astor had a mansion there. Martin Van Buren, Washington Irving, William Cullen Bryant and other New York intellectuals spent many week-ends in the Fields, feasted royally on local game and oysters.

One of the spots they'd encounter in their strolls along River Walk, directly under where the castle stands now, was the Sybil's Cave, a deep cavern that attracted romantic swains.

At daybreak on July 28 in 1841 a girl's body, kept afloat on the Hudson's placid surface by her ballooning petticoats and outer skirts, was taken from the river directly in front of the cave.

When it was identified as that of Mary Cecilia Rogers, the pretty clerk at John Anderson's, tobacconist, in the St. Nicholas Hotel at Broadway and Spring Street in Manhattan, hullabaloo welled up in town.

Mary was famous. Washington Irving and most of New York's gayer blades had hung around Mr. Anderson's shop in gallant bids for her favor, but she had given most of them the back of her bonnet.

The police figured out, soon as they had the body ashore, that Mary Rogers had been cruelly murdered. Her death was the great scandal of the day, but no one ever completely fixed the motive nor found the murderer.

Probably the best, and most lasting, theory, was put on paper by one of Mary's former customers at the tobacco counter. You can get it today in almost any public library. It is Edgar Allan Poe's "The Mystery of Marie Roget."

Sybil's Cave is easily found, directly under Castle Stevens, even now, but most of the interior has fallen in and there's not much turning space in it. Hardly anyone seems to remember that it figured in one of the city's great crime stories.

A visit to the castle and to Stevens Institute of Technology campus, of which it is a part, is rewarding for the glimpse you get of the New York skyline.

November 24, 1954

¶ A full year's preparation goes into the Macy Thanksgiving Day parade that will cover two miles tomorrow and last only one hour and two minutes. Plans for the next one start the following day—the talking stage, that is.

The production staff will be up all through tonight. The 700 store hands who will be in the parade will be up at dawn tomorrow.

At 9 o'clock tonight five huge trucks will carry the deflated giant balloons—the Turkey, Mickey Mouse, Spaceman, Dachshund, Toy Soldier, Alligator and Fish—to Seventy-seventh Street between Columbus Avenue and Central Park West.

That block will be mechanically swept and covered with canvas. The flat balloons will be stretched on it and truck-borne tanks will start filling them with helium at 11 o'clock. The process takes about seven or eight hours. All told, 25,-000 cubic feet of the gas will be used. All of it will be released after the parade because no one has ever figured a way to salvage it.

The balloons, incidentally, come all the way from Akron in Ohio on sharp schedule. They're stored in a Goodyear Tire and Rubber Company shed out there between parades. The Turkey had its Akron flight test only two weeks ago. The Spaceman, who was inclined to float face downward in former years, has been re-rigged to stand upright. The task kept engineers busy for months.

The nine oversize floats—freshening and repair of those started last April in a Macy warehouse in Weehawken, N. J.—will arrive at the Weehawken end of the Lincoln Tunnel at 6 A.M. All other traffic will be stopped to let them through.

They're due at the Manhattan mouth at 6:30 A.M.

Police escorts will lead them to Central Park West, where they'll line up from Seventy-seventh to Eighty-second Street. They're disassembled for the journey through the tunnel, reassembled outside the park. The job takes around three hours, and that's carefully figured out.

Eleven regional high school and institutional bands, all champion groups in their areas, roll into the city in buses from points as far away as Schenectady, N. Y., and from Lebanon, Pa. Some stay at hotels overnight; some go right into position from home points at 9 A.M. Macy's contributes to the school bands' funds in return for the units taking part in the parade.

Two bands of resplendent Mummers from Philadelphia—the most richly clad and probably the best-trained amateur string-instrument players in the country—will rumble up from Philadelphia. They're an ancient tradition down there. They leave their city only on very special occasions.

Macy employes who have parade roles dress in the store cafeteria and recreation room on the eighth floor in costumes ordered a year in advance, mostly in size twelves for girls. The men who hold the balloons captive are the strongest chaps in the store's employ. They wear coveralls.

Parade watchers sometimes feel sorry for the Macy girls on the floats, but a stern store directive tells the girls what to wear under costumes—"warm long underwear or pajama bottoms, long-sleeve sweaters, wool socks, saddle shoes or loafers."

The grotesque elastic heads worn by parade flankers are dumped in the basement of the Museum of Natural History the night before, right alongside stores of brown dinosaur bones and other prehistoric relics. The girls pick them up there just before they move.

The number of city permits required to make the procession legal is astonishing. Calls to the Weather Bureau are endless.

Store executives delight in getting into costumes and masks for the show. They're never identified, but John W. Straus of the owner family plays a cavorting clown down the two-mile stretch.

This year's Santa Claus is Charles W. Howard, who calls himself Dean of Santa Clauses. He runs a school for department store Saint Nicks up at Albion, N. Y. His expenses up and down are paid by the store. Macy employes in the parade, all volunteers, get a bonus.

The cost of the show seems to be pretty much a trade secret. Broadway men who have watched it over the last twenty-eight years figure each parade costs just under $100,-000. It's worth it. There's nothing like it anywhere else in the world.

December 3, 1954

¶ For thirty-five years a heroic Minerva has held her left arm in salute from a high hill in Brooklyn to her sister Goddess of Liberty in the Bay. Few ever see her and fewer know that she was assigned that gesture in 1919 when she was erected at the Altar of Liberty on the Plateau in the southwest corner of Green-Wood Cemetery.

Minerva stands erect in enduring bronze on a site commemorating the Battle of Long Island in the American Revolution. The plaque prescribes her eternal task—"Minerva, Goddess of Wisdom, Glory and Patriotism, here salutes the Statue of Liberty . . ." If you stand beside her on the silent height and look westward across Gowanus, you see the Green Goddess in the Bay signaling back with her torch.

Green-Wood, now 116 years old, has other curious monuments hidden among its 30,000 trees, twenty miles of roads and forty miles of footpaths, but few get to see them except birdwatchers who know that herons, storks and wild ducks abide there awhile in migration. Hawks and crows hover over the grounds in raucous combat.

Strangest, probably, of all the markers is a white marble that has frozen for eternity a sentimental moment in the life of Charles Griffith. It shows Jane Griffith, a slender woman in the forty-first—and last—year of her existence, standing on the steps of her cottage. Wisteria climbs on the cottage wall. The family pup sits on an upper step.

Charles Griffith is at the front gate, a light coat over his arm. He wears the stovepipe hat of the period—1857—and the swallow-tailed jacket. Behind the Griffith cottage a Sixth Avenue horse-drawn trolley waits. The driver leans out as if summoning Mr. Griffith to have done with his parting and hurry aboard.

The legend is dim now, but Green-Wood men have passed it down for almost 100 years. Tom Manning, the supervisor today, says that Charles Griffith assigned P. Piatti, a sculptor, to study the house, a photograph of Mrs. Griffith, and himself, the better to arrest forever the moment when Mr. Griffith saw his wife for the last time. It was the morning of Aug. 3, 1857, when the horse-trolley waited.

Mr. Griffith lived twenty-five years after that, until he was 69. During those years he made weekly pilgrimage to Green-Wood to study the monument, to look on the face of "Jane, my Wife"—that is part of the inscription above her image on the steps—and to weep over it. He was buried beside Jane on Dec. 15, 1882. The marker tells that, too.

December 6, 1954

⁋ Roland Taylor Ely should win mention in academic annals for the grim road he has taken toward a Ph.D. He has been four years at the task, now, toiling in a cavernous New York Public Library subbasement thirty feet under Fifth Avenue and Forty-second Street. He has another two or three years to go.

Mr. Ely is 6 feet 2, won his letter in track at Princeton and played freshman football there. He got out in '46. He is married, lives with his wife and three children opposite Dr. Albert Einstein's cottage in Princeton. He commutes to and from his research job, but stands the strain well. Gray begins to show in his college haircut, but only lightly.

Probably no other aspirant for a Ph.D. has ever had to equip himself for the task as Mr. Ely did. He works from 9 o'clock in the morning until 5 each evening with his whole face—eyes and all—covered by a special mask to filter dust and sand that rises from 1,000,000 brittle documents that should yield the material he needs for a booklength thesis.

His subject is Moses Taylor, nineteenth-century (1806-1882) New York banker and eccentric who started as a clerk with G. G. and S. Howland in South Street and in sixty years in trade acquired $35,000,000, a good part of it in railroads, in Cyrus Fields' Atlantic Cable and in Cuban sugar and French madder. Roland Taylor Ely is no kin of his. He wishes he were.

Mr. Ely will take his Ph.D. at Harvard. His theme was suggested by Robert G. Albion, Gardiner Professor of Oceanic History there. He knew from the start what the job would come to. He knew the Taylor correspondence and accounts, in sixty-three massive chests, had been in the library basement more than twenty years; they had been found under dust layers in the old Taylor office at 44 South Street.

He knew that the papers had not been catalogued because the library did not have the $10,000 it would have cost to assign professional workers to the task. He did not know, though, that someone in fairly recent years had stripped the rare stamps from the envelopes and

scattered the Taylor letters about in the chests, willy-nilly. He had to restore them chronologically.

Professional stamp collectors, incidentally, heard that the library had the Taylor letters, and a few unsubtle bribes were offered for first crack at the letters. They were coldly rejected by library officials and, as it turned out, it wouldn't have done the collectors much good. The strippers had done a thorough job.

Anyway, Mr. Ely toiled away— with the mask to protect him from the accumulations of sand used by Mr. Taylor's clerks to dry their inky script. He has the letters (incoming and outgoing) in perfect order, has invoices, bills of lading, ships' papers, bank drafts, ledgers all sorted. Fortunately he's a linguist, too, and can read them all. A quarter of them are in Spanish, a quarter in French; the rest in English.

He had no knowledge of bookkeeping or accounting, though. He spent six weeks acquiring a working knowledge of those before he could understand all the transactions.

Year in, year out, the scholar has toiled in the basement under naked lights, with massive blocks of shadow trying to close in. He bought an adding machine, and that clicked away in subterranean quiet. He did not hear the traffic. He did not know the weather until he stepped outside on his way to the 5:35 out of Penn Station. He wore a coverall in summer, a crimson bathrobe in winter, to protect his tweeds.

He would come out for lunch in

the library's basement cafeteria, but few there knew who he was. There was a quiet rumor that he was the Hermit of the Basement, but library hands see too many odd folk to ask rude questions. Few know his identity or his purpose even now. He smiles easily, though. He likes to tell how he fought boredom in the cellar one day, rigging a Boy Scout trap of cardboard to catch a mouse, which he let go.

Every now and then Mr. Ely comes out of the basement to fly to Cuba to check on Moses Taylor's vast sugar transactions. He'll take off just before Christmas, for example, to go through the accounts of Tomás Terry, a Moses Taylor contemporary, at Cienfuegos in Cuba, for about six weeks. He'll take his family with him. He's been in the old Terry warehouses before, and knows what to expect.

"Work in Cienfuegos," he explains quietly, "has this difference: It's hotter and you're forever brushing beetles, tarantulas and scorpions off the files. I carry DDT on that end."

December 8, 1954

❡ The good people who have lived for years in the six old red-brick houses in Grove Court sleep restlessly these nights. Their waking hours are troubled, too. They think they are under Blind Progress' lifted heel.

Word is out around the neighborhood, one of the quaintest old spots in Greenwich Village, that the City Planning Commission is toying with the notion of wiping Grove Court off the map, and some twenty other buildings with it. The report is that the city wants the space for a playground.

Local committees have come to meeting about it and there's talk of petitions, of appeal to historical societies and to architectural leagues, but there's no guarantee that those efforts can keep the heel from crushing the court.

Sentimentalists in the Village come close to tears about the possibility of Grove Court's evanishment. It is one of the few spots of its kind left in Manhattan—a cluster of dwellings more than 125 years old in a brick courtyard entered by an ancient iron gateway.

When you're past the gate, at the very spot where Grove Street bends, between Hudson and Bedford Streets, it's as if you had just stepped in from London's Berkeley Square—winter-stripped trees, lovely doorways, sleeping gardens, bits of statuary. The illusion is perfect at twilight and after dark.

There's some debate as to when the six three-story houses were built, but the best guess would put the date around 1820, when the Village was still semi-rural. All in the row except No. 4 seem to rest on ancient Dutch foundations and there are vestiges of Dutch ovens in them.

Mrs. Sidney Robbins and her sons Alan and Robert, sculptors, descendants of a long line of Congregational dominies, live in No. 5, which looks, inside and out, like something you might have come upon in late eighteenth-century London.

They've studied Grove Court's history. They know it was known at one time as Pig's Alley, at another as Mixed Ale Alley. When they came, thirty-five years ago, the pump in the court still gave clear water from what they think was a branch of old wandering Minetta Water.

The Robbins' have a large pewter tankard clearly dated 1784. It came up under a workman's spade when they dug cellar space for a heater a few years ago. They even thought they had a ghost for No. 5 that knocked in the walls around 1 A.M., but it turned out to be a young Naval officer at No. 4 knocking out his pre-bed pipe against his grate, which backs up to theirs.

Fairly authentic, they think, is the legend that O. Henry got his idea for the story "The Last Leaf" from a Grove Court vine. They own an old clipping of a city sound survey that says the court is, by decibel count, the quietest spot in Manhattan. It seems to be, at night.

No traffic noises penetrate to the court, none of the city's hullabaloo. Its nocturnal silences have dimension. Lying in their beds under the ancient rooftops and chimney pots, the tenants get only the heartbreak wail of groping river traffic on foggy nights—that and, now, the almost audible tread of Progress and the playground.

December 15, 1954

❡ Men sometimes set themselves to curious objectives. Cmdr. Thomas J. Keane, 65 years old today, hopes to complete next Sunday afternoon, if the weather is bright, a project he started a little less than four years ago—to walk in every street, avenue, alley, square and court on Manhattan Island.

He intends to start from the northern end of Broadway on Marble Hill around 1 o'clock in the afternoon and do the thirteen miles to the Battery. That will complete his self-imposed task. He thinks that at his normal walking pace, three and one-half miles an hour, he should make it within four hours.

The Navy Reserve officer is a rather short, brisk, blue-eyed man with remarkably good color. He has dropped thirty pounds on his walks, which he took only on weekends. He was 175 pounds when he started and his health, even in the Navy, was never better.

Even with brow-wrinkling and a decent time for harking back, Commander Keane can't quite remember what started him on his project. He thinks most New Yorkers are extraordinarily provincial, that they don't know much about neighborhoods six blocks from where they live, but he admits that comes as afterthought.

A pocket map guided the commander in his landlubberly rambling. He started at the island's tip, taking all the east-west streets. He had to weave and backtrack a lot in the crooked lanes and alleys in the financial district and in Greenwich Village.

He worked the flanks of Central Park as solid east and west blocks—took them from Fifty-ninth to 110th and then resumed his river-to-river hikes north of that point. The going was roughest where the marginal motor highways block easy access to the rivers' brims.

All told, the commander has covered 3,022 city blocks, which add up to roughly 502 miles. After he had done all the side streets he took the avenues, working from east to west. He left Broadway for the last, because it is the only avenue that runs the island's full length.

When visitors have only an hour in town, the commander recommends the walk from Christopher Street on the west, eastward along Eighth Street, as a stroll that offers the greatest variety for the eye and for the ear. "All kinds of people, all kinds of architecture," is the way he sums it. Takes him fifty-five minutes.

One thing that stands out from his island coverage is the city's children. In the richest neighborhoods and in the poorest, he finds, only the children are universally cheerful. Their laughter is the only relieving note in bitter slum surroundings.

The most curious things the commander saw were a goat farm, or stable, at 128th Street near the East River and the shacks on stilts on Harlem River around 223d or 225th Street. He kept no diary and isn't too sure of these locations.

There were little adventures. One day in lower Mulberry Street the commander wandered into a deserted Chinese herb, spice and tea shop, delighted with the heady odors. He lingered twenty minutes, pounded the counter, called with deck-range bellow. No answer.

He says, "Only the Chinese would be that trusting. Leave an open door in a shop like that. The smells put me right back in the Orient."

Another time, on a Saturday afternoon, he fancied a Virginia ham he saw in another Chinese shop (he forgets the street) and found that store deserted, too. He finally looked behind the counter and there he saw six Chinese chaps, shoeless and deep in sleep.

"Never figured that one out," he says. "They looked dead, though I'm sure they weren't. Crazy thing."

December 24, 1954

❡ The crèche on the high lawn at the northeast corner of Lexington Avenue at Sixty-eighth Street is triply significant. It represents the Stable at Bethlehem. The word crèche, according to Webster, means a nursery, sometimes a foundling hospital.

The old red-brick buildings that stretch from Lexington Avenue to Third on the north side of Sixty-eighth Street together constitute the New York Foundling Hospital —a series of nurseries, shelters and hospitals for the newly born and for infants up to 2 years old.

Its quiet corridors, its spotless crib-filled chambers, the silent movements of white-garbed Sisters of Charity, the solemn tint of light sifted through stained glass give it a cathedral air. It always houses from 270 to 300 babies, most of them marked at birth as unfortunates.

For the most part they are children left inside the hospital's main vestibule by unfortunate mothers who steal away without identification. Other foundlings are brought in by the police from doorways, from all manner of lonely places.

They seldom have names. Over their cribs in the Foundling Hospital, after the nuns and the nurses have bathed them and the obstetrician has examined them for illness, are cards that say with stark simplicity: "Aban. Male" or "Aban. Female."

They get names later, if they live. These are as appropriate as they can be. Notes left with some tell their creed. Some are of Catholic parentage, some of Protestant, some Jewish. Some are white, some are black, some brown.

Some, only slightly less fortunate than the rest, bring names. They are from homes freshly broken by anything from poverty to murder. You think you detect in their staring eyes, sometimes, something akin to hurt.

They nap at midday in rooms cast in twilight by drawn dark blinds, with gold patterns slipping through the sides. Some are just tiny heads above blankets. Little fists grope at air in convulsive dreaming. You hear weak whispers, deep infant sighs.

But yesterday the Foundling Hospital tried to look festive, and the 2-year-olds cannot quite understand it. The white-robed sisters and the white-clad nurses had covered the windows with winter scenes in soap and in powdered chalk, with Santa Clauses and with glittering sleighs with golden bells.

Sister Irene Marie pushed open a nursery door. Toddlers got up from their play on the immaculate linoleum and teetered toward her, like chicks, on uncertain limbs. They caught at her robes. Their upturned faces varied—smiled, stared in deep gravity, or were almost vacant.

A little blond boy slipped on the linoleum. He came last. Tears were golden beads in his eyes in the sunlight's flood, but the little face worked up a childish grin as he got a fist grip in a robe fold. Sister Irene Marie patted the heads.

One little girl in blue stared gravely from between crib bars, silent, unmoving. Somewhere, in another room, a radio softly played Christmas music. The baby in blue cocked her head. She put a pudgy finger in her mouth and the little eyes went dreamy. It was as if even before she had known a full year she had come to accept isolation.

Sister Irene Marie turned to accept a little girl's gift. It was a fragment of wet rubber from a blue balloon. The baby seemed eager to catch the sister's reaction. Her big eyes fixed on the nun's kindly features and when she saw a benevolent smile there, she smiled, too.

In the quiet corridor, Sister Irene Marie explained that the Foundling Hospital gets 1,000 babies a year. Some go back to mended homes, some are boarded out, some are adopted. The unwanted eventually go to orphanages. Wherever they go, the hospital keeps track and looks to their care.

Sometimes in his walks at night, Cardinal Spellman stops in and silently makes his way from crib to crib to study the sleeping faces. He does not think of all their futures as dark. From those same cribs have come a Governor, doctors, priests, artists, war heroes.

And at Christmas there is special hope. Good people flood the Foundling Hospital with toys, with clothing, with goodies, and the Christmas trees' sparkle. There is meaning in the raised letters on the main-entrance plaque. It says, "Home for the Little Homeless."

December 29, 1954

¶ Only a few hundred New Yorkers have the right and the equipment to tune in on radio station KEA 627, which operates on 43.5 megacycles and sends nothing but code numbers.

They subscribe to Aircall, a radio-paging service that provides an invisible extension of a telephone bell. If you are within thirty to fifty miles of your phone, the signal will reach you.

It has its little freaks, as all radio gadgets do. You may not hear it in a steel-hemmed spot in, say, a skyscraper or a subway, but shift a few inches or a few feet and it gets through to you. It always comes clear in open spaces.

Aircall is a subsidiary of Telanserphone, a telephone-answering service started in 1922 solely for physicians and surgeons. Now it answers phones for around 10,000 individuals and corporations in all fields for a fee.

One of its early clients was the Save-A-Life League, which existed

to divert would-be suicides. Its present customers include astrologers, who offer twenty-four-hour prognostications, and business-machine corporations that have repair men in the field.

Telanserphone is a vital link in the Alcoholics Anonymous night program. The American Red Cross subscribes for easy recall of executives in emergency. The New York State Nurses Placement Service relies on it.

The New York County Medical Association's Doctors Emergency Service, which has 250 practitioners available day and night, is hooked into Telanserphone. So are insurance adjusters, actors and actresses, elevator repair outfits.

Most hotel chefs, signing off for the night, leave fish, vegetable and meat orders with the service for transmission at daybreak to markets. Private detectives, narcotics agents, undertakers, slot-machine operators, newspaper circulation men also are on the lists.

When you call telephone numbers given on your TV screen with bargain offers your calls flow right into Telanserphone's main branch at 224 East Thirty-eighth Street. They're handled there by twenty to thirty clerks working top speed.

December 31, 1954

¶ Tugboats that churn past 10 Gracie Square almost always salute the slender gray-haired lady who spends a good part of her time from dawn to dusk, and sometimes even after sundown, painting on the third-floor terrace there.

Some of the tugboat men know the lady's name, but most don't. It's just that they've come to know her pretty much as they know all East River marks on which they take bearings to keep in the channel.

The artist is Mrs. Isabella Banks Markell. She has painted the East River for more than twenty years —all phases of it in all seasons. Her series of 150 canvases on the construction of the East River Drive, over which she lives, is a complete story of that operation.

Mrs. Markell's grandmother was a Lenox, member of the family out of Kirkcudbright in Scotland that owned a thirty-acre farm just east of Central Park at Seventy-first Street, where the Frick Museum is now. She is descended from James Lenox, whose rare book collection is now part of the New York Public Library.

During the war, Mrs. Markell's terrace studio was a kind of unofficial Navy observation post. She painted submarines, light aircraft carriers, whaling ships with vital cargo, crippled craft limping in from the sea—all for Navy records. She had swift contact with the Coast Guard when collisions occurred in the river within her sight.

Men who worked the derricks, pile drivers and cranes in constructing the East River Drive came to know her painting. They offered free, honest criticism on her rendering of their machinery. They went in groups to little luncheons in her luxurious apartment.

Mayor La Guardia was delighted with her East River Drive canvases. If he had lived he might have had them set in some permanent exhibit in one of the municipal buildings. He often said he meant to do that. She has sold quite a few since then and has lectured on them before the Architectural League.

It is a delightful experience to sit with the painter on a pleasant afternoon. She recognizes river craft 'way up or 'way down the river. Men wave to her from the decks—friendly, respectful gestures. She is a grandmother seven times over, and a born aristocrat.

The river under her window goes purple at dusk.

Huffing upstream in the twilight in creamy wake comes a pompous little tug. The figures on its deck are blurry silhouettes. But the painter knows the craft and the men.

She says: "That's the Bumble Bee. Railroad tug. They'll salute as they come by."

The men see the slender figure on the terrace. They wave, the bull-throated siren gives tongue, almost gaily, and the reverberations quiver in dimensional sound and die away.

1 9 5 5

T HE BRAND-NEW FACTS BOOK just issued by the Police Department is a neat job, but it deals perhaps a little too lightly with the 1857 period, the time when the state insisted on a Metropolitan Police Board. Fernando Wood, who was Mayor then, and something of a scrapper, hung onto his own Municipal Force, so the city had two sets of cops. They spent most of the time beating hell out of one another, with the Bowery Boys on the Municipals' side. Ought to make a spirited play, some day, that stretch of local history.

❡ A group of middle-aged gentlemen in town got talking about the weather the other day and how modern winters are sissy periods compared with those they passed through in youth.

One stubborn fellow insisted that in 1918, when World War I was on, he and a whole group of bold small-fry from Ninetieth Street walked across the frozen Hudson to a point on the New Jersey shore—Fort Lee, he thought it was.

The talk swelled to uproar at the bar, one faction holding that there has been no bank-to-bank freeze below Yonkers in modern times, though such a phenomenon was common in the seventeenth, eighteenth and nineteenth centuries.

Newspaper files show that a munitions worker named Fred Gabay crossed on the ice from Hastings in Westchester to a point on the New Jersey side in a freeze-up on Jan. 2, 1918. The same file indicated a Hudson River freeze-up just five years earlier but didn't say how far down it came.

The files also showed a photograph, published on Jan. 13, 1918, showing Dr. Lee de Forest, the inventor, and Miss Nancy Mayo crossing the Hudson opposite 230th Street, New York City.

Edward Ringwood Hewitt of Gramercy Square, son of Abram Hewitt, who was Mayor of New York in 1887, remembers that the Hudson froze almost every year around that period, mostly about February.

It sticks in his mind, he says, because he and other silk-stocking kids used to sail-skate from somewhere around Yonkers down to Manhattan's upper reaches. They did it year after year.

Mr. Hewitt, pushing 90 now, recalls clearly that one winter day in 1875 it was the East River that froze, and probably both rivers. That freeze is fixed in his memory because the cash boy for his grandfather, Peter Cooper, due at the office in Water Street that morning, didn't show up until mid-afternoon.

It turned out that ice had stopped the East Twenty-third Street-Greenpoint ferry, so the cash boy had come down the hard way. He had walked from Cooper's Bushwick glue factory to Greenpoint, then to the Manhattan shore and all the way downtown without wetting his feet.

The last ice-up anyone could remember was during the record cold of February, 1934, a bitter depression year when the thermometer only once struggled above freezing. By that time, though, river traffic was so heavy that there was no shore-to-shore ice bridge, only heavy floe accumulation.

¶ The new B. M. T. Jamaica Line subway cars that went into service the other day have an extraordinarily sensitive and well-hidden heat-control gadget that few riders seem to know about.

The core of these units, according to the Minneapolis-Honeywell people who designed them, is an almost invisible strand of wire that is at least 100 times more sensitive to temperature change than the most delicately attuned human.

Each of the fancy new cars has two of these thermostats, one to feel for outside temperatures, one to gauge interior temperature. Inside temperature varies, of course, according to the number of riders aboard.

The engineers who did the testing, incidentally, figure that 300 passengers jam-packed in one of the new cars generate enough body heat to warm a ten-room house.

No matter how dense or how thin the passenger load, the two balanced thermometers, which belong to the electronic brain family, call up, or reduce, the amount of power needed to make the conveyance comfortable. The engineers think it's the most perfect device of its kind ever put in a common carrier.

January 21, 1955

¶ The old Wesley Oak under which Methodism's founder preached in Georgia two centuries ago is up in this region now in the form of a dozen ten-foot beams.

They were brought here by Charles C. Parlin Sr., New York attorney who was one of the authors of the plan for the unification of American Protestantism, discussed the other day in Cincinnati.

Mr. Parlin is one of the country's leading Methodist laymen. He was in St. Simons, Ga., two years ago when the Wesley Oak was uprooted in a hurricane and fell across a highway.

The moss-hung giant live oak, one of a grove of stately trees surrounding Christ Episcopal Church and the graves of early settlers and soldiers, was already old when John Wesley stood under it in 1736 as a Church of England chaplain to exhort assemblages of red men and British troops from Fort Oglethorpe. It was in pretty advanced stage of inner decay when the high winds brought it down.

Mr. Parlin asked church and municipal officials at St. Simons whether there were any claimants for the ancient oak, and learned there was none. The authorities thought they'd just cut the tree for firewood to remove it as a highway hazard.

Mr. Parlin was told he could have it if he wanted it. He did. He hired local woodsmen to saw and hew out the sound portions, and arranged to truck the beams to his home in Englewood, N. J. He had smaller parts of the oak fashioned into handsome gavels. These he distributed to Methodist ministers at Sea Island for use at church meetings.

The beams have seasoned well in Mr. Parlin's garage and the time has come when he must figure the best way to use them. He thinks Methodist churches may bid for some of the Wesley oak wood, possibly to make into altar rails, lecterns and the like.

¶ The most clamorous show in New York's wintry dusk is the mass return to nesting of starlings from city parks and other open spaces that are bird feeding grounds. The flocks move in dark masses, blacker than thunder cloud.

Uptown, coming from Westchester, they have a way-stop at Trinity Cemetery in 155th Street off Broadway. Downtown, they swoop into the Municipal Building arches and into courthouse porticoes off Foley Square, usually a little after 5 P.M. Their combined twittering startles city dwellers who've never heard that sound before. The flocks take off for their feeding grounds again in frosty dawn with the same outcry.

January 24, 1955

¶ The newest lion in Chinatown's New Year celebration today will be the Chinese Community Club's. It was—for want of a better term—initiated on Saturday night at a lion's-eye-opening ritual on the fifth floor at 41 Mott Street, the club's meeting place. It will dart into the New Year parade from the doorway at 41 Mott, near Pell Street, at noon-stroke, to help bring in the Chinese year 4652, the Year of the Lamb.

The new lion, or what Westerners in error call a dragon, was made in Brooklyn by the venerable Henry Leong, one of the few Old China artisans left in the community who still practice lion and dragon manufacture. It replaces the tired and weathered lion of last year's advent of the Year of the Horse and is a brave thing to behold, all gold and silver, white and brown-furred, with great glass eyes, dangling white horsehair beard, lolling red tongue.

In Old China a monk would preside over the ritual. On Saturday night, because there are no Chinese monks here now, Dr. Arthur Liu, club president, acted as master. The new lion, stretched on stools, faced the altar. On the altar were sacrificial roast chicken, roast pork and a head of lettuce; red wax tapers, bundles of incense sticks, and the *gee tsa* or magic red dye made of herbs, with which the master or *see foo* (Dr. Liu, in this case) opens the new lion's eyes.

The club meeting chamber is about 30 feet long, 20 feet wide. The altar is at one end under a gilded old decorative panel done in wild-bird and palm-frond motif, all blackened with smoke and years. Around the side walls are dark teak chairs, like old thrones, with marble back insets. The elders were to have had most of these honor seats, but the five-floor staircase was too much for them. They stood in the streets, looking up, to listen to the *lo* (great gong) and the cymbals, or *po*, beaten with wooden drumsticks, the *pang ku*.

Dark-haired, bright-eyed Chinese boys in bright yellow garb and silken sashes handled the cymbals, the gong and the great drum. As they warmed up for the ceremony the sound was ear-crashing. The rhythm, though, was exciting, pat-terned to cue the lion in its movements when Dr. Liu gave it life. Other little boys were in yellow monk's gowns, their heads behind grinning helmet-shaped masks, all pink and blue. They just stood around.

The initiation began at 9 o'clock with shattering abruptness—gongs, cymbals and the great drum, with Pee Wee Wong inside the lion's head. The altar attendant lighted wax tapers set in tangerines, ignited the incense. The percussive cuing picked up pace with reverberating thunder. The dragon's white eyelids rolled upward. Dr. Liu dipped a brush in the *gee tsa*. He painted the lion's eyes with it. He instructed the new lion, as the master should, in how it should behave in the New Year.

He told it in Chinese: "You go out into the world. You go to bring peace, not to stir trouble. You go to find peace and to keep peace. I give you life, and you must be a good lion. You must be good to men. Now you know what to do."

Dr. Liu stepped back. Attendants passed little bundles of tiny firecrackers to guests around the altar. Another attendant set fire to gold and silver paper in a metal container. It flared, a tribute to the God of Wealth.

Then the drums and gongs and cymbals really broke loose. So did the new lion. Pee Wee Wong leaped, arms upthrust, and the lion's head shot high. It shot sideways. It dived at the floor, it turned on its silken length and glared at the rear end, where a hidden boy lion-dancer, with a kind of breast-stroke motion, kept the whole body aquiver. Firecrackers were thrown in bundles at the lion's feet to scare off evil spirits. It trampled them as they popped deafeningly and gave off spark showers. The place was incredible bedlam.

Pee Wee Wong was dripping and exhausted after ten minutes' violent plunging. Eugene Eng, a wiry student, replaced him in the lion's frame and, because he was fresh, the lion went into gymnastic frenzy. An altar hand dropped the lettuce at the lion's feet. It approached the offering with weird contortions and convulsive head thrusts.

It gobbled the lettuce and, with a sharp mouth twist, sent torn leaves scattering. Dr. Liu had explained what that signified: "He accepts the lettuce in token of all green things. He will eat only what the good earth yields. He will not devour man. He will be a good dragon, eat only grass."

The ritual lasted a full hour, with dancer changes. By that time a man could not hear. Mott Street was thronged with listeners. You could see them through the windows. Dr. Liu and the attendants passed out *lai see,* lucky little red envelopes holding gift New Year coins. Little boys got them, and bachelors, for a male unmarried remains a boy in the elders' sight.

The lion ended as he had begun, with three bows to the altar and to the master. He sank in quiet, toyed coyly with his floppy furred ears, winked his great glass eyes; he fell asleep.

He will awaken at noon today, a good lion. He will be in the parade with the lions of the Hip Sings and the Ong Leongs. His ears will ring with the shrill New Year greeting, "Gung Hay Fat Choy." That means, "Great good fortune for all."

January 26, 1955

❡ Old blotters in the West 100th Street police station, which is to be torn down this spring, make fascinating reading now. They show better than anything else how that part of the city grew out of semi-rural quiet into the teeming tenement and traffic-burdened quarter it is now.

The first blotter was started at 6 o'clock on Saturday morning, April 6, 1867, by a Sergeant Blake. He wrote the fine, heavily-shaded script of the period with flourishes and curlicues, as did most other desk men after him. He recorded that spring morning's first roll call:

"Captain Bogart in command. Sergeant Blake present. Three men answered—Lamb, Connor, Larkin —and were sent out on patrol. Roundsman Phenese to visit the men this tour of duty."

A good part of the precinct was covered by open fields—vestiges of the Mott, Striker and Van der Heuvel farms. To the west, by North River, rock outcroppings rose high. Squatter shacks with untidy barnyards were scattered everywhere. Bloomingdale Village had not quite vanished.

Day after day there was nothing in the blotters except reports of the patrol turning out and of its return with strayed critters. There was no major crime then. Outside precinct windows bees hummed, goats bleated, cows mooed.

The first business entry beyond roll calls was written at 1:20 A.M. on Sabbath Day, April 7, 1867:

"Officers Larkin and Connor brought to this station 11 head of cattle found astray in Broadway at 105th Street."

New York was host then to Civil War stragglers passing through on their way back to upstate farms. The blotter for this period reads like a hotel register: "John Burns, James Johnston, James McCann, William Hall, lodgers." The veterans were boarded overnight in the cell block back of the station house.

The precinct's first prisoner was brought in on April 14—"Michael Mott, 28, moulder, obtaining money under false pretenses from A. L. Eastman, Eighty-eighth Street near Twelfth Avenue. Witness Charles Tripler." The entry was made at "ten and one-half A.M."

On May 6, Patrolman Stoddard brought in a stray goat he found "obstructing travel" at Eighth Avenue and Eighty-third Street." A few hours later Officers Corey, Wilson and Stoddard with Roundsman Nicholson herded five more goats and two kids to the station-house door.

It was lush spring then. Mosquitoes were imprisoned between blotter pages and are there to this day. On June 30 a wandering bee, all black and gold, somehow got between the blotter leaves, and remains there. That was old 100th

Street precinct, in the beginning.

Little by little, as you read through the musty records, you see the town pushing northward. You see crime picking up. The first highway robbery, on June 3, 1867, curiously, was a juvenile delinquency job.

The precinct had its first homicide on July 15, 1867. Philip Monahan, 35, stabbed Thomas Cosgrove at Ninth Avenue and Sixty-first Street, then in deep remorse walked to the station house to give himself up. He was taken by wagon to the Tombs, 'way downtown. And men's wickedness increased as through the years the fields and lots became crowded with new flats.

Yesterday, West 100th Street's blotter had more crime on it for the day than old West 100th Street would have listed in a month. And men on seventy-three posts handled the usual scores of husband-wife spats that didn't quite make the book. They reported more vehicular accidents and injury cases than old Captain Bogart's clumping crews would turn in in a busy six months.

Today West 100th Street musters 275 men to cope with multitudinous problems. And this force is not enough, even with radios, automobiles and other modern gadgetry. You feel, with sadness, that the West Side was a happier, simpler, more pleasant place when the entries told of strayed kine and simple, two-fisted assault.

You stumble away from the untidy old building with its faded, feebly-lighted green lamps and wish, somehow, that time had stood still, without change.

¶ George Le Vind has been an engraver for sixty-three of his seventy-eight years. For the last fifty-eight he has worked for Gorham and for Black Starr and Gorham, jewelers and silversmiths. He is probably the dean of his vanishing craft.

He engraves the Davis cups, the dog-show trophies, the Gallant Fox Handicap Trophy, Princeton's Kafer Memorial Cup. He has done book plates for rich families all over the country. A generation ago he did them by the score, now he does fewer than twenty a year.

When President Hoover took office Mr. Le Vind was hired to engrave on a desk set the signatures of every man in the new Cabinet, which had purchased the gift. He did special cigarette boxes for the heads of each of the Western Hemisphere republics.

In 1938, after he had engraved, just for fun, six full alphabets on the head of a common pin, a British miniaturist heard of the deed and asked him to do something extraordinary for Queen Elizabeth of Britain.

Mr. Le Vind took a British farthing, sliced it layer-cake-wise with a jeweler's fine saw, fitted a reduced photo portrait of King George VI into the coin, drawer-fashion. When the drawer was closed the farthing seemed intact.

The Queen was delighted with the gift, and the engraver has a letter from Buckingham Palace graciously thanking him for it. He has made similar hidden-drawer coins since and is about to start another.

The latest coin project, though, involves a hunt for an American copper dated 1823, which hasn't turned up yet. Laurence Gouverneur Hoes, a descendant of President James Monroe, is searching for one, because the Monroe Doctrine was proclaimed in 1823.

When a coin is obtained, Mr. Le Vind will saw it as he did the farthing—and as he has done with American pennies—and engrave in the drawer slab the forty-seven words that embody the Monroe Doctrine, the part beginning, "We owe it . . ." and closing with the phrase, ". . . to our own safety."

Finished, the coin is to go into the Monroe Museum in Fredericksburg, Va., which already holds samples of the engraver's more delicate works.

A good many of Mr. Le Vind's assignments have been confidential. He has engraved secret symbols, hieroglyphics, sentiments, in almost invisible strokes in hidden places on all kinds of valuable gems, for positive identification by the owner in case of theft.

He thinks one of his oddest chores was changing the letters on a silver band on a homing pigeon's leg. Another unusual assignment was to engrave two sets of initials in a gold wedding band while it was on a woman's finger. She was superstitious about taking it off, once it had been slipped on.

A good part of the time, now, Mr. Le Vind engraves large silver cigarette boxes with all sorts of sentimental art works. He does the six

Augusta National Golf Club cigarette boxes each year, with an engraving of the clubhouse on top, faithful in every tiny detail.

These boxes go to top players, but he made an extra one for Mrs. Eisenhower. He did a handsome plate for "The Old Barn Gang," men who worked with the inventor Charles F. Kettering, that is a remarkable piece.

It incorporates the barn in which they worked, a true copy of Mr. Kettering's drawing for the first automobile self-starter, images of the men in the Barn Gang who labored with "Ket" and engravings of the plant that grew from the barn at Dayton, Ohio.

The master craftsman still turns out a large number of seal rings, though nowhere near as many as he did in the late nineteenth century. He does a lot of actual portraits of horses, dogs, cats and other pets for women's stationery.

One woman recently asked him to do a Diana engraving for her young daughter's personal letter paper, then coldly rejected it. It was beautiful, she conceded, but she preferred her goddesses in full dress. Mr. Le Vind quietly did a draped Diana.

February 23, 1955

MARGINALIA: ¶ There's a United States Senate building in town that not too many know about. It's an old apartment house at 235 Second Avenue. It has "U. S. Senate" across its façade in large, raised marble letters. No one in the neighborhood seems to know how it got that name, but there's a possible clue on the apartment house just south of it—the "Wm. L. Evarts." Mr. Evarts was, among other things, a Senator and counsel to the Republican party after the Civil War, about the time the house went up.

¶ There's a bit of Pennsylvania in the Rutherford Place courtyard of the Friends Seminary in Stuyvesant Square. The carriage block and hitching post there originally stood in front of William Penn's home in Letitia Street in Philadelphia . . .

March 7, 1955

¶ The telephone wire tap, which started, near as anyone can check, right here in New York City just sixty years ago as a police function, seems to have got pretty much out of hand.

It is used now in blackmail, in political spying, in divorce unpleasantness, even in business competition where unscrupulous men seek information to anticipate or thwart moves by others in their line. It has developed evil, quick-sprouting seed.

In the beginning, during Mayor William Strong's administration in 1895, it was a crude art. Tappers merely gouged bits of insulation from a set of wires leading into a home, an office, or institution, clamped headset wires onto the breaks, took notes at leisure.

From 1895 to around 1916, wiretappers stayed pretty much within bounds. They were mostly municipal cops and Federal agents stalking more or less legitimate prey—narcotic peddlers, murderers, kidnapers and kindred felons.

In 1917 the Government plunged into tapping on a vast scale. It set up a huge telephone switchboard in the New York Custom House, tapped the lines of hundreds of aliens into the board, and had relays of stenographers taking notes on conversations. It caught up with many war enemies that way.

The tappers' tempo stepped up during Prohibition. Every bootlegger in the country of any pretensions knew for a certainty that his lines were anything but private. The bigger alcohol dispensers hired counter-tappers to free their lines.

Around the early Thirties the practice spread and dribbled into fields that in no way threatened the public peace and safety. Blackmailers and the more unscrupulous private eyes began to wring a profit out of tapping, and still do, in increasing numbers.

Unfortunately for society, great progress in electronics, particularly in sound and communications, have been a boon to the tappers. They can now buy ready-made tapping equipment of extraordinary range and sensitvity.

They now tap wires by induction, without bothering to actually cut into them. They can hide pea-sized microphones in a telephone receiver.

Some of the breed are collectors of a sort. They keep their spiciest recorded items—bawdy conversation, between some yegg and his moll, or between some rich man and his mistress—which they play for one another or for the amusement of intimate friends.

The real technicians among professional wiretappers scorn ready-made equipment, in most cases. They're constantly at work in their private shops on research for improving their sets. They buy the parts in the Canal Street surplus shops and at sidewalk junk stands.

They're finicky in their terminology and don't share the public contempt for their operations. They "sit on a tap." Their calling is "wire work," not tapping (they dislike that term), "wire supervision," "censoring" or "bridging." They feel completely secure at it. No wiretapper has ever gone to jail —not for tapping wires.

March 11, 1955

❡ Vault demolition at the old Fifth Avenue Bank is under the supervision of a full-blooded Cherokee chieftain who was on Carlisle's varsity when Jim Thorpe battered opposing linemen. He is Leon Miller, M.E., hygiene instructor at City College and lacrosse coach there since 1931. He once was head of the Indian Council of Chiefs in the United States and is a former president of the Indian Confederacy. Mr. Miller is frequently called in as an engineer on difficult projects.

March 14, 1955

❡ A great man's word portrait of New York City after an all-blanketing snowstorm has turned up in a letter written 109 years ago by Capt. Robert E. Lee when he was stationed at Fort Hamilton in Brooklyn.

The letter is addressed to another officer, Capt. John Mackay. No part of it has ever been published. Ben Bloomfield, an autograph collector at 65 University Place, got it recently from Mackay kin in Georgia.

The collector says it is remarkable in that it presents Captain Lee (later General Lee, commander of the Confederate forces in the Civil War) as a gentleman with some instinct for a comely face despite his reputation for great dignity and austerity.

The captain wrote a lovely hand. He dated the letter "Jan. 30, 1846" and filled four full pages with delicate script. They are rich in pleasant chit-chat and with notes on military questions, almost innocent of paragraph breaks.

The New York portrait says: "We had a very deep snow some 10 or 12 days ago, and 10 inches on a level, followed by severe, cold norwesters for two or three days. This banked up the snow in parts of the roads higher than the fences and during the continuance of the wind rendered them almost impassable. After it subsided, it required two or three days to open the roads which had to be done by excavating with shovels. Then we had fine sleighing, but the last 3 or 4 days have been mild and rainy."

Captain Lee described how townsfolk stumbled and labored through thick mud and slid around potholes. Then he told about the sleighing carnival:

"Day and night the bells were going and those bitter cold nights the young women kept it up to 10 or 12 o'clock. During its height I went up Broadway to witness it. There was not a wheel carriage to be seen, but a rushing stream of sleighs of all sizes and descriptions flying in both directions. The corners of all the cross-streets into B. W. [Broadway] were crowded with spectators, the men hurrahing, the women laughing, and boys screaming with delight. There were some beautiful turnouts of sleighs and horses. I have never seen such fine horses in New York and the variety of the sleighs and the richness of the furs were beyond my anticipation. But the ladies with their smiling faces and gay dresses exceeded all. Some of the omnibus sleighs were very large. I was in one that carried 50 people. It was drawn by 8 horses. There were many of this size, and one belonging to the same line carried 75. Kip and Brown, I was told, was building one to be out the next day, that would carry 250. There was one called the Oregon drawn by 18 horses, all driven in hand by one man on a seat about 10 feet above them and on a platform behind him there was a full band of music. I did not learn how many passengers it carried, but they went 'the whole or none.' The girls returning from school were the prettiest sight; piled on each other's laps with their bags of books and laughing faces. Indeed there were [sic] no lack of customers at sixpence a ride, and you might be accommodated with a lady in your lap in the bargain.

"Think of a man of my forbiding [sic] countenance, John Mackay, having such an offer. But I peeped under her veil before accepting, and though I really could not find fault with either her appearance or age, after a little demurring preferred giving her my seat. I thought it would not sound well if repeated in the latitude of Wash'n [sic] that I had been riding down B.W. with a strange woman in my lap. What might my little sweethearts think of it, Miss Harriet among the number. [The captain was married to a direct descendant of Martha Custis Washington and had two children, too.] Upon reflection I think I did well, for though you know I am charmed when I can get one of the dear creatures on my knee; yet I have my fancies in this as in other things. I found, however, I was looked upon as such a curmudgeon by my fellow passengers that I took the first opportunity to leave them."

❡ Mr. A. C. M. Azoy of Ardsley-on-Hudson, who has searched the subject, says it is true that Secretary of State William H. Seward's head is superimposed on President Lincoln's body in the statue in Madison Square Park. It seems the committee that was supposed to raise $25,000 for the Seward piece fell 'way short of that amount. It compromised by accepting a body casting of Lincoln made some time before by Randolph Rogers, the sculptor. "The books under Seward's (Lincoln's) chair represent the Constitution," writes Mr. Azoy, "and the paper in Seward's (the President's) hand is the Emancipation Proclamation."

March 23, 1955

❡ For eleven days now, stout green canvas has swathed the monument that covers the grave of Etienne Marie Bechet, the Sieur de Rochefontaine, just inside the fence off the Church Street side of St. Paul's Churchyard downtown.

Passers-by have wondered at the mysterious covering. A few knew that the Sieur de Rochefontaine had rested in the yard for 141 years, and that his urn-surmounted monument had weathered and was crumbling. They figured the canvas might be protection against the harsh winter.

It isn't that. The original monument, gone from marble almost to brown flare and dust, has been removed by the New York City Post of the Society of American Military Engineers. A new monument of more durable material, granite from Westerly, R. I., has gone up in its place. It is that which is hidden.

Unless something forces a change in plan, the covering will not be peeled off until May 6 when thousands of members of the society assemble here for their thirty-fifth annual meeting. The unveiling and dedication are to follow a service in St. Paul's Chapel.

The monument switch is a sentimental gesture. The Sieur de Rochefontaine served under General Washington in the American Revolution until the surrender at

Yorktown. In 1794, when a Congressional act founded a Corps of Artillerists and Engineers, he commanded the unit and whipped it into shape at the encampment that evolved into the United States Military Academy at West Point.

Four years later, the French soldier-engineer dropped his title and set up as Stephen Rochefontaine, merchant, at 107 Reed (now Reade) Street. He died in 1814 in his fifty-ninth year. His daughter, Mme. Catherine Gentil, arranged for his burial in St. Paul's yard and set up a marble monument that was believed to be durable for centuries.

But the monument had a brick core with marble sides and cemented top. Temperature extremes eventually forced openings. Rain, snow and city grime invaded the breached seams. They caused bulges from within. Winds and slow-paced time gradually erased the lengthy inscriptions. Panels flaked almost at a touch.

Military engineers hastening in and out of 90 Church Street knew the story of the Frenchman who had commanded the original military engineers' unit, and they saw the monument's decay. They talked it over and picked a committee to do something about it. Trinity Corporation, which controls St. Paul's Chapel, consented to the substitution. It was achieved at a cost of $6,800.

The north and east panels on the old monument, worn almost to smoothness, pulverized when workmen tried to remove them. The more sheltered west and south panels held together. One, or both, are to be shipped to the Hall of Honor at the French Engineers Technical School in Versailles.

The New York Post of the Society of American Military Engineers plans to send with the panels a handful of earth from the grave, just as the Marquis de Lafayette, on his last visit to the United States, carried home with him a box of American soil to be strewn on his grave in France.

Curiously, there is a certain deposit of soil from Ay in France (where the Sieur de Rochefontaine was born) already on the engineer's grave. It was sent here in 1922 by the Mayor of Ay, along with a container of water from the River Marne, which flows by the city. The soil was consecrated in St. Paul's before it was taken to the churchyard.

One other thing. The monument restoration presented language difficulties. The stonecutters who worked on the original inscriptions used quaint, provincial word versions that baffled modern scholars a little. However, Claude Boillot, who represents the Suez Canal Company here and is an expert on old French, helped the engineers on that point.

The Sieur de Rochefontaine, most distinguished Frenchman buried in United States soil, should sleep well under his new comforter.

March 30, 1955

¶ Zelideth is a dark-haired girl, only 7 years old. Her sight is poor, or was until the Red Cross gave her glasses the other day. She is tiny and shy, as are many of the children of impoverished families who sit with her in Mrs. Bertha F. Smith's second grade class in Public School 75 at 735 West End Avenue.

Every morning for months, when she was on the way to class, Zelideth would see a pretty lady come out of a handsome house and climb into a taxicab. Sometimes Zelideth would linger until the lady came out, just to smile at her and to accept a smile in repayment. That little amenity took place at West End Avenue and Ninety-fifth Street.

A few days ago, as Zelideth waited, the lady came out with a large package done in brown paper, a package almost as large as Zelideth herself. The lady put it in the child's arms and said something, but Zelideth's English is something less than ample. The child did not understand what the lady had said. The lady seemed to sense that. She waved, smiled, popped into a cab and rode away.

At the school door, Zelideth's classmates closed in on her, shrill and wide eyed. They asked questions in Spanish. Zelideth could not tell them what was in the brown package. She stumbled across the threshold with it to Mrs. Smith's desk and surrendered it to the teacher. It took a little time, but Mrs. Smith got the whole story about the smiling lady and the morning meetings.

The second grade held its breath as Mrs. Smith cut the outer wrappings. As the paper fell away, the pupils joined in one sighing gasp. The lady's gift was a soft doll with golden hair and a dress of bright colors. Zelideth's eyes widened, too. Her lips trembled and quivered. Teacher found a card in the package. She quieted the children and read it.

It said: "Honey, here is a little Easter gift from me. One dolly is paper. The other is a dance doll. You slip the elastic under the doll's feet, and under your own. Hold the doll in your arms and she will dance with you. . . . I think you are a lovely little girl." It was signed, "Your friend, Muriel MacFarlan."

When teacher had finished, the children sat in a brief interlude of respectful silence. There was a class conference. Zelideth said she would not have a place for such a big doll in her parents' home, because space is crowded there already. The class joyously voted to keep the doll at school. It voted, too, to make a class project of building a cardboard doll's house—a big one—for it. The doll now belongs to the whole second grade. Each child gets a chance to fondle it a little while.

Mrs. Smith had Zelideth dictate, in broken accent, a note to the Lady of the Morning. It said: "Dear Lady. Thank you very much. That was very nice of you. I am happy about the doll. I love the doll. The doll's name is Sally Marie. I will sing to her to make her go to sleep. I will dance with the doll and I will sing a song to you. Love from your friend, Zelideth."

Teacher added a postscript. It said, "Your gift to Zelideth convinces me that this is really a good, good world."

April 1, 1955

¶ At the same moment two days ago that Congress was petitioned to establish a Theodore Roosevelt Centennial Commission for 1958, the staff at Roosevelt Memorial House at 28 East Twentieth Street was examining 780 letters written by T. R. between 1870-1918 to his sister, Anna Roosevelt Cowles.

The correspondence, a recent gift, is rich in the warm, frank kind of detail you'd expect between brother and sister. Some of the items disclose T. R.'s emotions as he tried to reorganize the New York City Police Department when he was Police Commissioner in 1895-96.

The same letters might be written today, sixty years later, by Commissioner Francis W. H. Adams, who is deeply engaged in the same problems.

On May 19 in 1895 Commissioner Roosevelt wrote, for example: "I have never worked harder than during the last two weeks; I am down at nine and leave the office at six, once at eight. . . . I shall speedily assail some of the ablest, shrewdest men in the city, who will be fighting for their lives, and I know well how hard the task ahead of me is. Yet, in spite of the nervous strain and worry, I am glad I undertook it; for it is a man's work."

On June 8: "I passed [the night] in tramping the streets, finding out by personal inspection how the police were doing their duty. A good many were not . . . and I had a line of huge frightened guardians

of the peace down for reprimand or fine, as a sequel to my all-night walk."

June 16: "Twice I have spent the night in patrolling New York on my own account, to see exactly what the men were doing. . . . The trips did good, though each meant going forty hours at a stretch without any sleep." On June 23: "I make some startling discoveries at times. These midnight rambles are great fun. . . . I get a glimpse of the real life of the [city's] swarming millions. I do really feel that I am accomplishing a good deal."

In February, 1896, as he neared the close of his commissionership, T. R. wrote that he thought his labors had not been wasted. "The work," he told his sister, "was herculean . . . even had I received help from the press and the politicians. As a matter of fact, public sentiment is apathetic and likes to talk about virtue in the abstract, but it does not want to obtain the virtue if there is any trouble about it."

In March, 1896, when it looked as though he was about to be legislated out of the job, T. R. told his sister: "The fact that our Police Department is far more efficient than ever is gradually growing evident even to the dull public mind. . . . If I am turned out it can hardly be until some time in May, so I will have had my year here, and I will have earned six months' rest."

April 4, 1955

¶ Elemental forces that once affrighted men or excited them to awe are entrapped today in vinyl for Atom Age entertainment.

On Friday, for example, the daily journals carried front-page accounts of an earthquake in the Philippines. On the same day, by coincidence, Emory D. Cook, sound wizard, released earthquake recordings for home use.

Six quakes are offered, disturbances that shook the earth between December, 1951, and July, 1952. They ranged from California to the Indian Ocean, deep off Madagascar.

Prof. Hugo Benioff captured them in sound on a seismometer at the California Institute of Technology laboratory in Pasadena. Mr. Cook transferred them from the Benioff tape.

Now anyone can step into a record shop and say, "Sell me an earthquake," and have one wrapped for him on the spot. In the parlor the purchaser can sit back and smugly hear Mother Earth in anger.

He gets the full earthquake effect. Cracking and sundering formations deep in the globe give off vibrations that make the ears slat like window shades. The rooms seem to shake. Some of the quakes burst like thunder. At one point the listener is told to watch the record to see his needle actually imitate earth's writhings in labor.

Probably more startling and awesome is the other side of the same record in which Mr. Cook has embalmed weird sounds from outer space—the music of the cosmos.

These sounds were drawn from the skies by Dr. Millet G. Morgan at Dartmouth's Thayer School of Engineering. They are weirdly patterned swishes, whistles, tweeks and peeps caused by electrical impulses that emanate from celestial spheres.

They bounce off the ionosphere, the fluctuating formation of cosmic dust and air that embraces earth at an elevation of roughly fifty miles. They skip shrilly from hemisphere to hemisphere, and the recording tracks them in their amazing gamboling.

April 6, 1955

¶ Mormons in New York will mark, this coming Sabbath, the 125th anniversary of the founding of their Church of Jesus Christ of Latter-Day Saints.

The actual anniversary is today, but members of the sect, a quiet, thrifty group, will in most cases go about their daily routine as on any other day. Even on Sunday when they meet in their main edifice here, the Manhattan Ward Church at 142 West Eighty-first Street, there will be no elaborate program.

The chances are, if the weather is nice, that some time between the morning and evening church meetings most of the Mormons in Manhattan will go "Eastering." That is an Easter Sunday picnicking tradition back in Utah's hills, and some families continue it here.

Mrs. Thora Allan, who lives in the West Eighty-first Street church with her husband Donald and their three children, said the other day that there must be around 2,000 active Mormons in this metropolis, with the largest concentration—

about 500—on Manhattan Island.

A goodly percentage of these are young men and young women enrolled at colleges and universities on or near Manhattan, but who still have their homes in the West. No one is certain, but Mrs. Allan says there must be around 10,000 Mormons in and around the city who are off the active list.

The ranking Mormon hereabouts is Bishop George E. Watkins. He lives opposite the Manhattan Ward Church, at 153 West Eighty-first Street. He works as an engineer for Consolidated Edison downtown.

G. Stanley McAllister of the Manhattan Ward is a stake counselor, which is a high office, too. (A ward rates about the same as a parish, while a Mormon stake is, more or less, like a diocese.) He is vice president and general manager at Lord & Taylor's department store.

Kenneth H. Beesley, who teaches philosophy of education at Teachers College, Columbia University, attends the Manhattan Ward Church. So does Mrs. Colleen Hutching Vanderweghe, who was Miss America 1952. A large number of men in the congregation are insurance company executives.

Because the Mormons adhere pretty sternly to a policy of self-sustenance wherever they are, men and women from the Manhattan Ward and from other wards and branches in the local stake voluntarily spend week-ends working the stake farm at Washington, N. J.

They raise wheat, corn, cattle, chickens, horses and hogs. The crops are neatly stored against a day of possible need and if a fresh crop comes in before the old is out of the silos, the earlier crop is sold in the open market. Nothing is wasted.

Many non-Mormons somehow have the idea that the Latter-Day Saints are a little on the grim side, socially, but that isn't so. Only last week local sect members held their lively annual Gold-and-Green Ball at the Roosevelt Hotel, with dancing and singing like anyone else.

They eschew tobacco and liquor, but, if anything, are a bit more apt to be merry in their leisure than a great many folk. The town is full of young people from Utah struggling for places on the stage, in TV, radio and in the other arts. It is this group, though, that is likely to slip out of the Mormon orbit, especially those who stay overlong.

The Mormons have had missionaries in New York for something like 110 years. The Eastern States Mission of the sect has headquarters in a house at 973 Fifth Avenue that was designed by Stanford White. It lies almost due east of Manhattan Ward Church, across Central Park.

Queens Ward has around 300 active members, with a church in Little Neck. Brooklyn, a small ward, has its edifice at Gates and Franklin Avenues. There are other branches in Leonia and Short Hills in New Jersey, at Uniondale on Long Island and in Scarsdale, Westchester.

Sect missionaries, always volunteers, do door-to-door proselyting quietly, and mostly through distributing tracts. Converts come in at a rate, roughly, of three or four a month. Baptisms, which call for complete immersion with the subjects clad all in white, are performed in the churches.

April 8, 1955

❡ The three City Fathers whose combined 635 pounds gave them some discomfort in a small taxicab on Tuesday are as babes in arms to the staff in Sig Klein's Fat Men's Shop in Third Avenue between Tenth and Eleventh Street.

The gentleman in charge said yesterday that since the weightiest of the councilmen tips it at only 225 pounds, two of his size would fit into some of the garments that are stock items in the shop.

Suits, underwear, pajamas, bathrobes, fancy vests, overalls, greatcoats and the like start at size 48 in the Fat Men's Shop and run up to size 70. On special orders they have gone to 74 waist size with 82 seat. One of those would fill a new cab.

Bedroom slippers and overshoes run to size 15. Shirts with size 22 neck are staple items, and belts go 'way beyond 70. Neckties for gentlemen who run these proportions are from four to eight inches longer than what the trade calls "basics."

Flipping through store files, the help recalled one customer—dead now—who worked as a mason for Consolidated Edison. He was the 74-waist, 82-seat man, and tipped the scale at 480 pounds up to the time he went off the company

books. They still speak of him with awe.

The store sometimes fills emergency orders. It fetched a 21-size evening-dress collar from Britain by air for the actor Francis L. Sullivan for his part in "Witness for the Prosecution." Close call, too. The collars got to Idlewild one hour before the show on opening night.

Sidney Greenstreet, the movie actor, was a customer until he died. "Actually," the Klein people tell you in a low whisper, "Mr. Greenstreet used padding for his pants toward the end of his career." They have many bits of such quaint information.

Steady shop patrons are, for some undefinable reason, gigantic undertakers and chauffeurs, clergymen, Senators, cattlemen. Several British M. P.'s are listed, too. The store's most poignant regret is that it never got Sir Winston. The staff speaks dreamily of him and estimates that he's a 50 or 52, a good potential.

Incidentally, deeds indicate that the two low gray buildings that house the gargantuan sizes date from 1804. They stand on the old Peter Stuyvesant Farm. Sig Klein, the store's founder, launched the specialty shop back in the Eighties, when most of his customers were German neighbors too fond of their beer.

"The more they drank the bigger they got," the current manager explains, "and Mr. Klein kept stepping up sizes to meet growing demand. Before he realized it he was making haberdashery history."

Fat men who have always had to suffer the jabs of jokesters, now come in for quips involving the small cab. One is about the corpulent passenger who shoe-horned into one of the tight-fitting vehicles. When the driver wanted to know the fare's destination, the anguished answer was: "Drive me to the nearest full-size cab please."

April 11, 1955

❡ The Metropolitan Opera has closed its doors for yet another season, but its vastness is not dark—and almost never is, year round.

All through the twelve months, whether there are shows or not, men toil within the huge hall, in the great storage house at 129th Street and Amsterdam Avenue where the scenery is kept, and in two buildings near the Met.

They make new sets, or parts of new sets. They plane and nail and hammer, paint and refurbish. They take inventory of the company's 10,000 costumes. They count and repair their armory of swords, rapiers, stilettos, shields, halberds, lances.

They assort, each set according to the opera for which it is intended, the great mounds of costume jewelry that performers wear. They inspect and refresh the tiniest props—rosaries, parchment scrolls, medallions and the like.

One man, the administrator of stage departments, oversees the endless task, worries about the almost infinite detail. Temperamental thunderbolts strike where he stands if a prop, a wig or a costume is not where it should be at a crucial moment.

He knows to the last nailhead what must be fetched from the warehouses for each of the sixty-five operas, which have from four to five sets apiece. Some are ancient sets, done over—"Pelléas," "Magic Flute," the old "Don Giovanni"—but they lie in brooding warehouse obscurity, sometimes for many years.

The oldest piece in the warehouse bays right now is the "Love of Three Kings" set, originally put together in 1913. The "Parsifal" scenes and props have been in use thirty-five years without major change. Some parts of sets date back a half century.

Right now the Metropolitan troupe is on a seven-week tour of the United States and Canada with pieces thirty to forty feet high—occasional pieces as long as seventy-five feet. It carries a variety of stage sky drops for thirteen road operas.

Shipping all this in twenty-two freight cars, and arranging nineteen sleepers for performers, is part of the administrator's endless chores, too. He still has nightmares about a "Carmen" set-up that was routed to Boston instead of Cleveland two years ago. Frantic signaling got it back, right on deadline.

Each year the master's crews must moth-proof and flame-proof each set. The Met's own tailors must make new costumes for new versions of an opera, or alter old ones for new performers. There are as many as five different-sized costumes, say, for the male lead in "The Barber of Seville," as many for the different Rosinas.

One of the stage administrator's

odd sidelines is moving among the pieces set up for a performance, especially at wing ends, to search for little indecencies that playful stage hands are apt to chalk on them. He sighs, rubs them out, and moves on. He is a patient, philosophical fellow.

He finds the "Don Carlos" sets the most difficult for handling. They are the most weighty, rich in heavy velour. "Boris Godunov" and "The Masked Ball" couldn't quite be tossed around by midgets, either. Those three, he thinks, are the toughest.

Set-up and breaking-set schedules are fantastic documents, and the movements of the trucks and trailers that bear them to and from the uptown storage bays to the Met, and back, have to be timed almost with railroad precision. A hitch could create a Seventh Avenue sidewalk traffic problem.

April 15, 1955

❡ The greater part of the 1,500 to 2,000 special buses that take Moslem pilgrims from Jedda in Arabia to the Holy Cities of Mecca and Medina were delivered for that service by the Overseas Equipment Company, which has its offices at 350 Fifth Avenue.

John Mermingas, who heads the corporation, started accumulating the buses after World War II. He sent the first freighter-load to Arabia in 1947. Since then he has sent several hundred each year and will have 319 more on the way out of New Orleans between this morning and the end of the month.

Through Mr. Mermingas' effort, and the cooperation of this country's leading motor car and car-body manufacturers, pilgrims now make the journey in a matter of hours. In the old days, when they went by camel, they were in the desert for months.

Six transportation companies in Arabia use the buses exclusively for pilgrims. Each vehicle is colored differently, but when Mr. Mermingas shipped an all-green job it was rejected. Green, it seems, is sacred to Mohammed. It is permitted with other colors, but not alone.

The buses have reclining foam-rubber seats for forty-five passengers. Baggage and tent space is on the roof. They carry drinking water for use between oases. Each bus has two fans, as the pilgrimages are made in July and August. Engineers employed by Mr. Mermingas have made the buses vermin-proof. The seats are plastic-covered and are easily hosed-down.

Special bodies, built for Arabian chieftains and princes, have air-conditioning and refrigeration. Like all the other Mermingas jobs, they have special radiators because of the scorching desert temperatures. The tires are special width, too, for better going through sandy stretches.

Mr. Mermingas has sent over quite a few armored buses, too, but not for pilgrimages. They're used in commerce and have steel-plate siding and shatter-proof windows, because Bedouins on horseback and on camels sally out every now and then for some wild pot-shotting.

Each pilgrimage bus has 800-gallons fuel capacity and there's plenty of oil in Saudi Arabia. It takes more than a tankful for the pull from Bahrein and Kuwait on the Persian Gulf, but a midway refueling oasis takes care of that. The runs from Jedda nowhere near drain the tanks. It's mostly Pacific Moslems from places like Indonesia who come up from the Gulf.

Mr. Mermingas' overseas technicians have had to break in Arabian drivers for pilgrimage service, because non-Moslems are not permitted to enter Holy Cities. The training is done in Jedda. The exporter reports that Arab boys, in spite of their centuries-old camel-riding background, do well behind a bus wheel.

There's no night-driving on pilgrimages. The faithful get out at sundown, pitch their tents before evening prayer, pray again on rising, take off before the sun is fully risen. Their ancestors probably wouldn't believe such a miracle had come to pass, even if they could return to see it.

Beats Sinbad.

April 20, 1955

❡ The city's grating anglers are a rather odd group. They're more than a little careless in their dress; they shuffle rather than walk because they make so many stops in their grate-scanning, and they're inclined, almost unanimously, to be somewhat on the misanthropic side.

Yet the anglers' dean, Sterling H. Parlee, originally of Hartford, Conn., is a neat dresser, moves with sprightly stride and weaves smoothly and easily among the city's populace; he is a genial conversationalist, too, He can't explain why he differs so from the common run in his calling.

Sterling Parlee has fished in subway and New York Central sidewalk gratings for thirty-six of his fifty-two years. He is as good at working the low Seventh Avenue grates, which in some places take only three feet of line, as he is on the difficult ones in streets off Park Avenue where they run as deep as thirty feet.

Men in the trade almost as long as Mr. Parlee won't so much as attempt to work the deep grates. It takes skill to maneuver a greased and metal-weighted line at thirty feet. They say the pendulum's too wide at ten yards. Such fishing calls for an extraordinarily sure hand, which most of them don't have.

Yet Mr. Parlee uses the same equipment that others do—regulation fishing handline, a half-pound weight and petroleum jelly for the stickum that adheres to coins, tokens, rings, trinkets and the long list of other odds and ends that New Yorkers keep dropping through gratings—and does very well at the greater depths.

He concedes that most of the anglers who shun the deep grates are "shakers"—lads who tip the flask too often and too long, and suffer from alcoholic palsy. That gives him the deep grates pretty much for himself, and he's honest enough to admit that he doesn't mind.

West Side subway gratings, generally, yield much more than East Side gratings—from $3.50 to $4, usually, in a six-hour day, which is about all Mr. Parlee ever works. The best fishing hours, he finds, are from daybreak through 11 A.M. After that human traffic gets a bit bothersome. You keep answering questions and don't have time to fish.

It takes an expert to fish things out of soft snow, but Mr. Parlee is good at that, too. Most anglers stay indoors in snowy or rainy weather, but not he. His secret for damp weather angling is a mixture of jelly with thinned-down G. I. soap, cut from the same brown bars that are issued to troops in the field.

The best fishing is at bus stops, subway stations, parking meters and newsstands where people keep dropping change. Mr. Parlee is a little bitter about newsstand owners because most of them have favorite anglers with whom they split, or do the fishing themselves. He thinks that unfair.

The 15-cent fare was a boon to grating anglers. Subway tokens are so small that people drop them as if they were so many peanuts. Times Square parking meters increased the anglers' profit, too. People wearing gloves, who try to put dimes in meters, are most apt to drop them. Mr. Parlee has an eye for that kind of detail in his trade.

The heaviest thing Mr. Parlee ever fished out was a cigarette lighter. That was a delicate job. He has brought up no end of keys; if they have their owner's name he mails them on and almost always gets a light reward. He has fished rings and bracelets, too; sometimes on request, and for reward.

Back in 1932, Mr. Parlee and five other top grating anglers formed a kind of syndicate, took desk space in Times Tower, and advertised special finds in The Times Lost Found column. It was a heroic step toward dignifying the profession, but worked out at a loss. The ads were a little too expensive.

When school lets out in June, Mr. Parlee turns to boardwalk chair pushing, a somewhat more exhausting task. It isn't that people drop less down gratings in summer; it's just that schoolboys swarm over the grates all through school holiday and kind of crowd out the regulars.

April 27, 1955

❡ Stalwarts who man America's gigantic jet bombers at freezing altitudes are not likely to know that the intricate and delicate coils in their ships' computer systems are hand-wound in many cases by this city's lame, halt and legless men and women.

The handicapped, it seems, are more patient and painstaking than normal workers. They are so pitifully eager to achieve perfection that the great aviation companies rarely have to reject an item they make. Rejections of the same kind of work from normal artisans may go beyond 40 per cent.

Air Force and Navy officials who get jet pieces from the work benches at the Federation of the Handicapped at 211 West Fourteenth Street marvel when they see the craftsmen—polio victims, amputees, the tuberculosis and cardiacs, among others.

A good part of the work done at the federation comes in on subcontract. The institution trains about 2,000 men and women every year and breaks them in as switchboard operators, bookkeepers, lettershop craftsmen, secretaries, receptionists, elevator operators and typists.

It gets special equipment for them. Men and women with only one arm, for example, work at left-handed or right-handed typewriters with rearranged keyboards on which they do fifty words a minute or better. Others do packaging for TV advertisers who use air pitchmen to get orders by the thousands.

It is a curious fact that the federation, which now takes on contracts from such concerns as the Bendix Corporation, Remington Rand, Bethlehem Steel and from the armed forces, was started twenty-three years ago by three men who, because of their handicaps, had been forced onto the city streets as panhandlers.

Mike Bertaro, one of the founders, who gets about on a dolly instead of on legs, is still with the federation as workshop supervisor. The two other men have dropped out of sight and even their names are forgotten. It was those three, ashamed of the situation in which they found themselves during the depression, who opened a small furnished room with their meager savings, to act as agents for the handicapped.

One of the artisans at the shop now spends twenty minutes each morning just getting into his car to go to work. Then he has to take another five minutes catching his breath before he puts the car in gear. The evening journey homeward involves the same tortuous routine, yet that man, like others released from slow decay within home walls, is grateful for the chance to earn a living.

The federation has done pretty well, too, with its project for the home-bound, men and women so hopelessly immobilized that they must work in bed. It takes the work to them—bead work, crocheting, slip-stitching for neckties, envelope-addressing, negative-retouching, print coloring—and delivers the end result to the manufacturer.

The visitor to the old Abbott Laboratories building, where the federation operates, may get lump-throated by what he sees. That is natural. But if he studies the faces and sees the inner light that comes through as the craftsmen bend over their tasks, he knows these are souls released from despair, men and women happily snatched from the human salvage heap.

May 2, 1955

¶ People who don't travel with the hunting set or who have no keen interest in firearms are apt to think that muzzle-loaders and flintlocks are to be come upon, these days, only in museums or in private gun collections.

Actually, there's a thriving trade in such weapons. Sporting gentlemen buy them all the time—powder horns and shot and all—and use them to go after birds and deer. You run into flintlock groups all over the country.

The biggest buyers, though, are primitives, mostly in Africa. It seems they're allowed no modern weapons—no quick-action (rapid-fire) repeaters such as white hunters carry—but are permitted to use the old flintlocks.

The Stoeger Arms Corporation in Fifth Avenue between Forty-second and Forty-third Streets, does a brisk traffic in flintlocks, in powder horns and in shot. It sells smooth-bore, single-barrel types at from $32.50; double-barrel from $65.

Modern flintlocks are modern only in their stocks and barrels. The locks themselves are all relics of the Napoleonic Wars. There seems to be an endless reservoir in France, where Stoeger has the weapons made up.

A great many find their way into the deep Belgian Congo. The natives use them to bring down big game. They'd prefer white men's equipment, of course, but colonial governments wouldn't dream of putting rapid-fire into primitive hands.

Experts say the old flintlocks are not too effective beyond about sixty yards. The hammer action is much slower than on later weapons. The black powder poured into them from steer horns (Stoeger sells those too) burns more slowly than newer powders, and flintlock shot is a bit eccentric when there's any wind.

Here in town and in suburban camps you're apt to find flintlocks on the wall. The shop sells quite a few to interior decorators.

May 4, 1955

¶ A third of the ninety-six steel workers putting up the frame for William Kaufman's twenty-story Grand Central Building on the east side of Third Avenue between Forty-fourth and Forty-fifth Streets are Indians who commute to and from Montreal in Canada on weekends.

Because there is so much building on the seaboard right now, steel crews for the assignment were more difficult to assemble than the contractors had thought it might be. Bethlehem Steel, which has the order, scouted from New Orleans to Nova Scotia to get the full complement on the job in time.

Most of the Indians putting up the Kaufman steel are from the Indian reservation near Montreal. They don't think there's much truth to the legend that they're better on high-steel because they're surer-footed than whites.

Des-Hu-Wagana, a young stalwart generally called Aleck, though his name means "Look At Me," says he thinks his tribe got into the trade years ago because the reservation is near the Dominion Bridge Company at Lachine, Quebec, and made a handy labor pool.

It's still true that the Indians don't talk much. On the job they rarely seem to exchange pleasantries, but that must be because rivet-clatter drowns conversation. When they do talk it is more likely to be Mohawk than English, especially if the riveting team is all-Indian, which it frequently is.

The Indians' label for the Nova

Scotia whites, incidentally, is "fish" in the steel trade. The term carries no opprobrium; it merely signifies that when the Nova Scotians are not on steel they're probably out with the home fishing fleets getting their living off the Grand Banks.

The Red Men, incidentally, have no difficulty getting to high-steel jobs anywhere in North America. They carry reservation identification cards that bear their photograph. The card is open sesame at all continental boundaries. They say that was all arranged by treaty.

Most of the married Mohawks have their families in cottages on the reservation near Montreal, which explains their week-end commuting. They prefer the social life up there. Though the ride is eight to ten hours each way, they're always back on the job at 8 o'clock Monday morning. The fact that they haven't slept all night doesn't seem to affect their high-steel walking.

The young, unmarried men are somewhat less likely to join the commuting car pools. Most of them spend their week-ends around Red Hook in Brooklyn, which has an Indian steel-worker colony of 700 to 800. They take their firewater, generally, in a Nevins Street groggery they call the Wigwam.

There's been for years a legend that municipal cops, sheriffs and constabulary can't lay a hand on an Indian if he kicks up after a drinking bout, because he's a ward of the Federal Government, both here and in Canada, and must be taken back to the reservation for tribal justice.

Look-At-Me says that's white-man's hokum. He says, "Red boy get whooping it up in New York, he gets thrown in the clink like any other guy." He didn't once say "Ugh!"

May 6, 1955

¶ A curious turn in the evolution cycle has compelled man to bring hundreds of thousands of his "ancestors" out of jungles in India and the Philippines to help fight the polio plague.

The forays have gone on for ten years now. In 1953 and 1954 men fetched at the rate of 70,000 monkeys each twelve months, a record that may be duplicated in 1955. Thirty thousand more monkeys have been flown into the United States since January—and still they come.

Roughly, three-fourths of the monkey cargoes are air-lifted out of New Delhi in India by Seaboard and Western Airlines. The planes put them down at Idlewild Airport in loads of 800 to 1,600. Then the creatures go to monkey farms and to laboratories.

Seaboard and Western, founded by Air Force men who flew the Himalayan Hump in World War II, has grown in less than a decade into the world's largest all-cargo line. It comes closest at this time to fulfilling Tennyson's prediction that the heavens one day would fill with commerce.

Flying livestock, wild and domestic, is the line's specialty. It started this in 1948 when it brought French racing fillies into Idlewild by way of Shannon and Gander to run at Belmont. In 1949 it flew six elephants to Idlewild out of Bangkok by way of Switzerland and Iceland.

The line has developed special techniques for coddling tropical fish, birds and beasts through subpolar stretches. It has crews standing by at stopover points with rolling machinery that pumps warm air into the cabins until take-off time comes again.

The line's manifests make interesting reading. They list such zoological items as crates of vipers, of pythons, gibbons, tigers, leopards, golden cats, heifers, hens, roosters, frogs, salamanders, chinchillas, bears, guanacos, nyalas, addaxes.

Two weeks ago the line flew 35,-000 day-old chicks to Greece with Harold E. Botsford, professor emeritus of Cornell University, to watch over them in their sky journey. The peepers were gifts from church, school and service groups to help Greek farm rehabilitation.

In its 35,000,000 miles of ferrying livestock above the clouds, Seaboard and Western has maintained a perfect safety schedule. It helped with the Berlin airlift and with the Pacific airlift during the fighting in Korea. It also brought wounded home from Tokyo.

The airline does a lush traffic in G.I. pets, especially dogs. Extraordinarily emotional scenes take place at landing spots when pooches, wriggling ecstatically, rejoin their masters. The line has carried as many as fifty-three dogs and one cat on a single run out of Frankfort in Germany. On one flight a German shepherd had a litter of three pups. They all came down in good shape at Idlewild.

When Doris Duke got lonesome for her two police dogs in Paris not long ago, Seaboard and Western wafted them across the North Atlantic for her. It carried Nathoo, the Aga Khan's 3-year-old, across the ocean three times in one month. Animals, it seems, take kindly to air travel, but are likely to get seasick on ocean liners.

Perhaps the most anomalous story told among the cargo-fliers is about Edmond H. Mitchell of Yonkers, an S. and W. pilot. He was with a B-29 group that destroyed the Palembang oil refineries at Sumatra in August, 1944, when they were enemy-held. Four years later, in May, 1948, he came down in Palembang with a load of materials for rebuilding the refineries.

There's a human touch, too, in the way the line is run. Crates that hold dogs and other domestic pets all carry pasters in red and buff. The labels say: "Handle With Love."

May 11, 1955

❡ New York's most interesting sandman is a woman. She sends sand to Saudi Arabia, to Liberia and to Algiers and gets good prices for it, though those places have no sand shortage.

Her sand is so good and so unusual that the armed forces eagerly buy it in lots up to 15,000 tons and fly it up close to the North Pole to use in concrete mix for weather stations, runways and other construction they don't talk about much. Britain's men-o-war buy sizable quantities of it.

The lady's special sand turns up on battleships and aircraft carriers to buttress gun emplacements. It is placed in sand traps on the best golf courses and is standard in the cigarette urns you see in theatre lobbies and such places. It was considered the very best mortar mix for use in constructing the United Nations building.

The sandwoman is Mrs. William A. Hannig, a gray-haired, soft-featured lady who wears rimless spectacles. She is a grandmother six times over. She has been in sand, so to speak, for twenty-five years—took over when her father died in 1930.

She was Carolyn Exner before her marriage. Her husband, retired now, was for years a Board of Education examiner. He keeps his hand out of sand. She runs her business as Exner Sand and Gravel Corporation on Westchester Creek in the Bronx. Sand scows come right up from Port Jefferson to the drying and sifting plant.

Father Exner never got as deeply into industrial sand as his daughter has. He hand-dried the stuff, distributed it to pet shops and to traction companies with a horse-drawn cart. Trolley lines found his sand better than any other in damp weather; it gripped where undried sand slipped.

All Mrs. Hannig's sand comes from Long Island Sound. At one time she had her own dredge—got it from a contractor who had defaulted on loans she made to him—

and her own tug. She sold them because she decided it wasn't wise to spread her efforts. She stuck to processing and selling sand.

East River Drive construction drove her from a site she had on the waterfront at 109th Street. She picked the Bronx spot and set up the new place in 1939 with the last batch of available construction steel before the Government monopolized the supply.

The Westchester Creek plant was expensive. Friends and family begged Mrs. Hannig to forego it. She quietly ignored them, put in an oil-fired sand dryer and the most efficient sand-screening system she could devise. Now her enterprise does better than $1,000,000 a year.

The Exner screens produce sand finer than most powders and grades up to pebble size; all for different uses. The finest stuff sells for $200 a ton; makes such tight concrete that damp can't get into it. That's what was flown to Thule, and beyond.

The grades that go to the desert countries are used for blasting oil scum from oil-tank interiors. They're used too, in blasting paint from old ships. These and other industrial applications more than make up for the loss that came when Board of Health regulations stopped skyscraper sandblasting in this city.

The sandwoman's product is sold all over the world for water-filtering systems, for replenishing private beaches, for weighting tumble-toys, for gravelling penthouse garden paths, in dental laboratories, in polishing marble, etching fine glass and finishing steel. The Plaza Fountain gravel is hers. So is the gravel outside the Frick Museum.

When the Japanese attacked Pearl Harbor, Mrs. Hannig hurried from a cocktail party to her plant and whipped her crews all that Sunday night to load special sand to replace what was lost at Pearl Harbor by the Navy. It was special foundry sand. It got across the Pacific all right.

Special sand is used on H-Bomb and A-Bomb projects, but Mrs. Hannig doesn't know exactly how. She bid for sand contracts on such Government deals, but somehow lost out. Altogether she serves around forty industries.

And she stands in her own sand when she's at her penthouse parapet on Park Avenue. That seems consistent in a sandwoman.

May 13, 1955

¶ The sleepy New York Public Library lions, forty-four years old today, have become international figures. Not infrequently mail for the staid institution they dreamily guard comes addressed to "The Lion Library."

Karl Kup, curator of the print collection within the pale walls, recalls that on a visit to Tokyo he was asked: "Are you from the Lion Library?" He said he was. A G.I. once got the library to cancel a date for him by directing a telegram to the girl "Care of the North Lion, Public Library."

The carved cats never got official names, except that Mayor LaGuardia once called them "Patience" and "Fortitude." Someone stole a nine-foot Christmas collar off one at Yuletide in 1953, but that was evened when some whimsical fellow, never identified, put a garland of daffodils around one lion's neck.

E. C. Potter, who carved the pair, originally gave them greater manes, but when the models were put up, passers-by wrote letters to the papers. They thought the lions' chests too hairy. So Mr. Potter shaved the beasts a little, and that's the way they were put up in pink Tennessee marble.

¶ When a fireman dies in line of duty tradition calls for city-wide tolling of a sepulchral 5-5-5-5 signal on all fire bells and over the department's radio.

On May 5 the toll went out twice—once for Fireman Andrew K. Wright, dead in a fire at Pitt and Madison Streets, then for Fireman Fred L. Cumming, who lost his life in a fire at 14 Ferry Street, ten blocks away.

No one seemed to notice it right away, but Commissioner Edward F. Cavanagh Jr. and Chief of Department Peter Loftus later realized the 5-5-5-5 calls had gone out by grim coincidence on the fifth day of the fifth month of "fifty-five," something that could happen only once in 100 years.

May 23, 1955

¶ Seed-corn-size transistors are being planted atop 8,400 street lamps on Manhattan and in the Bronx. They automatically switch the lamps on or off, according to the amount of light around them.

Broadway Maintenance Corporation, whose crews have the planting assignment, say the transistors should last almost forever. They replace the glass-tube photoelectric cells, which were much larger and apt to shatter. The transistors should need hardly any care, which means municipal saving.

If the city sky darkens under storm cloud, the transistors make the lamps glow; if the sun comes out a few seconds later, its light throws the transistor switch to "off." The corn-kernel gadgets are affected by dawn and dark, too, of course.

The installation crews test them by tossing their caps over them, which turns the lamps on. Lifting the caps off puts the lights out again.

May 30, 1955

❡ The city's—and the nation's—first Memorial Day was observed eighty-seven years ago today. It grew out of General Order 11 issued May 5, 1868, by Gen. John Alexander Logan, Commander of the Grand Army of the Republic.

It prescribed no specific form for the ceremonies, but called for "strewing with flowers or otherwise decorating the graves of comrades who died in defense of their country during the late rebellion, and whose bodies now lie in almost every city, village and hamlet churchyard in the land."

There was no parade in New York City nor in the City of Brooklyn on the first Memorial Day; only small groups of men in blue moving in carriages to local cemeteries with flowers and with battle flags still brave and new.

The First Long Island Volunteers, for example, bore to Green-Wood Cemetery in Brooklyn, where the greatest numbers congregated, the colors they had borne in battle.

George W. Collier, the city's last G.A.R. man, died eleven years ago.

June 22, 1955

❡ A tranquil spot, unchanged for more than 100 years in The City of Endless Change, is the four-story brownstone with brass handrail up the high stoop, with old picket fence and curtained high windows, at 110 Second Avenue, between Sixth and Seventh Streets.

It came briefly into the news the other day when the Lucy Stone League gave the House of Detention for Women in Greenwich Village a library as memorial to Abigail Hopper Gibbons, a Betsy Trotwood kind of Quaker lady who founded the Women's Prison Association here 110 years ago.

The old brownstone, built around 1830 and, like The Old Merchant's House in East Fourth Street, one of the few perfect relics of America's Neo-Classic period left on the Island, is called the Isaac T. Hopper Home. Isaac Hopper was Abigail's father.

The Home is run today pretty much as it was when Abigail Gibbons presided over it eighty years ago. It takes in for shelter, on its plain upper floors, girls and women freshly released from New York prisons; gives them a chance to steady their feet before they try to pick up the severed social thread.

The regime is nowhere near as stiff as it was in Abby Gibbons' time. Then, girls were taught trades to prepare them for self-support in the community. Many were Irish or German immigrant girls who had landed in the mesh because they had no skill or calling. There is less need, now, for such training.

The sad irons and fluting irons with which the boarders turned out crisp ladies' linens eighty years ago are piled, now, in the storage room. The old sewing kits are laid away. Miss Dorothy Koelsch, the gentle lady who runs the Home now, places the accent on social, medical and psychological aid.

In its early days the home sheltered as many as forty to fifty at a time; now, rarely more than nine or ten. The girls have a great measure of freedom—they date, go on inexpensive little picnics, on nights out that may mean dinner at the Automat and a movie. They must be in by 10 o'clock; and they almost always are.

Two quiet house mothers watch over them. They spend rainy evenings in the old English basement kitchen where the 100-year-old house call bells still dangle, mute. The old wooden settle still has its place at the table. Outside, Trees of Heaven shade the old patio and the girls sit under Manhattan's stars there on summer evenings.

Miss Koelsch goes out with some of the grimmer cases that come to the Home. She has spent quiet evenings in long strolls with girls and women who have been up for murder, with rebellious spirits who have flared up in felonies; with teen-agers who have tripped one way or another.

The girls form a kind of alumnae group. They drop in for calls long after they have left; write or telephone from distant places where they have comfortable homes and prosperous families; talk of the peace that came to them in the old brownstone on Second Avenue.

Miss Koelsch, who smiles easily, likes the familiar line that turns up in alumnae letters: "Give my regards to all the ladies in The Hopper."

June 27, 1955

❡ Among the gifts that will come today under Helen Keller's sensitive fingers as she marks her seventy-fifth birthday will be a lovely volume in dark-red morocco.

She will not see the color, but she will be able to trace with her fingertips the inscription done in raised letters on the top cover. It will read: "For Helen Keller, Beloved President, The John Milton Society."

Between the rich covering are bound 100 letters from different branches of the John Milton Society all over the United States. Most of these are typewritten.

The binding was done in a Dickensian shop under the skylights on the top floor of a rickety loft building at 39 Union Square West—an establishment cluttered with ancient book presses, old type cases, bookbinders' tools made more than 100 years ago.

Anton Bailer, who runs the shop, is the son of a bookbinder. He was apprenticed to his father, Karl, in Stuttgart when he was little more than 13, fifty-three years ago. So were three of his five brothers. Two are binders now in the Government Printing Office in Washington.

Anton is white-haired, now, of the vanishing breed of book craftsmen who set high standards in medieval times. He uses, basically, the same equipment they did—the same flour paste, the same wooden-frame sewing bench, the same instruments for leather tooling.

He still works with precious moiré silks, with hand-marbled, handmade end papers, with egg albumen where others have taken to modern synthetic sizing. He still fondles ancient volumes with the touch that betrays affection and reverence. He can do wonders with a foxed and bitten document 500 to 600 years old.

He has worked for the late Frank Crowninshield, for Lewis Douglas, Edith Wetmore, Clare Booth Luce, among others, through the years. But he put no greater care into the special bindings he did for them than into the red volume for the extraordinary woman who shall know it only by touch.

July 8, 1955

❡ Quite by accident the other day some file-worm stumbled onto a run of stories in The New York Times, written 100 years ago, that might well have carried the same general caption as a current series —the pieces labeled, "Our Changing City."

The first, on Aug. 11, 1855, told about street breakthroughs in the rocky regions east and west of what would one day be the Times Square-Rockefeller Center area. In open spaces between the rocks there, and by running streams, poverty-pinched Irish and German immigrants had built shantytowns, overrun with dogs, pigs and goats.

"Never before," The Times man wrote, a little breathlessly, "have there been so many improvements under way in our city as at present. There is scarcely a street in which one or more new, substantial buildings are not being erected in the place of others too old or too small to meet the requirements of advancing trade; and many downtown streets are being widened and straightened to accommodate their constantly increasing commerce."

The greatest single development, downtown, was the widening of Canal Street at a cost of $480,000. Old Knickerbockers in town had opposed it as rash; what had been wide enough for their forefathers was wide enough for them. The City Fathers, though, had visions; so did real estate men.

They predicted that Canal Street would replace Wall Street as the banking center. The Times man hedged on this. He wrote, "This may be too sanguine a belief." He must have carried a clearer crystal ball.

In another part of his story he showed "certain improvements being made in the upper part of the city, between Thirty-eighth and Fifty-fourth Streets, by the Corporation [the City] and by private individuals."

He reported Fifty-third Street being cut through "from the Seventh Avenue to the East River," and Watts and Seeley, two bold real estate men, running up a full block, sixteen new houses, in Fifty-third, between Eighth Avenue and Broadway. This was looked upon as downright mad. The horse stages did not run north of Forty-second Street.

From Thirty-eighth to Forty-second Street, reported The Times man, on the "Changing City" in 1855, the city was cutting through from Hudson shore to "the Seventh Avenue." He didn't think much would be done east of that. He wrote (and here his crystal ball clouded a little), "It will take immense labor to extend them (Thirty-eighth to Forty-second) through the rocky barriers to the east."

Thirty-ninth Street, he noted, was unfit for carriages; filled with sloughs and stagnant ponds. East of Seventh Avenue, from Thirty-eighth to Forty-second Street and northward, seemed impassable.

"Our reporter who has examined the rocks and the groups of wooden shanties scattered through them, reminding one of Indian wigwams," said The Times, "thinks it would be almost as easy to penetrate to Sebastapol [then under siege by an allied British-French force, and much in the news] in despite of its towers, to make carriages run here."

Another Times man did "Dutch Hill," a swarming immigrant shantytown that covered all the rocky land from Forty-first Street to Forty-fourth, East River to around Third Avenue, part of the land on which the United Nations stands in pale formation, now.

"The village called Dutch Hill, which with the neighboring shanties must contain thousands of people," The Times man reported, "is almost precisely like the poorest Irish villages; and poorer than most German hamlets."

Welfare agency reports told why. The immigrants were in full flood, then, and had been for several years, and there were no living quarters for them. Besides, they had no money for rents. They lived mostly on rag-picking and on what they could grow in beggarly gardens.

And the change goes on, endlessly on.

July 13, 1955

❡ America's oldest trade school, run by the General Society of Mechanics and Tradesmen of the City of New York, operates quietly in the six-story Indiana limestone and Roman brick building (originally the Berkeley Preparatory School) at 16-24 West Forty-fourth street.

The society was organized at Walt Heyer's tavern in Pine Street 170 years ago. Its 135-year-old school for apprentices is free. So is its library of 139,000 volumes, which started when the school did as "The Apprentices' Library." Its lock collection and its museum of general relics is open to the public.

On April 17, 1790, the society marched in a solemn body at the funeral of "our late brother mechanic, Benjamin Franklin." It turned out, full membership, for the funeral procession of "Lieutenant-General George Washington" in 1799; paced behind the coffin of Alexander Hamilton in 1804.

When work was started on City Hall in 1802, six brother mechanics had prominent assignments on the job—the architect, John McComb Jr.; the master stonecutter, Abraham Labogh; two master masons, Anthony Steenback and Arthur Smith; the master carpenter, Joseph Newton, and the construction clerk, James Hopson.

Eight years later the society started the Mechanics' Bank, the fourth chartered bank in the city, and after name changes—Mechanics National, Mechanics and Metal National—was merged with Chase National, now Chase Manhattan. In the Eighteen Forties the society's lecture rooms were used by Christy's Minstrels, though some of the sterner brother mechanics didn't like that idea very much. .

The society moved into its present building in 1898, less than ten years after it had been built for Berkeley Prep, which shared space in the block with the Vanderbilt stables and the stables of other wealthy New Yorkers. The school's drill hall, 85 by 100 feet and three stories high, is filled with library stacks now, but the old railed galleries still look down on it.

The building had one of the earliest air-conditioning systems when the society took it over—a smooth-masoned duct device with an electric roof fan to force out used air. This was done away with when the society added a sixth floor and machinery penthouse some time later. The Mossman Lock Collection, too seldom seen by New Yorkers, occupies one side of the gallery, the museum another. The whole place has a delightful Nineties air—white marble and dark paneling, everywhere.

School ritual hasn't changed much in 135 years, but the courses have. There were no railroads, ocean liners, motor cars, TV's, telephones, radios, airplanes when the society was founded, but as old trades vanished the society school replaced them with new ones. The curriculum is right up to date now, in virtually every modern trade. All told, the school has turned out around 120,000 graduates since classes started in 1820.

July 18, 1955

¶ Percy Griffith, a salt-water man with long sea duty behind him, does marine patrol now, on foot, landlubber fashion. He has served summonses to a Queen (the Mary), to the proud Ile de France, to fat-bellied ferryboats and to the harbor commoners, the tugboats. He has five-borough jurisdiction.

Percy is Inspector 71 for the Department of Air Pollution Control of the City of New York. He walks the shore spotting craft with powerful binoculars, as they come into or leave the harbor, to see whether they're blowing their stacks. He often tags big vessels right at quayside.

One busy day last week Inspector Griffith put the arm on both the Ile de France and on the Greek Line's Olympia as they lay, respectively, at the south and north sides of Pier 88 in North River, and on American Export's Exvrook at Pier 84.

Then he faced a puzzler. The slim-waisted French warship Jean Bart came up-river with heavy smoke billowing from her stacks. The inspector waited until she made her pier, learned that the United States Navy had some officers aboard and talked it over with them.

The upshot was that the Jean Bart escaped the indignity of a summons. The Navy men, though, undertook to pass to her chief engineer a French translation of Chapter 47 of the Administrative Code. It says, in effect: "Ocean-going vessels shall not operate soot blowers . . . within the waters . . . under the jurisdiction of the City of New York."

The city, Mr. Griffith confides, prints its warning notice only in English. He had just got the French version from the chief engineer of the Ile de France, who had had copies made for his own boiler-room crew.

Inspector Griffith holds a license as chief marine engineer. He held that rank on the Booker T. Washington through World War II as she ran troops and supplies to Eu-

rope and Africa. He was in the same post when the B. T. W. ran troops and supplies to Japan and Korea after trouble broke out in the Far East.

The smoke summonses are almost never served on ship's officers, the inspector explains, because ships often have to slip away before the cases come to court. The ship's New York agents, or its owners, get the summons instead. Fines generally run from $25 to $50, go to $75 if a violation is repeated.

When Mr. Griffith came ashore in 1952 to take the smoke patrol, harbor tugboats were the worst stack blowers. They've reformed since. The Queen Mary coughs up a bit of smoke now and then, but the Queen Elizabeth never does. The difference lies, the inspector says, in the type and age of their equipment. He's apt to get technical on that phase of his work.

Mr. Griffith has no jurisdiction over American warcraft, even in New York Harbor. The Navy can ignore his warnings, but since the Navy is traditionally polite, it always answers in proper form, promising cooperation, which, in truth, it gives.

The inspector, a soft-voiced fellow, knows all the ships by their smokestack colors even when he can't spot their names, but he always checks against official sailing and port-entry records to avoid an embarrassing error. He'd like a launch for his job, but the City Department of Marine and Aviation won't lend one.

The department has been in a

sort of huff, it seems, since the late
Clyde McGovern, Inspector Griffith's predecessor, used a department launch to chase after city
ferryboats with summonses.

One other note: Inspector Griffith got to scanning the summons
records at the office one day and
came across a 1951 entry that made
him grin. It told of a violation by
the Booker T. Washington, whose
chief engineer at the time was—
Percy Griffith.

July 25, 1955

¶ Probably the most active farm in
New York City lies, incongruously,
in the East River. It is on Rikers
Island, and is worked by men from
the city's penitentiary and work-
house.

The Department of Correction's
annual report, just out, tells quite
a bit about it. In 1885, you learn,
the island covered only eighty-
seven acres when the tide was in.
By 1930, with accumulations of city
waste dumped on its margins, the
island has grown to 500 acres,
which is just about what it is now.

Last year, felon farmers raised
10,895 pounds of chicken and gathered 5,917 dozen eggs on their poultry range. They brought in a vegetable crop that came to 59,315
pounds.

In the last sixteen years they've
grown 75,000 trees for the City
Park Department and 70,000 flow-
ering shrubs. They have a sizable
peach orchard—268 trees—and get
a crop from that, too.

The farm output is for city institution kitchens, mostly for city
prisons. The bakery on the island
turned out over 2,000,000 loaves
last year for the prisons and for
public school lunch rooms.

The report itself, a rather fat
volume, closes with a proud nota-
tion: "This report was printed at
the inmate print shop at the Penitentiary of the City of New York."

¶ Mr. Arthur Klar has sold refreshments to music lovers in the city
for more than forty years, most recently at Lewisohn Stadium and at
the New York City Center of Music
and Drama.

As the Lewisohn Stadium concerts near the season's end, he has
submitted a profound report on
music lovers' eating habits, based
on a careful survey of two years'
sales at the stadium.

"It is an irrefutable fact," the
learned vendor says, "that Brahms,
Beethoven and Bach go better with
beer; that Gershwin and popular
music go better with soft drinks,
though mostly with ginger ale."

Curiously, the sales figures are
about the same either way—twenty-
to-one for beer on long-hair music
nights at the stadium, twenty-to-
one for soft drinks on pop nights.

Mr. Klar contributes one other
important observation: that long-
hairs cannot stand the disturbing
crackle of popcorn and potato
chips, while crowds that go to popular music concerts consume those
noisy comestibles in quantity.

"These facts," Mr. Klar says
without qualification, "are con-
clusive."

July 27, 1955

❡ In the early morning on Sept. 16, 1878, a frightening rumble and clatter outside the window awakened a five-year-old boy in his bedroom over Lyman G. Bloomingdale's hoop skirt and ladies' notions shop on Third Avenue betwen Fifty-sixth and Fifty-seventh Streets.

A locomotive chugged by the window, chestily pulling a string of plush-seated elevated railroad cars. Their passage shook the ground. Morning sunlight through the railroad ties made interesting patterns on the cobbled street. It was something for a little boy to wonder at.

Now the little boy is a white-haired gentleman who counts eighty-two years of living. The morning when the Third Avenue train made its first run on the new stretch between Forty-second and Sixty-seventh Streets is only a dim memory, but because the boy was part of the road's beginning, he has been picked to be in on the beginning of its end next Monday at noon.

There will be an El wake at that hour. Then the wreckers will take over.

The boy was Samuel J. Bloomingdale, son of the founder of the Bloomingdale Department Store. He was born above the hoop skirt shop one June morning in 1873, and the Third Avenue El has always been part of his life. It helped his father to prosper until Bloomingdale's eventually covered the entire block from Fifty-ninth Street to Sixtieth between Third and Lexington Avenues.

In the beginning, when it was mainly a hoop skirt establishment —his father journeyed up and down the Hudson and up and down the Ohio getting orders for hoop skirts—that part of Yorkville was mostly fairly new brownstone houses, with brick and brownstone tenements farther north. The tough boys lived up north and the Sixties were Battle Row. The hoop skirt maker's son had to use his legs for quick getaways up in that region. The Battle Row kids were lusty fellows.

Samuel Bloomingdale remembers that in his boyhood Third Avenue was rich in spotless German restaurants shaded by willow trees in summer. He liked to look through the windows and study the Rhine scenes on the wall murals; to sniff the scent of good cooking.

He roamed neighborhood streets with other kids. They loved to watch the railroad men hitch an extra horse to the Fifty-ninth Street cars for the pull over Park Avenue ridge. He liked to roam in the Park Avenue hollows, among the shanties where goats and pigs foraged beside the New York Central Railroad cut; to engage in shrill snowball battles there; to feast on peanuts and bolivars sold at open-air stands where the Plaza is now. Bolivars were large round ginger cakes with scalloped edges. They sold for a penny.

In those days the Third Avenue line carried gentry as well as poor folk downtown to Wall Street and South Ferry. No one laughed at the elevated railroad then. It was new, and rather grand. Mr. Bloomingdale is saddened a little sometimes by the way folk came to scoff at its pot-bellied stoves and stained-glass station windows. He says they were part of a rich era, and wonderful for their time.

Mr. Bloomingdale remembers that when his father built his model department store at Fifty-ninth Street and Third Avenue in 1886, he got perpetual advertising rights at the Fifty-ninth Street station.

It was young Samuel's idea to give free red-and-white-wedged sun umbrellas to dray drivers in New York. Within a year more than 5,000 were dispensed, all proclaiming that "All Cars Transfer to Bloomingdales." One of the umbrellas even turned up, in some mysterious way, on a hotel lawn in far-off Carlsbad.

"Now," Mr. Samuel says, "all those are faded memories. The Third Avenue El will be only a memory, soon, and its pot-bellied stoves and its colored-glass signs will turn up in museums. That is the way of all things."

August 5, 1955

❡ Workmen digging in the lawn around lovely old St. Luke's Chapel at Hudson and Grove Streets the other day found dozens of century-old tombs under the topsoil.

They were untenanted. A search in chapel records showed that village parishioners who had slept in them had been taken up in their coffins about sixty years ago. They sleep now in Trinity's graveyard uptown, at 155th Street and Broadway.

Most of the tomb covers—flat marble slabs that cover the staircases leading down into the brick vaults—were back in place with their inscriptions still clear.

When St. Luke's new Primary Day School goes up on the Greenwich Street side of the ancient church grounds, the topsoil will be put back on the empty vaults and the grounds will be landscaped. A path will run through the north yard.

St. Luke's curates, when the tombs were first uncovered, checked the vault numbers. They found that famous as well as humble folk had slumbered in their yard. Under Number 18 had reposed Clement C. Moore, who had written "The Night Before Christmas." He had been a warden at St. Luke's.

The curates found records on Ten Broecks, Ketchums, Havemeyers, Pickwells, Warrens and Snowdens among other old New York clans. The sleepers had included at least one Mayor of New York, J. A. Westervelt, who had the City Hall high seat from 1853 to 1855.

A parish memorandum from William Waldorf Astor, dated May 25, 1882, when there was a motion to move the 700 sleepers from the old churchyard, shows his anxiety for secrecy in the transfer.

He wrote to the Rev. Isaac H. Tuttle from his house at 21 West Twenty-sixth Street: "It would be especially unpleasant to me were any mention of this inserted in any newspaper." He had kin in the yard.

St. Luke's and its auxiliary buildings make a charming study in ruddy, everlasting brick. When some of the houses in the chapel square came down a few months ago, decorators bid avidly for their doors and moldings. They were cut from primitive Greenwich Village forest trees.

In the beginning, in 1822, when the chapel was St. Luke's-in-the-Field—literally that—meadows and gurgling streams lay all about. Parishioners at Manhattan's tips sailed up to it on the Hudson, or rode the Indian trails or glossy mounts.

The red-brick vicarage, just south of the chapel, is the oldest (1823) in continuous use in the city. The companion structure just north of the church lawn was Bret Harte's boyhood home, guided across the meadows by its rich-toned bell.

In the chapel's sanctuary floor, in front of the red marble high altar, is embedded the white vault cover taken from the tomb of Good Dame Catherine Ritter, in whose village farmhouse the chapel congregation was formed.

The first worshipers in St. Luke's-in-the-Field were families that had fled the lower city when yellow fever raged there. The two Glastonbury thorn trees in the churchyard were brought from Britain by early communicants.

The legend is that they were seedlings grown from thorn trees that branched from the staff thrust into graveyard soil at Benedictine Abbey in Old Glastonbury by St. Joseph of Arimathea. In the same abbey, according to another legend, King Arthur slept. The St. Luke's thorns bloom at Christmas.

The Italian marble altar in the pale Lady Chapel in St. Luke's originally was in St. John's Chapel, another Trinity edifice that stood in Varick Street. The Rev. E. H. Schlueter, vicar of St. Luke's, saw it on the sidewalk one day in 1909, when St. John's came down.

He asked the contractor, "What is to become of that altar?" and the contractor blushed. He said, "We had an offer for it from a druggist. He wants it for an ice cream counter." The indignant vicar blocked that sale. He got it for St. Luke's-in-the-Field.

August 10, 1955

❡ Passers-by have been puzzled for years by the bronze rat-and-hawser rods that hold the heavy marquee of the Graybar Building, on the west side of Lexington Avenue between Forty-third and Forty-fourth Streets. No one in the building could explain what they stood for.

The other day, though, a letter came through from Herbert Metz, Eastern district manager for Graybar, to give the answer. He was advertising manager when the structure was finished in 1926.

"The architect," Mr. Metz explains, "tried to symbolize the fact that the Graybar Building was the focal point in the country's greatest maritime and railroad center. The rat-and-hawser motif is there to symbolize a ship and, in turn, a port. The rat on the hawser, baffled by the rat-guard, is trying to get into the ship. The circle of rat heads on the side of the hawser typify the rats *in* the ship.

"You will see some grasshoppers in the design, too, because, as in the song, 'Grasshoppers sat upon the railroad track.' And, too, you will see a number of albatrosses—birds of the sea—carved here and there."

August 12, 1955

¶ A little volume turned up the other day by Mr. A. K. Baragwanath, librarian for the Museum of the City of New York, will give no comfort to the grumps who hold that Gotham weather isn't what it used to be.

The book was published in 1850 by R. Craighead, a printer at 112 Fulton Street, for his neighbor, A. J. Delatour, who sold "medicinal waters, plain and flavored with syrups," at 25½ Wall Street, a business he had taken over from Lynch and Clarke.

The volume is titled, "Delatour's Record of the Thermometer from 1840 to 1850." It lists readings taken in the shade outside the waters shop four times each day over the ten-year period. Readings were at 6 A.M., noon, 3 P.M. and 6 P.M.

The earliest records in Mr. Delatour's work were written thirty-one years before the oldest existing official Weather Bureau readings. They tend to show that city temperatures 115 years ago were much like today's.

July was then, as now, the hottest month. In the decade of Delatour observations the lowest July high temperature was 90 degrees on the 27th, in 1842; the highest, 99 degrees, in 1844.

Annual average for the 1840-50 period was 54.3, which is more or less the same as now. The warmest year was 1848, with 56.5 average; the coldest, 1843, with 52.4 average. The only three-day August spell with readings of 90, or over, between 1840 and 1850 came in 1846 —Aug. 5, 91 degrees; Aug. 6, 93 degrees; Aug. 7, 90 degrees.

Mr. Delatour included in his little book readings kept at Bloomingdale Insane Asylum, on Morningside Heights, then well north of the city. The observers were Dr. Charles Nicholls and George W. Endicott, warden.

The entries have a delightful bucolic touch, as in the Asylum's 1849 spring weather diary:

"Mar. 5. First vessel seen bound up North River; March 6, River opened to Verplank's Point; Mar. 7, River opened to West Point; Mar. 14, Sowed peas; Mar. 16, Snow disappeared, bluebirds seen; Mar. 17, Crocus bloomed; Mar. 27, Cold blustering storm with snow. Many trees down."

A postscript advised that, "On the 9th there was an eclipse of the moon. The Aurora Borealis was visible on the evening of the 18th."

August 15, 1955

¶ A scrivener who earns his bread in town but lives with his wife and three young daughters in East Meadow on Long Island brought a relic of his own boyhood—he's around 40—into the house the other day, and the impact was astonishing.

Most of the scrivener's neighbors tend to follow the modern trend in child-raising. They have converted cellar space into bars for their sophisticated older boys and girls and stand a little in awe of their offspring's knowledge about electrons, TV, outer space, the jet principle and such subjects.

A somewhat wiser parent and less pliable in the hands of his Atom Age children, the scrivener thought it would be better for his daughters if he took them backward in time, if he brought them some of the flavor of his Third Avenue childhood.

He hit on the idea of converting the basement play space into some semblance of an old Third Avenue flat. He got a wood-burning stove, an iron sink, an old-fashioned round kitchen table and all manner of long-outmoded kitchen gadgetry, most of it in junk shops along Third Avenue.

He had fond memories of the pianola that had made evenings clamorous in his boyhood. He thought it would be no problem to find one, but the quest dragged through weeks until the scrivener, a gaunt fellow, just wasted and grew grim and somewhat bitter in frustration.

Wurlitzer's told him they hadn't handled a pianola in something like thirty years. Other piano shops said they got one now and then, but always sold it for the wood case. It seems men who build small boats find pianola mahogany perfect for that.

One day last week he landed a Winters Piano Company pianola, a dignified wreck with its insides rusted. The fever burned so brightly in his eyes that a Winters official had his repair men get it back in working order. One night last week it was maneuvered into the East Meadow basement.

Telling about his children's reaction, the scrivener went philosophically soft. He said: "Here were my daughters—9, 13 and 14—who confound me with their knowledge of everything new and modern, who know about cathode tubes and nuclear fission, about space flight and man-made satellites, but virtually nothing about the world I had known in my childhood."

The girls pinked the old upright's keys at random, managed limping tunes on it, but had no idea it was a mechanical piano. The scrivener had learned in his quest, incidentally, that piano rolls are still manufactured in the Bronx by the Modern Music Company, that Macy's keeps right up to date on them for the benefit of a long list of customers and that you can get the tunes of the latest musicals on pianola rolls for 79 cents apiece. Old rolls sell in junk shops for around 19 cents.

After dinner, the night the piano came, the writer cunningly told his daughters: "Daddy is going downstairs to see if he can still play the piano as he did at college. You stay here with Mother. I don't like people at my shoulder when I'm playing, any more than I do when I'm writing."

He got into the basement with a

smuggled-in roll version of "Dardanella" he had picked up at Macy's. He fixed it in place, worked the pedals and the volume gadget with a violence inspired by sheer sentiment. He heard his children squeal in delight and gave them a repeat performance.

Eventually, though, his spouse called an end to the deceit. She brought the girls down and let them in on the secret. Their astonishment thrilled the scrivener. They played "Dardanella" until bedtime. Next day they had forty classmates and neighbors in to listen. All the kids gasped at the wonder.

The scrivener hastened to the department store for more piano rolls next day, because his wife was working up a "Dardanella" psychosis. Parents in the neighborhood were distressed. Their children had abandoned TV, radio and hi-fi. They wanted pianolas.

And the scrivener's oldest daughter, warmed by her swollen prestige, hugged him for the gift. She said: "Daddy, it's so wonderful! What will the scientists think up next?"

August 24, 1955

❡ The New York Public Library announced yesterday that it had just acquired for its Science and Technology Division a complete set of Sears, Roebuck catalogues on microfilm. The catalogues date back to 1892. The microfilm version, worth $1,500, was a gift from the corporation.

That may not sound significant, but it is. Probably no other volumes in science and technology are used as much as the mail-order catalogues. Serious scholars say that though they make rather homely literature, they offer a complete picture of many facets of twentieth-century civilization.

The volumes are used in price research, in studies of the development of farm machinery and household gadgetry. Costume designers avidly consult them for recycling fashions. Movie writers, artists and novelists search them for authentic detail on home decoration. Historians delve into them, too.

The early rag-paper catalogues in the library's collection have stood up sturdily under almost endless fingering through the years, but issues after 1900 are brittle. They go to dust at a touch. Rutherford D. Rogers, chief of the Library's Reference Department, had worried over this before the microfilm came.

The middle-aged who riffle through the early catalogues will find that they stir memories hidden in memory's most shadowy corners; that they waft the scanner gently back in time. This is true for the city-bred as for the farm-boy and the farm-girl. There is no better record of America's Golden Age.

The pages of the 1896 edition, for example, confirm the dodderers' stories of incredibly low prices for almost all human necessities and for the luxuries and fripperies. They give a record of gadgets and utensils, proudly advertised sixty years ago as the ultimate of their kind, which have vanished from catalogues forever.

These would include sperm-oil dark-lanterns, King oak well buckets at 36 cents each; Oline's Improved Steam Washer, the hand-run forbear of the push-button washing machines; pot-belly stoves at $2.40 each; eleven-quart coffee pots; wood-or-coal stoves for only $7; hand ice-shredders, old-fashioned iceboxes; butter churns run on dog, goat or sheep power.

The 1896 catalogue lists coffees at from 12 to 36 cents a pound; five-pound tubs of apple-butter at 40 cents; a pound of rock candy in assorted colors, 10 cents the pound; blackstrap molasses, 13 cents a gallon; maple syrup at 67 cents for five-gallon jugs.

Bixby's Shoe Blacking was only 3 cents a box; flour was offered at $1 for forty-nine-pound sacks; a variety of health-restoring elixirs at from 38 cents to $1. Velvet capes went for $1.38; leg-of-mutton jackets of "finest imported broadcloth" cost only $6.60.

Untrimmed hat shapes—India leghorns, black cantons, Russian hair-braids, chantilly-lace models—could be had for 49 cents. Hat decorations—forget-me-nots, morning glories, French roses, orange blossoms and oversize daisies—sold at 16 cents a bunch. Delightful frights, all of them.

Emma waves and feather bangs for thin-haired ladies, "full-beards on wire" or "ventilated beards" for gentlemen who couldn't grow a crop of their own—they're listed. For the young buck who couldn't cultivate a decent mustache, Sears had handsome facsimiles that went at 10 cents each, 75 cents the dozen.

A man's suit was $9.75, a Prince Albert outfit cost only $13.95. The Encyclopaedia Britannica thirty-volume set sold for $29.50; a Columbia four-wheel buggy for $39.90 ($54.70 with jump seat); two-wheel road carts (sulkies), $8.45. "Young men's nobby stiff hats" (derbies) were 98 cents in black or brown.

You put the volume gently back on the shelf. You walk down Forty-second Street in deep reverie. You keep your eyes sternly away from shop windows and current price tags. To look would be to come awake with harmful shock.

October 14, 1955

❡ Between weathered tenements at 422 and 424 West Forty-sixth Street, east of Tenth Avenue, stands a high wrought-iron gate. It gives into a narrow alley that runs back thirty feet.

Beyond, in an ancient courtyard paved with random flags, stands 422½, a converted stable of red brick warm with time. An outside stone staircase leads crookedly up the front wall to a wrought-iron porch, something after the New Orleans type.

White statuary stands around the courtyard walls and pallid fragments of friezes show dimly on the porch wall. An ancient well in the courtyard is covered over.

Mistress of the stable in the courtyard, of the great studio beside it, and of the four-story tenements that hide it from the street is Miss Ruth Faison Shaw, an artist.

Miss Shaw is from Wilmington, S. C., and velvety Southern roundness shows in her soft speech. She bought the old stable about ten years ago, and made it her dwelling; filled it with ancient family pieces and portraits.

Architects who have examined the place think some parts of the stable—the door arches, mostly— indicate that the little building might be of the Federal period, possibly 140-150 years old, but they're not sure.

For years now, Miss Shaw has moved among her tenement neighbors, eagerly searching out the stable's history. She thinks the stable was part of a manor house; that it may have been owned by kin of Gov. George Clinton around 1809.

Miss Shaw has no documents to bear her out, but neighborhood gaffers, since slipped away, told her that part of the West Side was called Clinton more than 100 years ago and that Widow's, or Great Kill, Creek murmured by the manor door.

That is the way Miss Shaw likes to think of it. And because she is mystic, she tells of a delicate wraith in crinoline who sometimes materializes on the crooked staircase at dusk on summer evenings.

The ghost in crinoline, Miss Shaw thinks, is either the Irish wife of the Clintons' hostler, or Margaret, grandchild of one of the Clintons. Either one, or the other, died on the crooked turn. Miss Shaw dreamed that, but she feels in her heart it is true.

Miss Shaw lives with ghosts. She met one, twenty years ago, in her house on the bluff at First Avenue and Forty-third Street. She tells you, gravely, "It was a young mariner in a glazed hat, come to look for Kitty, his sweetheart, who had died there, back in the nineteenth century. He had come out of the sea to find her, and his hand was cut."

And below her stable-house, Miss Shaw says, somewhere near Forty-fifth Street and Tenth Avenue, there wanders the restless ghost of a Moor who was hanged at the Battery in Colonial days. She says, "His body was borne up here, far beyond the New York of that day, and it cannot find peace."

Much of this is gentle fantasy, but in the melancholy dimness of Miss Shaw's stable-parlor, with the Faisons and Shaws holding you with their eyes out of dark canvas, it is not difficult to forget you are in the heart of the worst West Side slum in 1955. It is not difficult to enter into the spirit of the stories.

October 24, 1955

❡ The Italian Historical Society with offices at 26 Court Street in Brooklyn, after months of research here and in Italy, has established that the first Italian settler in the city was Peter Caesar Alberti, a Venetian craftsman. He settled in Brooklyn in 1635 when the Dutch ruled there.

Since then, according to James Kelly, the Brooklyn historian, and John La Corte, the society's director, Alberti's kin (he married a Dutch hausfrau and they had seven offspring) have spread throughout the United States and number around 3,000. The original Alberti, incidentally, owned the land now covered by Fort Greene Park in

Brooklyn. He ran it as a tobacco plantation.

November 2, 1955

¶ At week's end the old frame farmhouses and the yellow-brick château-style retreat house of the Cenacle of St. Regis, on Riverside Drive between 139th and 140th Streets, will go dark, probably forever.

The fifty purple-habited nuns with their fluted wimples have already moved to their new convent at Mount Kisco. Only Mother Mary Judge, local head of the order, and a few aides still move through the old buildings, directing final house cleaning.

The order has been on the high bluff, looking westward across the Hudson to the Palisades, for sixty-three years. Countless thousands of girls and women have worshiped at its altars, or roved its ancient grounds in peaceful contemplation.

Mother Mary Judge, soft-voiced and calm-featured, makes no secret of the fact that she leaves the rocky bluffs with deep regret. She came to it, a young woman, more than forty years ago, and remembers when the grounds still had rural atmosphere—no motor din; only tree-whisper and bird notes.

She remembers when Cocoa, the convent horse, grazed in the lower meadow just off the Drive. She recalls that when the order took the place in 1892, in its first move out of France, the acreage had been used as summer residence by the Flemings and by the Schultzes, a brewing family.

The estate went all the way to the Hudson's shore in 1892. The Schultzes had their boathouse there, and a private bathing beach. Where the priests' cottage stands now, just off Riverside Drive, north of 139th Street, was the Schultz cow barn.

The tan-painted Schultz farmhouse still holds massive furnishings that were family relics. The carved doors and the paneling are rich and warm with many years. In the château, which had been an Episcopal home for wayward girls, late-afternoon sun gilds dressers, chests and wardrobes, richly carved.

Mother Mary Judge thinks all these must be left behind. There will be no space for them at Mount Kisco. Much of the furniture in the three-room apartment used by the actress Maude Adams through the years when she was a convent guest in the château is dust-covered now, and huddles in deep shadow.

Her books lie about, her personal voice recordings, some of her manuscript. Mike Doyle, the Longford man who tends the old grounds, points out the fire logs still on the hearth. He says, "Miss Adams, she'd have the fire lighted on the hottest days. She liked to just stare and dream into it."

There is a ghostly sound in the papery leaves that lie in the convent paths. Mike Doyle pauses under the massive poplar behind the château, and Mother Mary Judge's eyes go soft as she looks up into its branches. She says the Davey tree surgeon told her the tree may be the oldest in the city—300 years, possibly.

And Mike Doyle nods his gray

head. "The tree men," he remembers, "said that the feeder roots go out under the Drive and the highway, all that distance, to suck up water for the poplar." Neither he nor Mother Mary Judge knows what will become of the trees and the gardens, the farmhouses and the château.

The city condemned the property four years ago. It meant to raise a hospital for the tubercular there. Now that scheme is ended, because of the new TB drugs. Mother Mary Judge hopes the city may save the great old trees and the gardens, and change the grounds into a park. She loves the old place.

She turns, at last, and slowly climbs the stone steps between the boulders, but her moist eyes look right and left, and upward; then westward to the sun-flooded waters and the warm Palisades. The farmhouse door receives her into yawning darkness, into the silence of the empty rooms.

November 7, 1955

❡ The egg jewelers of Little Ukraine, just east of the Bowery around Cooper Square, will show their gemmed eggs all this week at the Women's International Exposition in the armory at Park Avenue and Thirty-fourth Street. The show opens today.

The egg decorators say their art goes back to Ukrainian prehistory, when their people were sun worshipers. They have been Christian since 988 A.D., but their eggs are done in symbols that often combine the two phases of their culture.

Myron Surmach, who runs a Ukrainian general store at 11 East Seventh Street, is the Eastern outlet for the jeweled eggs. Though they are most popular at Easter, they have a steady sale throughout the year. Some are mere parlor decorations, some are talismans, some are used in Ukrainian wooing.

The decorated eggs are called "pysanky." The term stems from the word "pysaty," which means to write.

The ten best egg jewelers who send their work to East Seventh Street are scattered over the country. Two work in Brooklyn, three in Philadelphia, three in Minneapolis, two in Manhattan. The three in Minneapolis, a mother and two daughters, are rated the best.

The two in Manhattan are Pani Kosciw, who learned the art in girlhood in the Carpathians, and Gloria Surmach, the storekeeper's pretty daughter. Gloria is a Cooper Union graduate and an art director. She teaches egg decoration in an apartment above her father's shop.

She has held classes the last seven years. Now her pupils have carried egg jeweling to remote places. In Honolulu, for example, the egg decorators are two women who studied with Miss Surmach.

The egg-decorating equipment is simple, little different from the articles used by the sun worshipers more than 1,000 years ago. Included are a hollow brass stylus that fills with liquefied beeswax, three bowls for yellow, red and blue Batik dyes, candle flame to melt the wax —and the eggs.

In the beginning even choosing eggs was ritualistic—the first-laid egg of a young hen was choice— but nowadays the artists work with any smooth egg, pigeon-size to ostrich. They work only raw eggs; boiled eggs get rough and porous, and dyes spread on them. The albumen and yolk of a decorated egg are said to dry up with the passage of time.

The artists work the design onto the shell with melted beeswax. Where the wax hardens, the shell stays white. They dip first for yellows, then for reds, then for blues, wax-surfacing in turn each color they want to keep. Each succeeding color is darker than the one before.

Greens are usually dotted, crosshatched or brush-stroked in, and when the design is finished, lacquer is poured or sprayed on for glistening finish. Fast workers usually handle three or four eggs at a time. They rest dye-wet eggs in wrought-iron egg trays. Commercially the eggs fetch from 69 cents to $3.50 each and more for oversize ones.

Designs and techniques are cunningly kept family secrets, usually centuries old. Symbolism is intricate. In wooing, a Ukranian maid offers her handsomest egg to the handsomest guy. That doesn't nail him. He may get twenty or thirty eggs at once, always on Easter Sunday, so he has some choice.

November 21, 1955

❡ Trini's grocery is like no other city grocery. It is a neighborhood institution with some of the flavor of the old village tavern.

You go into Trini's—it's at 3176 Villa Avenue, off the Concourse in the Bedford Park district of the Bronx—and sweet, sentimental music greets you. Stocky, dark-haired Johnny Gentile, who runs the place, has been a member of Musicians Union 802 since 1938. He plays request numbers for the good housewives who come to his shop.

Mrs. Nardiello will say, "Johnny, I am blue today," and Johnny will pull his guitar from behind the counter and play blues-chasing songs. Or romantic women will stay awhile to hear Johnny play "Young and Foolish" or "The Nearness of You" or "O Sole Mio," and they will dream a little before they take up their groceries to plod back to the flat.

Johnny keeps a tape-recorder behind the counter, too. If a conversation with a customer is interesting, Johnny keeps it secret until the customer comes again. He delights her with a playback. When the recorder picks up neighborhood scandal or dark gossip, Johnny destroys the tape. "It is not good to hurt people," he says.

He has used the recorder to correct easily irritated housewives. A playback of a blue-streaked conversation with one outspoken hausfrau left her so abashed that her store conversation now has silken edges.

Johnny collects old string recordings to play at home and in the shop—Segovias and numbers by the great Orey Engorren, who is 80 now and lives in a castle in the Argentine, or so Johnny says.

How the store came to be Trini's

is a fluke, the grocer-guitarist tells you. He explains that in the City of New York you may hold only one license. He, for example, has held a musician's license and a cab driver's license. When he opened the store almost five years ago, he couldn't get a beer license without surrendering his musician's paper. Trini got the beer license, and her name went on the window.

Trini is Johnny's wife. She tends store, too, but only in rush hours. She does not play the guitar. She does not run the recorder. Away from the counter she looks after the little Gentiles—six of them, 5½ to 15 years. But she, like Johnny, turns out a handsome "hero sandwich," lots of meat and cheese in a full Italian half-loaf. Men from the near-by subway yards go for these— and for Johnny's noonday concerts.

November 25, 1955

❡ Late this afternoon when early dusk enshadows Chinatown's ancient outward untidiness, Mai Que Chang will close the city's smallest post office, forever. It is at 13 Mott Street.

Mai Que Chang rolled on its worn wooden floor as a dark-haired, 4-year-old little girl when her father, Ng Que, became Chinatown's first postmaster on Nov. 15, 1918. Her mother's home has always been directly above it.

Ng Que was postmaster until he was called to his honored ancestors ten years ago. By then his dark, slender daughter was out of City College and married. She lives with her husband and two sons in Flushing, Queens.

Mondays through Fridays for ten years Mai nimbly handled all Chinatown's mail. Most of it now is registered letters for Hong Kong or Formosa. Her stamp sales have run to better than $100,000 a year.

She snatches stamps in strips with uncanny precision, as called for. She uses Ng's system—keeps the various denominations almost before her nose, in the manner of units strung on an abacus.

Her money order and parcel post traffic are extremely heavy, though with sizable parcels the three-by-nine office rarely holds more than two customers. In rain, in snow and sleet, patient Chinese queue outside.

As you go through the red-painted, latticed doorway you stand in a dark chamber lighted by one bare electric light. Nine feet ahead a grimy curtain hides from view a darker chamber that is a Confucian Temple.

In the temple's dim light the tarnished gilding on ancient grotesque carving, on grass prayer mats, on paper prayers clinging like bats to the south wall, the highly-polished worshiper stools, huddle in gloom.

In the thick shadow you do not, at first, see Chu Shee Que, Ng's widow. Chu Shee—Little Blue Flower—is a withered blossom, now. She dreams and murmurs in the temple's dark, in its heavy scents of joss stick and boiled bamboo shoots.

Mai Que hears the murmur above the thump of her busy rubber

stamp, above the scratch of her swift-gliding pen. The Little Blue Flower, when you can make her out in the dark, seems half asleep. The feeble temple light gilds her brown cheek.

Chinese elders move in and out of the temple on almost silent feet, past the customers at the grille. They do not seem to notice Mother Chu Shee. They seem to notice nothing of the living hour; only the draped and vanished yesterdays.

On Monday Mai Que will, as she puts it, move from the smallest to the largest post office in the city. At the General Post Office she will have clerk-typist status. "After this," she says, "that will be restful."

Monday morning, Contract Station 233, which is the designation for 13 Mott, will pass from Federal rolls. At 10 A.M. the Chinese Benevolent Association will set up barricades in Pell Street. For three hours Chinatown will celebrate the opening of the new post office which will have as clerks Charles Ho and Shuck Lee, Chinese-American boys from the regional office.

That is at 12½ to 14 Pell, a glittering wide-windowed establishment all chrome and with fluorescent lamps with 1,000 square feet of working space. Mrs. B. Marion Schaffer, wife of Robert Schaffer, Postmaster for New York, will cut a door ribbon signifying that the new place is ready for business. The Post Office band will play.

Shing Tai Liang, editor-in-chief of The Chinese Journal, will thank the Government for the gift. He has told his Chinese readers for weeks

that it was coming. Kock Gee Lee of the association will be heard, and the Postmaster, too. Then a Chinese celebration meal will be spread at The Pacific, upstreet.

Yet a sad note will linger. It is the poster in the window of Mai Que's cubby-hole post office. It says, "Goodby to Our Post Office Station."

November 30, 1955

¶ Few who plod by the home of the Chamber of Commerce of the State of New York at 65 Liberty Street, downtown, realize that in it dwells the oldest existing body of its kind in the world. The chamber was organized in 1768 by twenty local merchants to promote the "General Interest of the Colony, and the Commerce of this City in particular."

When it was born in a New York City of only some 20,000 souls, mostly below Canal Street, the town's total land value, someone has figured, would have come to less than the cost of a downtown city block now. Its members, all bluff fellows, held their first meeting in Fraunces Tavern, which still stands. A chair from the tavern's long room is among their relics; so are the original chamber minutes.

They met at eventide, usually, on the first Tuesday of each month. The day has been quietly worked around to the first Thursday, now, but actually, sessions haven't changed much. They're still more or less like a New England town meeting, with lively debates on grave commercial issues. In the beginning, lawyers were barred on the ground that the breed could mouth honest merchants out of any argument, but in recent years a few barristers have made the rolls—but only corporation attorneys.

The chamber's original account books show expenditures for "bread and cheese, beer, punch and pipes" —the old, long-stemmed Dutch clays—that members took round the tavern fire. It shows lists of fines for absenteeism, but duly notes absence for forgivable cause. A frequent entry of this kind gravely declared Mr. Whoever, for example, to be "in the gout." The first chamber president, John Cruger, was author of the Stamp Act Congress's "Declaration of the Rights and Grievances of the Colonies In America."

The chamber has always clung sternly to old parliamentary rule; it still does, pretty much. It was slow in other change, too; it did not give up handwritten minutes for typed versions until 1923. The first two minute books, scorched and lost in the great fire that wiped out lower New York in 1835, turned up again, years later, in a lumber box in a Front Street shop. Prosper Wetmore, the chamber secretary, found them there. The body's great seal, with the C. of C. motto, "Not Born For Ourselves Alone," was taken from New York by departing British soldiers in 1783. It was found again in a London curio shop long after. It is still used.

The chamber's portrait collection, which runs to more than 300 items, includes a Gilbert Stuart Washington, a Lincoln by Huntington, an Alexander Hamilton by Trumbull. Most of the portraits are in the chamber's Great Room, a vast room with chamber presidents, first to last, taking every bit of space behind the dais. The carpeting in the Great Hall, put down in 1902, doesn't seem to wear. Members like to prove the nap's depth by burying dimes in it. The ceiling lights come on like creeping dawn, though not because the architects planned it that way; the fuses available in 1902 wouldn't take the whole load at one switch-throw.

Some of the portraits have fascinating histories. The Cadwallader Colden painting had to be restored after Hessian troops, over-beered, had put their bayonets to it. Horace Claflin, member from 1865 to 1885, was originally painted, as Quakers apparently were inclined to do in that period, with his hat on. Years later that hat was painted out and put in his left hand. Now the rolling years have restored the first hat and you see two. The members like to point out those oddities, among others, but unfortunately few outsiders ever get to see the collection except during National Art Week.

Original members wouldn't like the modern rule that forbids smoking in the Great Hall and they might even frown if they knew that a few—very few—women have entered their sanctum, have even addressed the membership, which today is around 800. The distaff guests included Queen Maria of Rumania, Lady Astor, Dorothy Thompson, Barbara Ward and Clare Booth Luce.

December 14, 1955

❡ Probably one of the last places you'd expect to find a 345-year-old Jacobean room would be high in the Empire State Building, built less than thirty years ago. Yet that's where one is, linked by ancient doors with a Gascon chamber originally put together in a château near Dax in southwest France and a Georgian room made for the Guildhall in London in 1730.

The rooms were brought across the sea about ten years ago to be used as thirty-seventh floor dining space for Schenley Distillers Company executives and their guests. Even the handpegged chairs, tables and sideboards that stood in the chambers long ago are used every day at company luncheons.

The Jacobean room came from Rugeley Manor in central Stafford in Britain. It has green mullioned windows threaded with lead and stained glass images of poor Louis II of Hungary and his Queen, Maria of Austria. The legend around the king's image calls him Ludovico. It is dated 1522.

There are learned fellows in Schenley but none seemed to have heard that Ludovico was an extraordinary monarch, bearded and mustached when he was only 13, white-haired five years later; drowned, or lanced by Turkish invaders at the Battle of Mohacs in 1526, when he was only 20.

George Witten, the 73-year-old maître-de who gets up the executives' luncheons, says the Schenley people paid handsomely for special linoleum to simulate the original red-tiled floor of the Gascon chamber—even had it artfully aged and blackened for realistic effect. One day, though, a zealous new porter steel-wooled all that off.

Each of the three transplanted rooms came with its original fireplace. The one in the Georgian chamber—that room is the longest —is hand-carved, as is all the paneling in the whole suite. The fireplaces don't work, except with electric trickery. They won't burn real wood without smoking up the place.

George, the maître-de, is no ordinary fellow, and it is rather curious that his job in the ancient dining suites is only thirty-seven floors up from the job he held fifty-two years ago. He was a bus boy then—later a waiter—in the Waldorf-Astoria Hotel, when it stood on the site from which the Empire State soars.

George served the late Diamond Jim Brady, among others. He snorts at legends of Diamond Jim's generosity; says he was a niggardly tipper and a rather surly type, especially to waiters. George worked at Lüchow's, too, and gets misty-eyed about the place, its former owners, and the wild game he used to carry in for distinguished gentlemen in times now long gone by.

Still later, he opened his own place in Thirty-third Street opposite the Waldorf site. It was still going when the Empire State went up and he frequently had at his tables the late Gov. Al Smith, John Raskob and some of the du Ponts, among others. He sold out in 1945, heartbroken over loss of a son in the war, but the Schenley people called him out of retirement and he's glad of it.

George still owns a $125 custom-made evening suit bought for him on impulse by old-time gamblers on whom he waited one night in 1915 in the old Metropole Hotel. Johnny Walters, Spitty Shea and some of the other card-and-dice boys who had heard he was going to a Turnverein spree, chipped in and ordered the outfit.

When George tells about this, he's apt to stare, dreamy-eyed, westward through the Jacobean room windows at the hazy New Jersey shore, and tell you: "I cannot wear the suit now, not for many, many years, but Mamma don't want to cut it up or throw it out. She cannot forget that night when I first wore it, and danced with her."

December 26, 1955

❡ There live and toil in and around New York between 400 and 500 nuns of a 165-year-old sisterhood that is extraordinary. This is true if for no other reason than that most people of their own faith— priests, other orders of nuns and even close friends—have never heard of them, nor even suspect they are of the religious.

By far the greatest number of these nuns live in their own homes —"in the world," as they put it— and follow workaday tasks like other women. They are clerks, typists, secretaries, nurses, doctors, teachers, hospital help; employes in orphanages, in libraries, in girls' clubs. One is a woman of national

reputation; many are important executives.

Members of the order—the Society of the Daughters of the Heart of Mary—dress as do most other women, both the "externs" who dwell in their own homes and those who live the convent life in orphanages, schools for the deaf, for the blind and for the mentally ill. Each keeps to the garb dictated by her station in society.

These nuns are never addressed as "Sister," except in talks with one another; to all others they are simply "Miss"—as Miss Genevieve Ryan, a Cleveland woman, superior of the twenty-seven nuns who help her run St. Joseph's Home for the Deaf on Hutchinson River Parkway in the Bronx. Not one of the nuns, nor even the superior, wears an outward symbol to indicate she is of the religious.

Yet these are nuns in the strictest sense. They go through five years of instruction, take the vows of poverty, chastity and obedience, come "out of the world" for such periods of recollection and retreat as their work schedules allow. They are dedicated to prayer and to good works. The externs apply their earnings, or what they have left over after home needs, to the good of mankind.

In New York, girls of any age past 18 get their instruction in Provincial Headquarters at 103 East Twentieth Street, Gramercy Park. In a few rare cases even widows have been accepted for instruction, but no member of the order may marry after taking the vows. The society has about 6,000 nuns all over the world, engaged in all manner of work compatible with the religious existence.

The society established its first roots in the United States in Cleveland 104 years ago. It has centers now in Buffalo, Allentown, N. J., in Chicago and Batavia in Illinois, and in Holyoke, Mass. In spite of this long history the society was not even listed in the Catholic Directory until this year; then only because Pope Pius XII wanted it to become better known so that more women, yearning for a religious life but bound by home ties, might enter it.

The idea originated with a Frenchwoman, when the Reign of Terror impended. She pleaded that girls and women with pressing home obligations receive the chance for a religious life even if they could not enter the cloister. It was she who suggested that there be such nuns, and that they wear no visible token of their identity; suggested a life pattern that would save them from social embarrassment. Only a hint is given of their instruction—one postulate year, two of novitiate, two of juniorate. Each applicant must study literature, philosophy and theology.

Miss Ryan, a quiet woman with an easy, gentle smile and a light humor, worked in the New York Foundling Hospital, in the Fordham School of Social Service and as a teacher in Brazil on the Point 4 program before she took over as superintendent at St. Joseph's School for the Deaf. She knows one member of her order, a New York City school teacher who "lives out in the world" and devotes her wages to good works, who has bought twenty-five Christmas baskets for impoverished neighbors each year for many years.

December 28, 1955

❡ The world's most wealthy potters —men and women of distinguished New York families—labor in monastic quiet in a sub-basement in the former Ransom Hooker Mansion at 175 East Seventy-first Street.

Among them are white-haired dowagers, young Park Avenue matrons and, sometimes, retired brokers or bankers, lustily thumping clay as the ancients did 3,000 to 5,000 years ago. The best among them turn out pieces that art museums are eager to accept.

These potters are shy folk. Most have led completely sheltered lives and until they took to pottery had seldom soiled their fingers at manual labor. Now they toil earnestly day after day, fashioning all kinds of ceramics for sheer love of it.

Probably the most active potter of this school was the late Mrs. Robert Pruyn Goodrich, daughter of Robert Pruyn, an Albany banker. Some fifty of her best pieces were privately shown the other day in the mansion in East Seventy-first Street.

Mrs. Goodrich was 79 years old when she died a few months ago. She began—as all the rest in this group—as a pupil of Miss Maud Robinson, who lives in the old mansion surrounded by enough recent and ancient works to stock a museum.

The Goodrich show covered all manner of works from delicate miniature trays and flower holders to large garden drums, or terrace seats—each a superb ceramic example. Several museums have already bid for specimens of the Goodrich art.

Miss Robinson permits no short cuts in her courses. Each pupil, no matter how distinguished his or her ancestry, must learn every phase of pottery making—choosing and mixing the proper clays; working them by hand or throwing them on the wheel; firing them in the oven; making glaze from basic ingredients.

The great electric kiln built under the sidewalk in front of the mansion is a high-powered electric type. When it was first set up, no power line in the neighborhood carried enough current to heat it, but Miss Robinson was able to have a line run in from the old Third Avenue El's power system.

The studio always keeps on hand a stock of lead, feldspar, flint, borax; oxides for coloring—copper, cobalt, manganese. Until the Government swept up all available uranium for atomic projects in World War II Miss Robinson managed to keep a good supply of uranium oxide for yellow glaze. Now the supply is at an ebb and jealously doled.

Miss Robinson is a museum consultant, particularly on ceramic glazes. She has passed this expert knowledge on to her pupils. They have imitated with astonishing fidelity the finishes that all but died with ancient Etruscan and Egyptian cultures. Most of the pupils use their work for home decoration or distribute it as family gifts.

Among the treasures in Miss Robinson's collection is a chambered nautilus. When executives of the Electric Boat Company sought a perfect specimen of the nautilus from which to design the insignia for the U. S. S. Nautilus, the atomic submarine, they borrowed this one through Miss Robinson's brother, a vice president in the company.

1 9 5 6

THE CITY'S Civil Service examiners, who broke into print the other day with a plan to reshape eligibility requirements for men who want to take the test for patrolmen, form an anonymous group of sixty-five men and women purposely hidden from the public eye.

They prepare tests for 2,132 different city Civil Service jobs, mark test papers and grade them. Part of their work is proctorial, with some 3,000 reserve monitors—former teachers, clerks, Wall Street accountants and the like—hired at $7.60 a day to help keep test-takers honest.

Every examiner is a college graduate with a master's degree or its equivalent. He must have done graduate work in his specialty, or specialties, or must have had actual job experience in it. The group includes experts on the Police Department, Fire Department, on medicine, law, health, transit, various branches of engineering, social welfare.

For unusual examinations, expert outside help is called in. The test for city bacteriologists, some time ago, was prepared by a Nobel Prize winner, Karl Landsteiner, for example. The tests for jobs in the city's legal departments were framed by such men as Dean John Finn of Fordham Law School and Justices of the State Supreme Court.

When the examiners themselves undertook to qualify for their jobs, their tests were secretly prepared by experts both within, and outside, New York State. The test for Board of Education examiner, a $14,300 post, was framed by a group of the nation's foremost educators, rather than by local talent.

Four grim, massive multi-compartment safes lie behind locked doors in the Civil Service Commission offices at 299 Broadway. Each examiner alone holds the key to his designated compartment. He must put all test papers, at whatever stage, into the safe, even if he leaves his desk for just a few minutes.

Only Samuel Galston, director of examiners the last thirty-five years, holds a master key to the safes, and not even Joseph Schechter, City Civil Service Commission chairman, may handle it. The rule is inviolable.

No examiner may show a set of test papers to another, and each must ride alone to the printer with his copy. He must stay there until it is printed up, and ride back, seated on it. During printing, no outgoing telephone calls are allowed. One day a print-shop owner unthinkingly walked into his own plant while questions were going through. He had to stay.

Question papers are almost always printed on the eve of an examination and are kept locked in the safe overnight. Those who take examinations must not put their names on the papers; they use only their application numbers. These are on stubs, which are torn off and shuffled. Then the papers get new numbers. Test-takers are fingerprinted, too, so they can't slip in proxies.

The examiners are an astonishingly genial lot—not stuffy, as you might expect their top-security jobs to make them. They're proud of the fact that their safeguards have kept city Civil Service free of scandal since it was organized seventy-two years ago.

January 4, 1956

⁋ The fate of the last high-stoop building in lower Fifth Avenue, the 101-year-old Irad Hawley Mansion at No. 47, will be decided within the month by the 680 members of the Salmagundi Club, which quarters there.

Salmagundi is one of the oldest artists clubs in the world and the inclination of artists is toward sentiment for old things and old places, but there are business men in the club, too; business men who paint on the side, and they may vote for progress.

The club can spend $50,000 to $75,000 to remove the broad old brownstone stoop and to close in the ancient four-story stairwell; make other changes to meet existing fire laws, yet keep the old Washington Square atmosphere.

If the vote goes the other way, the Hawley Mansion will come down and, with adjoining properties, may be replaced by a $1,500,000 apartment house. That is the trend, anyway. It killed the Mark Twain House and the old Brevoort, among other places just above the Square.

If the moderns win, Salmagundi will hole up for a while, probably in the National Arts Club in Gramercy Square, then come back to modern marble and cold chrome when the apartment house is done. If that's the way it is to be, something lovely will die—something mellow and warm and friendly.

For Salmagundi was born in the warm and mellow tradition. It started one fall Saturday night in

1871, in John Scott Hartley's cluttered art studio under a skylight at 596 Broadway, above Prince Street, as the Salmagundi Sketch Club.

It was a lusty crowd of rowdydow intellectuals who painted, quaffed deeply and worked off animal excess after fried-sausage-and-coffee feats by impromptu boxing and wrestling bouts that always ended in panting laughter, never in anger.

The founders, the Villagers of their day, were great artists—Hartley, Howard Pyle, A. B. Frost, William M. Chase, Stanford White, George Inness Jr., W. A. Rogers, Edwin A. Abbey, among others. Writers belonged even then, and business men, too.

The club owns one of the best art libraries in existence. Its art collections are priceless; its art auctions famous. If the club votes to save the old place, the proceeds of auctions to be held Jan. 20, 27 and Feb. 3 would go toward a fund for doing over the smoky old quarters with their sixteen apartments for resident and transient guests.

Henri Laussucq, Salmagundi president, a Basque who won the Silver Star at 61 by heroic parachute jumps in World War II, seems to move with the sentimentalists, but withholds comment. The oldest members, men over, or touching 90, would be saddened by change. Even the Salmagundi Toast speaks for the old, rather than for the new:

Old Friends and new who gather here,
May kindly thoughts and friendly cheer

Pervade our feasts and warm our hearts.
May we play fair in all the parts
That life assigns. May art, not pelf,
Be boss, and Justice stand upon the shelf.

In 1893 the club moved to 14 West Twelfth Street. John Rogers, whose family-group sculptures got into almost every home in America, had worked there. The Salmagundians had a roof garden that looked down on the Square and on lovely neighborhood gardens. They filled the nights with laughter and song.

They took over 47 Fifth Avenue in 1917; burned the mortgage five years later. They filled it with the rich works of members, with smoke and with the clinging odor of good ale. They played billiards endlessly, have always had a good dining hall with waitresses who never seem to leave, or fade. And they, who were the Village wild ones in youth, are the Village conservatives now.

January 9, 1956

❡ At midday on Friday, winter sun lanced through Venetian blinds to spread gold bars on red carpet in the mosque that has been maintained for the last seventeen years on the ground floor of the old, rundown mansion at 143 in somber State Street on Brooklyn Heights.

At 12:30 the faithful assembled for the Juma Salat, the Sabat prayers. They made their ablutions in a yellow-stained bathtub in a tiny room off the mosque, shed their Western shoes and stockings and entered the living room to sit cross-legged, facing east.

To the east was a pale blue parlor wall with two white marble fireplaces. In a corner nearest the street windows stood the mambah, or pulpit, not unlike a lifeguard's platform. It was inscribed, in Arabic, with the legend "There is no God but Allah."

The faithful sat in deep, silent meditation, heads bowed—some swept by sun bars, some gilded by pale light from ceiling fixtures. A white-clad muezzin chanted the call to prayer. It closed with "Hayeya Salat"—"Come to prayer. Come to salvation."

For a half-hour, or more, against a background of dim traffic sounds in near-by Atlantic Avenue, the prayers were murmured. Sayful Al-Hassan, Prince of Yemen, delegate to the tenth session of the United Nations General Assembly, performed the services of Imam, reciting softly from the Holy Qur'an.

Shaikh Daoud Ahmed Faisal, spiritual shepherd of the Moslem Arabs in Brooklyn, a dignified, heavy figure in white robes, bowed and prostrated with his flock; touched forehead to the carpet, murmured the Moslem ritual. Beyond a curtain, in another large room, the Moslem women prayed.

When the service was ended, the men arose, put on the shoes clustered at the living room's threshold, spoke parting blessings invoking the Name of Allah and hurried out to their daily toil. They seemed to carry with them faint traces of incense and of perfume.

The Shaikh Faisal's flock is not large, but he says it grows. It has bought a Madina Salam, a Muslim village community site, part of the old Talbot estate in Wiccopee in East Fishkill, Dutchess County. It is to be the summer playground of the faithful.

Of the city's 40,000 to 50,000 Arab-speaking peoples the Shaikh's group is probably the smallest—somewhere around 300. He seeks funds to build a mosque with minarets that will include school and recreation hall.

In the main, however, the Arab-speaking peoples in Brooklyn are of different Christian sects. They are spread from the Heights to Bay Ridge. Atlantic Avenue below Court Street where they shop is not unlike a bazaar in Beirut or in Damascus—a market place for foods, sweets, water pipes, tambourines and all manner of things from the Near East.

Farid Alam, a stately gentleman who manages the Alamphon Records Shop at 182 Atlantic Avenue, knows the community's history. He is one of the Arab-speaking group that was squeezed out of Washington Street in Manhattan when the Brooklyn-Battery Tunnel was building.

Mr. Alam has done more, probably, than any other single person to keep the Arab tongue alive in this city. The new generations pick it up from the disks he sells, from popular songs taken from Egyptian motion pictures, like "The White Rose," that play in neighborhood theatres.

But the sterner Moslem Arabs seem to shun the gay music. Young and old, like their desert forebears, give their time to classes in the study of Islam and Arabic, to lectures on Islam and to the five daily prayers and the Friday Juma Salat.

January 11, 1956

¶ At noon today the Illuminating Engineering Society, with 9,000 members all over the country, will take luncheon at the Sheraton-Astor Hotel where the society got its start fifty years ago when the establishment was just the Astor Hotel.

Dr. Samuel G. Hibben, pioneer in modern lighting, a retired Westinghouse executive who is historian for the society, will hand over to Ralph Freeman, regional manager for the Sheraton Hotels, a bronze plaque commemorating organization of the society in the Astor.

There's a small problem to be solved when it comes to fixing the bronze plate into a hotel wall, because no one in the society today, not even Dr. Hibben, can find out where the society founders met. That's because the hotel has been through many alterations in a half-century.

Van Rensselaer Lansingh, one of the first members of the society— Dr. Hibben thinks he is around 90 now—can't recall the original meeting room and a search through hotel records was of no help. Dr. Hibben thinks the plaque may end up somewhere in the lobby.

The men in the society generally get credit for having put the United States into the lead in lighting just after the turn of the century, and

for having kept it there. Without them there would have been no Great White Way, no advance in street, school and home lighting.

Only a few years before the society got started, Dr. Hibben remembers, the carbon arc and the gas lamp lighted New York streets. It wasn't until 1891 that the first outdoor electric signs went up on the nine-story building that was on the site now covered by the Flatiron Building.

The first signs there advertised Spencerian Pens and Sapolio. In 1899 the space went to Manhattan Beach with the incandescent slogan "Swept by Ocean Breezes." Then Continental Tobacco took over and Heinz' 57 Varieties, done with bulbs hooded with colored glass caps.

By 1905, Dr. Hibben remembers, the Great White Way stretched from Herald Square to around Forty-seventh Street. The sensational signs were the Corticelli Kitten, the White Rock Nymph and the Heatherbloom Petticoat Maid tripping through the rain— in moving lights.

From 1910 to 1914 the wonder sign was the Roman Chariot Race on the Normandie Hotel at Broadway and Thirty-eighth Street, a 20,-000-light monster put up by the Rice Electrical Display Company. In 1917 it was the big Spearmint sign on Times Square's west side.

Dr. Hibben points out what most people seldom see or realize—that when Times Square's signs go off in early morning, it is no better lighted than any other part of the city; it lapses back into the semi-dark that brooded in the space before the engineers worked their miracles.

One other thing—the globe-covered lights on the Sheraton-Astor roof parapet were installed in the first major planned lighting job ever done in New York City, and haven't been changed, except for newer bulbs, since they went up fifty years ago.

February 8, 1956

¶ On February 16, 1868, the Benevolent and Protective Order of Elks was organized in Military Hall, a popular meeting place that still stands at 193 Bowery.

Originally the Elks were the Jolly Corks, a handful of wandering minstrels and song-and-dance men—about fifteen, near as anyone can make out now—who met on Sunday nights in Mrs. Arnold Geisman's boarding house at 188 Elm Street, north of City Hall, west of where Civic Center towers now.

Manhattan Sabbaths were somewhat on the dismal side in the Eighteen Sixties. The free-and-easies—drinking places where customers, waiters and bartenders impulsively broke into song—were tightly shut and the thirsty wandered as in a desert.

In November, 1867, Charles Algernon Sidney Vivian, an English parson's younger son, came to New York from the London music halls. He dropped into John Ireland's free-and-easy, The Star, in Lispenard Street off Broadway.

A few man-sized beers loosened his vocal cords. He took the floor and did four of his music hall numbers, and the sawdust quivered as other guests stomped and applauded without stopping to wipe the foam from their handlebars.

Mr. Ireland hurried Mr. Vivian over to the near-by American Variety Theatre, got him a contract and ordered Dick Steirly, the saloon pianist, to find him lodging at Mrs. Geisman's establishment for actors and for sporting gentry.

The parson's son had a strong turn for the convivial. He organized the Jolly Corks for Sunday evening cheese-and-beer parties at Mrs. Geisman's, choosing only other stage performers to share the spreads and the beery choruses.

The Jolly Corks swelled in numbers. They got the heave-ho from the Elm Street lodging house, but that didn't matter. Seventy-two years later, in the administration of Brother Elk Fiorello La Guardia, Elm Street was changed to Elk Street.

The Jolly Corks moved to 17 Delancey Street just before the end of 1867, then, a few weeks later, to Military Hall. On Feb. 16, 1868, they became the B. P. O. E. Vivian had suggested they call themselves the Buffaloes, after a London group, but that was voted down 8 to 7 for the Elks designation.

The legend is that one of the Jolly Corks knew that a second-hand elk's head was for sale cheap at Phineas Barnum's Museum at Broadway and Ann Street, and that rather than pass up the bargain the Corks bought it and made themselves elks instead of buffaloes.

Anyway, the order grew. Originally it was restricted to actors and kept picking up actor membership in all major cities on the song-and-dance circuit. But after a lot of wrangling in the Eighties the doors were thrown wide to all comers.

Today the organization that started as a Sunday night drinking club has 1,650,000 members throughout the United States and its possessions, with a city membership of over 20,000. Its 1,700 lodges own around $225,000,000 worth of properties; spend $7,000,000 a year for youth, physically handicapped and for war veterans.

¶ One of the oddest municipal assignments is "stick man," a Transit Authority post. A stick man's sole function is to ward off anyone who might attempt to touch a welder working on a subway third rail, because such a contact would establish a circuit ground that could be fatal.

February 10, 1956

¶ On the top floor of 41 Mott Street tomorrow night the dragon dancers will rehearse for the new year. They will wriggle and stomp under the goggle-eyed dragon masks. Firecrackers will explode at their feet and make the room dense with sulphurous odors.

Then they and the Chinese elders will go to their homes in ancient Mott and Pell Streets to make obeisance to the Stove King, or Kitchen God. They will offer him special dishes and dainty cakes. They will burn incense in his honor.

In that ceremony they will begin

The Year of Shun, the Monkey, deified during the Tang Dynasty as "The Great God Equal to Heaven." To the Chinese, Shun is the symbol of good health and of success for Mankind.

After midnight they will sacrifice to the gods of the home—to The God of The Front Door, to The God of The Kitchen Stove, to The God of The Main Hall (parlor), to The God of The Wall (kitchen sink, in town), to The God of The House Gate.

The elders will take down the red and black portrait of The Stove King, and it will go on the fire with special sacrificial dishes set before it. A new Stove King portrait will go up in its place and The Stove King, or god, should return to the household at month's end.

Chinatown doors and windows tomorrow night and for the next five days will be plastered with the Hsi-Hsi, or Double-Joy signs that have been tradition for thousands of years. The narrow streets will echo to "Gung Hay Fat Choy."

The dragons will charge into Mott Street before noon on Sunday —five of them. There will be one each for the On Leong Tong and the Hip Sing Tong, which are merchants' groups; one for the Chinese Community Club; one sent forth by the Gee Jong Tong, or Chinese Freemasons; one for the Oak Tis, a Canton District group.

All through the Sabbath, on the first day of the Year 4653, as the Chinese count, there will be shrill gaiety, the din of the Mon Jong or Ten Thousand Firecrackers. And there will be New Year feasting such as Western lovers of chop suey never see nor taste.

New Year is a happy time in Chinatown. It comes in The Seasons of The Great Snow and of The Great Cold, but it comes on the threshold of The Season of The Rain Waters, The Season of The Waking of Insects. Then can The Season of Clear Brightness be far behind?

February 15, 1956

❡ A gentleman in town, a China-Burma-India veteran, took his children to Chinatown on Sunday to watch the dragons dance on the Chinese New Year. Late in the day, having a Chinese meal in one of the local restaurants, the gentleman watched a CBS-TV version of the celebration. In it was an extremely active dragon. Suddenly the fore-end of the dragon shot its head mask high. The watcher jumped in his chair. The dragon's fore-end was Tech. Sgt. Andy P. Lee, Chinatown insurance man who had been his Army buddy in Counter-Intelligence in Calcutta. Hadn't seen him in ten years.

February 22, 1956

❡ A genial and earthy fellow who started a scholarly career as a bottle washer, who never studied in a high school or a prep school, or even won a medical degree, takes over today as president of the New York University College of Medicine Alumni. He is the first man without an M.D. chosen to head the group.

The new president is William Caruthers MacTavish, three-score and three, silver-maned and ruddy. He counts among many talents a flair for bocce, the Italian bowling game; plays it frequently with Carmine Street neighbors in Greenwich Village, most of them horny-fisted toilers who boom their joy at appearance of "Professore."

When Wullie MacTavish was 15, in 1908, he got a $2-a-week job in the late Prof. John A. Mandel's class as a chore boy in the Medical College's Biochemistry Department. He did the bottles, wiped the blackboards, swept floors, ran errands.

Between blackboard wipes he listened to the professor, got the hang of basic chemistry from what he saw on the slate before he sponged it and made friends with undergraduates, especially in the classes of 1911 and 1912. By and by, under Professor Mandel's urging, he became serious about chemistry, set about garnering Regents points.

From 1913 to 1917 he was a teaching assistant in chemistry, later an instructor, then assistant professor, then professor at the Washington Square College. He has been chairman of the Chemistry Department the past twenty-seven years.

Honors have come thick and fast to Mr. MacTavish. He is visiting toxicologist for Westchester County, special examiner in chemistry for the Civil Service Commission, academic adviser to the Italian Ministry of Education, is tied in with a dozen learned societies.

Mr. MacTavish truly loves mankind. He has an extraordinary record as godfather—he's acted in that capacity twenty-three times. Right now he's senior faculty member at N. Y. U. and will be torch-bearer at next commencement. He finds time, too, to coach the Jaguars, a soft-ball team of tough neighborhood kids.

Brave soul, MacTavish.

March 26, 1956

❡ The city's Health Department is ninety years old this month. The anniversary will be quietly noted at a meeting Wednesday in Commissioner Leona Baumgartner's offices. She has invited other municipal department heads to sit in on the session.

The Commissioner has dug from old department records the fascinating story of the pioneer days of the Board of Health. Those records are in an enormous hide-bound volume whose covers have dried and peeled. The pages, though, have barely aged and the shaded script is a delight.

The first entries tell of a preliminary meeting on March 2, 1866, and of the organization session three days later. The group was made up of grim, hard-hitting men —Dr. Willard Parker; Dr. James Crane, representing the City of Brooklyn; Dr. John O. Stone, Port Physician; and Jackson Schultz, layman.

They had a 500-page survey to work on—a job done by earnest young physicians, which, incidentally, has somehow been lost, though most other department records are still around.

They met in the gas-lighted Police Headquarters at 300 Mulberry, but got rooms of their own, right off, at 301 Mott Street. They laid in pens, ink, stationery and ordered the first permit blanks. The town's Police Commissioners were on the board with them to enforce health laws.

These came thick and fast, and a good thing, too, because cholera was then sweeping Europe and cholera-bearers were coming into New York Harbor. Cholera had taken more than 10,000 lives in the town in the fifty preceding years.

The Board of Health didn't want to give the disease a hold in a city that had grown to 1,000,000 souls. It deployed disinfecting crews all over Manhattan Island and Brooklyn, especially in the foreign quarters. Cholera deaths that year were held down to 1,137.

That was quite a drop in the cholera mortality rate. In 1832, with fewer than 500,000 inhabitants in Manhattan, the disease took 3,513 lives. When the population stood at around 500,000, the cholera death count went to 5,071. Physicians still in the department remember occasional cholera cases turning up as late as 1913.

New York was ripe in 1866. Though it wasn't rural any more, it carried strong rural whiff if you stood downwind. It had 200 slaughterhouses. Great droves of beef and mutton on the hoof were herded through its streets. Its glue factories and fat-and-bone rending plants, its countless stables—all offended.

Its food markets, huddles of fishmongers' carts and farm wagons that left their litter where they congregated, including prominent intersections as far north as Fourteenth and Twenty-third Street, were hardly ever cleaned. Private scavengers with leaky two-wheel carts did the only garbage collecting—and did it indifferently.

The Health Commissioners, with the Sanitary Police to back them up, really tried to duplicate the job Hercules had turned in for Augeas. They compelled livery stables and dray companies to cart 160,000 tons of horse manure out to near-by farms, forbade their letting new piles accumulate.

They chased hundreds of cowbarn owners beyond the city limits, drove 299 local piggeries far beyond Manhattan borders. They got 3,949 refuse-heaped back yards cleaned up, forced property owners to police 381 cluttered alleys, 230 basements and 3,067 cellars used as dwellings.

They introduced the first watertight garbage cans, got the scavenging cartmen to keep scheduled rounds and to ring handbells as warning to housewives to get their waste to the sidewalks. Fines were imposed for leaky carts. Fines were imposed for leaky wells—and there were hundreds then on the island.

The Commissioners ordered physicians to report "every or any patient laboring under any pestilential, contagious or infectious disease." They brought undertakers to heel; no more burials or exhumations without official permit. They set up an agency to record all births, deaths, marriages. The town had been free and easy in all these things before the board was organized.

Maybe the Commissioners beat their breasts a bit in their first annual report, but they had some justification for it. "Sanitary science," they said in the report, "has attracted considerable attention during the past eighty years, but it is only recently that an earnest interest in the subject has been manifested. This is a remarkable fact, considering the antiquity of the Mosaic Code, the greatest collection of health laws ever published, and the numerous examples of sanitary intelligence furnished by ancient Greece, Rome and Carthage."

The original board worked wonders, with virtually no budget. Its members might go popeyed at what their agency has come to—a staff of close to 5,000 men and women, an annual budget of around $25,000,-000. Or maybe they would not go popeyed. That first annual report said:

"In the City of New York, sanitary science will be compelled, in a very few years, to show how two millions of people are to be kept in health upon an area of less than twenty square miles of dwelling space [the habitable part of Manhattan Island then]. . . . It is entirely practicable to protect the health and give fresh air and domestic comfort to 200,000 people upon a single square mile."

That wasn't bad guessing.

April 2, 1956

❡ Fifty-two years ago, Julius Neergaard, a Dane, opened an apothecary shop in Brooklyn's Fifth Avenue just above Ninth Street. He set up an all-night-service policy. He has been one with the dust, now, for thirty-four years, but the tradition still holds. The doors at Neergaard's have not been locked in a full half-century.

William, son of the founder, a former cavalry officer just past three-score, would not dream of changing the all-night tradition, and his own son, William F., is dedicated to carry it on when he comes into ownership. He works in the shop now; takes the night shift when one of the old hands is ill or on holiday.

No other pharmacist in Brooklyn maintains through-the-night service, far as William Neergaard knows. If any shop in the greater city still offers drugs the clock round, he doesn't know of it. He likes to tell you that police stations in Brooklyn post the fact that his doors are never locked. Cab drivers know the Neergaard tradition and bring distressed nocturnal customers from every corner of the borough.

A goodly number of Brooklyn's hospitals maintain open accounts at the shop and no Neergaard late man is astonished when an ambulance pulls up at 3 or 4 o'clock in the morning with an emergency prescription. Holy Family, Jewish, Methodist, St. Peter's, Norwegian and Brooklyn Hospitals frequently send an ambulance driver over for the rarer biotics or some special heart medicine. Independent physicians come tearing through the night, too, for drugs for emergency cases.

Julius Neergaard opened his first drugstore in Brooklyn in 1888, at President Street and Fifth Avenue. In 1901 he bought John Kimball's place at 450 Fifth Avenue, an establishment that had started in 1865. He paid as much for Kimball's special fir balsam, a healing salve, as he did for the shop contents and goodwill, but lost nothing by the arrangement. Neergaard still sells the fir balsam; gets letters for it from customers who have drifted far from the neighborhood.

The shop, at 454 Fifth Avenue since 1904, two doors up from the original Kimball place, has a spacious, calm, old-fashioned air. Its high dark-wood shelves and bow-fronted cases are polished relics. The lovely stained-glass sign high above the prescription counter was made almost fifty years ago by an old-country friend of the founder who did exquisite glass for churches and colleges. It spells "Neergaard" in giant letters.

The older men in the all-night apothecary chuckle over trade yarns when business slacks off. They remember the New York druggist who, years ago, reaped a fortune with an odorless, nice-tasting dosage he labeled "Cod Liver Oil Emulsion." Other druggists struggled to find the secret of this formula, and finally did. The concoction was innocent of even the barest trace of cod liver oil. They talk nostalgically, too, of drugs that were forced off the market when the Pure Foods Act called for honest labeling—"tonics" that were taken by women for quiet alcoholic jags, so-called "liver invigorators" and the Indian remedies that were supposed to be good for anything from mild vapors to the most pernicious diseases.

April 6, 1956

¶ Rural flavor vanished from New York, especially from Manhattan, long ago, but The Rural New-Yorker, farm journal, has stayed on. Even after 106 years' existence it still flourishes here. It goes today to 300,000 subscribers from Maryland to Maine, from the seaboard to Western Pennsylvania. The journal got its start upstate in Rochester, and within a few years it took some offices way downtown in Gotham. Later it moved to the Scott-Bowne Building at Chambers and Pearl Streets, where Scott's Emulsion was concocted, then shifted to the old Times Building at 41 Park Row. It grew with each move.

Forty-one years ago, the plant was moved into the abandoned Chelsea Methodist Church, a simple red-brick building in West Thirtieth Street between Eighth and Ninth Avenues. The old brick parsonage at 327 West Thirtieth, one door east of the church, was included in the deal.

City slickers hurry by the plant but never seem to see the scaling black-and-white "Rural New-Yorker" sign over the main church door. They may hear the old Goss presses pant and wheeze, but the sound barely carries above traffic.

Step across the threshold, though, and you're in country-newspaper atmosphere—the pungent smell of printer's ink, splintery floors, un-washed walls and a folksy untidiness that carries you back into an earlier century.

Even in the old choir loft—or where the choir loft used to be—the editors' and business manager's offices are mid-nineteenth century. William A. O'Brien, a lean silver-head who is part-owner and has been with The Rural New-Yorker for fifty-two years, works at an old roll-top desk.

But that nineteenth-century country-newspaper background in West Thirtieth Street is a calculated thing. The Rural New-Yorker owners know that it would be grievous error to modernize the plant, to fancy up with heavy carpet, chromium and air conditioning. Their readers, who sometimes drop in to visit, would never understand.

Dirt farmers, the owners tell you, would look with suspicion on slicked-up editors in slicked-up surroundings. Mr. O'Brien said: "They'd just think none of us ever got his boots deep in stable droppings, and that could be fatal."

Actually, the president and publisher, William F. Berghold, runs a 300-acre farm at Hillsdale in Columbia County and goes deep into The Rural New-Yorker's territory to get his material. Jim Bodurtha, the other staff writer, drives or flies into rural areas all the time for first-hand stuff. Jim came off a New England farm.

Two years ago The Rural New-Yorker unhappily succumbed to Madison Avenue blandishment and dropped its sentimental bee-hive-bulls' head-plow and harrow-

old barnyard front-page decoration for a streamlined modern lettering job. That disturbed farmers who loved the ancient heading. Some had known it from remote childhood.

But the owners haven't changed the magazine's contents. They cling sternly to good technical stuff on fertilizers, poultry handling, farm machinery, livestock, horticulture. They retain the recipes, household hints and patterns departments for farm wives. The journal's price is still 50 cents a year, three years for $1.

The editors still get from 500 to 600 letters a week from readers, mostly on farm problems. They still find an occasional dead aphid or beetle in a letter sent by a husbandman who hasn't been able to identify the pest. Damaged fruit comes, too, for analysis.

There's no thought of ever moving the journal out of Chelsea. It's in the center of the territory it covers; it's convenient to the main post office. It would be difficult to find a better location for quick access to railroads for easy hop to farmers' conventions. The magazine has around 2,000 New York City subscribers, but doesn't encourage more.

Back of the plant, the old churchyard has eight or ten trees that bravely meet each new spring with hard-won greenery, but ask the printers and the editors what they are and it turns out they don't know. They're not ashamed to admit it. They shrug it off and say: "Heck, they're only city trees. No need to figure out what *they* are."

April 9, 1956

¶ It's almost impossible nowadays to find an American factory that turns out oversize bells—anything larger, that is, than ships' bells or bells for fire apparatus.

The alumni of the Industrial College of the Armed Forces found that out when they conceived the idea of getting American industry to chip in for a quarter-size reproduction of the Liberty Bell for their alma mater in Washington.

The job was done in time and the reproduction was turned over to the college at the first alumni dinner in the Sheraton-Astor, with due pomp and speechifying last Wednesday, but even the guests didn't know what a chore it had been to have the bell made.

The Copper and Brass Research Association undertook the assignment, but kept running into dead ends. Nowhere could they locate a bell factory that would do the job from scratch. Big bellmaking just isn't done here any more, though it is in France and in Scotland.

Before they realized that—and the bell had to be an American industry product—they had Capt. Bob Grimskold of the General Bronze Corporation make up a blueprint for the job. He's a painstaking draftsman, still active in his eighty-sixth year.

Captain Grimskold went to Philadelphia and asked permission to take measurements and rubbings of the original bell in Independence Hall. Federal Department of Interior men tried to tell him that wasn't necessary; that they had all the dimensions and inscriptions in the bell booklet they give to tourists.

At last they let him have his way, and a good thing, too. He copied the bell's crack and got his other rubbings. When he studied the result he learned that the name Pennsylvania as used on the old bell is spelled "Pensylvania" though the official booklet gives the inscription with two "n's" after the "e."

Then the copper and brass researchers learned it wasn't easy to get bell-metal ingots for big bells. They were in despair over that until Willard C. Peare of Carlstadt in New Jersey, an old bell foundryman, gave them a bell-metal formula that he'd jealously guarded. It's the one used for bellbuoys and lighthouse bells.

The researchers sent copies of the Peare formula to the Burndy Engineering Company in Norwalk, Conn., and to the Mueller Brass Company in Port Huron, Mich. They did a special job on the ingots, screening and rescreening the tin and copper for absolute bell purity; flew the ingots to New York.

Incidentally, they didn't just pick those two companies out of a hat for the assignment; they sounded out more than twenty-five before they found two that would tackle the job.

The final casting was done by the Roman Bronze Company in Corona, Queens. Sal Schiavo, who runs that plant, was a little worried about the job because his company hadn't turned out a large bell in over fifteen years. F. G. McLeod, a broad-burred Scot at Roman Bronze, had over-all supervision.

So much time had gone into trying to find old bellmakers that the alumni got fidgety. A fifty-ton bell like the one they wanted would ordinarily be three to four months in the making. Mr. McLeod pushed it through in four weeks, and just about made dinner deadline.

Though old Liberty Bell can't ring any more because it's cracked, Captain Grimskold's blueprints called for reduced crack depth in the reproduction. When David Sarnoff turned the bell over to Maj. Gen. Robert P. Hollis, college commandant, last Wednesday, its voice was richly vibrant.

April 27, 1956

⁋ City Clerk Murray Stand's brave statement the other day that he thinks it's about time to double the city marriage license fee—it has been $2 for thirty-six years—curiously found almost no dissenters. He got a few hundred letters on it, but mainly the writers said they thought $4 wouldn't be too much to pay for marriage privilege.

Actually the idea wasn't new. Mayor La Guardia mumbled about a $4 fee some twenty years ago, but energetic though he was he never got anywhere with it. Political-minded City Fathers shrank from it, afraid there might be loud outcry against a tax on love. Almost all other license fees have doubled and no one has hollered much about those.

Now, Mr. Stand will tell you,

about the only municipal items that haven't gone up in more than a quarter-century are the marriage license fee and the 5-cent ferryboat fare. If his notion is adopted—and he isn't too hopeful about it—he figures it would give New York around $200,000 in additional revenue.

There were no marriage licenses in the city before 1908. Up to then, ministers, magistrates, sea captains, aldermen or whoever tied nuptial knots in town simply sent a record of the wedding to the Health Department, and that's all there was to it. No fee. A $1 fee was voted in 1908, with hardly a gripe from the customers. In 1916 the city revoked aldermen's right to marry couples. In 1921 the license fee went to $2, without public clamor.

Marriage licenses, Mr. Stand will tell you, are less in some states— North Carolina and West Virginia, where they're still only $1—but much higher in others. They are $3 in Arkansas, Delaware and Florida, among others; $5 in Georgia, New Jersey and Washington; $6 in Kentucky. Several states get $4, with no complaint.

Marriage conditions are set down in the state's Domestic Relations Law. There was a change in this law in 1943 to allow a couple to pick up their license in any city, town or borough in the state. Before that the license had to be taken in the borough in which the prospective bride lived.

The most puzzling marriage license problem that came up within memory, the City Clerk thinks, was when Siamese twin sisters with the circus appeared to ask for a license for one-half the set. Publicity men were back of that. The clerk finally denied the application, on moral grounds, a phase sternly covered in the Domestic Relations Law.

April 30, 1956

¶ Peculiar behavior of Bronx Park ponies at one spot on the pony track outside the Children's Zoo last week puzzled the staff there. At that spot the animals shied, leaped and tended to get skittish, which isn't characteristic of the breed. They were ploddingly calm before they got to that stretch and after they had passed it. Park investigators were brought in to figure out what was up. At first they thought that perhaps the ponies were frightened by a ladder that leaned against a tree near the trouble spot, but experiment established it wasn't that. Passing the hoodoo point, the park people noticed a bright yellow car visible through thin greenery. That wasn't it, either. Finally they got it: A power line passes under the track. It had corroded and had lost its insulation. It sent a mild electric charge up through the turf and the ponies' hoofs picked it up.

¶ Mrs. Harry Thurlow, a woman in Mount Vernon, wanted to know the other day, "Could you explain to newcomers to this area why residents of New York City live in Brooklyn, Queens, Long Island, Manhattan and THE Bronx? Is it simply that it is easier to say 'THE Bronx?' " Well, it turns out that no one has an official, documented explanation. James J. Lyons, the Borough President of the Bronx, and members of his staff have had lots of queries on the subject and they've fabricated a legend that they'll not defend too stanchly. They tell people that Jonas Bronck, the Dane who was the first white settler up their way 320 years ago, was a hospitable fellow and that visitors down in New Amsterdam used to say, "Let's go visit the Broncks." Stephen Jenkins, who wrote "The Story of the Bronx" a long time ago, guessed that the borough was named not for Jonas, but for the Bronx River, originally the Aquenounck, that flowed through his acreage. Mr. Jenkins maintained that you never mentioned a river but that you put the article before it—the Army of the Potomac, for example, or the Valley of the Hudson. That's not too sturdy an argument either, because New Jersey has Hudson County, not the Hudson County.

Bronx County never carries the article before "Bronx," nor does the Post Office list any such place as THE Bronx. The official city directory calls the borough THE Bronx and so do all official borough documents. All this tends to bring on migraine, but that's the way it seems to be. It might have been better to have kept the old Indian name for the area—Keskeseck. The Dutch West India Company, incidentally, bought THE Bronx for less than it paid for Manhattan— for "2 gunns, 2 kettles, 2 coats, 2 adzes, 1 barrell of cider and two bitts of money." Jonas Bronck's farm, surveyors figure, must have stood at Southern Boulevard and Willis Avenue.

May 9, 1956

¶ Only one resident on Gramercy Square has the right to enter Gramercy Park without the special key, whenever he's minded to do it. He moves around the Square at his own slow pace with no fear of rushing cabs or trucks. If a motor vehicle bears down on him, he merely pulls in his head and waits. If it hits him he just sticks his head out again and goes his quiet way. He's a large, dark-shelled turtle that has lived on and off the Square for years, though no one seems to know how many. Gramercy ladies feed him moistened bread and dainties. Park birds can't stop him from sharing their hand-outs. In winter, near as anyone can make out, he holes up somewhere in the Friends Meeting House in Twentieth Street. The sexton knows it's spring when the turtle stirs from somewhere in the hedges, tests the sun and starts moving across the pavement toward the park.

May 16, 1956

¶ Through all four seasons, year in year out, the Sun Mee Company's cellar farm at 32-34 Division Street is like tropical jungle: air heavy and moist, steamy as a laundry. The crop yield is one and one-half tons of nga choy—bean sprouts—

every twenty-four hours. This is about half the amount used in the metropolitan district, though some of it goes as far north as Connecticut, some down to Philadelphia. The Sun Mee crop represents, roughly, half the total yield of four such cellar farms in Chinatown.

C. P. Liu runs the Division Street operation, a curious venture in hydroponics, on pretty much the same lines as did the Greeks of Homer's time, or the ancient Egyptians. His output goes into chop suey, into all manner of Chinese meat dishes, though mostly with roast pork and cut beef; into egg foo yung, an omelette. Almost all Chinatown boys like to experiment with miniature nga choy gardens. Some of the elders will tell you that tolerant teachers used to let them grow the sprouts in water-filled classroom inkwells. Even today, thrifty Chinatown housewives often raise their own.

These amateur sprouts lack the flavor of cellar crops. They're likely to come up green because light gets at them. Green sprouts are bitter. Anyway, house-grown or inkwell sprouts are not kept at a constant 75 degrees as they should be, and that affects flavor, too. It also accounts for the miasmic atmosphere in Mr. Liu's cellar. He germinates the mung beans—they look like undersized dry green peas—in deep pans filled with water and kept at 75 degrees. After they've had six straight hours of that he dumps them into the large cans.

The beans come in 100-pound bags and Mr. Liu gets his from different sources—from Oklahoma, Texas, Thailand and Peru.

His hot-water bills are his chief expense. In the big receptacles, the beans absorb seven to eight times their weight in water. Fifteen pounds of beans will end up as 100 pounds of sprouts. A crop comes through in five summer days, or in seven winter days. Oilcloth over the cans keeps out the light from naked overhead incandescents. When a crop is finished it goes into bushel baskets. Noodle companies in Chinatown handle restaurant distribution.

Mr. Liu is a crisp, businesslike chap. He got his Master's degree in business administration at the University of Missouri, tried teaching and selling life insurance before he turned to cellar farming. He has put bean sprouts in chain stores with pamphlets telling housewives how to use them in cooking, but chain store clerks won't keep the sprouts under refrigeration as they should, and he loses by spoilage. He speaks learnedly of the sprout as a cure for burns and of its application for snake bite; knows that the Greeks called the sprouts erebinthos and that they sometimes come under the names of chick pea, Asiatic gram, adsuki bean, Egyptian pea and Bengal pea.

He didn't know, though, that his cellar stood directly on the old boundary line between the old Delancey and Rutgers Farms, and that Division Street got its name because it divided Delancey and Rutgers acreage. "Never heard that before," he concedes, "but I only bought this farm two and a half-years ago."

May 18, 1956

❡ The Trail of Tears on which American Indians set their moccasins when white settlers first started taking over their hunting grounds more than 300 years ago is still poignantly real to members of the New York Metropolitan Group of American Indians.

They think that now they are really making a last-ditch stand—that unless sympathetic white folk help, their last reservations, their arts, ceremonies and culture may vanish. They hold regular monthly meetings in town in brave attempt to save what is left.

Right now the New York group, one of a chain of national units, is small—about fifty, all told, all western Indians. The president is a Cherokee; one vice president is a Pawnee, one a Sioux and the treasurer is a Winnebago. The secretary, Tzika Subbas (Indian for the Sun Bird) is a California Modoc, a soft-voiced woman who sings professionally. She went to Mills College in California, then took her B.A. at City College in New York.

Sun Bird is probably the most earnest toiler in the New York group. Her little flat in Leroy Street in Greenwich Village is a museum of her people's handiwork—their weaving, painting, bead work, pottery and talismans. She gets out all the group's correspondence there, works up Indian programs for schools, churches and for such places as Town Hall and Carnegie Hall. She has a wardrobe of authentic Indian costumes.

She has preserved many of the songs of the Old Ones, the few tribal ancients who remember traditional prayers and chants. She knows more than forty Indian calls by heart—summonses to ritualistic dances, to powwows and the like. They roll liquid from her tongue, to hand-drum obbligato. She assembles her people for weddings, for funerals and for parties; she helps with suggestions for moves to try to stave off politicians' reservation-grabbing.

Sun Bird says: "Few white people know how poor and how unhappy some of our people are." She says there is a move right now to dispossess the Shononi and the Bannocks at Fort Hall Reservation in Idaho. Her great fear is mostly for the Old Ones. She thinks they will die off fast if they are taken from the reservations to be turned loose in large cities to a way of living they have never known.

There are between 600 and 800 Indians around Red Hook in Brooklyn, most of them Mohawks who work on bridges and on skyscraper construction, but neither they nor the tribes on reservations around Buffalo, N. Y., face the same problems as the western Indians. Sun Bird and her group meet them socially once in a while, but haven't enlisted them against the reservation grab, because New York State takes pretty good care of them and doesn't try to seize their acreage. Many white church folk help, though, chiefly the Society of Friends.

The Sun Bird—she is Anita De-Frey off the reservation—does not tell you the names of other Indians in the New York group. She says: "I speak only for myself. They might not welcome identification in print without their permission."

One of the group is a psychiatrist in a New York hospital; several, odd as it may seem, are accountants, and a number of the Indian women here are hospital nurses. Some members work in city shops that sell Indian artifacts—places like the Wigwam, Tepee Town and the Plume. Those places, incidentally, serve more or less as the Indian grapevine in New York when there's need to spread a message.

A few of the Indian women here make doeskin dresses for wear at big powwows and ceremonials, and decorate them skillfully with bead work. The only powwow of any size in the New York area is the Labor Day assemblage on Shinnecock Reservation on Long Island. Sun Bird goes to that and also manages to make a lot of the Western powwows, water dances, corn dances and sun dances. Other local Indians who go to those are Red Wing, the old Winnebago movie star; Princess Atalie, a Cherokee, and Green Rainbow, a Winnebago.

May 21, 1956

❧ Vantage spots for visitors in town: Fort Tryon Park, for sweeping views of the city, of the Hudson and of the Palisades, morning or evening. . . . Brooklyn Bridge at dawn or at sundown, for watching lower Manhattan come alight after dark. . . . The 5-cent ferryboat ride across the bay to St. George, S. I., for harbor and sky-

scraper views, for watching gull flight. . . . Morningside Drive, as spring greenery turns lush and trees come to flower. . . . West Side Highway for spring color. . . . Shore Road in Brooklyn, for great craft and small, entering and leaving the harbor.

May 23, 1956

❧ The country fair, or weekly market, has pretty much vanished from the American scene in the last fifty years, at least within hollering distance of big cities. In the New York area only a few hang on in vestigial form.

The only regular weekly fair with bucolic trim that holds out inside Gotham seems to be the Farmer's Fair off Victory Boulevard in Greenridge on Staten Island. Its cries, its mixed scent of cabbages and roses, its itinerant peddlers briefly settled at stands and booths, its lost babies, leather-lunged barkers and wheedling pitchmen are rural hangovers strangely holding on within the Great City by the Sea.

The genius behind the Farmer's Fair is Ernest W. Johns, a florid giant out of Sault Sainte Marie, a triple-degree man from the University of Michigan who has been schoolmaster, deputy motor vehicles commissioner and Methodist parson, each, of course, at different times. His chief aide is Duke Lanihan, former golf pro.

Most of the merchants and farmers who show at Greenridge every Saturday from noon till midnight through the four seasons are circuit riders. They're at the Columbus Fair in New Jersey—at one spot or another almost each day in the week. Some are just farmers who make the Staten Island market on Saturday and no other.

Probably the most popular vendor at Greenridge is a hulking good-natured fellow who runs a general store on wheels; sells an astonishing variety of hardware, seed, house furnishings and gimcrackery from a stand set up at his truck's tail. Customers call him "Uncle Al." His name is Alfred Tyrza; in his youth he worked rural carnivals.

Farmers show their wares in rented stalls set out on the fairground. So do florists. They, like merchants who have their stock in three old airplane hangars on the grounds, pay monthly rental. Pitchmen pay by the day. Mr. Johns supplies space, floodlights for night operation and water.

Most of the stuff displayed, except the foods, seems to be low-grade (bargain-rate) catchpenny stock, strong on color and glitter, weak on honest sturdiness. But children and flat-pursed working folk seem to go for it.

The air's heavy with the stinging scents of hamburgers, hot dogs, ice cream, pizza, apples-on-the-stick, beer, cosmetics and assertive lotions of one kind or another. Kids splash the whole canvas with color as they trail balloons, horns, hand-run noisemakers.

To one side of the market a very blonde young lady, Miss Carolyn Kisker, runs an archery range. Next to her place lusty farmers and pale Wall Street clerks flail at baseballs malevolently shot at them by an automatic jigger.

On an adjoining lot—all these concessions pay Mr. Johns—Bob Tobacco, a former combat pilot, teaches flying, rents hangar space and offers overnight "tie-downs" at $1 for impecunious airmen. The small Tobacco ships offer barnstormers flights for $2, and the planes add their decibels to the din.

Mr. Johns and Mr. Lanihan get around a lot, letting tenants' complaints roll easily off their shoulders. They arbitrate little trade disputes, call lady concessionaires and sales girls "Honey"; cry recovered babies over a public-address system set up in their air-conditioned trailer; announce lost keys, umbrellas and the like.

The whole set-up has a dreamy, nostalgic effect. It's a bit of the pattern that faded from the tapestry of the happy Golden Age.

May 25, 1956

❡ The memorial service for the Civil War dead of both sides, to be held Sunday afternoon in Old Cypress Hills Cemetery on the Kings-Queens border at Hylan Boulevard and Jamaica Avenue, will be, near as anyone seems able to tell, the first of its kind since the dead were buried there roughly ninety years ago.

Confederate dead in the cemetery represent virtually all the southern states. Judge William M. Beard of Westfield, N. J., past commander of the Sons of Confederate Veterans, will speak at the service. He will mention, among other things, the men taken from the Confederate privateer Savannah and held as prisoners at the Old Tombs, or City Prison here, until transferred to Fort Lafayette in the bay off Fort Hamilton, Brooklyn.

Miss Desiree Franklin of this city, past vice president general of the United Daughters of the Confederacy, who helped locate the graves of the 460 southern dead in Cypress Hills, will be heard, too. Confederate and Union Army songs will be sung by northern children and by children of southern descent.

Caretakers in the National Cemetery in Cypress Hills have always kept 18,000 American flags for the graves there, but at the service on Sunday there will be intermingled with these 150 flags with the Stars and Bars, all that Confederate groups here could raise money for this year. By 1957, Miss Franklin thinks, there will be Confederate flags for all the southern dead in Cypress Hills.

June 4, 1956

❡ Horse players almost never know or understand much about jockeys' silks, possibly because they are insensitive to any color but long green. Yet racing silks have a long history.

They were first used at Newmarket in Britain in 1762 "for the greater convenience of distinguishing" one rider from another.

Silks are sternly watched against duplication, must be the same colors and design front and back, must be registered at $5 a year or $25 for life. The oldest in the United States are Howell E. Jackson's maroons, adopted in 1825. John A. Morris' scarlet ones are almost as old.

Terry Farley, custodian of silks at the New York tracks, knows 1,428 sets of silks by heart. He didn't pick that up overnight. He first got the job fifty-one years ago, after he had been, from 12 to 14 years old, an indifferent jockey at old Gravesend and Sheepshead Bay.

Around New York, silks are made by the Jockey Valet Service in Jamaica, Queens, which also cleans them for any stable; by Wilner in Manhattan, by Thybens' Saddlery near Belmont Park, L. I., and by Arcaro-Dan of Elmont, L. I., a service in which Jockey Eddie Arcaro has, or had, an interest. Some stable owners' colors are made by Merry in Britain and some by Paris concerns. One woman seamstress works in a motor trailer that follows the horses around the New Jersey tracks.

Probably the best known seamstress, though, is Marion Frances Dondas Legere, a smartly dressed, good-looking woman who is almost jockey size herself—4 feet 10 and weighing 110 pounds.

Mrs. Legere has sewn for Sir Winston Churchill (a gift set ordered by Bernard Baruch when Sir Winston acquired Colonist) for King Ranch, William Helis, C. V. Whitney, the Lit stables, John W. Hanes, Joshua Reed, Edward and Jane Lasker, Frank Rand, Eleonora Sears and Arthur Godfrey among others. Her father, William Dondas, a racing secretary on the Southern circuit, nicknamed her Taddy-Faddy when she was a rolypoly baby; wherefore she's Tad Legere around most tracks.

She gets $40 for a set of silks, though most other seamstresses rate only $25 to $35. Since she went into the business sixteen years ago, she has worn out three electric portable sewing machines.

Mrs. Legere finds an astonishing number of clients are color blind. She has had to do sets over for stable owners who ordered red, for example, when they meant cerise. Blue is the most popular shade for silks. Reds run second, yellows third. The favorite combination is blue-and-white.

Some designers, to hear Mrs. Legere tell it, skimp on silk and jockeys find that the shoulders tighten when they hunch over or that sleeves stop blood circulation at the wrists or forearm. She always gives extra measure to avoid such restriction. She knows all jockey head sizes—large for Conn McCreary and for Pete Anderson, for example, and small for Arcaro. She can rattle right down the list.

Superstitions creep into the business. Some jockeys and owners won't have buttons, because they consider them jinxes; some shun bows. Jockeys always claim as souvenirs the sets they wear as winners in big stake races. Warren Mehrtens wouldn't part with the silks in which he rode Assault to the triple crown—the Derby, the Preakness, the Belmont.

Mrs. Legere isn't altogether innocent of superstition herself, though she's well-read and calmly sensible in most matters. She likes to point out that 1,300 first-time winners have carried her silks. Her own color inclinations are blue and white. In her own dressmaking she tends to grays and light blues. She wears them like a winner.

June 15, 1956

¶ Uneasiness stirred two days ago by the scientists' report on radioactivity might be eased a bit if folk in town knew that the Fire Department had been turning out a corps of monitors to detect danger spots. Forty-nine men in the department's new Radiological Unit were graduated yesterday at the Fire College in Long Island City, Queens.

This was the second group to finish the intensive course in the new department specialty. By June 28 the last of five groups of volunteers will have been graduated. That will give the department a total of 144 men, enough to provide one expert for each of the city's forty-eight fire battalions, in every hour of each day's twenty-four. This service comes in good time, since by last week's count 199 hospitals and industrial plants within the five city boroughs were using isotopes in their work.

The city's 158 engine companies now carry ion chambers to pick up radioactive emanations. Battalion chiefs pack their own equipment. Department telegraph and radio dispatchers have complete lists of isotope-using plants and flash warning to companies rolling toward them. Each company has such lists, too, for its own immediate area, and the listings grow apace.

The detectors now in the department's hands can pick up minor or insignificant radiations. They could measure dangerous and lethal exhalations in, say, an area where an atomic or hydrogen missile had spread its evil content. The gadgets are actually owned by Civil Defense, but it would be the Fire Department's job to use them in war time, anyway, as they do now during uneasy peace.

The chief isotope users in town are the hospitals and Columbia University, which does a lot of research work. Printing concerns use radioactive strontium to counter static in their press rollers. Some companies use it to gauge micrometric differences in layered materials, and it is used in food preservation. The department's monitors keep a pretty sharp eye, too, on concerns that rent out isotopes. The firemen have a check on it all through Atomic Energy Commission records.

June 20, 1956

❡ A telephone book expert pantingly reports that the classified telephone directories in town have caught up with a truism uttered over 300 years ago by Francis Bacon. In his "Advancement of Learning" he wrote: "Cleanness of body was ever deemed to proceed from due reverence to God," a sentiment that John Wesley in a sermon 100 years later reduced to "Cleanliness is next to godliness."

Well, on page 368 in the classified book, the scholar discovered that the top-of-the-page listing in 1956 is "Cleaners-Clergymen."

❡ Because there are more fires in mail boxes than you'd think, the United States Post Office in Washington asked the Fire Department here recently to try to find the best way to put out such fires without using water. Water makes letter addresses fade and run; it reduces a mail receptacle's contents to pulp.

The Post Office Department sent three regulation mail boxes to the Fire Department College in Long Island City—a big parcel post holder, a middle-sized mail box and a small one. It shipped newspapers, magazines and dead letters with them for use in the tests.

The experts at the college set the boxes up in a lot alongside their establishment, started fires in each, let them burn for ten minutes, then ran two series of tests— one with carbon dioxide, one with carbon tetrachloride.

The carbon tetrachloride worked out best; it had the fire in each box out in thirty seconds, with minimum damage to the mail. The carbon dioxide got about the same results, but it took about five minutes to do the job.

June 22, 1956

❡ The soft-eyed Panamanian olingo, kin to the kinkajou, that was shown for the first time at Bronx Zoo two days ago was the gift of Richard Van Gelder, assistant curator of mammals of the American Museum of Natural History. He is the youngest man ever to hold that post, yet it came to him seventeen years after he first applied for it. Wild things had been his passion, even in boyhood. One day, when he was only 10, he prowled the museum's mysterious backstage quarters, gravely seeking employment. He was turned down, though gently, advised to come back later, which he did.

He found the olingo in rather a freakish way. Some weeks ago he was in Los Angeles, shopping for a kinkajou for his own collection. A pet-shop owner told him of a shipment that had come up a short time before from Panama. He disclosed that it had included what he called "a low-grade specimen." He described it—gray head, golden-brown body, ample tail twice body length; altogether something like a cat but much more slender. He said a roadside zoo in the Yakima Valley in Washington State had reluctantly taken it.

Mr. Van Gelder knew from the description that the "low-grade kinkajou" was an olingo, a rare thing, first discovered in 1876. The roadside zoo was happy to accept a kinkajou for it. Mr. Van Gelder shipped it East. The Bronx Zoo had never owned one before.

July 2, 1956

❡ The Sirdar Haripal Singh Jaaj spends his days in town handling the affairs of Maharajahs, Inc., on the sixth floor at 150 East Fifty-second Street. At night he stays close to his FM radio in his apartment in the building's second floor, recording on tape the softest and most tender melodies that come over the air, mostly from WBAI and WQXR.

The tapes are flown to the Sirdar's friends and to his family in New Delhi in India, who dance to the music or merely sit and listen, enraptured, to the latest from the United States. The tapes usually reach New Delhi within three days after programs are recorded. For special teas or garden parties, the Sirdar tapes his friends' requests.

Last week, for example, the Sirdar's sister, Mme. Komal Dhindsa, wanted something new and lovely for a garden party. The Sirdar called WBAI to ask if it would put on the air for him the Jackie Gleason albums, "Lonesome Echoes" and "Romantic Jazz." They did, and the tapes took immediate flight to India.

Haripal Jaaj wears the traditional Sikh turban, or pugree, the full beard and mustache. He explains that he does not take just *any* music from the air; he searches for pieces that bring in flutes, oboes and strings that are related to such Indian musical instruments as the citar and the sirod, a stringed, sobbing device calculated to induce pleasant sadness.

The Sirdar leaves house parties or functions, as he calls them, to hurry home to his recorder when something special is scheduled to come in over FM. His friends understand. They have heard him repeat that "music speaks from the soul of geniuses living and dead," that "it can dwell forever in the heart," that "it is truly the language of the angels."

Haripal got his first tape recorder in New Delhi on his twenty-first birthday, five years ago. It was the first ever seen there. It was flown to him from New York by his father, Sirdar Sardul Singh Jaaj, founder of Maharajahs, Inc. The young sirdar took Voice of America broadcasts from the air, British Broadcasting Corporation programs, music from the New Delhi radio station, and live material.

They excited wonder. A complete tape of a religious ceremony was played back before friends and family. They bowed and were reverent, as if at the original service. The young Jaaj had a tall aerial built outside his home near India Gate beyond Delhi, the better to bring in clear versions of distant broadcasts.

He takes 16mm. color movies, too, to send home. He recently did one of Times Square at night, got sound effects for it by putting his tape recorder microphone out his window at the evening rush hour to pick up traffic roar and street cries. He did the Third Avenue El in color before it came down, used a hair-dryer before the microphone to simulate train thunder. Worked out fine.

The elder Jaaj started Maharajahs, Inc., seven years ago to sell Indian artcraft and handicraft in the American market. He began with the output of ninety workers around New Delhi. Now he has 2,000 working in their homes and in factories. He sells to chain stores and department stores all over the United States and Canada.

Part of the profits go for medical treatment for the Indian workers, for spectacles for those who need them. Sirdar Haripal says: "We are ambassadors of commerce. We would have our people help themselves rather than expect bounty from other countries."

And while he speaks in the dimly lighted chamber where the walls display pictures of his family and paintings of the Himalayan foothills near his home, four hidden loudspeakers flood the room with the all-but-muted language of the angels, so dear to the Sirdar's ear.

July 4, 1956

❡ The man responsible for the building of the new Rockaway extension of the city's subway system will never be identified because he wouldn't know he brought it about.

This point is made by Transit, the Transit Authority magazine, in its summer issue. The fellow who set the Rockaway project in motion, the piece says, was an anonymous Long Island Rail Road commuter who, on May 8, 1950, flicked a cigarette butt out of a train window. The butt started a fire that burned down 1,800 feet of trestle. The road couldn't afford to rebuild at the time. It sold the branch to the city, which had been toying since 1917 with the idea of rapid transit for the Rockaways.

Transit authorities, mindful of

that butt-flick, have fireproofed the trestle. Their enginers, they let on, also had to go in for exhaustive research on bivalves and their habits, because mussels had done a lot of damage to the old trestles. They had a way of forcing themselves into cracks in uprights and enlarging them. This opened the door, so to speak, for other marine creatures to get into the wood to start greedy mining for tidbits. Vic Lefkowitz, one of the engineers, found they had reduced some 500 posts to skeletons, much as termites do.

Men who worked on the new Rockaway trestle ran into another hazard—mother gulls protecting nests in the long-abandoned structure. They'd come diving and screaming like kamikazis when crews got anywhere near unhatched eggs. When sand was dredged out of other points in Jamaica Bay, great gull swarms followed the loads to where the Transit men were creating new islands to reinforce the subway line. The dredged-up sand was filled with goodies that the birds never could have reached without the dredges to serve them up in tremendous portions. The gulls, incidentally, have taken over the new islands. They are a gulls' paradise.

July 6, 1956

¶ A new memorandum for tourists just put out by the Postmaster in New York discloses, among other things, that the inscription on the Post Office's Eighth Avenue façade isn't pure Herodotus, as most persons seem to think.

The late William Mitchell Kendall, senior architect for McKim, Meade & White, who designed the building just before the first World War, rewrote Herodotus. He was qualified for the task. His father had taught classical languages and young Kendall himself was no ordinary scholar in Greek and in Latin. He got the idea for the inscription while reading Herodotus in Greek; he found it in Volume 8, Chapter 98. First he tackled all available English translations of the passage—Rawlinson's, Macauley's, Carey's—but thought they hadn't quite caught it.

Mr. Kendall was a Harvard man. He asked Prof. George Herbert Palmer of the old school to work up a translation, and the professor came up with: "No snow, nor rain, day's heat, nor gloom hinders their speedily going on their appointed rounds." The reference in Herodotus, incidentally, was to Persian couriers who figured in the to-do between the Greeks and the Persians five centuries before Christ. Anyway, not even the revered professor's translation suited Mr. Kendall.

He chewed his pencil a bit, night after night, before he worked out his own version: NEITHER SNOW, NOR RAIN, NOR HEAT, NOR GLOOM OF NIGHT STAYS THESE COURIERS FROM THE SWIFT COMPLETION OF THEIR APPOINTED ROUNDS and boldly added the signature: HERODOTUS.

The quotation was approved by the Post Office and up it went. Mr. Kendall seemed to get a greater thrill out of his literary achievement, almost, than he did out of the over-all design. He chuckled over it right up until he died in 1941, aged 85.

There are quite a few of his creations around town, besides the Post Office. He did the Morgan Library, the Columbia University Library and the local Municipal Building, among others.

July 9, 1956

❡ The Statue of Liberty in the harbor is not the only work of Frederic Bartholdi on display in this city. He did the Lafayette for Union Square in 1876. New Yorkers of French descent paid for it. Not too many know, incidentally, that Alexandre G. Eiffel, who did the Eiffel Tower, has an invisible work in this city, too. He built the framework for the Statue of Liberty.

❡ The tune you hear from Metropolitan Life Tower as the half-ton minute hand on the tower clock trembles at quarter-hours is a bit from Handel's "I Know That My Redeemer Liveth." The designers chose this to fit the quaint old verse:

> *O Lord our God be Thou our*
> *Guide*
> *That by Thy help no foot*
> *may slide.*

❡ Keene's English Chop House in West Thirty-sixth Street has three-dimensional menus, now—stereoptican color slides showing all available courses, including desserts.

The diner studies them through a viewer.

July 11, 1956

❡ Town dwellers may be astonished to learn that for all its soot and weather change, spired Manhattan has among its dwellers a goodly number of men and women who breed orchids right in their flats and apartments, and do rather well at it.

They meet the fourth Wednesday of every month in the American Museum of Natural History to plunge into exciting discussion of the 15,000 or so kinds of orchids, of how they coax seed along with tomato juice, white sugar, cornstarch, coconut milk, agar, among other kinds of orchid feed.

Dr. Harold E. Anthony, deputy director of the museum, is one of the enthusiasts. So are the broker Ira Haupt, and Mrs. H. H. Schwartz, who brings orchids to bearing in her apartment at 944 Fifth Avenue; E. Bradley-Martin, the steel man; R. W. Jones, who sells netherware, and Dr. Howard N. Scal.

Raymond McAdam, an airline purser who lives uptown, also does very well at it, using turkish toweling in his apartment as a humidifier and fluorescent lamps for proper light. One member grows orchids on his fire-escape in summer, keeps them in his flat in winter.

One gentleman in town is up to his hips in orchidology through happenchance. He is the photographer Valentino Sarra. Down in

Miami, about fourteen years ago, in a backroads greenhouse, he came upon a homesick New Yorker who owned the place.

They talked for hours about New York. When Mr. Sarra left, the expatriate thrust two orchid plants at him—Trianae, a not very expensive kind—and insisted he keep them. Mr. Sarra coddled them in his Sutton Place apartment by the East River and they thrived.

By and by, he filled an extra room in his apartment with new acquisitions; bought a thermostat to keep humidity and temperature right, installed special lighting. He loved to distribute the lovely yield to friends and associates. And the mania grew.

Before he knew it, Mr. Sarra owned greenhouses full of orchids out in Albertson on Long Island. He got into the habit of rising at 5 A.M. to drive out for a few hours with them every morning, including Sundays, before beginning his day at his photographic studio. He still maintains that schedule.

He specializes in cattleyas, dendrogiums, cymbidium and cyprideum, but raises an almost endless variety, patiently cross-breeding and pampering new kinds. He still raises some in his East River apartment, too, but the Albertson greenhouses now hold around 200,000 plants and need the services of nine men. He sells to local florists.

Mr. Sarra has worked for seven years on a new yellow variety, but the true orchidist figures that as hardly any time at all. A new shade can net $1,500 or more for each stud plant. Mr. Sarra says: "You get so deep in the thing that even that isn't the prime attraction. It is like a deep love."

MARGINALIA: ¶ Patrolman Harry Eginton of the Police Department's Sixth Division goes his rounds, sometimes, in a sparklingly neat black Model A sedan, the kind that sold as a de luxe model thirty years ago for around $580.

¶ Most islands in New York Harbor are larger today than when the white men first saw them more than 300 years ago. They were widened at the margins with rock and soil taken from subway excavations and from skyscraper foundations. Even the Hudson River shore was built up that way. Part of it is rock from The New York Times extension in Forty-fourth Street.

¶ Urban sophistication is blind to poetry, else early names about town might have survived. When the town was young, the junction of Grand and Center Streets was Bayard's Mount, or Bunker's Hill; East Thirteenth Street at Avenue D was Burnt Mill Point; just north of City Hall stood Windmill Hill, and around that spot were Gallows Hill, Potbaker's Hill and Cowfoot Hill. The inlet that cut into Seventy-fourth Street from East River was Sawmill Creek and the great dimple east of Riverside Drive between 129th and 132d Streets was, quaintly, Mother David's Valley.

July 13, 1956

¶ Something in a tycoon's thought patterns seems to incline him to seek high places, even when hunger signals. In the city this is reflected in the so-called "sky-clubs" up in skyscraper eyries. There the diners see motorcars and vans as mouse-sized, far below, and plodding humankind as even lesser figures. It must be a godlike feeling.

The newest of these clubs is forming now. It will have the forty-second floor of the Socony-Mobil Tower at Lexington Avenue and Forty-second Street. The vast main dining hall is just getting its plaster and flooring, and lesser private rooms with awesome views line one whole side of the floor. A man just couldn't help thinking big thoughts in them.

He sees the rivers as rippled, dull tinfoil, the bridges as toys, harbor craft as a child's ships fit only for bathtub maneuvering. His eyes look far and beyond the Queens flats to the east, far out over the Jersey meadows to the west. Chrysler Tower blocks some of his sweep on one side and Chanin Tower on another, but the view south is unbroken, clear to Wall Street's haze-shrouded stalagmites.

¶ Town moles seem to be a little slow in trying the new gray-tiled and generously lighted tunnel that leads out of the new Socony-Mobil Tower to Grand Central Terminal, to the Commodore, the Chanin and Chrysler Buildings, to the cross-town shuttle, the Graybar, the Post Office, the Biltmore and—if you know the old route—clear up to the Roosevelt at Forty-sixth Street.

On a rainy day, a knowing mole might work his way from Forty-first Street and Third Avenue all the way to Forty-sixth and Madison without feeling a drop. The first leg would take him through the Socony-Mobil concourse. The warren to Grand Central was dug primarily to drain off the thousands who will work in that building; to keep them from flooding into Forty-second Street rush-hour traffic.

A lobby guard in the new skyscraper was approached the other day by a middle-aged couple who had just ridden the shiny new escalator up from subway level. "Where are we?" they wanted to know. "We got lost down there. We're from California."

July 16, 1956

¶ The old Wanamaker store was unroofed and skeletonized by fire over the week-end, with astonishing volumes of smoke for its funeral shroud. It had stood for ninety-four years. It was built in 1862 as an uptown counterpart to the Marble Palace, a cavernous dry-goods establishment raised sixteen years earlier at Broadway and Chambers Street by the merchant prince, Alexander Turney Stewart of Lisburn in Antrim. It was, like his Palace, a wondrous thing for its day, built around a cast-iron front, then the newest architectural twist. Ground for it was leased from the estate of the Revolutionary War privateer, Robert Richard Randall. The plot, like the land for the newer store that went up south of it in 1906, was the east end of the old Randall Farm. Under the terms of the privateer's will, tightly drawn by Alexander Hamilton in 1801, no part of the acreage was ever to be sold outright. Randall wanted income from the properties to support Sailors' Snug Harbor, which it does to this day. The current ground lease on the two plots, incidentally, runs to 1994.

The district that lay under a smoke pall yesterday has a fascinating history. In Astor Place, onto which the lower Wanamaker store faced, adherents of two rival Hamlets—William Charles Macready and Edwin Forrest—locked in bloody riot one May day in 1849 with nothing more to stir their anger than who was the better actor. The Seventh Regiment was sent on the double from Centre Market and, when battle smoke cleared, the street was strewn with 200 dead and dying. In the Colonnades, a bit farther south in Lafayette Street, President John Tyler married Julia Gardiner of Gardiners Island. Washington Irving lived in that row, and so did John Jacob Astor, who built the Astor Library just across the street. The Colonnades are 125 years old.

There's history, too, in the bend in Broadway that shoots abruptly westward just beyond the northern end of old Wanamaker's. The bend is there because a stubborn old Knickerbocker, Hendrick Brevoort, wouldn't let city planners cut down his favorite shade tree that stood in the line laid out for Broadway in 1807. There's no Eleventh Street between Broadway and Fourth Avenue because the same old Knickerbocker wanted no cuts through his farm. Grace Church stands on his

acres, now. It was a peculiar twist, too, that ended old Wanamaker's history at almost the same time as that of the old Bible House, just east of it that wreckers had just taken down. The Bible House cornerstone was laid in 1852 just ten years before the store went up. Cooper Union, just southeast of the store, was started in 1853 as "The Union for the Moral, Mental and the Physical Improvement of the Youth of This City, the Country, and the World."

The store building passed into the hands of Hilton, Hughes & Co., A. T. Stewart associates, after the old man died in 1876. Oddly, there was no rest for the merchant even after he was buried in the churchyard at St. Marks-in-the-Bouwerie. Grave robbers took up his body one dark night, two years later, held it for ransom, which they eventually got.

July 25, 1956

❡ Forty years ago, Prof. Edmond Bronk Southwick, entomologist and Shakespearean scholar, designed for the west side of Central Park what he called The Garden of the Heart. It spread over two acres of rocky hillside near the Swedish Cottage at Eightieth Street, a glory of posies.

That year happened to be the 300th anniversary of the Bard's birth. The garden's name was changed to The Shakespeare Garden, and a search was started for the 180 trees, shrubs and flowers mentioned in the poet's works. Professor Southwick got the list from

F. C. Savage's "The Flora and Folk Lore of Shakespeare."

Stratford oaks were brought from Avon. York and Lancaster roses, rue, bittersweet, savory, balm, flax, mint, eglantine, ash, woodbine, rhubarb, primrose, wild thyme, cowslip, lavender and columbine— everything from aconitum to yew —were added.

A marble bust of Shakespeare went up in the garden, a gift of the local Shakespeare Club. A Shakespeare collector, H. C. Folger, gave $1,500 for garden maintenance. Much of the growth could not long survive in Manhattan's uncertain climate. The lemon tree and the orange tree, for example, withered in island blast. So did other tender growths.

Today even top gardeners in Central Park don't seem to know how many different species exist in the Shakespeare acres. The number has dwindled greatly. Mrs. Cephas Guillet, a gentle, white-haired woman who guides the Riverside Church nature class to the park in seasonable weather, generally on Fridays, worries a lot about that.

She keeps writing to Park Commissioner Robert Moses and to other officials to do something about the Shakespeare Garden and about the bulldozers' bucking down old park trees. When the park was new, 100 years ago, Frederick Law Olmstead, who laid it out, figured on using 450 arboreal species for a total of 140,000 individual trees. Mrs. Guillet says a census now would show there's nowhere near that many.

She can tell you what destruction the bulldozers have wrought in some spots, and she does, with some anguish. They've pushed down the hawthorns, willows and black cherries near the pool at 103d Street, killed an old Chinese elm and four of the five persimmons that made lovely huddle near one of the new boathouses. She fears they may have brutal intentions against five rubber trees near the embattled Tavern-On-The-Green.

What wounds hew-to-the-line Shakespeareans more than anything else, you learn from Mrs. Guillet, is the invasion of Stratford Will's garden by plants he could never have known—Dorothy Perkins roses, for example, and fancy chrysanthemums. Worse than that, though, is the fact that the Parks Department has not replaced Will's nose. Someone knocked it off five or six years ago. Mrs. Guillet shakes her head over that when she sits in the garden's rustic bower.

"Here," she sensibly points out, "is Shakespeare in his own garden, without a nose to enjoy it."

July 27, 1956

¶ An attorney's existence can be a drab thing, bedded deeply in whereases, wherefores and most deadly legal flubdubbery. But sometimes it can have odd twists, too.

Last June, when the bloom was on the rose, a stately dowager who had long holed up in her Times Square hotel room, with only her pet Pomeranians for solace, went at last down the last, unbending road. In her will, offered in local Surrogate's Court for probate the other day, she directed, that, "my executor, herein named, have my body cremated . . . and I further direct my executor . . . to mingle my ashes with those of my late beloved toy Pomeranian dog, Mr. Ming Toy, in the same container, and that the ashes, when commingled, together be flown in a private plane over the area of Miami Beach, Fla., and strewn with pictures of my late beloved Pomeranian dog, Mr. Ming Toy, which are presently in my possession. . . . I have bequeathed all of my property [it comes to well over $15,000] to the American Kennel Club, because of my great love and affection for dogs . . . and hope that this bequest to the American Kennel Club will aid in the care, breeding and general improvement of dogs."

The executor was the woman's attorney. It will be his odd mission to throw the commingled ashes to the wind from a private plane, and one day, soon, he will. The lady left no kin but a husband from whom she had long dwelt apart.

July 30, 1956

❡ On Saturday morning a crypt was opened in the basement of the Roman Catholic Church of St. Paul the Apostle at Columbus Avenue and Sixtieth Street and the body of the Rev. Richard Stearns Cartwright, a Paulist father, went into it. The crypt was then sealed.

This was one of the rare crypt burials in Manhattan in modern times. Health laws now do not permit the use of crypts within Man-

hattan, except in places that retain the old rights. These would include Trinity Churchyard, St. Marks-in-the-Bouwerie, the old and the newer St. Patrick's Cathedrals, the Church of St. Paul the Apostle.

At St. Paul's there are seventy crypts in facing rows of thirty-five, all under the south church tower. With Father Cartwright's tenancy, sixteen remain open. When those fill, the church community may ask for new crypt space under the north tower, but that would not be for many years, if ever. At this date there would be no telling whether such a request would be granted. It has never been taken up officially.

Among those who sleep in the crypts is Father Isaac Hecker of the family that founded the old Hecker Baking and Flour Company of New York City. He founded the community. The church, incidentally, is rated among the most beautiful in the city. It probably is surpassed only by St. Patrick's Cathedral and the New York Cathedral (St. John The Divine). In the early Eighteen Seventies plans called for a thirteenth-century Gothic edifice. Stanford White, Augustus Saint-Gaudens and John La Farge were consulted.

Jeremiah O'Rourke, the chief architect, died before the Gothic church plan was finished. Paulist Father George Desho, who had been U. S. Grant's room-mate at West Point, took over. His military training is reflected in the church design; it has some of the aspects of a fortress. A goodly part of its stonework was done with materials taken from the walls of the reservoir that had occupied the space that is now Bryant Park.

The deep blue vault in the church, richly studded with stars, is a quaint decoration. The heavenly bodies are placed in the pattern of the stars and planets as seen from Manhattan the night of Jan. 25, 1885. That was church dedication date, the time of the Feast of the Conversion of St. Paul. The stars were plotted by Father George M. Searle, a member of the community, a man learned in astronomy.

¶ When City Hall, just made like new again, went up on the City Common 150 years ago, the City Fathers were so anxious to open its beauty to public view that they ordered the destruction of ancient Babylonian willows, sycamores, maples and walnut trees that had graced the park when the first white men landed on Manhattan.

August 6, 1956

¶ For seven years Mrs. Winifred Walker, born in England near Hampstead Heath, has sternly devoted her time to painting the 116 trees, shrubs, plants and flowers mentioned in Scripture. Her approach has been reverent but realistic. The end result is a portfolio of rich loveliness. It is believed to be the first complete work ever done on the subject.

Though the paintings took only seven years, the project can be traced to Mrs. Walker's remote childhood. She would run in from the garden in front of the Hamp-

stead Heath cottage to ask her headmaster father, a Biblical scholar, or her writer mother about myrrh and frankincense; about rare spikenard and gall, all mentioned in the Bible.

Grown up, Mrs. Walker went to good art schools—two of her brothers are members of the Royal Academy—and won lush commissions. She was artist to the Royal Horticultural Society, became a Fellow of the Linnaean Society, painted flowers for catalogues put out by American seed growers, taught art at the University of California at Berkeley.

It has taken almost 200 years to identify the green things of Scripture for what they truly were. Botanists have quarreled over identifications. Theologians plunged in to keep the record as it stood. But from the time Linnaeus, in mid-eighteenth century, suggested proper classification of plant life in the Holy Land, experts have worked fiercely at it.

Fifteen years ago, the New York Botanical Garden exhibited seventy-five plants named in Scripture. Dr. Harold N. Moldenke of the staff did a scholarly summary of those, and others, for the botanical garden's journal. Mrs. Walker found this guide most helpful. She located many of the plants growing in California; others she had to take as pressed specimens. One group came from an archdeacon's wife in Devonshire. The woman had gathered them between Jericho and Jerusalem in the Holy Land.

Startling facts develop as you examine the Winifred Walker paintings. You learn, for example, that the "apple" of the Garden of Paradise was not an apple at all, but an apricot. That the bulrushes in which Moses was cast away are not common cattails, but Cyperus papyrus, from which the ancient Egyptians made the first paper. That the "burning bush" was crimson-flowered mistletoe.

The "gall" of the Bible was a kind of poppy. The Rose of Sharon was a tulip. The rose that grew "by the brook of the field" was the oleander; the rose in Isaiah xxxi was the Narcissus tazetta; the "rolling thing" (Rose of Jericho) was a resurrection plant. Hardly any of the Scriptural lilies were really lilies; they were anemones or poppies. The glowing blossoms referred to in the passage "Solomon in all his glory was not arrayed as one of these" were poppy anemones, "the lilies of the field."

Frankincense and myrrh were not Holy Land perfumes. They came out of Tibet and Arabia. Spikenard (the nard plant) came out of hidden Himalayan vales in alabaster boxes 4,000 years ago, Mrs. Walker assures you—and it still does. It has never been grown elsewhere, though many have tried. Persians, it seems, still like it to perfume their beards, still pay high prices for it.

Mrs. Walker says you can find some Bible growths right in and around New York. Hemlock—not the hemlock spruce, but the weed that yields the poison that filled Socrates' bitter cup—grows now in local ditches and meadows. Dill, onions, leeks, the fruiting almond and beans are to be found in urban and suburban gardens.

You start downtown, and when the cabbie asks your destination, you get a good whiff of something the Scriptures mentioned. Common garlic (Numbers xi, 5).

August 8, 1956

¶ A career woman in town opened the top desk drawer in her apartment in one of the nicer apartment houses in the East Fifties last Saturday morning and stared in mystified disbelief at a man's calfskin wallet that lay in it.

In the wallet were, among other items, a Social Security card, some Florida and Pennsylvania addresses, three $1 bills, 1 cent in the coin pouch and papers clearly indicating that the owner was a young Philadelphian. One card showed a club membership in the Frankford section of Philadelphia.

In another pocket the woman found a business card with the same last name as the wallet owner's, but a different first name. It indicated that the man whose card it was worked in an executive job with a Madison Avenue advertising firm.

Suddenly the woman knew weird panic. She always kept her apartment door double-locked. She knew neither of the men whose names had turned up in the wallet. Besides herself, only her maid held a key to the suite. If the maid had found the wallet, she had left no note about it.

The woman knew a tortured week-end. She could not reach her

maid in Harlem—no telephone. She looked in the telephone book for the name of the advertising man; he was not listed. How had her room been entered? Why had the wallet been put in her desk drawer?

Imagination took over—wild imagination. Was the placing of the wallet in the drawer part of some plot to involve her in heaven knows what kind of deviltry? Could it be a murder frame-up? Would the cops be at the door to tell her they had found the body of the young Philadelphian?

Hysteria set in. The woman thought of calling the police, but would they believe that she had not seen the wallet until she opened the desk drawer? That story would make no sense, though it was true. The woman started calling a few friends for advice.

They were no help. They could no more figure out a likely explanation for the situation than she could. They thought it sinister, and offered her shelter for the week-end. They warned her to keep her door bolted and chained, which she did, wracking her brain for solution of the mystery.

She tried the telephone of the advertising company named on the business card, in the desperate hope that someone might be working on some emergency task over the week-end. She heard the audible ring—then silence.

The poor woman was aquiver when she got to her office desk on Monday. She had been awake most of the night, fearfully expecting the plot—whatever it was—to develop.

But she had had one happy inspiration: the wallet could have been dropped by the cleaner's boy when he had called for the laundry on Friday morning.

She figured: "That's it. He dropped the wallet. The maid found it and put it in the desk."

When she called the cleaner, though, that idea shattered. They had no one on the staff whose name answered to the name of the wallet-owner.

The woman called the advertising man's office. The receptionist told her the man had left the firm some time ago to go to another advertising firm. The woman finally got him. She told him who she was and where she lived. She said: "I'm terribly upset over something I can't explain. I found a wallet with your card."

The advertising man laughed, and the laugh was not sinister. He said: "I've been expecting your call."

The woman's spine stiffened. "Just a moment, sir," she told him icily. "I don't know you. I don't know the man who had your card in his wallet. You couldn't have expected this call."

But it turned out he could. He had, only a few weeks before, taken an apartment four floors directly above the woman's, then had left on business for Chicago. He had told the apartment house staff that he expected his son in from Philadelphia and wanted the son let into his suite when the boy got there.

The elevator man misheard the suite number. Instead of letting the boy into his father's rooms, he had let him into the woman's, four down in the same row. The boy began to undress for a shower when it struck him the fittings in the place were too feminine for his dad —that the photos in the living room were of no one he recognized.

The boy redressed and got the elevator man to let him into his father's suite. He had a good time for a few days, then left before his father got back from Chicago. He told his father: "I think I left my wallet in that wrong apartment, but I may have lost it outside somewhere."

The father went to interview the elevator man who had let his son in, but the elevator man had quit house service and had left no forwarding address. He had not told the management of his error, probably afraid of reprimand.

"Anyway," the advertising man said, "I knew that sooner or later whoever found the wallet would probably call."

The woman sighed deeply in sheer relief. She said, "I'll leave the wallet with the lobby desk," and she did. She is grateful, now, for the conversation piece the incident created. "Couldn't have happened anywhere but in this crazy New York," she tells people.

August 10, 1956

❡ Rare items in the Metropolitan Museum of Art, the great mural in the United Nations Building lobby, relics in the Bedloes Island Museum and displays in Fifth Avenue store windows are protected from sunlight's destructive ultraviolet rays by a new plastic window coating.

The compound, called Solar Screen, changes the ultraviolet rays' wavelength so that when the rays fall on priceless paintings, documents, costumes or the like they no longer have the quality to cause fading or deterioration. It is used to protect foods, drugs, photographs, wines and liquors—almost anything—exposed to sunlight.

Fluorescent lamps give off ultraviolet beams, too, so the Solar Screen people have made roll-up shades and frame-glass coated with the plastic to protect exhibits or displays that might encounter fluorescent light.

The plastic is poured on glass when it is to be used for windows. It is as colorless as glass; does not hold back or diminish light passing through; is made to last indefinitely.

❡ A tape-recorded starling distress note captured three years ago by Dr. Hubert Frings and Joseph Jumber of the Department of Zoology and Entomology at Pennsylvania State University is offered for sale now as a device for ridding starling-plagued districts of those raucous birds. It was used first on sound trucks on large farms where starlings were cutting themselves in on crops; then was taken up by public institutions that found themselves grackle-infested. Here in town, the Metropolitan Museum of Art and property-owners under 125th Street Viaduct have been starling targets, off and on, for years.

Near as Dr. Frings and Mr. Jumber can make out, the distress call throws all starlings within hearing in bird panic during which they give off some undefinable exhudation. It clings to an area for some time and until it wears off, the whole flock shuns the spot. Mr. Jumber got onto that by accident. Working on a thesis about starlings four years ago, he caught a bird in a Pennsylvania barn one day. It give off the weird, crow-like scream —the distress call. When he went back to the barn for other bird specimens, the birds cleared out— and stayed out. That got Mr. Jumber thinking. He talked things over with the professor, and after a few tests they pinned the thing down. Mohawk Business Machines Corporation in Brooklyn heard about that; started making the tapes and found eager buyers.

The Federal Government has Professor Frings and Mr. Jumber at work now on seagull and on crow distress calls that they hope may be as effective as the starling's scream. Oddly, no one has urged the team to try their stuff with pigeons, though you'd think they might. Mr. Jumber, strange as it may seem, does not aim to make a career of distress calls, or even bird study. He wants to be a dentist.

¶ Well-to-do gentlemen, mostly retired business men from Park and Fifth Avenues, keep Joe, the Central Park Zoo's chimpanzee, in fancy cigars. They unselfishly give Joe their own favorite brand; rarely pass him a stinker. Monkey-house keepers don't let the chimp carry his own matches, but light cheroots for him when he's in the mood to smoke, which is two or three times a day. If the mood passes before a good cigar's burned down, Joe sticks the butt high in the cage for future reference. Curiously, Joe never worked for a circus or in vaudeville. He came out of Africa, a primitive, when he was 18 months old, eighteen years ago; just picked up the nicotine habit from customers passing him lighted cigarettes. He's been strictly a cigar-chimp, now, for eight or nine years.

August 13, 1956

¶ The original constitution and by-laws of the Society of Tammany, or the Columbian Order, written almost 170 years ago, have just come into the hands of Charles Hamilton, dealer in autographs here in town. Sheer accident brought the document to him on the eve of the Democratic Convention.

The writing is in a kind of ledger on sturdy hand-ruled rag-paper pages. The cover is simulated marble veining, a bit rubbed but otherwise in good order. Mr. Hamilton got the book from descendants of William Mooney, a New Yorker who ran an upholstery business at 23 Nassau Street after he had been a soldier in George Washington's Army.

Mr. Mooney was Tammany's first Grand Sachem. A note in the volume says, "William Mooney, Founder of Tammany," but his right to that designation could be challenged. There were Tammany societies in almost all the original thirteen colonies before Mr. Mooney's New York unit started in 1789.

Chief (sometimes called King or Saint) Tammany was a Delaware sachem, traditional friend of the white man, the Red Nestor of Eastern tribes late in the Seventeenth Century. He had been kind to William Penn. His name meant "The Affable," roughly speaking. He was a liberty-loving savage and a national symbol of democracy.

Tammany, as Mr. Mooney and his New York cronies shaped it in the constitution—it is dated Aug. 24, 1789—was a fraternal and patriotic body. Its members dressed and paraded as Indians, used tomahawks instead of gavels, spoke with an Indian dialect and took fearsome oaths to guard their grip, their password and other ritualistic humbug.

All ritual details are in the volume, but not the password or the details of the grip, plainly because alien eyes might get at the volume and steal those secrets. They were passed to the membership only orally and under threat of extreme penalty. Rituals were conducted by torchlight at the Tammany wigwam.

The wigwam, incidentally, shifted with astonishing frequency in the earlier years. You get the notion that perhaps the brotherhood may have been over-fond of blood-curdling outcry at their meetings. The ritual arcana in Mr. Mooney's book call for stamping of the feet by assembled brethren, too, and that must have made them rather noisy tenants.

"Et hoh" (Indian for "Yes") and "Yaugh-ia" (the term for "No") are still part of Tammany's infrequent induction ceremonies, but few braves in the present wigwam seem to know the meaning of other ritualistic shouts, like "Sago, Sago, Olie," which are in the Mooney document.

"If any Brother [brave]," the Tammanial laws provide, "shall reveal any of these [ritualistic] secrets to any other than a member . . . without a caution to 'Beware of eve-droppers' [Mr. Mooney's spelling was delightfully erratic] he shall be impeachable and shall be reminded by the proper officer that by the breach of his obligation he has approached The Gates of Infamy . . . that willful repetition of the crime shall be a capital offense."

They couldn't have meant that literally. Even in a New York of only 33,000 souls, huddled at Manhattan's foot, civilized braves did not actually take scalps.

Grand Sachem Mooney and his braves had themselves roaring times in all public demonstrations. They stalked down muddy Broadway in full regalia, puffing at calumets, in New York's Louisiana Purchase celebration in 1804 and were the welcoming delegation when the Creeks—real red men—came to town in 1790 to meet The Great White Father (George Washington).

One last thing. When latter-day Tammany meets in social conclave, which isn't often, the Sachem and the Sagamores don't wear the original feathered headdress or any other Indian trappings. These were dropped in 1813, when townsfolk soured on Indians because of atrocities in the War of 1812. Today, gentlemen like Jim Farley and ex-Sheriff Charles Culkin wear silk toppers, instead. Et hoh, they do.

August 27, 1956

¶ The Pharmacie Legoll specializes in French herbs, drugs, liqueur components and imported nostrums dear to the hearts and palates of Gallic patrons all over the United States. It seems a tiny shop, hidden behind a pale green and gold front at 581 Tenth Avenue, above Forty-second Street, but behind a modest partition it swells out in vast space crowded with French stock.

The shop has stood on Tenth Avenue the last sixty-two years, but its history began 110 years ago. A Mr. Crawford—his first name seems nowhere on record or in memory—started it as a common apothecary in 1846 in Seventh Avenue between Twenty-sixth and Twenty-seventh Streets. M. W. Caswell bought him out in 1870, kept the place for twenty-four years, then sold it to Edouard Legoll.

M. Legoll, fresh out of Alsace, changed the shop's character, or, rather, had it changed by French families that then lived in the neighborhood. The women sighed for herbs they had had in France, for extracts for homemade liqueurs, for patent medicines their parents and their parents' parents had trusted. M. Legoll was an astute man. He imported all the items for which they seemed nostalgic. By and by he printed ambitious catalogues to send to Frenchmen far outside New York who heard of his wares.

The coming of the Seventh Avenue subway changed the avenue and the neighborhood. The fur trade took over the area. The French families left. M. Legoll, sensitive to this change, drifted uptown with his countrymen. Because he was thrifty, he took the shelving and other fixtures with him. The warm-glowing cherrywood, the intricate carving, the noble mirrors that were secret doors, the bowed glass either side of the mirrors stand today in Tenth Avenue as they did in the original Crawford apothecary.

A wise one, that Uncle Legoll. Stray moderns who see the shelving and the old cherry front have bid high for just portions of it. One man with an estate in Connecticut offered $3,000 for a one-tenth part. Another man wanted it for an apothecary museum. He told Joseph C. Legoll, who has run the shop since his uncle died in 1939, that it was one of the oldest in the United States. He has begged that if ever Joseph gives up the shop, he be permitted to bid for it. Since Joseph has no sons to follow him, that day may come.

Anyway, to linger in the pharmacy with eyes closed to all outdoors is to think you stand in a shop in, say, the back streets of Montmartre. The customers give their orders and their gossip in fluid French. The shopkeeper answers in kind. The shop's advertising signs have Gallic flavor. Many are from Paris, advertising French products.

The main traffic is in herbs for gentle teas—for verveine, for peppermint, camomile, tilleul (linden), for orange blossom and for powdered orange leaves, all for aromatic brews.

French chefs in town order their basil, their thyme and other cooking herbs from the shop. Men and women from the United Nations and from the French Embassy go there, nostalgic for items they miss elsewhere in New York. Sailors from the Ile de France and other vessels of the French Line buy their drugs there, or go to replenish ship's stores. Until they moved, some years ago, the workers for Pernod at Thirty-seventh and Tenth and the bakers for L'Etoile in Forty-second Street, just around the corner, shopped at the Pharmacie Legoll for specialties.

Withered old women go for French mineral waters, tonics and cough syrups they had known in France; stock up on extracts that, with judicious amounts of water and alcohol, turn into prunelle, curaçao, menthe, crème de noyau, and the like. The old Mouquin Restaurant bought its extracts from Uncle Edouard. And Joseph has kept the shop as his good uncle kept it—simple, neat, a little on the dark and broody side, with barely no concessions to modern drugstore pile-up of items in no way associated with the trade.

Joseph, though he got his chemist's and pharmacist's ratings at Columbia University—he came here as a lad of 10, out of Alsace in 1910 —thinks, "It is better so."

October 15, 1956

❡ What is most likely the greatest single collection of reproductions of the world's art masterpieces— 11,482 items—is kept in a rather dimly lighted but neat, small room on the ground floor of 234 East Fiftieth Street. It is part of a family flat.

The collection includes the greatest paintings, old and modern; outstanding works in sculpture, in ceramics, porcelains, tapestries, prints and drawings, arms and armor and jewelry. They are the pick of public and private treasures.

The collection is mounted on Kodachrome slides for use with hand, or table, viewers or for screen projection to natural—or larger—size, in true color. They are owned by one family—Francis G. Mayer; his wife Adele; their sons, Peter H. and Charles T. Mayer.

Francis Mayer, tall, slenderly built, with frost in his mustache and at his temples, was a Viennese machine engineer and master photographer. Peter is a lieutenant in the Air Force Reserve; Charles a lieutenant in the Army; both have World War II records.

All three have worked at assembling the collection. The father started it—he had worked in the Lumière color process fifty years ago when he was only 15—with *his* father's Lechner camera and ground-glass magnifier. He still uses the sixty-five-year-old magnifier.

The Mayers' establishment of the collection grew out of happy accident. Francis Mayer was asked, fifteen years ago, to photograph Flemish paintings for a friend, a Belgian diplomat, who was to tour the United States to lecture on Flemish art.

Photography had been his hobby since childhood, as it had been his father's. He got out his ancient Leica, bought floodlights, and copied the Flemish masterpieces at New York museums for his lecturer-friend. They made perfect transparencies, were admired around the circuit.

The art department head at the University of Minnesota asked for copies for study purposes. Other schools, colleges and women's clubs put in bids, the demands snowballed and, quite without ever meaning to, Francis Mayer was in business.

He now works for the Metropolitan Museum of Art and for most other great museums throughout the country. Paintings in miniature, on sale at countless art centers, are likely to be his handiwork. He has done the Thyssen, Liechtenstein, Lewisohn, Dale, Clarke, Frick and Lasker collections, among others.

The Mayers also have a tremendous collection of famous cathedrals, both interiors and exteriors; some with fine detail of stained glass. They have done beautiful places and castles, famous gardens, public buildings; even pets such as peacocks, but only a few portraits.

In the last fifteen years the Mayers have combed the museums of Europe and the United States for subjects; have made slides in the Vatican, in the Louvre, the Ufizzi Palace, Pitti Palace, the Villa Borghesi—have been virtually everywhere except Russia and her satellite countries.

The slides are used mainly for educational groups. If they are sought for any commercial purpose, permission for reproduction must come from the owners, who usually consent if they are to go into books on art, into new Bibles, or the like. For these purposes the Mayers copy the subjects on larger films, mostly Ektachrome.

They are so adept with their equipment that they have come away with as many as 2,500 slides in a single day. They never miss. They not only take a full canvas, but take separate shots of important detail for study purposes. Some of the Velásquez shots are about to go on the back of new playing cards.

Their work goes to the world's farthest corners, mostly to schools and to lecturers; some as far off as Ceylon, among other remote spots. They filled a large order for a convent, which puzzled them; all were religious subjects but one. That one called for Matisse's "Nude In Reclining Chair."

Not long afterward they got a note in rather disturbed phraseology from the convent's mother superior. She never mentioned the Matisse item by title, only by number. Someone had made an error. She asked for a replacement (by number) and got what she wanted —Bellini's "Madonna and Child."

October 24, 1956

❡ In 1886, when Lizzie Reincke and Martha Koester were 5-year-olds, they lived on the East Side where Manhattan Bridge approach is now. They had golden blond pigtails done up in bright ribbon, stiff little dresses of calico. Hand in hand they tripped to class in Public School 7 at Chrystie and Centre Streets. They grew up together in a changing world.

Fifty-seven years ago, Lizzie got a job at Purdue, Frederick & Co. It paid $7 a week for six full days. The job was just pasting labels on Dr. John P. Gray's Compound, a kind of tonic with sharp sherry (11 per cent alcohol) flavor to it. Seven years after Liz had been pasting labels, she got a similar job for Martha. They liked the work. They never married.

First they worked at 15 Murray Street. When the plant moved to 298 Broadway, they moved with it. About thirty-four years ago, another move took them to Christopher Street, west of Hudson, still pasting labels; still wrapping the bottles. Forty-eight years ago Lucy White, a Bronx girl, was hired. They worked on through the years.

When the Strattons owned the plant, long ago, the girls not only made their own lunches, but broiled the chops, each day, for the Strattons. One day Liz would buy a cake or a pie on the way to work. Another day it would be Martha, or Lucy. They always made their own coffee—and still do. They were happy; never dreamed of, or wanted, change.

The Dr. Gray bottles changed a little. Once they were white-topped, now they are black. The label was never altered, nor the 11 per cent

sherry. In the first few decades the girls did the bottles in tissue paper and tied them with pink cord. They don't do that any more. They walked to work in the old days, or rode the horse cars; now it's the subway.

They rarely stayed away from the shop. Lucy and Liz have only five days of absenteeism on their records; Martha has only four. City pace stepped up all around them—planes spanned the skies, motor cars thronged the city streets, movies came, and talkies; radio and TV; wars disturbed the earth and ended. They went happily on with their labeling.

Three years ago Dan Schneider, master pharmacist, took over Purdue and Frederick. In his tour of the shop in Christopher Street he paused in the labeling room where a south light made lovely halos around pleasant-faced, white-haired women—Lucy and Liz and Martha, and Ellen Newman, a Greenwich Village girl, born and bred, who joined up only five years ago. They looked up at the new owner and smiled—and went on pasting Dr. Gray bottles.

Mr. Schneider looked up their service records, and whistled; studied their absentee records and whistled again. He saw that their wrinkled hands, even now, never stop at their work; that their little coffee klatsches and cake sessions do not interrupt. Whatever sweeping ideas he had at first just melted away. Instead, he raised them from $35 a week to $50. They glowed.

Mr. Schneider is glad, now, that he did not follow the blind Atom-

Age policy—"off with their heads, if the heads are silvered." At 2 o'clock on Friday afternoon he will call a plant halt so that all hands may gather around the labeling and packaging table to honor Liz and Martha and Lucy and Ellen, all past 70 and all happy and tireless; girls who never changed in a world of constant and violent change.

October 26, 1956

¶ About a year ago Tom Manning, historian at venerable Green-Wood Cemetery in Brooklyn, discovered the unmarked grave of Capt. Samuel Chester Reid, who designed the stars and stripes that first flew at the Capitol in Washington in 1818.

The Granite Craftsmen's Guild of New York, made up of some forty dealers in monument stone, designed and has set up in Green-Wood a simple granite monument to mark the forgotten grave. It will be unveiled at 2 o'clock this coming Sunday afternoon. The stone, meant to be everlasting, bears the legend: "Samuel Chester Reid 1763-1861. Designed the flag of the United States of America with thirteen stripes and one star for each state. Approved by Congress April 4, 1818. First flag of this design, made by Mrs. Reid, flown over the Capitol at Washington, April 12, 1818."

The epitaph also tells how Captain Reid, commanding the frigate General Armstrong, engaged three British men-of-war at Fayal in the Azores on Sept. 26, 1814, and delayed their journey with reinforcements and with military supplies, to enable Gen. Andrew Jackson to win the battle of New Orleans.

October 29, 1956

¶ For sixteen months from July, 1955, to mid-October this year, fifty-six of the seventy-two bells in the Riverside Church's 400-foot tower were missing from their dark belfry. So was the master carillonneur, Kamiel F. LeFevere. Yet the carillon through all those months kept bonging the quarter hours with the Parsifal theme, day in, day out, and on the Sabbath it pealed its clangorous repertoire of sacred music and calls to service, as always.

There were many, even among the church's own congregation, who didn't know through that long interval that the music that wafted down to the great nave, over the town, across the Hudson, was ghost music. It came from tapes recorded by Mr. LeFevere before the bells were lifted from their perches. Many were taken down in the still of the night, to avoid clustering of curious onlookers. The bells were then quietly crated, carted to a Black Diamond freighter, and borne across the Atlantic to Heiligerlee in the Netherlands.

Heiligerlee is a tiny town, away off the beaten track, but there the Van Bergen Bell Founders, an ancient establishment, turn out a major portion of the world's carillons. Mr. LeFevere went there to supervise the casting of new bells for the Riverside Church tower. Over twenty-six years the old set had flatted; had lost a half-note over its full six-octave range. Mr. LeFevere had been painfully aware of this defect. So had visiting carillon-neurs and a few among Riverside Church's own parishioners with an especially sharp ear for music.

The Van Bergens accepted the fifty-six old bells as part payment toward the new. As the fresh set was cast, Mr. LeFevere and three other experts stood by to test them for true sound. One of these was a blind man, because Mr. LeFevere believes that a blind musician has quicker ears for a bell-fault than you'd find in a sighted man. As it was, between them, they rejected six of the newly cast bells because they were infinitesimally off. In his talks with the bell-founders Mr. LeFevere explained that the River-side Church clavier—the keyboard for playing the carillon—had ped-als and manuals for seventy-four bells, though the total of the church's tower bells came to only seventy-two.

The magnanimous Van Bergens pondered that fact a while. Then they cast two additional high-note bells—they'd correspond to the sel-dom-used notes at the right-hand side of a piano keyboard—and of-fered them as a gift to the Laura Spellman Rockefeller Memorial. That's the true name of the caril-lon, largest of its kind on earth, a tribute from John D. Rockefeller Jr. to his mother. The new set got back to New York last February and, again without attracting pub-lic attention, was carried through the church to the tower elevators. Then the riggers were called in,

and they spent months setting them into position.

Now the carillon is sharper and clearer in the high end of the scale, and is utterly without flaw. The great bourdon—the twenty-ton bell that rumbles lowest of all the tower set—and its deep-throated kin have always been perfectly true. Mr. Le-Fevere, who loves them all with deep affection, sits in his lofty office in the tower's twenty-first floor, writing new music for them all the time—sacred things, ancient songs done for the lute as far back as 1,100 years ago. Between notes he stares out far across the Palisades and the New Jersey meadows, on the Hudson running far below, re-flecting autumn's rich coloring. He is happy now. His bells have found their tongues again.

November 9, 1956

¶ Any old stage-door Johnny yearn-ing to know again one of the thrills of young manhood might achieve his wish when, from cocktails at 7:30 well toward dawning, the Ziegfeld Club, Inc., made up solely of former Follies steppers, will stage its annual ball.

The stage-door laddies wouldn't know their old favorites now. Some are in their 70's, or close to it. Many —there were about 1,500 in twenty-two Follies editions—are snow-crested; a few have somehow main-tained the raven or platinum color they had under stage lighting long ago.

The Ziegfeld Club, Inc., got its charter twenty years ago. It was dreamed up by the theatrical press agent Bernard Sobel in 1936 after he had rounded up a cluster of former Ziegfeld beauties to add luster to the opening of the motion picture "The Great Ziegfeld," which he was crying up at the time.

The girls, Mr. Sobel found, had such a merry time at that first reunion, talking about their heyday, that in the beginning all they had in mind was a social club. By and by, though, it dawned on those who had married wealth, as quite a few had, that some of their sisters-of-the-Ziegfeld-line had come upon unhappy—some upon utterly miserable—days.

In that hour the more fortunate set about helping the less favored. They went at it seriously, and still do. Many give annual donations, send in contributions of dresses, furs, shoes and hats. One woman, gray now and a grandmother, gets a $50 check every year from a former admirer who never gave up. She turns that into the fund, too.

But the club treasury depends on the annual ball for its largest income. The events yield anywhere from $7,500 to $10,000 a year. Local merchants send in some 200 prizes for the ball each twelvemonth, and some are quite handsome, too. Guests buy tickets for these, on blind-grab privilege, at $7.50 each. That swells the coffers.

Some of the money goes out to former Follies girls who, strange though it may seem, are in homes for the aged. Some goes to train other old Ziegfeld girls for jobs as receptionists, seamstresses, typists or saleswomen. These are girls who have married unfortunately or through illness and other misfortune have walked long on the dark side of the street.

The gifts of clothing, of funds, the training expenses, are distributed so that none but the top officials—Mrs. Gladys Feldman Braham is president—know to whom they go, or in what amount. Some of the richer ex-Follies girls have even taken old dressing-room companions into their own homes to get them back on their feet. When the girls turn up at the annual ball, though, you won't know the fortunate from the unfortunate.

Of the very first Ziegfeld row, the cast that had the Johnnies gaping at the Jardin de Paris, and at the old Liberty in 1907, the club has turned up only two. They are Vi F. Bowers Simmons, who celebrated her fortieth wedding anniversary not long ago, and Florence Arkell Jacoby. Both have done well since they left the stage.

Annette Simonet Tanner, who has five grandchildren now, will be at the ball. So will Madeleine Janice Courter. Justine Johnston, one of the rarer beauties of the happier days, is now Dr. Justine Johnston, an expert in medical research. The other members didn't know whether she would be in from California. Nor do they expect Gladys Glad. She lives up in Canada. One of the thrilling beauties of the line is blind, now, but is looked after by the others.

Rae Dooley, who appeared in ten different versions of the Follies, will be a performer tomorrow night with her husband, the producer Eddie Dowling, and with Fred Coots, who wrote music for the Ziegfeld productions. John Steel, who introduced "A Pretty Girl Is Like a Melody," will sing that song again. Will Rogers Jr. will do some of his father's old rope tricks. Lorelei Kendler Hess of the old line will be at the party. She won't perform, but her daughter, Judy Tyler of "Pipe Dream," will.

Old stage-door Johnnies who go must expect to meet silvered versions of the dream girls of their youth.

November 12, 1956

❡ The Merritt-Chapman & Scott Corporation in town, which has its fingers in a multiplicity of maritime enterprises, has a piece in its Black Horse News, a house publication, about shipbuilders always setting silver coins, heads up, under ship masts.

It seems that Bill Wall, who worked in the company's New York Shipbuilding Yard for years until he retired a few months ago, first told the company's white-collar lads about the custom. The tradition is so old and so steadfast now that New York Shipbuilding architects always design a spot for the silver under the masts of ships abuilding.

Merritt-Chapman researchers got interested in the theme. They decided, finally, that the tradition began, most likely, in prehistory when men first learned to launch watercraft; that in the beginning there were human sacrifices to propitiate pagan deities of wind and of water. Later this got down to offering foods and wines to the gods. Finally the food offerings were withheld. Now filled champagne bottles are swung against new ship's prows.

In most cases the silver—dimes, quarters, dollars—is contributed by artisans who actually labor at shipbuilding, but when the Navy's Princeton was put together at the New York Shipbuilding Yards the silver came from Princeton undergraduates.

Mr. Wall told the Merritt-Chapman researchers that the change from human sacrifices and food-and-wine offerings to silver facing heaven must have been dreamed up by the early Greek mariners. It assured their ferry fare across the Styx if storm or wreck got them or their passengers. The United States Navy, to this day, has memory of an old tradition of putting a penny in a dead seaman's mouth before he is committed to the water in sea burial. That must trace back to the Styx fare idea, too. It was called a Coin for Charon.

November 14, 1956

❡ Earl Van Sickle has been a gentlemen's tailor for more than sixty years. He started as an apprentice in Indianapolis, his home town, in the Nineties, worked in Cincinnati and St. Louis. He got to New York in 1903 with $100 in savings and a wardrobe he had made for himself.

He knew no one in town then and had no kinsmen here. On Sundays he strolled with the rich in

Fifth Avenue. He wore a double-breasted Prince Albert with satin facings, silk hat, pointed patent leathers; he swung a jaunty stick. He went to John D. Rockefeller's Sunday school class in the West Forties off the Avenue. He rode the horse-drawn Fifth Avenue omnibus on the box, when he could, to have the driver point out the merchant princes' mansions.

His money had all but run out when the Everalls, at 259 Fifth Avenue, took him on. They had rich customers. The Avenue was filled, then, with smart, sparkling carriages. Mr. Van Sickle often watched Alfred Gwynne Vanderbilt tool a coach-and-four down the cobbles starting a run from the near-by Holland House to Ardsley in Westchester.

"Mr. Vanderbilt," he remembers, "usually wore a pearl-colored frock coat, black ascot, gray felt topper. His footmen wore tan gabardines and high hats with side cockades."

Most eccentric of all who came to Everalls, Mr. Van Sickle thinks, was John Gottlieb Wendel, the grim and fabulously wealthy real estate operator who kept his six sisters virtually imprisoned in their mansion at the northwest corner of the Avenue at Thirty-ninth Street, for fear they would be courted only for their riches.

Mr. Wendel had a horror of dyed wools. He thought they caused skin afflictions. The Everalls selected certain Scottish herdsmen in the Highlands to raise special wool for the Wendel homespuns—enough each year to make sixty yards each of black sheep's wool, sixty of gray.

Woven together these made up a hound's tooth pattern that Mr. Wendel dearly loved and always wore.

Mr. Van Sickle recalls that Mr. Wendel had another phobia—a fear that disease could come at him from the pavement. To guard against this he wore special shoes with inch-thick soles and what Mr. Van Sickle calls "one-inch verandas"—wide sole flanges.

Walking home from Everalls, Mr. Van Sickle often saw old Mr. Wendel reading by gas light in his ground-floor study in the mansion, behind partly pulled shutters. In later years, Ella and Rebecca Wendel sometimes appeared in the neighborhood, always in black bombazine. Most of the time they carried shopping bags. Their poodle, Tobey, was exercised in the $3,-000,000 back yard that knew no other use.

Georgianna, one of the six sisters, rebelled. She broke out and went to live in a hotel, Mr. Van Sickle recalls, but her brother immediately got commitment papers that would have sent her to an asylum. She went back to the mansion to die there, as the others eventually did, behind a front door that was never opened.

In 1909 Mr. Van Sickle had his own clients. He opened his shop at 10 East Thirty-third Street, and prospered beyond his boyhood dreams.

He likes to remember that as a lad of 14 he sold newspapers at Illinois and Washington in Indianapolis opposite another boy who had his eye on a high place. That boy became one of his customers—Roy Howard of the Scripps-Howard newspapers.

In 1922, in Paris, Earl Van Sickle ran into another home-town boy who had made good in a big way —Frank Williams, a dentist. Dr. Williams had him down for a weekend at the Count Brion's sixteenth-century Chateau Plessis-Brion, and Mr. Van Sickle loved the place so much he had it photographed from all angles and reproduced in Larchmont in Westchester.

The gargoyles for it came from the Vanderbilt mansions in Fifth Avenue; its gates from the old Watson mansion at 18 East Fifty-third Street, where, curiously, Mr. Van Sickle has his upstairs shop now, with twenty persons on his tailoring staff. He filled the chateau with relics—tapestries, armor, paintings, statuary. He finally sold it in 1941 to Paul White, a paper manufacturer.

Mr. Van Sickle has seen his trade change. In the beginning he made hunt clothes all the time, but hasn't had an order for a scarlet fox-hunting outfit in more than twenty years. He still turns out suits that start at $280, top coats for as much as $800, but thinks men's wardrobes now are simpler. He only owns about twelve suits himself now, and four coats. He finds the demand today chiefly for dark, conservative suitings, mostly flannels and worsteds.

Mr. Van Sickle is still ramrod-straight, but his hair is gray. He inclines to pencil-stripe blues in business hours. His eyes soften when he remembers the gas street lamps spilling golden light pools in Fifth Avenue; John Jacob Astor, tall and lean, purposefully striding homeward; Diamond Jim Brady, Bet-a-Million Gates and John Drew at the old Waldorf; Stanford White, Dan Reed and William Leeds, familiar Avenue figures. Gone, now, all gone.

November 21, 1956

❡ The close of a 121-year-old business dynasty in town was hidden the other day in a brief financial-page item. The item merely said that the House of McAleenan at 1330 Broadway had sold out to Modell Pawnbrokers at 1178 Sixth Avenue and had turned over to Modell somewhere around 3,000 pledges.

McAleenan's is the dusty five-story brick and brownstone establishment at the southeast corner of Broadway at Thirty-fifth Street, the last building on Broadway before that street jumps west at the north end of Herald Square, behind the bronze bell-ringers Stuff and Guff, who, incidentally, appeared on McAleenan stationery.

Before the McAleenans took over the building it had been the Sixth National Bank. The old bank vaults, eighty to ninety years old, were used to hold the diamonds and silverware on which the McAleenans made loans. The house rarely took in anything for pledge other than precious stones and silver.

When the McAleenans moved up to Broadway back in the Seventies the neighborhood was mainly snooty brownstone. The genteel folk who lived near-by begged old Henry McAleenan not to hang out the traditional golden spheres of the pawnbroker, for fear of what their visiting friends might say. So he never did.

He opened a discreet side door for prominent men and women to use, to spare them the anguish and publicity of the Broadway door, and by-and-by the very folk who had shuddered when he took over from the old bank became steady clients. They stayed on when the later Henrys, son and grandson, replaced him.

When the Modell deal was worked out, H. Alvin McAleenan, Princeton '16, mailed notices to all his customers that what they had pledged with him was about to be transferred to the Modell vaults. Many came to redeem their stuff.

Among these was a prim, quiet dowager. Fifty years ago she had placed with the McAleenans a gold sewing kit—gold needle, gold scissors, gold thimble in a gold case— on which she had borrowed $20. In the half century since, she had paid $300 in interest on the loan. She didn't need the money; it was just that she felt the article was safe with the McAleenans.

The favorite legend of the establishment has to do with a man who came in thirty or forty years ago and left his coin collection for a loan. He never turned up again. Among the pieces in his collection was a gold medallion with Queen Elizabeth's likeness on it.

Some instinct told the current McAleenan's father that the Eliza-beth piece was rare, but when he sent it to the New York Numismatic Society experts they had never seen nor heard of such a piece. Old Mr. McAleenan boldly labeled it "$500," and stuck it in the window, anyway.

About a year later a Dutch gentleman stepped in and asked to see it. He studied it through a glass, quietly peeled off five $100 banknotes, and left. He never identified himself. Not long afterward the Elizabeth piece turned up in a sale at Christy's in London. It brought $20,000.

It was a medal Queen Bess had had struck for Sir Francis Drake for his victory over the Spanish Armada.

A McAleenan pledge ticket, picked up during World War II by the F. B. I. from a German espionage suspect, led to the arrest of German agents put ashore at Montauk Point, L. I., in a U-boat. Mr. McAleenan's accounts showed that the last interest payment on the ticket had come by Post Office money order from Montauk. The G-men closed in there.

A precursor of the business was started in 1835 by Patrick Fullan of Newry in Down in Ireland. The shop was in North Moore Street. The first Henry McAleenan married Patrick's daughter Ann and opened his own shop in 1844 at 52 Mulberry Street. Later he moved to 194 Eighth Avenue, then to 1330 Broadway, ever more prosperous.

In his Mulberry Street shop he used to allow Chinese gamblers $18 on $20 gold pieces, thinking that a good investment—but it wasn't.

The gamblers, it seems, had a wee trick. They would violently shake a full bag of gold pieces until they had worn off a goodly bit of the metal, so that what they pawned was actually worth less than the $18 they got.

Mr. McAleenan will sell the building, a choice corner. Charles Kelly, who has been his manager for almost fifty years, and Tom Norton, custodian, who raised his family on the top floor in the same half-century, are about ready to retire. So the doors are to close, soon, forever, on the House of McAleenan.

December 3, 1956

❡ The New York Convention and Visitors Bureau makes the point that the first tomb to an unknown soldier in the United States is not in Arlington Cemetery in Washington. The bureau says that the first unknown soldiers lie under the Martyr's Monument in Trinity Churchyard. They were unidentified Colonials who died in British prisons in New York City during the American Revolution.

❡ Scattered within the city limits are some fourteen or fifteen old houses and mansions that have somehow escaped the mechanical digger's maw—quiet, serene dwellings into which a step removes you from the shrill clamor of our age.

Dorothy and Richard Pratt, who have done several good works on early American homes, have a new guide out that includes pictures and information about examples within

and outside the five boroughs. They have pieces on Fraunces Tavern (1719), the Old Merchant's House (1830), Theodore Roosevelt House (before 1858), Jumel Mansion (1765), Dyckman House (1783), Van Cortlandt Manor (1748), Poe Cottage (1812), Bartow Mansion (1820), Stillwell-Perine House (1679), Voorleser's Cottage (1695), Billop Conference House (1680), Lefferts Homestead (1804), Bowne House (1661) and King Mansion (before 1750).

The first five are in Manhattan, the next three in the Bronx, the next three on Staten Island, where seventeenth-century Cocclestown (Richmondtown, now) is being restored; the next two in Brooklyn, the others in Queens. For some reason the Pratts have left out Smith's Folly, the Abigail Adams high-seated eighteenth-century house at 421 East Sixty-first Street, but it's worth a visit, too.

December 5, 1956

❡ It is only thirty-three years since the National Democratic Club moved into the granite pile at the northeast corner of Madison Avenue at Thirty-seventh Street, but even senior club members seem to have forgotten the establishment's romantic history. Some are inclined to weave weaker legends of their own to impress visitors.

Hardly any remember, for example, the real name of the mysterious financier who built the mansion in the Nineties directly across the way from the princely J. P. Morgan house. One version you get

is that he was called de la Mer—
He Who Was Taken from the Sea
—because he was found, in infancy,
afloat and unattended on an ocean
raft.

There's a trace of fact in that, if
you dig into the records. Capt.
Joseph Raphael De Lamar, born in
Amsterdam, did begin his career on
the sea. He worked in sail, became
a skipper at 23, went diving for
ocean salvage in 1872, traded in
Africa. And in 1878 he sold his
mine holdings in Leadville, Colo.,
to a British syndicate for $2,000,000.

Within fifteen years Captain De
Lamar owned mines, cable companies, beet sugar plantations. He
held directorates in the American
Bank Note Company and International Nickel, bought vast mineral
tracts in Canada and in the Far
West and served as State Senator in
Idaho. He had homes in Paris, New
York and the West. He owned the
yachts Savarona and Sagetta and a
collection of art masterpieces.

Newspapers of the Eighties and
Nineties got into the habit of calling him the American Monte
Cristo. They described him as
taciturn, secretive. They worked up
high ink pressure when he married
Nellie Virginia Sands, an American
apothecary's daughter, a beauty of
the period. It was for her, as club
members tell it, that the captain
paid $254,000 for the Madison Ave-
nue corner, and $1,000,000 for the
granite mansion.

The De Lamars had one child, a
daughter, Alice, but they were di-
vorced in the late Nineties. The
Democratic club members say that
Mrs. De Lamar never lived in the
granite mansion, that she refused to
cross its threshold, though it was
one of the city's showplaces, but
that her daughter was brought up
in its vastness. Even today, the
chambers glow with warm murals,
sparkle with crystal chandeliers.

Rich stained glass lets in the
wintry light to cast blushing colors
and lovely greens and blues upon
old floors and walls. In the great
ballroom the light picks out a
golden Steinway decorated with
plump cherubs and rosy garlands.
Between the captain's death in
Roosevelt Hospital in 1918, and
1923, when the National Democratic Club bought the place, art
thieves stripped some of the murals
from the ballroom walls. They were
replaced with blue velour.

The captain's art treasures were
sold at auction in 1919, but some
old boys at the club still seem to
think that the gold-framed paintings in the mansion were paintings
he left behind. Actually, most were
donated by club members. Among
these is a Blakelock oil of Seventh
Avenue and Fifty-fifth Street, done
in 1883 when that corner was still
Shantytown, and a painting of High
Bridge, done by Charles Miller in
1876.

Mostly, though, dark Tammany
chieftains frown and glower from
the mansion walls—old Charlie
Murphy, John Curry, among others. Presidents Wilson, Jackson,
Polk, Van Buren and Cleveland
brood in large old frames. In the
awesome stairwell, spiraling down
six stories in lush crimson carpeting, is a magnificent staircase with
a pallid marble statue set in a wall

niche, midway. Members insist that Stanford White designed the house, but old clippings credit Cass Gilbert.

Below street level the old De Lamar kitchens are still white-tiled, and of extraordinary proportions. The old heating boilers, changed over to oil, look almost new. The old front conservatory in the white marble lobby is a caged cloak room now and the sidewalk elevator that lifted and lowered the De Lamar Baker electric is used only for kitchen freight. In the sidewalk in Thirty-seventh Street you can still make out the crescent sweep of the old carriage drive. The wiring put in by the captain is changed, but his call buttons remain on every floor.

Tom Dunleavy, who went to the club as custodian in 1923 and is still on the staff, likes to show the dawnlike lighting on the ceiling murals. He loves to tell about the massive French clock and sidepieces, done in bronze. They were the captain's, too, set on a magnificent pale fireplace mantel. Thieves got them out and into a pawn shop just before the club took over in 1923, but they were found, redeemed and restored to their old position. One club legend is that Alice De Lamar, who is still living, came in one day and identified them.

The clubhouse is one of the few old city palaces kept more or less intact, a haunting, melancholy home fortress of a period when penniless boys could come to the New World and rise to rival Croesus.

Within its walls you fall back into the dark velvet arms of yesterday and know a kind of forgotten peace.

December 19, 1956

¶ On the desks of 400 of the most distinguished men on earth, even in remote corners of the world, a visitor is apt to see a silver paper cutter that is a miniature reproduction of the dress sword worn by Lord Nelson. Presidents, kings, shahs, princes, prime ministers, great military leaders, ambassadors, cabinet members, chiefs of staff own them.

Each silver sword is evidence that the owner has spoken before the Calvin Bullock Forum on the thirty-third floor at 1 Wall Street. No other person may own the sword. That goes for Hugh Bullock, head of the House of Bullock, that has specialized in investment management the past sixty-two years. And it goes for all his top executives, too. The sword must be won by speech.

Nor may any man or woman own two of the swords, although some speakers have appeared as many as three times. For the second, and later, appearances, the gift is some valuable trinket from Tiffany's, which, incidentally, makes up the swords, too. They are ordered by the dozen, but come in singly after the speaker's name has been engraved on them.

The Bullock Forum is unusual in financial history. It was started in 1937 by the late Calvin Bullock to educate financiers, lawyers, industrialists, among others, on the latest developments, especially in periods of national or international crisis. The talks are always behind closed doors and off the record. The speakers are always key men.

When the Suez turbulence broke out, for example, the speaker was Sir Pierson Dixon, United Kingdom representative at the United Nations. When the pot boiled over in Hungary, the forum speaker was Msgr. Bela Varga.

For each session 140 invitations go out on engraved stationery. The guests are picked from a list of 3,000 names—the cream, so to speak, of the world's Who's Who, names that are in world headlines. Men fly in from Europe, from South America—from almost everywhere for important sessions.

With each invitation goes a green-and-white admission card, sternly nontransferable. Each is numbered; must be given up at the door. No unapproved proxies may enter. Two failures to respond to invitations put a man in the doghouse category at Bullock's, and they call it that. Forgiveness is rare.

Every forum speech starts at 4 P.M., at the close of the Wall Street day; each ends at 4:30 o'clock, and an electronic clock on a special I.B.M. rostrum—a rising, tilting, falling gadget, all button controlled, gift of the late Thomas J. Watson—calls irrevocable halt. Questions may be asked for fifteen minutes after that, but not one moment beyond.

Women have addressed the forum—Lady Astor and the late Anne O'Hare McCormick, among others—but women may listen only when there are women forum speakers, as when the Queen of Greece appeared with her consort. The ban traces to 1945 when the commando chief of the Frasers, Simon Lord Lovat, was to speak.

Mr. Bullock told him there might be women in the audience. They had clamored for sight of Lord Lovat because he was one of the most romantic figures in World War II. But he was distressed. "Mon," he pleaded, "what's this? I'd understood the forums were stag." The ladies were ruled out of all forums thereafter where the speaker was male.

The Bullock offices are, in effect, a rich museum of Napoleon and Nelson relics. That partly explains the Nelson sword for speakers. Calvin Bullock worked at a Napoleon desk, beside the chair the Emperor used at Elba. He died at that desk in 1944, surrounded by the priceless relics he had been years collecting. His room has not been altered since.

Hugh Bullock keeps it that way as a memorial to his father. The forum is maintained as a memorial, too. And the original Nelson sword, Mr. Bullock likes to explain, was bought for his father at auction at Chrystie's in London to the great distress of the British Museum, whose agent nodded—or failed to nod—when it was put up. A curious item in the museum is Field Marshal Viscount Montgomery's beret. He left it as a souvenir after he addressed the forum in 1945.

It has become a matter of pride for a man to be able to say that he has been a speaker at the Bullock Forum. Lester B. Pearson, Canada's Secretary of State for External Affairs, sometimes puts it quaintly. He's apt to say, "I'm a graduate of the Bullock Forum."

1 9 5 7

MOST MEN, when their last counter is tallied and they are put to rest, leave few ripples to mark which way they went. But there is an old tombstone among the many in the north graveyard beside old Trinity Church downtown that has given passers-by reason to pause and frown these last 162 years.

The epitaph is simple: "Here lies deposited the body of James Leeson who departed this life on the 28th day of September 1794 aged 38 years."

Masonic symbols decorate the stone—the square, the compass, the hour-glass, the lamp and the flame.

Carved into the stone are peculiar dots, or depressions, spaced as ordinary writing is. Some units have one dot, some have two. Who James Leeson was, or what his role in life, the legend does not say.

Men thought that more of his mortal history lay behind the dots; that the depressions were a cryptogram.

Whether the living of James Leeson's time ever figured out the cryptogram, no one can now say. In the February, 1889, Trinity Record, though, the key to the cryptogram was published. Whether the solution to the puzzle was fresh then isn't at all clear.

But the dots were dispersed on the stone as follows:

$$\vdots \; \cdot \; \vdots \; \cdot \; \vdots \; \cdot\cdot \; \vdots \; \cdot\cdot\cdot \qquad \cdot$$

The solution was worked out with a tick-tack-toe chart.

Working left to right, line after line, in the chart the cryptographer placed a single dot in each chart section. On a second round he put two dots in each section. On the third round, each section was separated, but left without marking, to complete the alphabet. On the first round of single dots the ninth, or last section, was used for two letters, "I" and "J." That is the only double use of the single dot.

In the end, the cryptographer came up with this:

R E M E M B E R D E A T H

If the inscription was intended to stay the churchyard wanderer long after James Leeson was dust, it succeeded. Whether James Leeson himself devised it no man, probably, shall ever know.

January 7, 1957

¶ Most New Yorkers know how the Dutch bought Manhattan Island from the Indians on May 6, 1626, for a mere $24 in trade goods. Fewer know that twenty-eight years later, almost to the day, the Canarsies, a tribe across the river in what is now Brooklyn, sold to the same corporation, the Dutch West India Company, another island—Coney Island—at a higher price, considering the comparative size of the places.

The original bill of sale drawn up for the Coney Island deal is part of the official record of Kings County in Brooklyn and is kept in the Hall of Records there.

The Coney Island deal was made on May 7, 1654. The bill of sale conveyed a certain "Neck of Land" and "an island called Conyne," both at Gravesend, to the West India Company for "fifteen fathoms of sewan, two guns and three pounds of powder." James A. Kelly, official Brooklyn historian, figures the sewan (wampum), the guns and the powder were probably worth $15, if that much. City folk on Coney Island holiday 300 years later probably burn up more than three pounds of gunpowder every hour of a summer day at the shooting galleries.

The Indians who made the deal were the Sachem Mattanoh, and the Indians Guttaquoh and Iveta Chen, who, when you stop to think of it, weren't poor salesmen at all.

The Indians called the neck of land Manahamung (it was all meadow and marsh at the time) and the other plot in the deal Narriohk, which was their term for "The Island." Curiously, somewhere on the land involved in the deal, the first white murder occurred. The Canarsies killed one of Henry Hudson's sailors there in 1609, when he landed for fresh water.

January 9, 1957

¶ In early evening when thin winter light begins to fade in Chambers Street, starling flights drop through the dusk to twittery homing in the portico of the Old County Courthouse just north of City Hall. They roost there in thousands and their bedding song is as of thousands of nail files, synchronized.

Joe Hanlon, who lives on the top floor in the courthouse, sometimes hears melancholy owl hoots from the portico. So does his daughter, who has spent all her twenty years in the Hanlon apartment and teaches now at Washington Irving High School.

The nine City Court justices who have chambers in the ninety-year-old structure are accustomed to starling feathers floating in on their papers. Some even like that touch. They say it gives them the feeling they are in the city, but not of it.

Sometime within the next five years the courthouse will be leveled. Then lovely City Hall, pale in restoration shell, will have the park to itself. Its architectural beauty will be open to view, then, from all sides.

When the courthouse was new, it stood a monument to graft. The octopine Tweed Ring charged the city between $12,000,000 and $16,000,000 for building and furnishing it, and at least five-sixths of the charge was booty.

Now the building has pretty much lived down that smudged part of its history. Some of the judges speak proudly of its four-foot-thick walls and twenty-foot-high ceilings. Since New York Steam was introduced, twenty years ago, the chambers are airy and comfortable.

Justice Harry B. Frank has dug into the building's history. He likes to relate that it stands on the site of the old Alms House that was burned down in 1854, and that some of the Alms House inmates must still be buried in surrounding lawn.

In mid-nineteenth century the building was called "New City Hall" or "City Hall No. 2," because the City Watch, the District Attorney and the Supreme Court had offices in it. To this day Joe Hanlon watches over both the courthouse and the City Hall.

The great central glass dome, the galleries, the indestructible flooring, the stained-glass windows are still in good shape in most places. Romantic souls point this out. They say the fact almost justifies the millions spent in construction.

Bronze memorials to jurists who sat in the old courthouse long ago now lie in the well-swept basement, deep below the park—memorials to Frederick Smyth, Henry Rutgers Beekman, George Pierce Andrews, Henry Bischoff. They stare through dust at eternity.

Justice Frank says an architect named Kellum started plans for the courthouse, but that Leopold Eidlitz finished it. He says: "Even though it was probably the most costly municipal building, when you think of the Tweed graft, it might have been worse. The original plan called for a tower 210 feet high."

January 23, 1957

❡ Park Department researchers report that they have traced the origin of the red ball as the signal that park ponds are ready for ice skaters. They say the inspiration came in 1862 in Prospect Park, Brooklyn. It seems that when the ice was ready that year officials looked around for some public signal to announce conditions safe for skaters. They sighted a tall pole on a hill at the north end of the park, and lying on the ground near by were some red sighting disks that had been used by surveyors on a job there. That's all there was to it. Now, instead of a fixed disk, they use the red ball on a white flag because it's simpler to lower and hoist a flag than it is to shinny up a pole as they did with the metal disk in the beginning.

February 4, 1957

❡ José Arnold, King Saud's steward, is a Zurich-born Lutheran—a merry foot-loose sort of fellow who is the only Christian in Saud's household. He came to the United States with the royal party but will fly the seas in a day or two to Riyadh in Arabia to prepare the palaces against the monarch's homecoming.

Mr. Arnold runs the King's fabulous kitchens, which he says have no equal on earth; he orders all foods for the palaces, supervises eight Italian master chefs, moves with the royal entourage on falconry expeditions—goes everywhere with the King except to the holy cities of Mecca and Medina, which are forbidden to all but the faithful.

A chicken cacciatore dinner got Mr. Arnold the stewardship. He prepared it one day in 1951 on an air-conditioned train of the Arabian desert railway for executives of the Arabian-American Oil Company. The King was their guest at the feast.

When the dishes were cleared the King—then Crown Prince—wanted to know, "Who put this meal together?" He was told and right after that Mr. Arnold got a gold watch from him for his achievement.

Three weeks later a radio message summoned Mr. Arnold to Riyadh. He was under contract at the time with the oil company—had been for four years, running the oil company Ras Tanurah—but the camp boss told him, "You're through working for working stiffs. If His Majesty wants you, you go." And he did.

José Arnold knew enough Arabic by that time to issue orders around the palace. Besides, he rather fancied it as a kind of adventure. He had worked before that in Paris, in Istanbul, in Peru; had served as wartime steward on troop runs across the Pacific on Matson liners.

He had been in the States as early as 1928 and had won citizenship here in 1933. He had been a bank clerk in Boston, had washed dishes in cafeterias in Pasadena, had run his own hamburger joint, the Hannibal, in Las Vegas; always had gravel in his socks, had to keep moving.

He comes of a long line of hotel folk in Switzerland and had been to schools there for hotel training. He was baptized Joseph and his family called him "Sephie," but a passport twist in Peru gave his name the Iberian twist and he's kept it.

No kitchens in the world—and Mr. Arnold says he has seen, or worked in, the greatest hotel kitchens including those at the Waldorf-Astoria—compare with the

King's. All were specially designed and made in the United States to Mr. Arnold's specifications.

They are fully electronic, of gleaming stainless steel, with tremendous walk-in refrigerators all set in tiled rooms big as caves, and all air-conditioned. The foods are almost exclusively American, come in regular shipments from the United States in refrigerator ships.

In the two new palaces at Riyadh —pink creations of an Egyptian architect, furnished with Puritan severity except for the lush carpeting —the King's dining halls easily seat 500 at a time. His Majesty rarely has less than sixty people at table, mostly entourage.

No women appear at these meals. There is no music. There is no smoking or winebibbing, because these are proscribed by Koranic decree. Although the King favors Western foods and stays pretty much on a salt-free diet, there is always ample rice and lamb, the native staples, for his guests.

On royal pilgrimage to Mecca, the steward stays at Jidda, makes up hot meals with all the fixin's there and sends them to the Holy City in what he calls "giant air voids"—enough to feed from sixty to 100. Air voids, it turns out, are special vacuum cylinders.

In his magnificent kitchens the steward wears Western garb. In the desert he goes completely native in costume—wears the sheep-lined aba, or outer cloak, on cold evenings and a black camel's-hair bisht indoors. His ghutra, or head-shawl, is pure white with embroidered corners fitted over a white gafiyah, or skull cap. It is shaped to the head with the double-banded, crownlike agal.

Mr. Arnold's best joke, he thinks, is about his return to Zurich in 1947 after having been away a full twenty-six years.

He tells it like this: "My mother, when I left to wander, was a handsome brunette. She might have been Mme. Pierre Curie—the radium man, you know—because she had found favor in his eyes when they were both at the Sorbonne.

"Anyway, when I came home she was white-haired. She looked at me. She said, 'Sephie, that money I gave you when you left was for white bread. Now you bring me whole wheat.' "

March 1, 1957

❡ Few townies stop to search the limestone trim on skyscrapers with eager eye, as Robert G. McCullough does. He finds the stone rich in sermons about forgotten millenniums. In it he's likely to find, among other fossils, all manner of Brachiopoda, invertebrates that wiggled and crawled in Paleozoic ooze 200,000,000 to 400,000,000 years ago. He finds that fascinating sport.

Mr. McCullough's interest in primeval wrigglers fixed forever in stone would be less astonishing, somehow, if it were not for his bread-and-butter calling. He is head bartender at the Racquet and Tennis Club in Park Avenue and has served there for the last fifteen years. Not many dispensers of spirits, he finds, are apt to be avid rock hunters.

Some of the architects and engineers in Racquet and Tennis know Mr. McCullough's passion for rocks, minerals and fossils. When they come across items they think might take his fancy, they pick them up for him. The other day a member came in with a cut of red Italian marble that put the bartender into quiet ecstasy. He found a perfect nautilus fossil in it. Curators at the American Museum of Natural History, where he spends a lot of time, figured the nautilus might have lived 75,000,-000 to 100,000,000 years ago.

Mr. McCullough was born in Chicago. He came to New York about twenty-five years ago, and because he had always loved nature study, began to look around here. In no time at all, he learned that rich finds frequently turn up in the city at sites where foundations are put down deep, as for skyscrapers or subways. He started a collection of his own and pretty soon was scooping up garnets, beryl, tourmalines, jasper and the like though he's still shy quite a bit of the total of the 177 varieties of rocks and minerals that lie in Manhattan's ancient deposits.

Mr. McCullough finds city contractors kindly and tolerant of amateur rock hunters, but a little worried lest they injure themselves scrambling around foundation excavations. When the Seagram Building foundations were a-digging, Mr. McCullough timidly—he's not at all brash—asked the superintend-

ent on the job for rock samples. He said, "I'll come on Sunday because that's one of my days off, and just pick up a few bits here and there," but the official went right out with him instead and had a Mr. Saunders, of his staff, do the collecting.

It isn't all pavement hunting with Mr. McCullough. He gets out into green countryside a lot with Boy Scout Troop 318, which meets in the Duane Methodist Church at Seventh Avenue and Thirteenth Street. He has taught the troop a lot about bird life, about wee creatures of the woods and fields, but mostly about rock-hunting. His favorite out-of-town bunks for rock hunts are in the New Street Quarry in Paterson, N. J., and all over that area, which he has studied quite a bit. He's scoured the lower Catskills, too.

The Scouts are deeply infected with rock fever now. Whenever they go any distance on vacation, they search for fossils and minerals, and mail or express them to Mr. McCullough. He led a group, not long ago, into a prehistoric lake bed about a mile north of New Bergen on the New Jersey shore, and came in flushed and triumphant. He had turned up sharp, distinct fish fossils in rather slaty gray shale. At the Natural History Museum one of the curators knew the fish at a glance. "Diphoris," he told Mr. McCullough, "primitive lung fish of about 175,000,000 years ago."

The bartender left with a deeper glow than most men would get from a triple scotch.

March 27, 1957

¶ Wherever the Rev. Dr. John Sutherland Bonnell moves these days, he jots little notes. He writes on envelopes, on invitations, on cards. He writes in subways, on buses, on his walks.

His jottings are messages of hope for men and women crushed by despair. He couples the messages with brief prayers and they go, fresh each night, on the Dial-a-Prayer telephones set up under Fifth Avenue Presbyterian Church, where he is pastor.

Ten telephones carry the messages and prayers, all on Circle 6-4200. They are in use around the clock. If you stand by them in the sealed rock chamber under the church, you hear the relays' metallic click as they pass each call.

The system has brought floods of mail to the minister's desk in the two years since the installation was set up in the basement. And it has brought him some weird experiences.

Most of the letters just pour out thanks for a message that lifted an overburdened heart, but sometimes prayer listeners ask for spiritual aid beyond the dialed prayer.

Some weeks ago, a deep voice called the minister's study. Dr. Bonnell answered. The voice told of having heard the prayer for that day: "We thank Thee, O Lord, that there are no hopeless cases in Thy clinic. Grant to every seeking soul now Thy healing and salvation."

The voice said, "Do you really believe, Dr. Bonnell, what you said about no case being hopeless to God?" The minister said he did, with all his heart.

The man begged for audience, but not at the church. Dr. Bonnell sensed that the man was desperate; the voice was not an old voice, but it broke and quavered. He agreed to meet the man in Central Park, near General Sherman's statue.

The man would wear a carnation. The minister was to carry a paper-wrapped book. They met, and the man opened his heart in full flood. His home was shattered; his wife and children were apart from him; he could not concentrate on his office work and his career faced disaster.

Dr. Bonnell knew that the prayer had unlocked the troubled soul; that this talk in the park—it lasted more than an hour—had provided outlet for something black and bitter that had found no previous gap.

The man told the minister, "I had meant to die today because there was no door out. If you will let me keep in touch, I know I can fight through." He begged Dr. Bonnell to take a small phial, filled with clear liquid, that he took from a coat pocket.

Dr. Bonnell forgot about the little bottle until his hand fell upon it in his overcoat, days later, as he passed a Madison Avenue drugstore. He went into the shop and asked the apothecary if he could identify the phial's contents.

The man lifted the cork and sniffed at it. He said, "Potassium cyanide. Enough to kill five men." The minister asked him to keep the poison, but to let him have the bottle, which he did.

The man who had turned over the phial has his feet back on firm ground again. So have other folk who have lifted a telephone in the dead of night to listen to the dialed messages and prayers.

There is a letter from a nurse in one of the large East Side hospitals —". . . terribly discouraged and homesick; afraid of the future"— who found new faith in a prayer. One from a daughter who knew agony as she watched a mother die in the low hours when the indifferent city slept. One from a Wall Street man, hard-driven, who responded to, "Eternal God, help us to know that amid all life's busyness, in a moment of prayer we may drink at the deep wells of Thy peace."

Dr. Bonnell's congregation passes Dial-a-Prayer cards to friends and to co-workers and the cards spread. Mail shows that men and women even call from other states for a voice to sustain them over bitter hours. One letter said of the telephone prayer service: "I believe this is the greatest ministry that our church has ever exercised."

It is one of the miracles of a great city that the voice of a clergyman, rising from a Fifth Avenue church basement, can reach so many, to lead them out of depression's darkness.

April 8, 1957

❡ Harry Graus, a bedspring mechanic who retired a few years ago, got to brooding over too much leisure. People kept telling him, as they do all retired fellows, that what he needed was a hobby.

He found one. He hit on the idea of working on the world's smallest gardens. He planted lemon seeds, orange seeds, grapefruit seeds, podocarp, ardisia and begonias, among other bits, in the tiniest containers he could think of.

He used toothpaste-tube caps, beer-bottle caps, whisky-bottle caps and thimbles. In the beginning, this experiment at a Lilliputian garden didn't work out too well. The plantings withered and died.

But Harry Graus, big and broad, is persistent, too. He gave up straight watering for eye-dropper sprinkling. His chief garden tool, now, is a toothpick.

The metal thimbles he used poisoned the plant roots. He gets around that now by lining the inner thimble wall with waterproof glue.

Mr. Graus is inclined to be a little secretive about his special fertilizer, but lets on that it is a mixture of distilled barley soup and tea.

He uses only sandy soils and humus. He thinks one secret of his success at bottle-cap horticulture, is kitchen planting. Kitchen steam, he says, is good for keeping plants moist. He keeps his plantings out of drafts, too.

Mr. Graus doesn't know the names of most of the plants he works with. He is apt to call the different ivies "iv'ries" and he does amazing things with names like philodendron. The names just don't interest him.

He has an extraordinary affection for his plantings. He calls them his "babies," or "little wonders." He has only rich scorn for folk who use ordinary pottery for their greenery.

Mrs. Graus, who shares a three-room flat with him at 1630 Forty-first Street in Brooklyn, was openly disrespectful of her spouse's first efforts, but no more.

When Harry sits up late o' nights, gardening with toothpick, eye-dropper and safety-razor blade, she keeps him faithful company, makes up all the barley soup he calls for.

"Both of us, now," Harry says, "we are proud of our babies."

December 25, 1957

❡ On Christmas Eve the city glowed. Last night it was truly the City of Light. It wore its Christmas jewels—millions of rubies and emeralds, golden tiaras, blue gems, azure and sapphire and turquoise, all softly bright.

Fifth Avenue was an Avenue of Light from the Plaza to Washington Square. At the north end, just beyond the park's roped golden beads of road lights, the Christmas trees shimmered like cloth-of-gold and the trees and window boxes in the Plaza Hotel were spangled with a deep mysterious blue.

The great Fifth Avenue shops had their windows outlined with Christmas lights, like giant jeweled buckles. Hotel marquees in the side streets were rimmed with red and white and blue and green. At 666 Fifth Avenue, Santa Claus and his elves clawed their way up the spotlighted façade and thousands stood to watch.

In Rockefeller Center the sixty-five-foot tree from the White Mountains bathed the area all about it with wondrous glow, and the path to it was lined with tributary trees, cone-shaped and man-made that bloomed in pale green with inner lighting.

Angels in samite descended from white cloud in the Lord & Taylor windows. The Tree of Light that reaches from roof to sidewalk was radiant on massed, upturned faces. Carols sweetened the night and the throngs nodded, unconsciously keeping time.

The Library's façade and its lions were pale and the lions wore their giant neck wreaths, studded with electric gems. Below the shops, in Madison Square Park, a lone tree stood in the darkness, a happy beacon; then comparative loneliness and unlighted windows to a point below Fourteenth Street.

Lower Fifth Avenue was a fairyland of light, gem-studded at the First Presbyterian Church, at the Church of the Ascension, the Hotel Grosvenor, at No. 1 and at No. 2. Christmas candles burned in the little old houses and in the skyscraper apartment houses.

Unsold Christmas trees cast great blocks of shadow in Paddy's market in Ninth Avenue. Chestnut venders' carts gave off their charcoal-fire glow. The waterfront on Hudson River lay dark, but candles and trees sent cheery beams through even the meanest, blackened tenement windows.

The city's own tree was gem-be-decked on City Hall lawn. Trees sent their colored mass out of darkness at St. Paul's and at Old Trinity. Down on South Street the tugs wore their running lights like Christmas rubies and emeralds. Great freighters had small lighted trees at top mast and the reflections danced and spread on the black tide.

The wide spread of windows in the Al Smith Houses showed thousands of golden panes, with blazing jewels on some levels; whole windows trimmed with colored glimmer facing East River. So up all the east shore, a glory of holiday glow, wondrous, probably without parallel anywhere else on earth.

Jeweled trees on hospital lawns and hospital terraces. A huge jeweled tree in front of the Mayor's home in old Gracie Mansion, on the front of Doctors Hospital. Eighty-sixth Street from First Avenue to Lexington was arched with golden lights and red Christmas bells, which is Yorkville's traditional canopy at Yuletide.

Park Avenue was a row of lighted mall trees from the Nineties to Thirty-fourth Street. Trees glowed in Park Avenue and in Fifth Avenue lobbies and Christmas candles spread gold on rich window draperies. From the park's west end a watcher could see the effulgence re-written in the dark lake mirrors.

One Hundred and Twenty-fifth Street in Harlem, where poverty stalks, did not show its poverty last night. Looped ropes of light made a golden canopy over the pavement from Madison Avenue, west to St. Nicholas. To the south around Columbia University subdued Christmas lighting gleamed like spangles and sequins against nocturnal velvet.

This was Christmas Eve in New York. This was the city dressed in richest stones and trinkets. This was the city trying to match the gems from her endless treasure chest against the winking and sparkling brilliants in Heaven's vault. This was a city bathed in Christmas peace, breathing carols into the night. This was the City Magnificent.

1958

MARGINALIA: Satellite fever has inspired a wintry star-gazing course out at Jones Beach. Percy Proctor, supervising principal of public schools at Babylon, L. I., takes from 500 to 1,500 persons every second Sunday night into Parking Lot 1 and points out the stars and the planets. Free telescopes are handy, but lots of people bring their own or use binoculars. Abraham & Straus, a Brooklyn department store, sponsors the show. The deserted beach is used because there is no outside light to interfere with viewing. The next session will be from 7 to 8:30 P.M. this coming Sunday.

¶ Ten years ago the historian Allan Nevins of Columbia University saw a stumbling block ahead for historians of generations yet to be. Before the twentieth century, men had relied chiefly on letters to keep them in touch with associates in their calling, or in government. They wrote when they were on holiday; kept diaries.

When the telephone came into wider use and radio communications developed, the letter and the diary came to figure less and less in the daily scheme. Men could speak to one another though whole oceans lay between. Fast planes swept them in brief time to friends or kinsmen and that cut down a lot more on use of the written word.

Professor Nevins finally figured a way to build a source-material stockpile for tomorrow's historians: get competent researchers to make tape-recordings on interviews with men and women notable in law, medicine, the arts, government, journalism, industry, advertising—in all fields.

The Oral History Research Office was created. It operates out of Columbia University's Butler Library. Finished tapes are transcribed there in triplicate—one copy for the subject, two for the files. The tapes are used over and over again, but small sections are cut off from time to time so the historian may hear the actual sound of the subject's voice.

In ten years Oral History Research has accumulated 100,000 pages of manuscript in interviews with some 450 persons. All are stored in the Butler Library. Some will not be available to historians while the subjects still live, some will stay closed to from fifty to eighty years after a subject passes; one or two are not to be opened to historians until the Year 2001.

Columbia University does not own the manuscripts; it merely has them in custody. Ownership, it is explained, might make the university liable if any libel action resulted from a historian's use of the material; mere custodianship would not. Each subject owns his own manuscript. At his death ownership passes to his estate. Closed items are locked away with rare books in the library's fireproof vaults. Open manuscripts may be scanned by qualified scholars.

Researchers and transcribers are carefully chosen. They must be persons who would not be likely to disclose restricted material. Only the other day a girl transcriber resigned. She was working on an almost legendary police case, which is still unsolved. She told Oral History Research executives, "I'm afraid I couldn't go on listening to this material without blurting some of it out somewhere." Her resignation was accepted.

The project owns seven tape-recorders. Their newest models will take up to twelve interview hours on a single reel. Wherever they're available, researchers pick up any diaries, pertinent documents, photographs or drawings and put them in with the Mss. Several open biographies already have gone into books, or into parts of books—J. M. Burns' "The Lion and the Fox," A. M. Schlesinger's "The Crisis of the Old Order," among others.

Columbia has hired its project researchers out for special projects —to Book-of-the-Month Club, to the Ford Motor Company, Radio Pioneers, Weyerhauser Timber Company, McGraw-Hill. The material will probably be used for corporate or institutional histories. The fee comes to around $90 an hour, which leaves a small profit margin. The margin is applied to other projects, although most of the work is done on special grants.

Not all subjects want their names made public now, but among those who have left their material open are Sir Norman Angell, Nobel prize winner; John W. Davis, the barrister; Senator William J. Fulbright; Edward J. Flynn, the late Democratic leader; John R. Gregg, the shorthand man; James W. Gerard, the diplomat; Mrs. Fiorello H. La Guardia, the former Mayor's widow; Mrs. Alice Roosevelt Longworth; Geoffrey Parsons, the late journalist; Keats Speed, the journalist; Norman Thomas; Henry A. Wallace; the Rev. George Barry

Ward, parish priest. Frances Perkins' manuscript, more than 5,000 pages, is to stay closed until five years after her death.

One of the subjects, a minister, is 100 years old. Close to fifty of the persons interviewed since the project started have died since. "Some of us," one of the project people said the other day, "keep thinking of it, in some cases, as a race with death."

January 17, 1958

❡ At sundown next Thursday the sexton of St. Paul's Chapel, oldest religious edifice in the city (1764-1766 were the building years), will close the right-of-way through the churchyard from Fulton Street to Vesey Street. No public traffic will be allowed on the path until sundown on Sunday, Jan. 26.

The gate-closing ritual is a legalistic maneuver. Dates when the gates are closed are written into the official church record to protect St. Paul's against any move by the City Fathers to declare the churchyard path a public thoroughfare. Gate-closing periods almost always include Jan. 25 because that is the date of the conversion of St. Paul.

The barring of the churchyard path is a comparatively new ritual. It was started in 1918, and for a long time the gates were kept closed for a whole week. In 1928 the period was reduced to two full days. The chapel's Broadway door, however, is always accessible for services and for private worship.

St. Paul's is a chapel-of-ease of Trinity Protestant Episcopal Church, which lies just south of it. That simply means, under English ecclesiastical law, that it is an offshoot of Mother Trinity. Trinity has its own gate-closing ritual about the same time as the chapel's. It will shut off its churchyard path between Trinity Place and Broadway from next Friday evening through Saturday. Trinity started its gate-closing in 1939.

St. Paul's, incidentally, isn't just the oldest religious edifice in Manhattan; it is the oldest public building, too. Old Trinity was put up earlier (1696, for the first one), but the first two buildings burned.

George Washington's pew is maintained in St. Paul's under the Great Seal of the United States. Across the aisle from it is the pew in which Gov. De Witt Clinton worshiped. The chapel was used by the British when they held the city during the Revolution and a number of Britons lie buried in its churchyard.

Vesey Street, which is one of its boundaries, was named for the Rev. William Vesey, Trinity's first rector. He took the pulpit in the Mother Church in 1746. Immediately after George Washington was sworn in as President on April 30, 1789, he went to St. Paul's with his aides for a special religious service.

January 31, 1958

❡ The first professional play ever staged in New York, near as research can prove, was "The Recruiting Officer," a farce by George Farquahar. English players put it on in a windy barn in Pearl Street at Maiden Lane Dec. 6, 1732, about twenty-seven years after it had opened in London's Drury Lane with David Garrick and Peg Woffington, among others.

The charge here for the opening was one shilling (about 4 cents), and the players sold tickets door to door. The piece went on, intermittently, for roughly 153 years. Its last recorded showing was at Augustin Daly's in Thirtieth Street with Ada Rehan, John Drew, Otis Skinner.

February 5, 1958

MARGINALIA: ¶ A purist in town holds that the place name "Greenwich Village" is tautological. "Wich," he stubbornly maintains, is borrowed from the Saxon "wic," which meant village. The Saxons stole their "wic" from the Latin "vicus," which means pretty much the same. Green Village, the fussbudget argues, would be proper, but Greenwich Village really comes to Greenwich Village Village.

February 17, 1958

¶ The white moon of the winter solstice has faded. The bitter moon of the twelfth month is gone. Tonight, after midnight, lions will rage in Chinatown's narrow streets. They will drive off the evil spirits who threaten the Chinese household at the advent of the New Year. And the New Year, by Chinatown reckoning, is 4656—some say 4655 —the Year of the Dog.

The lions will issue from the portals of the Hip Sing at 16 Pell Street, from the doors of the Chinese Merchants Association at Mott and Canal Streets; from the halls of the Chinese Community Club at 47 Mott. The Ong Leong Tong, the Chinese Free Masons and several family groups will have lesser lions raging in the streets. But the show tonight is mere warm-up for tomorrow. Then the lions will have their big day.

If lions clash on the Chinatown pavement after the New Year festivities get going full-power at noon tomorrow, strangers must not take alarm. Peter Lee, Chinese merchant (and Columbia University graduate, too) explains that it is in the nature of lions to have at one another. In ancient China, he says, the lion sent out by one village might be met on a narrow bridge by a rival hamlet's lion and the way would be contested.

The lions would not devour one another, it seems; they would just try to outdo one another in traditional leonine gymnastics—arbitrary cavorting and lunging, in a kind of athletic shindig. Damage to the loser would come, not from the stronger or better-drilled lion, but from the winner's village followers. They might strip the losing lion of his fancy banners. They might kick in his drumheads, or offer other insults.

Even such unkindly acts, Peter says, would not be final. The losing lion's followers can retrieve the lost paraphernalia with an offering of roast pig or barbecued chicken. "When you get the hang of it," Mr. Lee explains, "it's like Princeton tearing up Yale's goalposts after a Princeton football win."

Certain traditional rules must be observed in the lion-gos, which some call dragon-fights. No young (black-bearded) lion may seek combat with an old, or revered, lion. The oldest lion in the streets tomorrow will be the Chinese Merchants Association entry, who has stomped up and down Mott and Pell Streets for more than seventy-five years. The other white-beard is the Hip Sing roarer. Most of the black-bearded challengers are comparative upstarts. They may go for one another where the pavement narrows, but not for a grampaw lion.

No outsider can ever estimate the skill of the lion-dancers. There are fine points in the art, especially for the man in the lion's head, that call for sophisticated judgment. The tail end of the lion doesn't just leap and kick around, either. He has centuries of lion-tailing to abide by; no fancy Western tricks allowed. Where you really get to see neat lion work, is in a two-story garb; when the head man, leaping on the shoulders of his firecracker-throwing followers, tried to snatch a head of lettuce from a Mott Street or Pell Street balcony. You bring one of those off, Peter says, and you're one good lion.

New York hullabaloo will carry on through the first moon, the spring moon, in mid-April. Tomorrow and for the first fortnight, Chinese will swarm in from Bridgeport, Newark, Washington, Baltimore, Philadelphia and from the suburbs, for the New Year feasting. Because

there are not enough Chinese restaurants to hold all the large family and village clans at one time for the great feast, the New Year dinners will spread out a full two weeks. Just the Chins, Lees and Wongs are too many for the feasting, not counting other families in this area.

There will be hardly any mui guai (rose wine) for this year's feast because good rose wine was made only on the Chinese mainland and Chinatown folk do not trade with Communists. Neither will there be much ng ga pei, which is bark wine. But Peter, a philosopher, thinks that won't darken the feast. He said: "There's always Scotch. What's better, in the Year of the Dog, than a hair of the dog that bit you the night before?"

February 24, 1958

❡ For more than a year the windows of the black-painted, white-trim brick houses in Sutton Place on the East River between Fifty-fifth and Fifty-sixth Streets have worn the wreckers' doom mark— the whitewash cross. Scaffolding went up around the old dwellings last week. Soon the row will be rubble. A nineteen-story and penthouse cooperative to be called Cannon Point North, straddling Franklin D. Roosevelt Drive, will soar from the old plot. It will be a companion development to Cannon Point South, now under construction.

Indians speared and netted fish off rocky Cannon Point for ages. They found it rich in oysters, too, and feasted on them at that same spot. After the Britons took Manhattan from the Dutch in midseventeenth century, Sir Edmund Andros granted sixty acres there to David Du Fou, a native of Mons. The Du Fou family later turned up in deeds as Du Fore and Devore. The original rental of the sixty acres was "one bushel of good Winter wheat."

Capt. William Kidd, the pirate, came to own a farm a mile north of Cannon Point, on the shore, in the eighteenth century. He got it through marriage with Sarah Cox Oort, a lively lady who managed in one lifetime to dispose of no less than five husbands including the captain. As a matter of fact, his death by hanging left the title to the farm "attainted," as they put it in those days.

The river acres off the mid-Fifties were lush and rich in fruit trees and nut trees, especially walnuts. In 1782, the gentleman who had the property up for sale described it in local journals as "that most delightful and elegantly situate farm of Ruremont . . . within four and three-fourths miles of the City."

Eighty years later, though, the whole aspect had altered. Grimy coal yards, breweries and fat-rending plants made it untidy. Effingham Sutton, the dry-goods merchant who built the row of houses on the ridge that sloped to the river, went broke on the venture.

The Sutton mansions, all brick and from three to four stories high, with sweeping river views, changed from one-family dwellings to blackened, untidy tenements. In the Nineteen Twenties, Mrs. William K. Vanderbilt, Lady Mendl and Miss Ann Morgan, J. P. Morgan's sister, led a sort of Drang Nach Osten from Fifth Avenue to Sutton Place to live in converted or newly built brick houses in Sutton Place. In 1928, however, a poor writer or artist could have an apartment in the river row for as little as $15 a month. The catch was that there were no utilities.

By that time the property had come into the hands of Henry Phipps, an Andrew Carnegie partner. He left the buildings just as he found them, but William L. Laurence, one of his $15 tenants, installed hot water, a hot-water heating system and a bathtub, and did a superior interior decorating job.

Dorothy Draper, a visitor at the Laurences, was inspired. She induced the Phippses to give her a free hand with the row, and they did. With black paint for the brick, white paint for the handsome fire escapes and balconies, formal back gardens and brightly colored doorways she transformed the dwellings.

The flats, all walk-ups with lovely river views, attracted new tenants, mostly affluent. The Bohemians who had enjoyed what they called "The Ark," were nudged out of it. Henry Huddleston Rogers Jr. was a new tenant. So was Bradley Martin, a grandson of Henry Phipps. McAdoos and Hartfords, Fred Gevaert, the film man, Clarence Francis of General Foods came to live there. So did a titled Briton who loved to take pot shots at river wild life from his back window. Young Rogers practiced marksmanship from his flat, too.

A genial concierge appropriately named Boom—Fred Boom of Cannon Point—kept the row tidy. James Flanagan, a handsome doorman, did all manner of chores for the tenants—hung out dress suits to air, shook out ladies' minks, helped at back lawn cocktail parties on summer evenings, rode herd on Dead End kids who liked to assemble in an old life-savers' shack just back of the row. They remember that a Mrs. Ackerman, one of the tenants, always hid eggs in the garden at Easter for children to find; that beery loafers were apt to sneak in their for a snooze in the sun.

Now Cannon Point Row is dead.

March 26, 1958

❡ In the spring some men's fancies turn to frankfurter wagons—to neoclassic hot-dog carts of chrome and stainless steel that kick sun glare back into the sun's eyes. Itinerant peddlers start polishing their equipment when the robins coast the air slopes into Central Park.

Most carts winter in vacant tenement-district stores in dust and in brooding dark, singly or in huddles, and some hibernate in neighborhood garages. A few are out the seasons round, but more than 60 per cent of the cart owners are older men. Because they chill easily, they stay on the pavement only eight or nine months.

For fifty years or so, between the Eighteen Nineties and 1948, most trundle carts were made by Old Weisbard at 16 Catherine Street, off the Bowery. Ten years ago the master died and the Dickensian shop

fell into the hands of Edward Beller, a tinsmith, and Marc Monies, City College, '47, who had a good Air Force record and had hoped to be a physicist.

Old Weisbard's carts—hot-dog men bought them, and so did peanut venders, ice-cream peddlers, hokey-pokey merchants and soft-drink criers—changed hardly at all in the half-century of his domination of the hand-cart industry. The chassis, wheels and compartments were always of wood, sturdy but creaky.

The oldest street peddlers still cling to part of the original Weisbard design. They grumblingly accept the shiny new-style cooking compartments and refrigeration units, even the gleaming white-metal chassis, but they won't give up the Pennsylvania-made wooden wheels or the old-style German-made leaf springs.

Younger men, though, eagerly go for the Satellite-Age wagons turned out by Beller and Monies. They like the smooth-riding quality of English bicycle-tire wheels; the new compartments for broiling hamburgers and frankfurters; glass-lined sauerkraut wells and the three-gallon coffee percolators.

Forward-looking venders like Giuseppi Patalano have improved on even the Beller-Monies creations. Giuseppi tired of pushing his food cart along the West Side docks. He had the artisans hitch it to an Italian scooter. As he added more and more equipment to his rig and its weight increased, he got a more powerful scooter.

The little Catherine Street shop

turns out models for use in television and motion-picture production. It creates rolling barbecue pits for country folk; made one for a Cissie Patterson garden party in Washington. It builds rolling flower carts for big department stores and gets up rolling hot-cold food units for roadside trade.

The Catherine Street store has shipped frankfurter, peanut, ice-cream and soft-drink carts to far places—ten to Puerto Rico, two to Tegucigalpa, Honduras. In those places most of them were for wandering frijole peddlers. Gypsies have begun to use the carts, too, and concessionaires at country fairs have bought motorized units.

Special hot-cold carts are sold to large offices in the city and to factories, so that employees can take coffee breaks without leaving the floor. The partners are working now on a trailer-type barbecue pit that will cook stuff while in motion, using gasoline or charcoal. The gasoline stoves are made by the Colman Lamp people.

Nothing, you see, holds static in a restless city. Even so simple a mechanism as a hot-dog cart— there are roughly 400 in town, all unlicensed—must conform to the modern scheme or go into limbo.

April 7, 1958

⁋ The fuss and hubbub over the sites for the Lincoln Center for Performing Arts, for a Fordham University campus and for a Lincoln Square housing project would have been way beyond the wildest imagining of the husbandmen and gentlemen farmers who settled the area almost 300 years ago.

They could not have dreamed that their Bloemendaal (Dutch version) or Blooming Dale (later English form)—their Valley of the Flowers—would one day be a tight and untidy huddle of weathered brownstones and decaying tenements swarming with contending hosts of middle-class and impoverished city dwellers.

Eighteenth- and nineteenth-century visitors and guidebook scribblers thought that the Valley of the Flowers, with its lush gardens, fruit orchards, great-girthed elms and dreamy views of the lordly Hudson, was one of the loveliest spots on earth.

Frances Trollope drove the five miles from City Hall in 1831 to visit with gentry who had summer homes there. She wrote later: "Hardly an acre of Manhattan but shews some pretty villa or stately mansion. . . . Among these perhaps, the loveliest is one situated in the beautiful Village of Bloomingdale."

Dutch farmers broke Lincoln Square soil and ran ox-drawn plows across Indian trails down to the Hudson as early as 1660. Indians and mynheers alike found monster oysters, giant lobsters, sturgeon, shad and crabs. There was good hunting, too.

Flocks of passenger pigeons would virtually shut out the sky some days. Foxes, wolves and bear roamed the woods. Blooming Dale made ideal country seats for English squires who owned great numbers of slaves. Silver streams, branches of the Great Kill that came in at Forty-second Street, were alive with fish.

The squires hunted wild foxes, raised blooded horses; lived pretty much as they had in Merrie England—until the American Revolution. The war tore neighbors apart. James Delancey's Bloomingdale farm was burned by patriots. After the war it went, at auction, to John Somerindyke.

The Reign of Terror in France brought royal refugees into the area. Mme. D'Auliffe, lady-in-waiting to Marie Antoinette, built a French cottage near Broadway, a half-mile above Lincoln Square. She and her daughters entertained Talleyrand there and Louis-Phillipe, King of France. Louis-Phillipe taught school in Bloomingdale in 1799.

Edgar Allan Poe wrote "The Raven" in Bloomingdale's upper reaches. George Pope Morris' "Woodman, Spare That Tree" flowed from his pen in Bloomingdale after he and an unidentified "old gentleman" on a walk in the Flowery Vale had paid $10 between them to persuade a woodcutter to swing his axe at some lesser giant than the primitive elm he had set his heart upon.

The area's loveliness was doomed from about 1825 when J. L. Norton, William De Peyster and others of the gentry allowed the City Fathers to put the first streets through. In 1826 a stoneyard was built on the lovely river bank between Fifty-eighth and Sixtieth Streets. Squatters filtered in during the Fifties.

Hip-to-hip brownstones and cob-bled pavement hid a good part of the Valley of Flowers by 1885, although there were still some wide spaces in and around Lincoln Square. The gentry's family gravestones were kicked over in the frenzied population push that came with the subway cut-through around 1904. Then new theatres threw their brazen lights, but they were death candles. The area turned slummy.

Now the Valley of the Flowers will change again. Metropolitan Opera stars will lift their voices where the larks sang. Fordham undergraduates will walk green sod where the crude plow and the ringing axe echoed three centuries ago. That's the city's way—churn and bubble, hurry and hustle, endless change.

April 18, 1958

❡ A Lexington Avenue spirits dispenser prints this sales pitch on the back of his business cards:

"Since you cannot refrain from drinking, why not start a saloon in your home? Be the only customer and you will not have to buy a license. Give your wife $55 to buy a case of whiskey. There are 240 snorts in a case.

"Buy all of your drinks from your wife at 60 cents a shot and in twelve days, when the case is gone, your wife will have $89 to put in the bank and will have $55 to start in business again.

"If you live ten years and continue to buy all your booze from your wife and then die in your boots from the snakes, your widow will have $27,085.47 on deposit, enough to bury you respectably, bring up your children, pay off the mortgage, marry a decent man and forget she ever knew you."

April 21, 1958

⁋ For close onto fifty-five years New York subway companies have run underground excursion trains, although scarcely any regular riders seem to know there always has been, and still is, excursion service.

The first official run the afternoon of Oct. 27 in 1904 was an excursion of a kind. The 600 riders were city officials, road owners, clergymen, their wives and friends. F. B. Shipley of Philadelphia made history that day—the first man to surrender a subway seat to a woman. It's a sad fact that no one took her name.

Most excursions now, except for large groups from Brooklyn or Queens going to uptown communion breakfasts, are for out-of-town folk. Travel agencies bring in parties of from 500 to 1,000 at Easter time and at Christmas, sometimes on midsummer tours. There are between thirty and fifty of these underground pleasure runs each year.

Excursion trains are ten cars long and rent at $75 a string. Where there are more than 500 passengers, the rate for each additional rider is the normal 15-cent charge. Excursion runs for city school groups —to zoos, museums, parks—get a special rate.

Out-of-town groups are picked up at Grand Central Terminal, Penn-

sylvania Station or near the Liberty Street Ferry. The trains assigned for the underground run await them on special sidings, of which there are many.

The principal destinations are Rockefeller Center, Baker Field and Yankee Stadium; Rockefeller Center for Easter and Christmas visitors; Baker Field for college football; the stadium for pro football.

April 23, 1958

⁋ There is a green world high above the pavement that city groundlings rarely see. Familiar and exotic growths flourish in this sky acreage. The same birds, insects and crawling things that invade open countryside plantings climb to apartment house and skyscraper gardens —as high as thirty-eight floors at Radio City—to rob or destroy crops.

The rural housewife who puts up jams, jellies and preserves from the fruits of farm acreage has a silk-gowned bediamonded sister in town who loves to fill Mason jars and cans with penthouse-grown fruits and berries—when she doesn't have the hired cook do it.

The green-thumbed sisterhood— better than 95 per cent of the tillers of penthouse soil are women—organized the Rooftop Gardeners six years ago. The movement was started by Mrs. Carolyn Hannig, who lives atop 875 Park Avenue and runs the world's largest sand-processing industry.

She got the notion at lectures given by the New York Horticultural Society in 1952. It came to her at one of the sessions that while she could study and enjoy neighborhood penthouse gardens, she knew none of her sky neighbors. She suggested that they meet and exchange ideas, and they snapped at it.

Membership in the Rooftop Gardeners is thirty right now, with the committee considering 101 new applications. These are only a small portion of the 2,500 to 3,000 New Yorkers who use the short-sized rake and hoe on skyline acreage. Many are rich, many are humble.

The busiest and most knowledgeable top-floor husbandman is Hal Lee, a freelance writer on horticulture. He has more than 2,000 plantings on the eleventh floor at 1394 Lexington Avenue, near Ninety-second Street. His crop includes figs, bananas, strawberries, peaches, cherries. He maintains a rich compost heap of leaf mold and kitchen leavings.

Mr. Lee has worked his Lexington Avenue soil the last eleven years. When the Rooftop Gardeners organized they made him president. By and by, though, he turned professional consultant. He wanted to resign then, on the ground that he was a pro, but the resignation was unanimously rejected. He still gets all their business.

Pioneer of the penthouse Maud Mullers is Mrs. Harry Schwartz. She has kept up her penthouse garden atop 944 Fifth Avenue a full thirty-five years. She owns the tallest penthouse trees—a forty-foot honey locust, wide-branched Russian olive growths, magnolias, fifteen-foot high privet hedge and white birch, peach, apple and cherry trees, among others.

The Schwartzes, like most other crow's-nest horticulturists, grow thousands of annuals and perennials. They put their fruits and berries up in jars. They fight off crows, woodpeckers, bats, pigeons, aphids, tent caterpillars and go after all sorts of crawlers with spray guns. They grow magnificent orchids. Their pet dachshund, Penny, cremated, sleeps inside a miniature grave fence under an olive tree.

The Rooftop Gardeners eat under whispering leaves with flower scent drifting across their candle-lit tables. Some sleep in their gardens, under the stars. Some have forsaken the country entirely; just live on their green roofs. One gentleman, a United Nations delegate, has worked a broad putting-green into his garden scheme.

The secret of sky gardening seems to be peat moss. It overcomes the drying effects of lofty winds. Mr. Lee says that dampness from rooftop soil and plantings acts as a humectant—keeps a woman's complexion smooth and soft. He got that from Mrs. Lee, an expert on beauty.

And there's an advantage in having neighbors under you when you're gardening. Last spring Mr. Lee got a telephone call from a tenant three flights down. The man said: "Mr. Lee, get your spray gun handy. Tent caterpillars just passed my window, headed up." It took another hour or so, but Mr. Lee met the invasion at the parapet. The tent caterpillars never established a roof beachhead.

April 25, 1958

¶ The northwest corner of the Tenth Street-Second Avenue crossroad has been used without break for houses of worship close onto 300 years—longer than any other church site in the city.

It was primitive wilderness when Peter Stuyvesant built his chapel there in 1660. Later it served the rural hamlet, Bouwerie Village. Fashionable folk drove to it in shiny carriages in the eighteenth and nineteenth centuries.

At the end of the nineteenth century immigrant floods marooned it. Its well-to-do communicants fled, singly and in groups, to uptown parishes or to Brooklyn. In the last forty years it has known only hard times.

One brave pastor after another tried in vain to revive old St. Mark's-in-the-Bouwerie, and failed. For the last fifteen years the Rev. Richard E. McEvoy, out of Ohio and Iowa, has stood his ground there, though he floundered as in shifting sand.

When he came, there were barely twenty at Sabbath service. He has time and again brought his congregation up to as high as 100 or 150, only to lose about 20 per cent each year. Communicants were compelled to pull out of low and middle-class housing projects on the East Side because their families had grown too large or because their incomes had risen.

Each time the pastor from the West has tramped his alien-crowded parish to restore his flock. He has allowed men and women of St. Ann's Church for the Deaf, the oldest congregation of its kind in the city, to take old St. Mark's for mute worship on Sunday afternoons.

For the last ten years his little church has stood in the stream of displaced artists streaming eastward from Greenwich Village to low-rent studios, apartments and galleries between Third Avenue and East River.

He opened his arms and his parish hall to these Bohemian refugees, as he has to all new elements. For three years, now, he has let the Lower East Side Independent Artists hold their annual show in his parish house.

He says with classic simplicity: "No church can live that does not make itself part of the living community."

If you say that choleric old Peter Stuyvesant must squirm in his tomb in St. Mark's churchyard because of some of the weird daubs hung for the show, the tolerant pastor just smiles. He tells you: "Perhaps these works are a vital kind of expression."

Other New York pioneers in the old graveyard—Mayor Philip Hone, Gov. Henry Sloughter (a Briton), Daniel Tompkins, a Vice President of the United States; Matilda Hoffman, who was Washington Irving's childhood sweetheart; the famous Colonial printer, Hugh Gaine—would blink in amazement at the canvases, if phantoms could see.

But the Rev. Mr. McEvoy knows only that he must keep their old church alive. The church porch, built 100 years ago, needs rebuilding ($25,000 would do it), the whole edifice needs repainting, plastering and paint, redecoration. He dreams of bringing these improvements to pass before St. Mark's celebrates its 300th anniversary in 1960.

He says, "Old St. Mark's must not die."

April 30, 1958

¶ Most New Yorkers who feed peanuts and popcorn to Central Park's gray squirrels do so out of the goodness of their hearts. It may startle them to learn that this diet may encourage blindness and baldness in the little gray beggars.

Richard G. Van Gelder, assistant curator of mammals at the American Museum of Natural History, has been studying park squirrels since last August, mostly in early morning walks with his Doberman pinscher. One phase of his study has to do with diet.

He isn't certain that blindness and loss of fur come from peanuts and popcorn, but his own observations so far and squirrel studies by other men in his field tend to confirm the theory.

Like most scientists, Mr. Van Gelder doesn't want to be guilty of snap, or hasty, judgment, and it may be years before he pins down his facts, but he has some interesting notes that will bear following up. They shape up to this:

Park squirrels definitely cluster more thickly at pedestrian gates, probably on the wise assumption that this gives them first crack at potential feeders.

They have degenerated because

the Park Department provides wooden tree-houses for them. Ready-made housing saps their nest-building initiative. (Mr. Van Gelder comes across an occasional do-it-yourself job in, or just outside, the park, but the percentage of squirrel-built shelters doesn't begin to compare with what you'd find in natural woods, remote from pavement.)

Municipally built squirrel tree apartments may be fostering promiscuity among the grays. The tenants have no privacy. You'll find five or six tenants in a single tree apartment, with no dormitory rules or house mothers to enforce stern morality.

Park squirrels lack a fine taste in foods. Mr. Van Gelder has mounted mixed fruits—walnuts, almonds, filberts—in the grass to try to find out which the grays prefer. Turns out they just greedily grab at the nearest tidbit. No discrimination at all.

It seems likely that the Central Park tribe is hopelessly inbred and probably has been since the park was laid out 100 years ago. Like many humans, they're frightened of motor traffic and rarely venture into the street.

That would prevent them from, say, visiting kin over at Riverside Park or at Morningside Park. The end result of this isolation means they have a limited number of genes, with no possibility of producing mutations. No new blood, and that's bad.

Townsfolk should be taught that park squirrels hoard only whole nuts, with shell. If the nut is opened for them, they have to eat it on the spot; shelled nuts spoil when they're buried.

That doesn't mean, the mammalogist says, that the park grays are likely to starve if they don't get material for deep-freeze. Kindly New Yorkers feed them more generously after a snowfall than at any other time.

Passers-by frequently mistake Mr. Van Gelder's note-taking in the park. They see him stare up into a tree and jot a line or two, and can't figure him out.

He expects, eventually, to get mimeographed park maps. He'll hand these out to park dog-walkers and ask them to help him with a census.

To check on squirrel movements he may get a special park hunting license to go after the grays with a water pistol and dyes; scientists do that—dye animals' tails, shoulders or legs, the better to keep track of them.

Mr. Van Gelder, youngest assistant curator at the museum, started studying mammals when he was 7, up on Washington Heights. One of his early pets, a Bronx Park gray, nested in his mother's drapes. She didn't like that too much; made him carry the squirrel to the Bronx Zoo.

Young Van Gelder turned his pet over to Leonard Goss, who was zoo veterinarian at the time. The boy Burroughs said: "You can have him, Mr. Goss, he's completely tame."

The vet reached out. He said, "Thank you, so—ouch!"

The "tame" specimen had bitten a piece out of his forefinger.

May 7, 1958

¶ A record factory in the basement of the New York Public Library branch at 127 East Fifty-eighth Street turns out seven-inch disks that cannot be bought for love or money.

The factory's record titles are most unusual—items like Kant's "Prolegomena to Any Future Metaphysics," "Einstein on Relativity," A. S. Edwards' "Outline of Abnormal Psychology," Plutarch's "Lycurgus and Numa," C. A. Robinson's "From Prehistoric Times to the Death of Justinian," "Hartman and Vickers on Hatchery," D. C. Bryan on "Building Church Membership Through Evangelism," Leage and Ziegler on "Private Roman Law."

Day in, day out, except on the Sabbath, the basement plant throbs with air-displacing electronic impulses that beat against the ear like a warm breeze. You hear mouse-like squeaks from turntables turning slowly with the seven-inch plastic disks in which soft-treading operators embalm a tremendous spread of knowledge from tape recordings done from standard texts by volunteers. Rarer works are turned out three at a time, more popular texts in batches of ten or twenty. The factory was designed without fee by Dr. Peter Goldmark of Columbia Broadcasting System Laboratories. He is a master technician.

Most of the recordings are in English—a few in Elizabethan or Chaucerian English—but there is no human tongue this factory will not transcribe. The disks are substitutes for textbooks for sightless students striving for college degrees or for some special skill that may be learned through text. They are done on student request, without charge, by Recording for the Blind, a seven-year-old volunteer group of kindly, efficient men and women.

They started the factory for blind service men. Now they fill orders for civilians, too.

They have headquarters at 745 Fifth Avenue, do the initial readings on tape in the Yorkville branch of the New York Public Library; the final disks at the factory. They have done more than 4,500 books so far, have established branches in thirteen American cities. The group has no direct connection with the New York Public Library; just gets the use of space free.

The group has found that older volunteers make better readers for the blind. Their diction seems to be clearer. Professional commentators and stage folk do some of the reading—people like Ruth Draper, Cornelia Otis Skinner, John Mason Brown, Alistaire Cooke—but some stage folk tend to be over-dramatic and blind students find themselves hypnotized by voice quality so that they lose text meaning.

One dramatic class, offered as a unit, had to be rejected for just that reason, whereupon the head of the drama school ordered a

sharp change in the school's course in diction in an attempt to get more natural delivery.

A committee of blind folk judges volunteers for reading jobs. If men and women on this committee find that a particular voice diverts them from text, it's thumbs down. Many men and women who make tapes from books for Recording for the Blind have had no special voice training but are wonderful at it. Mrs. Winthrop Aldrich, for example, makes an ideal reader. Women who have led sheltered lives are likely to be shocked, sometimes, by the stuff they have to read for students, but gallantly get over it. One woman blushed and stumbled over biological passages in James Joyce's "A Portrait of the Artist as a Young Man," gulped, then sternly got on with it.

Right now R. F. T. B. has about all the readers it can use, but needs men and women to paste labels on recordings, to help with filing, with punching Braille numbers on disks and with all kinds of clerical chores. Volunteers can work days or nights, as they choose. Some couples hire baby sitters so they can help with the project.

Men and women from the United Nations give a voice with foreign texts, physicists at Oak Ridge, Tenn., read complex mathematical works; engineers of one kind or another read in their specialties. Physicians read on medicine; have even gone through a medical dictionary for use by a blind typist who does medical papers.

Although R. F. T. B. is purely

nonprofit and depends on private contributions for all its work, it must get releases from copyrights on every text it handles. On anthologies, sometimes, the number of releases may run up to forty or fifty, but there's no cutting corners for fear of legal complications. The disks are cut to run at sixteen and two-thirds revolutions a minute, which is half the speed of ordinary home long-play recordings. The average textbook takes about thirty disks and most students keep each set about three months. No recreational reading is undertaken by R. F. T. B. but other agencies take care of that end.

May 12, 1958

⁋ The Hudson River steamboat Mary Powell was to small fry between Rondout (Kingston) and New York City what the massive sternwheelers of the Mississippi were to Huck Finn and Tom Sawyer. They dreamed romantic dreams about her. They would sit for hours on the river bank of a spring or summer day, hynotized by the rise and fall of her walking beam, by the creamy foam curling from her sidepaddles.

Like the small boys of Hannibal, Mo., in Mark Twain's time, they day-dreamed themselves into her pilothouse, guiding her smoothly past slower, lumbering river craft. They saw themselves in blue uniform and glittering gold buttons like her masters, Absalom L. Anderson and, later, his son, A. Eltinge Anderson. Or they would have settled for the grandeur that was

Dan Bishop's. Dan was bucko mate from 1861, when the Mary Powell was launched, until he died in 1890. She was used as Dan's funeral barge.

The Queen—men and boys called her that in honest awe and reverence—was the fastest thing on the river for almost all of her fifty-six years. When the black smoke poured thickest from the twin stacks set aft of her paddlewheels she could breast the tide at twenty-four to twenty-five knots. Even today not many river craft do better. She slid through moonlight like a slender ghost and music from guitars played by Negro waiters threaded the night with silver. The Queen was something for men and boys to fall in love with.

Hundreds of men and women still living can remember the picnics, school reunions and excursions on which the Mary Powell bore them. Couples now snow-thatched can recall summer evenings when they held hands in her deck chairs as she slid them through onyx-black water between brooding hills and mountains veiled in moon magic. City people and rural folk alike boarded her for one-day family parties, staggering up her gangplank with shoeboxes or hampers filled with boiled eggs, fresh tomatoes, homemade apple pie and soda pop.

Rich men commuted in her. J. P. Morgan often went aboard to sit on her deck between lower Manhattan and Highland Falls. General Grant was a passenger. When she was finally broken up for scrap in 1917, her two gilded flagpole balls were saved for Mr. Morgan and were set up on his Highland Falls estate gateposts. Part of the Queen's engine heart is in the Ford Museum at Dearborn, Mich. Old Captain Absalom and his son, who loved her beyond all else, arranged matters so that when her end came she was not to be sunk to make background for some Hollywood film. Even in death she was to keep her dignity.

When Gen. George Armstrong Custer's body came into New York from the disaster at Little Big Horn, the Queen, draped in black, carried it to West Point. She was a gleaming white unit in ceremonies attending the dedication of the Statue of Liberty. She led the sea parade that marked the centennial celebration of George Washington's first inauguration; stood offshore on the day when Grant's Tomb was dedicated.

Her run through a fierce storm as she was headed upriver in 1899 made legend. Off Haverstraw Bay winds of cyclonic ferocity tore out her starboard funnel, blew her campstools clear off the deck and carried them through the air for astonishing distances. She shuddered through it. Her 200 passengers were shaken and pale, but none was lost.

After the Queen was dismantled in 1917 the clear-toned Meneely bell that woke sweet echoes along the river where she passed was set up at Indian Point, to sound last call for excursion departures. Later it was brought to Manhattan and mounted on the Hudson River Day Line Pier at West Forty-second Street. It sounded departure time there, too.

But Alfred Van Santvoord Olcott, former Day Line president, who loved even the memory of the Queen, wanted to make certain that the bell should last forever. Today he is to turn it over to the New York Historical Society at Seventy-seventh Street and Central Park West for a place of honor in the society's Port of New York Gallery.

May 16, 1958

❡ When Red Wing was a girl, about fifty-five years ago, her pretty face and her lovely eyes were known almost all over the world. She played in the earliest silent films—"Squaw Man," "Thundering Herd" and "The Mended Lute." She starred in "Pioneer Days," an Indian whooper staged in the old Hippodrome, where the pale concrete parking garage stands now, opposite Stern's.

Now Red Wing is 74 years old. She is broad and her hair is frosted. She works all day, sometimes through the night, in her dark two-room lodge in the walk-up at 189 West End Avenue. She sews authentic Indian war bonnets, war shirts, beaded suits and leggings of buckskin, cowhide or elk.

Some of her handwork goes to her own tribe, the Winnebagos in Nebraska, but she sews for other clans, too. A good part of her output is for the Improved Order of Red Men, a national lodge of whites. Right now she is turning out stuff for Iroquois Tribe 590 of New Dorp, S. I., whose sachem is Dan Iatauro, a New York City policeman.

Red Wing's Winnebago name was Rupa-Hu-Sha-Win.

Her father was the chieftain Waunk-Shik-Sto-He-Gah—He Who Gathers His People. Her mother was Nah-Gu-Pingah—Pretty-Hair Woman. Their photographs, and pictures of Red Wing's five brothers and sisters, fade on the dark tenement wall. So does the image of Young Deer, the Delaware she married in 1906.

Red Wing's eyes often lift from her work to look upon her vanished kin. When she speaks, the syllables are soft and low. She tells of how Episcopal missionaries put her through private school in Philadelphia; how, at Carlisle School, she knew the great athlete Jim Thorpe and Chief Bender, pitcher for the Philadelphia Athletics.

In girlhood, Red Wing lived for a while in the home of Senator Chester Long of Kansas as Mrs. Long's protégée. She learned the whites' customs and graces, but never forsook the ways of her own people. When she first came to New York in 1902, she had a few Indian neighbors but even the last of these, two Seneca families who lived nearby, are gone.

The two-room lodge where Red Wing toils is crowded with her stock—with skins and jars, with millions of beads, with feathers, fur ends and leather strips. She would prefer eagle feathers for her headdress work, but the law forbids that. She plods to the millinery center for turkey feathers, instead;

steams them over a tea kettle spout to make them flexible.

She gets her skins in the old swamp beside the Brooklyn Bridge approach, an area that has been crowded with tanners for almost 300 years. For the rarer hides she goes to Mayer & Son in North Bergen, N. J., a concern that sells to tribes all over the United States. Fur fragments for ear drops can be picked up in the garment center.

There is a bitterly ironic twist in the fact that white men who play at Indian, and even genuine tribesmen, can now buy do-it-yourself kits: sets for war bonnets, for breech clouts, peace pipes, moccasins, arm bustles, brow-bands— even for full-size tepees costing up to $162. Red Wing scorns such kits.

After Red Wing got out of the movies in the early Twenties, she worked on Indian costumes for F. A. O. Schwarz and for the Eaves theatrical costume company. The buyers in those places who knew Red Wing and her work died and she lost that trade, though no other worker in the city maintained her high standards.

Every color used by Rupa-Hu-Sha-Win has definite traditional meaning—red for life blood, blue for sky, yellow for sunlight, green for earth, orange for the light of the harvest moon. Beaded triangles in her brow-bands stand for mountains; floral and leaf designs go into bead work for Indians of the plains and forests.

Red Wing doesn't, as she puts it, "do much socializing now," but whenever the Friends, the Quakers, ask her to sing, dance, or lecture for them, she puts on her ancient buckskin dresses and hurries to oblige. "The Friends," she tells you, "have ever been good to my people. I would never refuse them."

Sometimes she cooks special Indian dinners for church groups. Sometimes she entertains for the benefit of mentally retarded children. Then she goes back to her dark tenement lodge to sit with the faded wall pictures, far from the home of her people, but always with them in spirit.

May 19, 1958

¶ At dawn, now, night herons flap over the marshes to feed in the waters on Grover Whalen's vanished World of Tomorrow on Flushing Meadow. Pheasants light in tall, swaying meadow grasses to hunt for weed seeds and for insects. Cottontails break from brush and hedge; show their white flags in hoppity flight.

Beside the rustic summer house on the edge of the old Gardens on Parade—the Queens Botanic Gardens now—a wild duck has laid seven large eggs in ground ivy. A few weeks ago majestic swans sailed down from April skies to light in Flushing Creek. Wee things creep in the grass. Wild birds whistle and flute in old fair-ground trees.

Fishermen plod to the meadow to dangle bait in the creek, in old Fountain Lake and in Willow Lake just beyond the stretch where the Amusement Center made brazen clamor nineteen years ago. The anglers catch carp, catfish and sunnies. In twilight, frogs swell

their throats in batrachian chorus.

From early morning into early evening, from fifty to sixty old men and women come each day to the Meadow with burlap bags slung from their shoulders to search in dandelion-starred greensward for dandelion greens and for button mushrooms. They look like Millet's rustics—figures in "The Gleaners" and "The Angelus."

Park Department foresters prune the Meadow's pin oaks, red maples and weeping willows on the 1,200-odd acres where Mr. Whalen's gardener-army planted them nineteen years ago. The paved roads that ran between glowing World Fair pavilions are carefully patched, but weeds grow in the cracks as in a ghost city.

The new world fair in Brussels seems to have made people think of yesterday's World of Tomorrow. They wander on the Meadow in vain search for the buildings that wrote lambent loveliness against the sky there in 1939 and 1940. Only two structures still stand— the Building of the City of New York and Billy Rose's Aquacade.

The city operates roller- and ice-skating rinks in the New York building at night and police rookies study there by day. On summer nights, water shows are staged in the Aquacade and children use the pool up to noon. But of the dream houses that stood in the meadow— the Futurama, the pallid Trylon and Perisphere, all the pastel pavilions—there is no sign.

Local hausfraus set up easels and paint the gardens and the lakes. Amateur botanists, including women deep in the winter years, look after the rock-garden plantings. One great patch near the old Gardens on Parade throbs with the color of 12,000 enormous tulips, a gift of Louis Dupuy, a greenhouse man in Whitestone. Azaleas flame at wide intervals over the whole meadow.

No other green spot so close to granite-towered Manhattan has quite the sylvan lure of the old fair grounds. It is a place to dream on a spring or summer day— among the grasses, beside the creek or on the lake banks, with bird music pulsing all about. El train rumble comes in like mild thunder from the Roosevelt Avenue trestle, but only after wide silences.

By-and-by you come upon a dark marble cylinder that reaches up out of the meadow. Its inscription says:

"This Time Capsule deposited fifty feet beneath this spot by the Westinghouse Electric and Manufacturing Company on September 23, 1938. Preserving for The Future a record of the History, Faiths, Arts, Sciences and Customs of the People then alive. . . . Scientists and Engineers designed it, Scholars chose its contents . . . to endure for 5,000 years."

May 23, 1958

❡ Fifty years ago this week A. M. Kidder & Co., stockbroker, one flight up at 14 Wall Street, took on a new hand, Jimmy Mount Jr., 18 years old. Jimmy was a provincial from Brooklyn's Bushwick district. His first job, at 14, had been as of-fice boy for Parker-Wilder, a Leonard Street woolen merchant. Later he had run errands for F. N. Saunders, coffee broker, at 70 Wall.

In his new job he was up early every working day to catch the rackety elevated train that took him from Gates Avenue in Bushwick to the Manhattan end of the Brooklyn Bridge. He'd walk the rest of the way. He took his lunches in dark little basement sandwich shops on, or near, the waterfront. In those days meat sandwiches were a nickel. So was pie or coffee. Some lads got by on 6 cents—a 3-cent meat sandwich or frankfurter at Max's Ann Street Busy Bee and a whopping big waffle covered with ice cream. Good, too.

Jimmy got $1 a day for a six-day week at Kidder's. That wasn't poor pay, then, for an 18-year-old. He ran securities and clearing house tickets around to neighboring brokers, helped the order clerks at the telephones—did anything that was asked of him. He stood in awe of Charles L. Morse, the partner who had hired him, and was reverent in the presence of the other partners, Charles E. Marvin and George S. Coe. He never speaks of them, even now, without a certain awe.

Anyway, the years hurried by. Open-flame gas lamps went out of fashion and gas mantles shed a mellower light in the streets. Low, red-brick buildings vanished from Wall Street and skyscrapers reared where they had stood. There was less and less daylight in the man-made canyons, but Jimmy hardly noticed, it came so gradually. The horse and carriage disappeared, but you forgot the cloppety sound of a horse's hoofs in downtown Manhattan. Underground, the new subways rumbled; you got used to that, too.

Jim worked hard at whatever chore he drew. His climb at Kidder's was slow—runner to mail clerk, to relief man in the wire order room. Other young men came and left, but now Jim can't remember the name of even one. He kept scratching away, entering transactions in the company's blotter in pen and ink.

A few highlights stand out—the day he carried $5,000 in cash and about $200,000 in Norfolk and Western paper out to R. B. Davis' house in Summit, N. J., by train; the time he was told to clean out Mr. Vernay's desk and tried one of Mr. Vernay's Puerto Rican cigars, just for kicks. He was sick for three days.

If volume got up to 250 shares, forty or fifty years ago, that was a big day at Kidder's, but the business grew and you didn't realize that it was heavier and that the time was sliding by. Before you knew it you had put in twenty-five years. The company gave you a handsome wrist watch at an office party. People said heart-warming things, and you choked up a little.

Another twenty-five years, your hair all gray, forty-five years of marriage behind you with two children born and gone; up at 6 o'clock every morning to make the 7:15 out of Darien; the 4:48 back in late afternoon unless things were hopping, as they often were. Gosh, where did the years go?

"All the big men I worked for at the start are a long time gone. Now only C. L.— that's Mr. Morse, who hired me—is still alive down in Virginia Beach, down South. He must be past 80. And here I am, almost 69.

"I know I look healthy, and all, and I am, except my legs. You stand all the time, working the wires, and by and by your legs begin to go. I handle all the American Exchange business here—have for years. No more pen-and-ink entries now. We're too big for that—sixty telephone lines, twenty-eight branch offices, fifteen corresponding firms. Without the I. B. M. machine we'd be buried by the volume.

"No, I never got to be a member of the firm, but I've had a good time. I really have. They're giving me a dinner at Lüchow's next Wednesday night and I retire the end of the month. The party's supposed to be a surprise but I've known about it for weeks. I'll miss this place. I can't figure how it will be, not making the 7:15, and all. No, I never had any hobbies. I just hope that if things get busy here in the office, they'll call me and just say, 'Come on in, Jim; give us a hand.' I hope they will. I'll be happy to help out."

June 11, 1958

❡ Alfred Altman's talk almost always comes in lactic flow, and for good reason. He ran a milk route before school hours in boyhood in Clinton, Mass., where he was born. For many years now he has been head of the National Dairymen

Association, Inc., with offices at 17 East Sixty-fourth Street. He had a lot to do with development of the milk-tank truck and canned milk-product baby foods.

Horses have figured in his life since childhood, too. He won his first blue ribbon when he was 10. Later he was one of the Early Riders, a group that cantered in Central Park before going to the office. He thinks he was the last man to drive his own horse and buggy to work; kept it up until 1942 when he had offices in the Borden Building at 350 Madison Avenue.

Most of the Early Riders were important names in the city forty-fifty years ago—Judge Elbert H. Gary, John McEntee Bowman, C. K. J. Billings, James W. Gerard, William H. Vanderbilt, among others. George Crouch, now 92, oldest living typewriter salesman, was another. He owned the last private stable at 26 West Seventy-sixth Street; sold it in 1930.

Mr. Altman likes to reminisce about the early riding days—about horseback cotillions, costume parties on horseback, even formal dinners on mounts. All that faded in the Black Days after October, 1929.

But it isn't always horses and milk. Dear to the dairyman's heart is the story of Mary Sawyer, whose kinsmen still live in the 150-year-old cottage on Sawyer's Lane—now Maple Street—in Sterling, Mass., a little way down from Mr. Altman's summer home.

Mary Sawyer inspired the rhyme, "Mary Had a Little Lamb." Mr. Altman always keeps in his office desk here copies of a pamphlet that tells her story. Although Sarah Josepha Hale, nineteenth-century editor of Godey's Lady's Book generally gets credit for the verse, the booklets owned by the dairyman contain affidavits to disprove it.

Mary Sawyer was born in the old Sterling farmhouse in 1806. One March morning when she was 5, according to the Altman version, her father gave her a puny newly littered lamb. She kept it in the house, bottle-fed it, washed it pure white every day, combed it, picked burdocks from its snowy wool, even sewed pantalettes for it.

Mary stopped in the sheep meadow every morning, to pet the lamb before she went to school. One morning it trailed her and her brother Nathaniel. They were almost at old District School 2 in Sterling before they heard its plaintive bleat. It came right in. Miss Polly Kimball, the teacher, let the class laugh a minute or two. Then she ordered Mary to shut the lamb in a schoolyard shed until lunch time.

John Roulstone, a divinity student boarding with his uncle, the Rev. Lemuel Capen, in Sterling, heard the lamb story. He wrote three simple verses about it, left them with Miss Kimball next day. Years later someone—possibly Sarah Hale—added three more verses. The record on that isn't clear.

Anyway, Mary Sawyer herself later taught school in Sterling. The old schoolhouse was bought by Henry Ford and is now on the Wayside Inn property in South Sudbury, Mass. Mary's portrait, and her mother's, still hang in the old Sawyer house, which is filled with family relics, kept now by William Sawyer, an architect.

Mary's lamb was killed one day by a cow whose grain-feeder it had invaded. Mary's mother made two pairs of home-knit stockings from its wool. The little girl always kept those. In 1882, seven years before she died, Mary (then Mrs. Columbus Tyler) raveled the stockings, sewed bits of the yarn to cards on which she printed: "Knitted yarn from the first fleece of Mary's Little Lamb." The souvenirs fetched a total of $100 for a fund for preservation of Old South Church in Boston.

July 11, 1958

❧ Wreckers have torn the heart out of blackened old Broome Street Tabernacle near Police Headquarters in Centre Market Place. The inner walls, the pews, galleries and partitions have been pounded to splintered board and lath.

In a few weeks the stout stone outer walls, put up in 1884, will come down in rubble—all but the light-brown cornerstone, which is probably the only one of its kind in all the city. More than 100 years ago it was the top step of the stoop of a policeman's dwelling in almost exactly the same spot where it is now.

When the New York City Mission Society sold the Tabernacle a few weeks ago there was a provision in the contract that the cornerstone was to be carefully removed. When it is, there should be a Bible in it,

opened at Psalms 27:10, "When my father and mother forsake me, the Lord will take me up." The story behind the cornerstone is one of the Mission Society's warmest legends.

On Dec. 7, 1847, John Dooly, a 6-year-old orphan, was homeless in the bitter-cold streets a little north of where Police Headquarters stands now. His father had died, a pioneer in Ohio.

Mary Dooly, the boy's mother, got him to New York, hoping to earn passage money to take her back to Ireland, her birthplace. They lived in utter poverty in a small boarding house off The Bowery. One night Mary Dooly, delirious with yellow fever, wandered out of the place. The best guess is that she died in the street somewhere and that, like other plague victims, was buried in Potter's Field.

A Patrolman Dunne, whose first name is lost, found little John Dooly, blue with cold, and learned about the dead father and the vanished mother. He left his beat to take the boy to his own dwelling on the upper floor at the corner of Broome Street and Centre Street. Mrs. Dunne fed the orphan and next morning she and her husband gave the lad into the custody of the Leake and Watts orphanage uptown.

By and by, John was bound out to a Dr. Benjamin Bevier upstate. Eventually he went to Rutgers University in New Jersey. In the Civil War he fought at Gettysburg in the New Jersey Brigade. After the war he married and was the father of four children; opened the first Bowery Y. M. C. A. in 1872 and was blessed, in that street of unhappy men, for his kindnesses. The City Mission Society voted to build a church in the district and to put him in as minister.

The Mission Society Board bought five buildings at Broome Street and Centre Market and one of the five—the corner dwelling—was the one in which Patrolman Dunne had lived and sheltered John Dooly. The board didn't know that when it took the property. The Rev. John Dooly saw the Divine Hand in the transaction. Most of the money for the Tabernacle was put up by William E. Dodge, whose family down through three generations has backed the society's good work.

When the minister told the story of how Patrolman Dunne had brought him to the corner house, and put his footsteps in the way he was to go, Mr. Dodge and other board members took the top stoop of the old Dunne dwelling for the cornerstone. In the cornerstone they placed the Bible with the significant passage from Psalms. A merchant who had been at Leake and Watts with John Dooly, on the site of the Cathedral of St. John the Divine, donated the bells, anonymously. The largest bell bore the inscription: "Remember December 7, 1847" and the quotation from Psalms 27:10.

Years later the Rev. Mr. Dooly left the city. He was pastor of a Congregational Church at Monterey, Mass., eventually died and was buried in Oxford, Mass.

The last service was held in the old Tabernacle on Sunday, June 1. It had served changing congregations for almost seventy-five years.

Patrolman Dunne's old doorstep, John Dooly's symbol of Divine rescue, is to be used as an altar table or is to be fitted into the scheme of one or another of the Mission Society's chapels or missions, and a tablet is to be made to tell the story of the Bowery waif and how the Lord took him up.

July 25, 1958

¶ Tomorrow night before the sun is down, Japanese in New York and Japanese from Toronto will have met in the green park on the Hudson shore at 103d Street.

They will have set up their yagura—a platform for ritual dancers. Many of the guests and all the performers will be in richly dyed Japanese costumes. The park will be strung with paper lanterns and bright streamers.

The ondo—the dances—will be slow and measured, done in ancient patterns. Gongs will pulse through the twilight and all through the night. Ritual drums will throb. Men, women and children will sing in chorus.

Most of the hymns will be joyous—greetings to the dead; to kin and friends long gone, but returned under the full moon of Ullambana, the Buddhist period for meditation and for self-inventory. There will be gaiety because the spirits are released for just a few hours for reunion with those they loved and who loved them.

Buddhist priests of the New York Buddhist Church at 171 West Ninety-fourth Street say that though the evening is popularly called the Feast of Obon, it is actually the Feast of Ullambana. Obon is a contraction of Ullambana.

Behind the feast is hoary legend. Mogallana the Virtuous, a Buddhist of time long gone, redeemed his mother from the Torture Place through selfless giving. By living without greed or passion, he won a place for her in Paradise.

The New York Buddhist Church group has held the Feast of Obon these last nine years, and the nights have been nights of music and color.

It is a bit sad, the priests tell you, that they cannot bring the night to the same lovely end that is possible by still, easily accessible waters.

When the feast is ended, the spirits rise beneath the moon to go back to Heavenly Paradise. It is the custom, then, for celebrants to light pretty colored candles and set them adrift in colored paper boats, to light the spirits home. The Hudson shore is not an easy place for launching paper boats.

August 15, 1958

❡ Vincent Sardi the Younger is grown, now. He is 43 years old, a lieutenant colonel in the Marine Corps Reserve with South Pacific background. He is a father, risks his frame in supercharged motorcars; has a snug interest in the family's two restaurants.

Sometimes, after the customers have pushed on to the playhouse, Vincent thinks of his Times Square boyhood; how, when he was only 6, his father and mother opened a little eating establishment in the brownstone basement and garden where the St. James Theatre stands now.

Father Sardi was indulgent. He let Young Sardi keep rabbits, chicks, cackling fowl, guttural pigeons and two dogs in the yard, though great players ate there in summer against rather ripe wall murals of Italian sunsets done by a paisan out of Canelli in Asti Province, where the Sardis had their roots.

Ardito, one of the rabbits, was pugnacious for his breed. He table-hopped, nose a-twitch for lettuce handouts. He begged from notables —Guthrie McClintic, Katharine Cornell, Winthrop Ames, Frank Craven, Wally Ford, the Shuberts, Miriam Hopkins and John Golden, among others. Young Vincent's other pets were always underfoot.

On summer mornings when the sun washed fresh gold on the Forty-fourth Street brownstones, Vincent, the boy, would hop on the neighborhood milk wagon. Sometimes he got to handle the reins. The ice-wagon man would take him as far west as Ninth Avenue, and would filch jelly doughnuts for him from ice-buying groceries.

As a spratling, young Vinnie would shoulder his bee-bee air gun and go on the prowl in and around the Square for red men. He would tear down the block on his home-made scooter; flash by the West-over Apartments a-whooping. When Bobby Walthour, a neighbor famous as a six-day bike rider, came by, the boy would just trail him, in awe.

A fella could hitch on horse-drawn hacks; ride the blind side of open-air trolleys through Times Square. He opened limousine doors for sweet-scented ladies and silk-hatted gentlemen at theatre-break to earn pocket money; got the feel of a car by sawing at the steering apparatus of parked vehicles during playtime.

His fiddle-scraping in the Sardis' apartment just above the restaurant was torment for yard diners. They were more delighted when he was allowed to abandon music than he was. His scholastic career in Holy Cross in Forty-third Street was smoothed and speeded by French pastries and cold lobster he swiped for the teaching sister.

There were picnics in Central Park and on Washington Heights. His mother would pack the lunch and take him on the Fifth Avenue bus. He wandered backstage in the five theatres in his own block and in Forty-fifth Street. He knew all the players, electricians, stagehands and doormen, a privilege rare even for a Times Square Huckleberry Finn.

At 6 he was cast as an Italian urchin in "The Master of the Inn" in the Little Theatre, down from the restaurant. He wore a sailor suit in the part, reclined on a bear-skin rug and endured the embraces of Vera Teasdale, the leading lady. Ian Keith and Robert Lorraine were in the play, too. The pay was $75 a week and he toured with the company.

The family moved to Flushing, in the country, when Vincent was 11. The years sped. He got out of Columbia University in 1937, after casual study of business administration and a wishy-washy interest in medicine. He went through all the menial jobs in his father's prospering establishment and then, one day a few years ago, took over. His responsibilities multiplied and the great and near-great sought his favor.

But even a busy grown-up can dream and the dreams of Vincent the Younger have mostly Forty-fourth Street and Times Square boundaries.

August 20, 1958

❡ Awesomely remote in the firmament are the so-called "faint variable stars." Actually they are not faint. Most of them are more brilliant than our sun—more than 10,000 times more brilliant.

They seem faint because they are, in some cases, 50,000 light years away in space. To compute the distance, each light year is counted, roughly, as the equivalent of six trillion miles. If the Rev. Walter J. Miller, Jesuit astronomer, is right, and he should be, one ends up with a 3 followed by seventeen ciphers—and migraine.

Father Miller, a blue-eyed priest with thinning hair, is one of a handful of astronomers who specialize in the study of faint variables. It is a painstaking and highly exacting form of research, done mostly with oversize glass plates.

The supersensitive photographic

emulsion of such plates has caught, through powerful telescopes, heavenly bodies too distant for steady observation with the naked eye. A single 12-by-12 plate may capture up to 600,000 separate stars; a larger plate up to two billion.

For ten years—first in the Vatican Observatory in Castel Gandolfo and for the last three in a dark, book-littered study in ivy-covered, stone-walled Dealy Hall on the Fordham University campus—Father Miller has given his full time to the faint variables. He may spend the rest of his life there, tracking them among the star-spatterings on the glass plates.

He has written thirteen brochures on them and has a backlog of many that are still unpublished. Astronomers all over the world know them as the "VV Series"—"Vatican Variables."

The latest is a report on the peculiar variation cycles of "VV-48," a plate-speck caught through an opening of the Milky Way, VV-48 seems to breathe and pulse 50,000 light years out.

No one is certain what makes VV-48 expand and contract, but the best guess is that it is due to hot-gas flare-ups. Some faint variables seem to go through their breathing cycle in as little as ninety minutes. VV-48 goes through its rise and fall about every fifty-four days; some variables change shape only once in twenty-seven years.

Father Miller has had to study as many as 1,500 plates to compute the complete cycle of just one faint variable. He borrowed his oldest plates from Harvard University.

They go back sixty-four years. Around him, in his enshadowed cubby, are some 4,000 plates taken through the years—3,000 from the Vatican Observatory, 500 from Yale and Harvard and 500 from Mount Wilson and from Palomar.

When one stares at the spatters of stars on the plates, it seems that the astronomer could mistake a mote of dust for a faint variable. But he doesn't. Dust is apt to have ragged edges under the microscope; the stars are more or less round—or seem to be.

The bracket that holds the microscope looks a bit odd, and it should; it is made from a fragment of a Flying Fortress that crashed in Ciampino Airport, ten miles south of Rome, in World War II. An inventive Jesuit passed it on to Father Miller.

Differentiating between spatter spots on a plate that holds two billion of them sometimes gets tedious. When it does, Father Miller, who was born in Rochester, N. Y., may slip away to a Yankee game. For briefer intervals he carries a pocketful of peanuts for the gray squirrels and black squirrels that invade his splintery-floored hide-away.

His work has made him a compulsive counter and he keeps track of his furry visitors. He has had as many as nine begging for handouts at one time. In the winter he feeds chickadees, juncos and grackles with sunflower seed.

"Never had a cardinal," he tells you, sadly, but the blue eyes twinkle. At dusk he watches the bats flap out of Dealy Hall's untenanted top floor.

Father Miller studies his stars to muted symphonies played on a hi-fi record changer. He has a rig of his own invention that can play the same record over and over from early morning until past midnight.

"I need it," he explains, "for variation from the music of the spheres."

August 25, 1958

¶ Of the city's eighty-one police stations, only seven have stood for a whole century, or for close to a century. Of these, six are in Manhattan. Brooklyn's Bedford Avenue station house counts 103 years.

Manhattan's oldest is at 160 East Thirty-fifth Street. It went up in 1854. Emergency Squad 6 at 209 East 172d Street was built in the same year as Bedford Avenue in Brooklyn; West Forty-seventh Street and Mercer Street date back to 1860; the Sheriff Street house to 1862, and 327 East Twenty-second Street to 1863.

Last Wednesday Police Commissioner Stephen P. Kennedy tolled the bell for Mercer Street, the sad-looking, gray-painted, stiff-fronted relic that has been a station house in lower Greenwich Village for ninety-eight years. Actually, the building may have a full 100 years or more. It was a double-dwelling unit before it became a station house.

As a police precinct, Mercer Street dates back 113 years. It started in 1845 in Ambrose H. Kingsland's stables across the way from where the station house is now. The cops of that day, mostly without uniforms, were members of the Municipal Day and Night Watch. They shared quarters with Volunteer Fire Engine Company 4 and with sweet-scented coach and draught horses.

The lower Village still had the semi-bucolic look—sandy hills, marshes and glittering streams. Only a few years before, men had fished Minetta Brook for trout and had shot wild fowl in what is now Washington Square. Fourteenth Street was the city's northern boundary. Men still lived who had fought in the Revolution.

In 1845 the stable station was called the Fifteenth Ward house. The first entry, on Nov. 1, is still bold on the flyleaf in old-fashioned script: "New Station House Wants: Draws [drawers] for blanks; stove, shovel, poker, scuttle and sifter; fixtures for privy; bin for coal; locks for cells, spittoons." Five men did day watch. Nine walked by night.

The richest man in the precinct was John Jacob Astor in Astor Place. Washington Irving was a neighbor. Business men rode "to town" in their own equipages or in horse stages. Lower Fifth Avenue was building up, though Union Square seemed to have more rich folk. Sewers were just going in and the men on beat had to make blotter entries for each house connection.

In the beginning there were no murders to speak of, but a spillover of Bowery b'hoys and bewildered famine-fleeing immigrants from Ireland roamed the area seeking jobs and shelter. The earliest entries are strings of "assault and battery" and "intox" and lines on strayed or stolen "horse and waggon." Every policeman was "Mister." Because the stable was damp and odorous, even the reserves slept at home.

Service entries were polite and in flourishing hand: "Mr. Irwan and Mr. Barnes will look at Thirteenth and Fourteenth Streets." "Mr. Smart will look after Fifth Avenue." "Mr. Taylor and Mr. O'Dell will take a good look at Broadway and The Bowery." Each night there was a list of homeless under the heading "Lodgers." Beggars were rounded up and listed at the rate of thirty-five to fifty each day.

Thefts were all petty—silk weskit, woman's shawl, frock coat, napery, silver spoons. Chronic drunks signed a station house pledge promising "that for one year he will not drink any ardent spirits, cordials or wine" except as medicine under a doctor's orders. Boys were scolded for running foot races in the public highway to the embarrassment of cartmen and haughty coach drivers.

The years brought change. The blotters show varying population wash. Horses, stages and carts vanish from the entries. Buses and motorcars, subways and trolleys take their place. The station house that opened in 1860 was hemmed by loft buildings that blackened with time. Where fourteen men had been ample in 1845, the roster grew to 125.

And time left grim blotter tracks: The Astor Place riot of May 10, 1849, in which twenty men died over an actors' feud, many right in the station house. The draft riots of July, 1863, in which men of Mercer Street were crippled by brick-throwing ruffians. The $2,247,-000 robbery of the Manhattan Savings Institution on Oct. 27, 1878. The murder of Col. Jim Fisk by Ned Stokes in the Grand Central Hotel in Broadway on Jan. 6, 1872. The death of 143 girls and men in the Triangle Shirtwaist Factory fire, March 25, 1911.

By and by the old blotters will be stored away in the Police Archives room downtown, probably never to be opened again. Capt. William E. Coleman and his men will be scattered. The station house where in the spring the watch snored in the stable doorway 113 years ago will have passed forever from police annals. Time's tide, receding, will leave no trace of it.

October 1, 1958

❡ Dry leaves skitter down city walks. The air has promise of autumnal pinch. High above the pavement the flocks fly south. The gypsies tune their Cadillacs for the run to warmer places—to Memphis, Atlanta, Birmingham, Chattanooga, Miami and New Orleans. They will hold off longer than the birds. They will wait until there is more ice in the wind's breath.

The Rev. Alexander Chechila will be happy when the gypsy caravans pull out. The Tsigani are a plague to his little Russian Orthodox Church of SS. Peter and Paul at 121 East Seventh Street, which he bought at auction forty years ago for $1,800. They give nothing into the collection plate and they prey on his parishioners.

Father Chechila's peeling old church building lies almost at the heart of the East Side. The interior is creaky and dark even at midday. The scarlet carpet runners in the halls, on the stairs and in his third-floor study are faded. The church organ has been silent since Mrs. Chechila died, long years ago.

It is a struggle to keep the little church alive. Father Chechila was young and vigorous when he bought the church at auction in 1918 with help from officials of the Bowery Savings Bank. Now he is silver-haired, tired and gaunt. His only attendants are two old women, heads kerchiefed as in Old Russia. They live in the church basement. They keep the altars white. They do the stairs and his study. They sweep the sidewalks. They draw no pay.

Now, the women of Father Chechila's flock are hard-working women. When darkness comes to the East Side they leave their babies with neighbors and move northward by the hundreds to clean the thousands of offices in Rockefeller Center. The bulk of the city's charwomen come from the parish of SS. Peter and Paul. They are away from their tenement flats through dawn.

Almost all these toilers retain the superstitions and fears that they, and their mothers before them, brought with them out of Russia. They cower under the threat of the evil eye. They still believe in soothsayers, in black magic and in the Tsiganis' vaunted power for calling evil upon them, or of removing afflictions with gypsy mumbo-jumbo.

The dark-eyed gypsy Romni, with their red and green low-necked dresses, with their necklaces of gold coins, their slippered feet, move from door to door in the old tenements. They coax or they threaten, and the charwomen admit them, and are compelled to pay for the sorcery the Romni sell. Then, on the Sabbath, in Father Chechila's church they have little left for the plate when it is passed.

Father Chechila passes a thin, high-veined hand across his tired eyes in his brooding old red-carpeted study. "A man of God," he muses, "must not hate, but I have no great warmth in my heart for the gypsies. When they come to my church for a wedding or for one of their funerals, I must perform the services to which I am dedicated, and I do. But I pray for the season when they go south."

He says, "The gypsy never changes. For countless centuries he has held ignorant men and women under his sinister influence. Now, even in the time of the Atom, the power holds. I am glad the fall has come. They will leave my people in peace now until Easter. Then they will come swarming back. I wish there were some way to hold them off. But no man ever has. Perhaps no man ever will."

October 3, 1958

❡ The Practising Law Institute, a school for lawyers and prosecutors, was twenty-five years old yesterday. Close to 500 grave barristers, judges and teachers of law assembled in the Statler Hilton Hotel at sundown to quaff a discreet cup or two to the institute's astonishing career.

The institute was an unusual venture in 1933. It was founded by Harold P. Seligson, now an authority on corporate law, a little more than eight years after he got out of Columbia Law School in 1924. Earlier he had experimented by teaching his own law clerks at night with his office as a classroom.

In Abraham Lincoln's time a young fellow could "read law" in an older man's office. He could absorb courtroom technique by a kind of osmosis. Young Seligson found when he came out of law school that, although he was crammed with the theory of law, he knew nothing of actual practice. You don't get much of that in law schools.

It came to him then that the modern law office had no time to give individual instruction to apprentices as the older men could in Lincoln's less hurried age; that the year of clerkship was virtually worthless, a dead tradition. He thought that, if he won success in law, he might find some modern substitute for it.

The late Prof. Herman Oliphant, one of Mr. Seligson's teachers at Columbia, agreed there should be courses in actual law practice for law school graduates. Mr. Seligson easily found twenty-five eager young men for his first institute students; taught them four nights a week in a borrowed classroom at New York University.

The institute grew. In the last twenty-five years it has trained more than 30,000 men and women in practice. Its classes for prosecutors have helped 1,000 district or city attorneys throughout the United States. Similar institutes now flourish in other regions—in Boston, Los Angeles, Toledo, San Francisco and in Texas.

Big law firms send their newest staff men to the classes and pay instruction fees, which may run from $25 to $40 for a course. The same firms contribute generally to the institute's support. The Carnegie Foundation chipped in $50,000 because the institute is a nonprofit venture.

The State Board of Regents chartered the institute. Twenty years ago the Court of Appeals ruled that if a law school graduate took a year's study in the school he did not need to go through the one-year clerkship that had been tradition. The greatest specialists in law were the teachers, many serving without fee or for nominal fee.

Classes now meet in the New York County Lawyers Association rooms in West Forty-fourth Street. They hear men like James D. C. Murray, famous at the criminal court bar; Emile Zola Berman, outstanding expert in negligence cases; District Attorney Frank S. Hogan on criminal investigation and prosecution. They hear handwriting experts, tax authorities, men versed in medical law.

Some of the great lawyers have eventually faced former pupils in the court chamber, and had to listen to counterargument based on their own teachings. In one negligence-case class, a student asked an insurance company official whether his company kept its office open at night for case settlement. It never had, up to then, but now it does.

Mr. Seligson tried, almost in the beginning, to get the Bar Association to take the institute over, but it never did. The president now is Nicholas Kelley of Kelley, Drye, Newhall & Maginnes; vice president, James A. Fowler Jr. of Cahill, Gordon, Reindel & Ohl. And the founder is still stuck. He teaches corporate law.

October 6, 1958

¶ From dawn through sunset on Oct. 12, islanders, fliers and voyagers in the South Seas will see varying phases of 1958's last solar eclipse. Scientists will watch it from Motu Koe in the Danger Islands in the South Pacific.

Because it will be the year's last big sky show, lecturers at the Hayden Planetarium this week and next will talk mostly about solar eclipses and show their track on the man-made heavens. They will tell listeners that no total solar eclipse will be seen from New York until April 4, 2024, and none after that until May 1, 2079.

Then the lecturers will bring in the solar eclipse of Saturday, Jan. 24, 1925—New York's so-called "Uptown Eclipse," a rather freakish phenomenon.

Astronomers had figured that city folk as far south on Manhattan Island as Eighty-third Street would see totality that bitter morning. There was a gale, and the thermometer reading was 5 above zero.

The lower island was empty when the eclipse started at 9:11 A.M. Freezing throngs covered the Columbia, N. Y. U. and City College campuses. Hundreds of thousands stood at Eighty-third Street, staring at the sky.

But the astronomers had missed in their guess by a half-mile or more. The southernmost viewing point for totality fell between Ninety-sixth and Ninety-seventh Streets and the best views were north of that. South of Ninety-sixth watchers thought they saw totality, but didn't, quite. Downtown Manhattan was deserted, an asphalt desert.

Superstitious people were a little uneasy that freezing day. A Seventh Day Adventist spokesman in Washington had told newspapers that the stars might fall when the earth and the skies went dark. He even hinted at the world's end.

At the moment of totality, the city came under full darkness. The moon's shadow fell across the rivers, the island and the Palisades. Harbor craft broke out their red and green running lights. Skyscrapers turned on their lights.

Manhattan and its waters took on a weird, coppery glow, and great throngs murmured in awed concert. The corona flared and the glorious spectacle of the "engagement ring" effect with its great gem of burning white light thrilled the people.

It was one of the most brilliant eclipses the city had ever seen. The man in Washington was wrong. No stars fell. On Monday morning President Coolidge was back at work in the White House. Mayor Hylan was busy at City Hall.

¶ For almost ten years, now, passengers in cars that use the southbound roadway under the New York Central Building in Park Avenue have had the protection of a silent guardian—Our Lady of the Ramp. She will have watched over the ramp a full ten years next May.

Our Lady of the Ramp is a statue of the Madonna in the offices of America Press in the terminal building at 70 East Forty-fifth Street. The Catholic magazine America is put together there. So are other publications.

The offices are at ramp level just below Forty-fifth Street. The Lady of the Ramp is in the southernmost corner. The twenty or more girls in the office bring fresh flowers every day to place at her feet. They get them from home gardens, but subscribe to a fund to buy flowers in winter.

After dark, when the girls and the priests have gone, a ceiling spotlight is trained on the silent figure in blue, gold and white. Cab drivers are familiar with it and tell riders about it. Many motorists write in to find out the shrine's history. Some come to visit.

In the beginning the statue was on an office filing cabinet, not easily seen by riders in ramp cars. Then the girls thought of placing it closer to the window. Lillian McGuire and Lucy Quigley undertook special care of it.

They started collecting flower money and there is always a reserve of a few dollars for fresh blossoms. Miss Quigley knitted a lace canopy for the shrine. At Christmas time the display is bravest, with poinsettias and silver tinsel.

It was the Rev. Joseph McFarlane of America's staff who thought of naming the Madonna Our Lady of the Ramp, and on each May 10 there is a special recitation of the rosary before her in the office, because May is the month of Mary.

MARGINALIA: ¶ New York's first World's Fair came to a fiery end 100 years ago yesterday. The Crystal Palace in Bryant Park, which held the exhibits, went up in flame that day. Two thousand visitors got out before the dome fell. The last thing they heard before the alarm was sounded was a steam calliope version of "Pop Goes the Weasel." . . .

October 16, 1958

¶ One of the curious collections in town—and there are many—is the Pawnee Bill Archives kept in rather ill-lighted offices on the second floor at 1165 Broadway by Allan Leonard Rock, an advertising man.

Mr. Rock was promotion manager thirty years ago for Gordon William Lillie, part owner of the Buffalo Bill-Pawnee Bill Wild West Show. He started the collection then. G. W. Lillie was Pawnee Bill's true name. He left his material to Mr. Rock.

It has expanded a lot since 1927. It now includes close to 2,000 volumes on the Wild West, mounds of original photographs of bad men and law men and Indians. It contains original Wild West show posters, Indian Agency records, old Western newspapers, dime novels, Pawnee Bill's correspondence, Wild West medicine show literature.

Writers of Westerns have borrowed from the Pawnee Bill Archives. So have museums. Pawnee Indian Agency ledgers in the Broadway files helped the Pawnee tribe only last year to win its litigation over 23,000,000 tribal acres in Nebraska.

Mr. Rock, a shy, modest fellow, doesn't mention it often, but he is a Pawnee by adoption. His tribal name is Rah-wis-tah-rika (Smoke Signal Son), which is as close as the Indians could come to finding a word for an advertising man. Smoke-signal paintings are part of the archive's office decorations.

Mr. Rock is a stickler for factual presentation of the history of the Old West. He is forever trying to straighten out what he calls "the distortions" or cockeyed notions of frontier history that people get from inaccurate biographies.

He says he can prove that Gen. George Armstrong Custer was not scalped at the Little Big Horn and that the story of that engagement is one of the most distorted in frontier annals. He has loads of stuff on Phoebe Ann Moses, who lives in Western history as Annie Oakley.

Pawnee Bill was born in Bloomington, Ill., in 1860. He was a hunter and trapper with the Pawnees in 1872. At that time Adlai Stevenson's grandfather, Gen. Adlai

Ewing Stevenson, assigned him to teach English to the Pawnees. He eventually became White Chieftain of the tribe.

Mr. Rock spent a lot of time with him between 1927 and 1942, when Pawnee Bill died. Effie Judy Lillie and Lena Little, the showman's sisters, kept up the contact and turned over to Mr. Rock all the material their brother left at his death.

Traveling Wild West shows, Mr. Rock says, first came East in 1883. They were staged then in a lot in Atlantic Avenue, Brooklyn, where the old Brooklyn baseball team played. Buffalo Bill and Pawnee Bill first came to the old Madison Square Garden in Manhattan in 1908.

The two Bills, Pawnee and Buffalo, had their offices in the same building where the archives are now. Due south, on the southwest corner of Broadway and Twenty-eighth Street, Thomas A. Edison held previews of his first important film, "The Great Train Robbery," in which he used cowboys and Indians.

Mr. Rock isn't quite sure how he will eventually dispose of his Pawnee Bill Archives. He thinks, though, he may display them first in banks, museums, schools and in historical societies.

"Mainly," he says, "I want to use the archives to get the Western Frontier record straight. The true cowboys and Indian stories were exciting enough without exaggeration. I think people should get that history unadulterated."

October 15, 1958

¶ By 1970, if the Downtown-Lower Manhattan Association achieves its aims, Manhattan Island south of Chambers Street will have lost what it retained of nineteenth-century flavor and atmosphere—of the city-that-was.

Close to 3,000 low, moldering architectural relics, mostly of warm red brick, of soot-covered yellow brick or of sagging clapboard with dormered top floors, will go to rubble under the wreckers' blows.

Almost all the properties, huddled in the long shadows of skyscrapers, were handsome dwellings a little over 100 years ago. Then their owners, one by one, moved northward on steady residential tides and commerce claimed the houses.

Commission merchants took the houses, dealers in fish, in fruits and vegetables and spices. Ship chandleries set up in what had been magnificent nineteenth-century parlors. So did seamen's groggeries and restaurants. In other parts of the city, streets widened. These remained narrow and crooked.

South of the Brooklyn Bridge, leather merchants kept on with their 300-year-old city trade on the Swamp—it's still called that—although their noisome tanneries, dating back to Peter Stuyvesant's city stewardship, had to pull out to open areas, far outside city limits. The Swamp is doomed, too.

There is a sleepy, melancholy charm for the wanderer, stranger or native, among these hangovers of a bygone day, especially on week-ends when they are silent, barred and shuttered, staring with dust-covered, bleary panes on the narrow thoroughfares.

Yet that lower part of town has fought against chromium-faced, white-vested progress, and for an astonishingly long time. The area from the Brooklyn Bridge to the Battery, which has always been the market place, has maintained the pleasant blend of fish, coffee and spice smells for long years.

The great, lumbering trailer trucks now bring in the stores of foods and fish that at first sailing vessels, later steamships, dropped on the downtown waterfront, handy to the commission merchants' shops. Yet the merchants somehow hung on in the sway-backed, decaying converted town houses. Now they will vanish.

The practical-minded group bent on redevelopment downtown will work with the Municipal Art Society on what relics should be preserved, but there will not be many. Fraunces Tavern, built in 1719, will stay. So will old Federal Hall, the nation's first Capitol, now the Sub-Treasury Museum. So, probably, will the Catholic Mission at 7 State Street, which was Moses Rogers' dwelling 150 years ago.

City Hall will be passed by, of course, as beautiful now as it was in Moses Rogers' time, but the old Almshouse, the so-called Old Tweed Courthouse back of it, is on the wreckers' list. It was marked for demolition before the Downtown-Lower Manhattan Association started its plans.

Fate probably never meant Lower Manhattan to attain any semblance of hoary antiquity anyway. Almost every vestige of the original Dutch village was burned away by great fires in 1776 and 1778. The area was leveled to ash again in 1835.

When the markets are swept away by redevelopment—old Fulton Fish Market, the half-mile of ancient produce and spice buildings between Barclay and Hubert Streets, the Swamp, the dusty chandleries and coffee-roasting plants in and around the Wall Street district —only names will linger on street signposts to preserve city history.

Maybe men will remember that Wall Street was named for a real wall that the mynheers built to keep out Indians. Maybe they will recall that Mill Lane took its name from an old Dutch mill; that Marketfield Street was Petticoat Lane, the hausvrows' road to Bowling Green market; that there were once aromas and trades and events identified by every name that will then be only a signpost.

October 20, 1958

¶ A small part of a world-wide glossary of policemen's cant collected in the past two years by Patrolman Redmond O'Hanlon of the New York Police Department's publication, Spring 3100, runs in the October issue. Writers of cops-and-robbers fiction or television thrillers will benefit by it.

Contributions came from as far off as New Zealand and Alaska, but the Police Department in Greece, a town near Rochester, N. Y., stiffly

answered Patrolman O'Hanlon's questionnaire with the comment: "This is a department of seventeen men and has been in existence for twenty-five years. We call a complaint, a complaint; nightstick, a nightstick." No cant, or slang, there.

Some of the items in the New York Police Department glossary are interesting. A-men are men in the automobile squad. A uniform is a bag. A policeman calls his arrest and summons record his batting average. Detectives are brains. The broom is the station house custodian. A detective's shield is a button, potsy or tin. Any stretcher case is a carry.

Unidentified dead destined for potter's field are C. C. (City Cemetery) cases. Chopper coppers are helicopter fliers. Any spot that takes a policeman out of the rain is a coop, or a heave. A motorist who drives with one eye on his rearvision mirror is a cutie. Departmental charges against a policeman are didoes, or small ones.

A motorcycle policeman revving up in pursuit of a violator is dumping it in. The foxy motorist who slows almost to a halt when he senses pursuit drops dead. A transfer from one police command to another is flying. An easy arrest is a grounder and a speed violator is a heavy foot. A cutpurse who goes after women's off-the-shoulder bags is a hanger binger, and a cop assigned to narcotic cases is a hombre, or the Man.

A man a long time on the police force is a hairbag. The man who wins a promotion is "made." The precinct captain is the Old Man or

Skipper. The policeman who hands a summons to a motorist puts him in the satchel. A fine for violation of police regulations is a rip. A spying department superior is still a shoofly. A salute to a superior officer is a slam, or a highball. A man on desk duty has the stick. An informer is a stool, or stoolie. A complaint is a squeal. When you follow a suspect you give him a tail.

A policeman doesn't subdue a truculent prisoner; he tranquilizes him. A man who leaves home is a walk-out to the Missing Persons Bureau; a man on motorcycle duty is on the wheel and a lieutenant who leads a detective squad is the whip.

Even the Communications Division has its own terms. A busy switchboard at Police Headquarters is, by poetic touch, a Christmas tree.

¶ This week or next, depending on when the first sharp frost bites Times Square, crews hired by Douglas Leigh, the sign man, will add 3,000 gallons of anti-freeze to the waterfall display in the square. The anti-freeze goes in every year about the same time. A 1,000-gallon tank of the chemical is kept on the roof behind the waterfall to make up for evaporation loss, which varies from 250 to 500 gallons a week.

October 22, 1958

¶ An unusual new guidebook is out. It is for men and women who get about in wheel chairs or on crutches or both.

It tells what city establishments have steps, and how many; which provide wheel-chair ramps, which have staircase hand rails; in which theatres it is easiest to transfer from a wheel chair to a regular house seat.

The booklet covers restaurants, theatres, museums, colleges, municipal bureaus, parks, sports arenas, boat rides, churches, shopping, art galleries. Under "Marriage License Bureau, Municipal Building," there is a line: "At the south end of the building there is a revolving door. If this is impossible for you to use, send someone in to inform them and the door will be opened."

The booklet sells for $1. Its author, Sandra Schnur of 2255 Cruger Avenue, the Bronx, took to a wheel chair seven years ago when she was 16.

¶ Horse-drawn carriages, mostly family-size, reached three blocks in all directions from the Metropolitan Opera House when it opened for the first time at 8:30 seventy-five years ago tonight. Brisk ushers in bottle green with gilt buttons led ladies and gentlemen to seats. The opera was "Faust," with Christine Nilsson as Marguerite, Italo Campanini in the title role.

The William H. Vanderbilts had Lord Chief Justice Sir John Duke Coleridge in their box. Astors were there, the Belmonts, the Russell Sages, the Goelets and Carl Schurz. In a box where the dress circle is now sat Adam Weber of 203 Second Avenue, who had made his fortune in chimney brick and as founder of the Union Square and

Germania Banks. The Sirovich Day Center occupies the old Weber mansion now.

Mathilde Weber was only 16 years old when the opera house opened. Her father did not take her that first night, but within the week she saw a performance from the family box. She cannot remember now which opera it was, but few teen-age memories linger when you've reached 91.

Miss Mathilde has attended the Metropolitan Opera House almost every week through the seventy-five years that have since passed, and still does. She and Miss Frances Weber, her brother Oscar's daughter, have held front-row seats since 1903. Miss Frances has occupied one of the Weber seats since she was a little girl. She is 70 now.

The Webers have seats 101 and 102 on Saturdays; seats 103-104 on Fridays. None of the conductors or performers today seems to know them, but sixty and seventy years ago almost all the principals would bow or wink at them in friendly recognition.

Enrico Caruso often came to the Weber house during opera time in New York. Mathilde and Frances Weber have portfolios of letters, cards and cartoons from him. He never came on stage without a sly wink at Row A. They worship him as much today, long after his death, as they did when he and they were young. His portrait as Canio the clown in "Il Pagliacci" faces Frances in her bedroom.

The Misses Weber have lived in the fortress-like Dakota apartments at 1 West Seventy-second Street since 1903. They remember when no towering multiple dwelling houses faced them across the park from Fifth Avenue; only low stately mansions. They still speak wistfully of the family gardens in Second Avenue, especially of the old wisteria their mother had trained over the arbor. They have stopped by for visits at 203, but not a soul there remembers the Webers of the Eighties and Nineties.

Aunt and niece love to talk about Christmas Eve, 1903. Alfred Hertz, the conductor, and most of the principals who had performed in the American première of "Parsifal" at the opera house that night came down to Second Avenue. They stood around the Webers' drawing room piano and around the Webers' tree—"It was lighted with tiny wax tapers," Miss Mathilde remembers—and raised their drinking vessels. They sang rich sacred music and old German folksongs.

But the opera stars of that period live in Miss Mathilde's and Miss Frances' memories and in faded autographed photographs, kept in the same box with the delicately colored Parsifal Christmas cards they sent to the family fifty-five years ago. Miss Mathilde hasn't made up her mind what she will do with the family opera relics—items signed by Marcella Sembrich, Olive Fremstad, Andreas Dippel, and photographs taken when the Webers went to Bayreuth in the Eighteen Seventies to visit Frau Cosima Wagner, after her husband's death. It has been suggested they go to the Public Library Music

Division, and most likely they will, one day.

October 24, 1958

¶ The largest and busiest apiary in town, a five-hive establishment, is on the fourth-floor terrace at 44 East Sixty-fifth Street, facing south. It was inherited with the lease for the terrace apartment last May by Ted Ralph and Milburn Butler, young decorators.

The gentleman who owned the flat and terrace before the decorators took it over has a young son, a student in a progressive school. One of his class projects some months ago was bee study. His father promised to cooperate. He bought a wooden hive and some Italian bees.

It turned out the little buzzers liked the East Sixties. It is only a short flight to Central Park, where the pickings are good, and on less windy days the bees forage in neighborhood penthouse gardens, even the highest, and there are many in the territory.

Although it was not written into the lease, the original owner made it clear that he could not let the terrace and the apartment to anyone who would not keep the apiary. The decorators gave a gentleman's agreement. They were promised part of the honey yield, too, a sweet inducement.

All spring and all summer the decorators watched their little charges with a wary eye. They saw them swarm out at dawn and settle down for the night between 5 and 6 o'clock. The bees never invaded the decorators' privacy and never went after table sweets or the shower.

The man who started the hives has been up a few times with head net and thick gloves, to poke around and remove filled combs. He had intended to carry the boxes up to the country after the first frost, when the bees would have gone into winter doze.

Now the man has changed his mind. Mr. Ralph and Mr. Butler own the bees and the hives, and like the idea. They're a bit foggy on bee-counting—don't know whether they own 5,000 or 50,000, but they're proud of one thing. They say, "We own the most snobbish bee colony in the world; the only flight that takes its nourishment from Manhattan skyline penthouse gardens."

¶ A telephone cock-crow is offered now for slugabeds.

Bill Adler, a young advertising man, has started a Wake Me Service—he calls it that—that will rouse you from slumber, give you the time, the weather of the moment with exact outdoor temperature, and a forecast, too.

Telephone-answering services have done some wake-up business in town, but the new venture will start round-the-clock wakings on Nov. 3 at $8 a month a person.

Instead of using a switchboard for the work, Mr. Adler has rounded up twenty housewives who are up very late or very early to do the calling. He got most of them through church organizations. If Wake Me builds up as he hopes it might, he expects to add a telephonic reminder service, too—one that will warn of birthdays, appointments and wedding anniversaries.

¶ A lively trade in second-hand brick is growing steadily in town. It started a few years ago when tenements were coming down all over the city to make way for new housing. The men who clean old brick with trowels and other sharp tools have come, for some unexplained reason, to be known as Klondikers. They usually get one cent for each brick they clean.

Dealers move in on piles of their finished work, haul them away to their yards and sell them to builders for about 2½ cents each. Most of the brick is used for walling. New brick is used for outer facing.

Several architects have used them for facing as well as backing, with a pleasant effect. A good example is the De Witt Memorial Church on the edge of Baruch Housing at Columbia and Rivington Streets. An irregular pattern of blackened brick enlivens the facings. The black brick came out of tenement flues, or fireplaces. Edgar Tafel, the architect, has even worked natural rock found on the slum site into the sunken gardens around the church.

¶ East-West Item: Gentleman with high-piled turban in Times Square cutting through wind-blown rain yesterday with plastic cover protecting the turban.

October 29, 1958

¶ Fifty years ago the Bohemian Benevolent and Literary Association built an annex in East Seventy-fourth Street between First and Second Avenues. That part of Yorkville then was flooded with Czechs and Slovaks. Their chief meeting place was the association's main building in East Seventy-third Street, directly behind the annex. It still is.

The annex was used as a ballroom because the main ballroom in the original building wasn't big enough, vast though it is, to handle all the Czech and Slovak weddings, which were lusty, highly musical and colorful. When the immigrant tide ran low, the annex became a motion picture theatre, mostly for Czech and Slovak films.

Now Pantheon Productions, Inc., an off-Broadway play group, is doing the theatre over. It found the original marble box office hidden behind a false wall; the original white marble staircase hidden under layers of paint. It has restored the green-and-gold baroque decorations in the theatre proper.

It also has converted old skylights for air-conditioning. It has built a rotating stage on a second-hand piston-type hydraulic garage jack—the kind that lifts big cars with ease. The owners—the producer, Day Tuttle, and Howard Kane, a former drama student of his at Columbia—have cut through the movie house wall for rehearsal space and dressing rooms in the cavernous association hall.

An alley along the theatre's south wall is to be trellised so that patrons of the new East Seventy-fourth Street Theatre may drift out the side doors and move back toward the quaint, broodingly dark bar in the Bohemian National Hall where Czech and Slovak gaffers linger over their beer all afternoon and evening, reminiscing mostly in their native tongue. There's a genuine Bohemian restaurant, too.

It is an odd joining of old and new. Some twenty clubs that meet in the big building have obligingly removed their cast-iron safes from a basement storage room so that players in the new theatre may have the space for dressing. There will be nights when the big ballroom in Seventy-third Street will echo to a Czech, Slovak, Hungarian, Italian or Arab wedding while the players are performing in the annex.

There will be evenings when the main ballroom in the Bohemian National Hall will be showing a rival play, or opera, by amateur association members in Bohemian costume. They did very well, not long ago, with a production of "The Bartered Bride." They like that one best of any. Friedrich Smetana, a Bohemian, wrote it.

¶ All through the week until Saturday Richard Loderhose runs an eight-story paste and glue factory in Renwick Street, downtown. Week-ends he putters around pipe organs—very large pipe organs. He keeps collecting and changing them; swapping parts with other members of the American Theatre Organ Enthusiasts, which has contact with other organ collectors as far away as India and Mozambique.

Mr. Loderhose's most recent acquisition came to fifty tons, which made five big van loads. It is the Mighty Wurlitzer that had occupied a good part of the eighth floor in the Paramount Building. Mr. Loderhose thinks it could not be duplicated today for less than $250,-000. Paramount had it made in 1928.

Miss Ann Leaf of the Columbia Broadcasting Company, who probably does more soap-opera background music than anyone else, played the Mighty Wurlitzer for years. Now she uses an electric organ for her radio shows. Jesse Crawford used the big Wurlitzer for recordings. Bing Crosby and Gladys Swarthout have used it for background.

Mr. Loderhose bought the organ about a year ago. He kept it in an East Side warehouse until he could build a special hall for it back of his own home in Jamaica Estates in Queens. The housing was ready last week—70 feet long, 25 feet wide, 16 feet high with fifty seats for listeners.

There will be private concerts from time to time, and when the mood comes on him the paste and glue man with the romantic heart will wander out to the organ and let his fingers wander idly over the noisy keys. Word that the organ has been set up has already spread along the pipe line. Mr. Loderhose will keep open organ house for the Enthusiasts.

¶ A neatly painted placard in the boxed fall blossom display in front of Stern's Department Store in Forty-second Street begs passersby: "Don't Eat the Chrysanthemums."

October 31, 1958

¶ Operation Inferno, a singular marine enterprise has evoked alarms in New York Harbor since last May. Seamen, housewives, fliers and fishermen have called the Coast Guard and municipal departments in high distress to report vessels ablaze in the shallows in the Lower Bay between Staten Island and Sandy Hook, but in each case it was just great mounds of wood burning, mostly old New York piers.

The fires are set by Burn It, Inc., a subsidiary of Hughes Brothers, 17 Battery Place, who specialize in solving what they call "marine difficulties." They dump radioactive slag heaps 300 miles at sea, jettison left-over poison gas, and use their great scow fleet for all manner of hauling and disposal.

Grandfather James Hughes started the business in 1870. His son, James H., took over after him. Now William, Robert and James, the third generation, carry on, rotating in executive posts.

There was a time, quite within recall for all middle-aged townfolk, when the city's poor scoured tenement neighborhoods in eager search for stove-wood. Today, though, the housewreckers can find no one to take it. Some contractors try to burn it on a wrecking-operation

site, but that often means a fine for air pollution.

The municipal Department of Air Pollution Control has been worried over the problem for years, but so far hasn't been able to get the city fathers to loosen up for incinerating plants for wood-burning. Between January and July this year wood from close to 6,000 tenements had to be burned within city limits, which increased soot-fall appreciably.

Disposal of pier wood, jobs where old beams run sixty to ninety feet, worried George Rodgers, a pier contractor, early last spring. He talked it over for four hours with Bill Hughes at the Whitehall Club, and out of that talk Burn It, Inc., was created.

Mr. Hughes finally worked out a tentative plan. He adapted two of his all-steel barges—200-footers —for the work. He decided to strengthen the decks, cover them with eighteen inches of sand, load the wood on the sand, have the barges towed to the shallows west of the ship channel, and do the burning there.

First he anchored a steel barge out on the flats in fourteen feet of water and decided to leave it there permanently. He would secure the Burn It barges to that with three-inch battleship chain and use a 30,000-pound battleship anchor on the permanent barge. In that way, the barge became a pivot and the pyre units could swing into the wind.

The Fire Department, the Police Department, the Coast Guard,

Army Engineers and the Navy were consulted. They approved the initial experiment in May. A load of pier wood 20 feet high, 200 feet long and 40 feet wide was towed to the shallows. A Hughes man climbed over it with an oil-sprayer and doused the wood with Diesel oil.

Patches of burning cloth were tossed on the pyre. The oil caught with a whoosh and the flames leaped high. Bill Hughes had consulted the Weather Bureau before a Moran tug pulled his loads out. He had learned that he would always need a west wind for a burning, if the smoke and soot were to carry right out to sea. They did.

The technique has improved through the months and a trade jargon may develop. Instead of loading their own oil for pyre-soaking, the Hughes men get Diesel oil from the tow tug under high pressure. When they toss the burning rag that's a "touch-off," or a "set-off."

A burning may take only six to ten hours in dry season. It may last two days under steady rain. The fires are spectacular. So are the smoke clouds, especially with old pier piling. Now the Hughes office notifies all Government agencies when burnings are due—they usually start around dusk—or all hell breaks loose.

Airplane and helicopter pilots have reported the burnings as ship fires. So have dwellers on Staten Island, Coney Island and New Jersey. On an early burning, two city fireboats went out to extinguish the blaze because the Fire Department then had had no official word there was to be a pyre.

Hughes Brothers hasn't worked out a future for Burn It, Inc., but they seem to think there's likelihood of their getting contracts to burn housewreckers' wood heaps; inshore wrecks, of which the harbor has hundreds; great mounds of telephone cable, and metal litter from auto junk yards. The cable-burning would call for all ash to be saved, to be sifted later for copper and silver.

Burn It is being watched by other marine companies, in other port cities, by groups that aren't sure yet whether the enterprise will show a decent profit. Spokesmen for these groups and the pier and housewreckers don't ask for Bill Hughes any more, when they want him on the telephone. They say, "I'd like to talk to Nero."

November 3, 1958

❡ The last trolley car that ran in New York State on regular passenger service—Trolley 601 that covered the route from the Manhattan end of Queensboro Bridge to Queens Plaza in Long Island City—was hauled out of the city last week by highway trailer-truck. The truck lumbered across George Washington Bridge early Tuesday morning, took a bridge route from New Jersey to Staten Island, where there is a trolley museum. It used the spans because no ferry could contain it. The trip was arranged by Everett A. White, the museum's

curator, who has offices at 481
Twelfth Street in Brooklyn. Old
601 made its last pay run on April
7, 1957.

¶ The energy, time and money that
go into preparing temporary political headquarters is astonishing.
Early in September, on Republican
order, Roosevelt Hotel housemen
stripped the seventh floor of everything except the carpets, draperies
and television sets. The sets were
kept because Mr. Rockefeller
wanted his staff to keep up with
campaign developments.

When the floor was cleared,
brand-new office equipment was
carried in by the carload. Countless
reams of stationery were piled up.
Three hundred telephones were
hooked up with a special three-po-
sition headquarters switchboard.
Forty more telephones will be installed in the Roosevelt's Grand
Ballroom tomorrow. So will extra
circuits for radio commentators
and television men.

The Rockefeller men tried something new with good results. They
set thirty telephones aside to carry
Mr. Rockefeller's stand on major
issues. His voice was recorded on
tape. The numbers of the special
telephones were advertised so that
any voter who wanted to brush up
on Mr. Rockefeller's platform could
hear it in his own words, in his
own voice.

¶ Someone asked Bernard Baruch
the other day how to decide between political contenders in any
election. The adviser to Presidents
quietly told him: "Vote for the

man who promises least; he'll be
the least disappointing."

November 7, 1958

¶ The future of the three heroic
figures above the door of the old
St. Paul Building on the east side
of Broadway between Ann and Fulton Streets will be weighed this afternoon in the chambers of the Architectural League of New York at
115 East Fortieth Street.

The sculpture was created in
1896 by Karl Bitter. It shows three
men—Mongolian, white and Negro
—bowed and on their knees, sharing the burden of human respon-
sibility. The figures are massive, a
shade under ten feet in height, im-
pressively muscular; their faces are
sad and tortured.

When the Western Electric Company bought the Broadway block
between Ann and Fulton Streets
many months ago, prominent artists
pleaded that it save the Karl Bitter
work, and the plea went to the corporate heart.

Western Electric agreed to save
the group and to pay for its transportation to any chosen site,
though the cost might be as much
as $200,000.

At first there was an attempt to
ship the statues to Austria, where
Bitter was born, because Austria
owns no major Bitter masterpiece.
The idea was that the group would
be a fitting gift to a country op-
pressed in political and social
agony. For a number of reasons that
plan never worked out.

Then bids came in from a number of colleges, parks and commu-

nities. These have been narrowed down, now, to four. The Committee to Preserve American Art is to sit this afternoon to consider those. The committee's decision, though, may not be made public for another week.

The Bitter group may stay in New York, or may go into friendly exile. New York University and Columbia University would like to have it. Fairleigh Dickinson University wants it for the great lawns of the old Twombly estate in Madison, N. J., which the university took over some years ago.

A strong bid has been made by the City of Indianapolis. It wants the group for its Holliday Park. David V. Burns, an architect, has drawn tentative designs for the Holliday Park installation.

New York University would put the Bitter group near new buildings in the green sweeps of campus on University Heights. Carroll V. Newsom, president of the university, told the judges who are to sit today:

"We . . . believe that the presence of the sculptures on the New York University campus would provide the appropriate environment in keeping with their value and meaning."

Columbia University wants the statues for its proposed new East Campus. It would use them for a huge fountain, which is the idea that the City of Indianapolis submitted, too. A fountain with a wide pool would give back the powerful figures in mirrored image.

Francis Keally, head of the New York Federation of Fine Arts, will be chairman at this afternoon's meeting. At the board with him will sit Adlai S. Hardin, president of the National Sculpture Society; Karl Gruppe, vice president of the National Academy of Design; Charles Baskerville, president of the National Society of Mural Painters; Thomas M. Beggs, director of the National Collection of Fine Arts at the Smithsonian Institution in Washington.

The Bitter statuary is now enclosed in stout boards, to prevent possible damage when the wreckers start to pound the St. Paul Building within the next week or so. They will work so that when they have finished, only the statues and the ledge on which they kneel will remain intact. The City of Indianapolis wants the ledge, the facing stone and the doorways, if it can get them.

The St. Paul Building stands on the site of the Eighteenth Century Spring Gardens, later the site of Barnum's Museum. It went up in 1896. Western Electric will replace it with a new office structure.

MARGINALIA: ¶ The Humane Society of New York figures that while there has been a 40 per cent increase in human population in New York City in the last twenty-five years, the number of cats and dogs has gone up 200 per cent; 350,000 dogs in the five boroughs now; 575,000 cats. Cats and dogs live longer now, too: an average of ten years as against seven or eight a couple of decades back. . . . ¶ Honors for being the oldest off-Broadway company probably belong to the sightless Lighthouse Players, now in their thirty-fifth season. They are in rehearsal at the Lighthouse Little Theatre, 111 East Fifty-ninth Street, for "All My Sons." It will open Nov. 19.

November 10, 1958

¶ One of the oldest houses in the city—it may even be the oldest in the state—lies under the Interborough Parkway at Vermont Street in Brooklyn. It is a mere collection of boards and doors, windows and barrels of house hardware, waiting in darkness for the time when the Brooklyn Museum can raise enough money to set it up again.

The house was built 303 years ago in Flatlands, then called Nieuw Amersfoort by settlers from Amersfoort in Holland. They were the Schencks—Jan Martense Schenck van Nydeck, two sons and his grandson, Capt. Jan van Schenck, all master mariners. Down through the centuries there has persisted the legend that Captain Jan was a pirate, but no one ever proved it. For years, though, the dwelling was called the Pirate House.

Captain Schenck's ships' carpenters were the real builders. They set the rough-hewn timbers as they would have set them in a sailing vessel of their time—with the major beams resting on ship's knees.

There is no way of telling now, but the timbers may even have come out of a ship. The narrow staircase to the second story is an obvious sailing-ship ladder; just as steep and just as narrow. The builders set dormers in the upper story; used Dutch tile for a great fireplace; built a giant Dutch oven. True bunks were nailed to the attic beams. This was sleeping space for the Schencks' slaves.

The same carpenters put together Schenck's Wharf and a grist mill that was worked by tidal ebb and flow. It was on a creek off Mill Island close to the west shore of Jamaica Bay, roughly where Avenue U and East Sixty-third Street cross now, or a bit to the east.

If the location were not a buccaneer's hideout, it could have been; just the kind of rendezvous which pirates could slip into from the sea of a dark night, with muffled oars.

The Canarsie Indians still lived in Flatlands when the house was built. The Indians' long house was within easy walking distance. It was the Canarsies who sold the land to the Schencks and to other Dutch settlers not long after the historic land buy in Manhattan.

The Hollanders loved the spot because it was so much like home —flat, marshy, with wide salt meadows where snipe and wild geese and other waterfowl assembled in season. The Schencks added an Old World touch; they built dikes, too.

The records are not too clear on what happened to the Schencks. The Captain just vanishes from history. So does his wife, a pretty girl he was supposed to have kidnaped from Holland on one of his voyages.

Anyway, the house, with additions, was handed down from one

family to another—to the Martenses, to the Catons for whom Caton Avenue in Brooklyn is named; to Gen. Philip S. Crooke, to a Florence G. Smith who sold it to a real estate promoter, who, in turn, passed it on fifty years ago to the Atlantic, Gulf and Pacific Oil Company.

The company let one of its supervisors use it as a dwelling. Then, in 1953, after the primitive willows, marshes and meadows had been taken over by contractors for highways and home development, it was carefully taken apart and turned over to the Brooklyn Museum, a gift from the company. The Park Department gave it the storage space under Interborough Parkway.

Some day it will be restored and furnished so that tourists and native Brooklyn folk may have a good idea of how the first settlers lived. When that will be, the museum people tell you sadly, no one can say right now.

❡ A sleek new purring Cadillac slid through Times Square a few nights ago with a metal sign athwart the hood. The sign said: "Made in Las Vegas—The Hard Way."

November 12, 1958

❡ In the basement of the made-over old dwelling at 54 West Forty-sixth Street you stand, after you have passed through a series of doors protected with burglar alarms, among crates of rocks—blue rocks, green, golden yellow,

pink, red, purple, some that look like anthracite. Some—the brown ones—look like beer bottle shards. Grays look like housewreckers' chippings. They are worth a maharajah's ransom.

These are semiprecious stones, roughs from mines in near and faraway countries—jades from Wyoming, lapis lazuli from Chile and Turkestan, opal from Australia, moss agate from the Deccan plateau in India, rutilated quartz (arrows of love) from Brazil, amber with ancient imprisoned insects brought up from the Baltic Sea, malachite from the Belgian Congo, meerschaum from Turkey.

High on a dusty shelf are great elephant tusks, ivory that sells at $7 a pound because it is soft and without cracks, taken from beasts that lived in well-watered jungles. Watergreen peridots wink blandly from the depths of a crate by the wall. They came from the Island of St. Johns in the Red Sea.

King Helmet shells from the shores of East Africa look like a hippo's gums. They are used by cameo makers. There are diamond roughs, too, but not in sight.

Much of this hoard goes out to commercial gem cutters, but a vast amount of it is mailed to amateur lapidaries all over the world, including New York and almost every large city in the United States. Men and women make gems of these roughs as a hobby.

Lots of teen-agers have taken up the art. These young ones are called "pebble pups." The older hands, who go hunting for quartz and other semiprecious stones, are "rock hounds." They increase apace.

The establishment on West Forty-sixth Street has sold rough stones of gem quality for almost ninety years. The business started in Holland in 1870. Now the concern is owned by Gottfried Parser and his sons, Edgar and Donald. They import some of the roughs by the ton, some of it by the gram. Great quantities are shipped out now to the Idar-Oberstein district in Germany, now the busiest gem center. Before that it was Czechoslovakia and Italy.

Amateur lapidaries in New York City and across the world spend what they can for working equipment—for grinding wheels, buffers, polishers, spindles, dops. Some work with home-made tools and second-hand motors. Some fit up workrooms that may cost as much as $15,000 to $20,000.

The late John Kraft of Kraft foods had one of the most imposing amateur shops in the world. Much of his work was as good as that of some professionals.

There is hardly any spot on earth where you don't run into amateur gem turners. One group operates near the South Pole. This is a bunch of Navy men who bend over roughs during the long nights at McMurdo Sound. They reported to the Parsers only a few weeks ago that they had sighted some new crystal deposits on a helicopter flight from the I. G. Y. base, and they were trying to get up a rock-hunting expedition.

Capt. John Sinkankas, a Navy flier, is one of the foremost amateur lapidaries. He writes learnedly on gem-making techniques in the Rock and Minerals Magazine and is a member of the American Gem Society with the title "Certified Gemologist."

The Parsers sell loads of roughs to Veterans Hospitals. They are used in rehabilitation programs.

Beginners in the art work on cabochons—smooth rounded forms. Advanced amateurs do complicated gem faceting and speak a peculiar jargon. They gabble about "cutting a pavilion," "cutting to the girdle," doing an "octagon step-up"—terms that have to do with faceting that are borrowed from the trade.

At regular intervals, the Parsers send out a rock caravan, a station wagon loaded with rough semiprecious stones. The caravan calls at all conventions held by amateur lapidaries from the East Coast to the West; drops off orders for workers in inaccessible places.

The Parsers fly once a year to the State of Goiás in the Brazil interior, where they control five square miles of rich mine territory. Indians work for them.

Manhattan Island's pavements hide more than 100 different kinds of semiprecious stones—garnets, tourmalines, jasper, beryl, amethysts are included—but the Parsers have never had anyone turn up with any that might be counted true gem quality. Beginners, when they do find some in excavations of one kind or another, lug them home, but mostly just for practice. An exhibit at the American Museum of Natural History has a representative New York City collection.

MARGINALIA: ¶ A Quebec automobile bowled merrily up Madison Avenue the other day with a weird decoration whipping at the windshield. It was a parking summons. . . . ¶ In chalk lettering inside a chalk heart on the wall of the public library branch at Ninety-sixth Street and Lexington Avenue, the delightful scrawl: "Billy Maher Loves Everybody."

November 14, 1958

¶ Tolstoy wrote that "time is infinite movement without one moment of rest." Plato called time "the image of eternity." Seventy-two years ago the Pratts and Bedfords, Brooklyn aristocrats who had made fortunes in oil, conceived of time as something to sell. They organized what is today the Self-Winding Clock Company, Inc.

From 1886 to 1957 the corporation made clocks and sold time from a Pratt-owned building at 205 Willoughby Avenue in Brooklyn, next door to Pratt Institute. Then it moved to Varick Street in Manhattan. It still makes its own clocks, but as in the beginning has them installed and maintained by Western Union. There are more than 50,000 in the United States, more than 5,000 in New York City.

A little over a year ago, the corporation started to install the first of 2,500 clocks in the New York subway system. So far 111 have gone into thirty-three stations. These are shaped like grandfather clocks laid horizontally. The clocks are at the left. Where the case would be is space for an illuminated advertising sign. When all have been installed the city will have more than 8,000 of the corporation's clocks.

Western Union keeps all the clocks in the system synchronized to its own master units. These are in a sealed chamber in the wire company offices. They get the exact time from the Naval Observatory in Washington.

Each corporation clock is equipped with two long-life one-and-a-half-volt dry batteries. These keep the clock spring wound. If a clock varies two minutes off true time either way, the batteries supply the power for automatic adjustment every hour on the hour. Clocks properly oiled and with no worn parts are accurate within tenths of a second.

The corporation has had clocks in service for fifty and sixty years in some cases. It has installed tower clocks—the four-sided Metropolitan Tower clock is an example— and revolving clocks with two faces. It provided the clocks used in the House of Representatives and in the Senate; on great battleships and on flattops; clocks for the countdown for the moon rockets and for other missiles. It installed the clocks in London's subway, in the nation's broadcasting stations, in several of the large skyscrapers, in schools, hospitals, department stores, stock exchanges, hotels and universities.

The big ball clock above Grand Central Terminal's information booth was specially made by the corporation forty-five years ago; so was the giant clock with the 200-pound dial hands on the terminal's south wall. Railroads across the country take their time from the system. So do some of the airlines. Jewelers subscribe to the service, mostly to set true time on watches or clocks they repair. Special installations have gone as far away as Indonesia, Saigon and Pakistan. A special clock mechanism for a giant bell in Tokyo was turned out in the corporation factory.

The Strategic Air Command, to which split-second timing is vital, operates a special Strat-Com system developed by its engineers and by the clock corporation. It has extra sweep hands, automatic adjustments for all possible time-zone differences.

The Navy's sea-going clocks have a modified version that permits the changing of all clock units when a vessel slides over a time rib. The change is made by press of a single button. Sea-going units synchronize their clocks by radio signal trapped by FM waves. Land clocks work on Western Union land wires.

In wartime, the corporation has been diverted from the peaceful measuring of time's pace to turning out clock mechanisms for military mines for both sea and shore use. It puts together a lot of airspeed and ship-speed indicators then, too.

Basically, the corporation clocks have changed but little since Chester H. Pond, an engineer, worked out the dry-cell battery idea for automatic spring-winding and syn-chronization adjustment a little over eighty years ago. Before that there had been only manual adjustment by clock key. Another engineer, William F. Gardiner, perfected the system for transmitting official time signals from Washington to New York and to other cities where Western Union maintains its sealed master and submaster control units.

The batteries, incidentally, are good, in decent climates, for at least eighteen months.

Martin Marquard, an old hand with the corporation, is its chief trouble-shooter. Whenever a unit misbehaves because of climate or because of worn parts, he wings to the spot to set things right. He flies as far west as the State of Washington and to Oregon and California, as far south as the Mexican border and Florida.

He thinks the new subway clocks should do all right because they've worked for years in the London underground. If a problem does develop in the subways here, it will be from oily steel filings from grinding subway brakes and from lint. He doesn't think vibration will give trouble. The clocks are well cushioned against that menace.

November 17, 1958

⁋ Throngs on their way to, or from, trains in Grand Central Terminal stopped last week in the Main Concourse between Tracks 25 and 26 to watch a half-hour show that they seemed to think was color television on a twenty-four-inch screen. Actually they were looking at a behind-the-screen projection of a half-hour 16 mm. film, "The Big Train," produced for the New York Central Railroad to let the riding public know what the country's railroads are doing in electronic research for faster and safer transportation. Late this week the display is to be moved down to the commuters' level. A New York Central executive hurrying to his office the other morning a half-hour late stopped dead in his tracks in the Main Concourse when a familiar voice boomed out, sharp and clear: "It's good to see you. I'm Alfred Perlman, president of the New York Central." The tardy official guiltily broke stride. Then he realized it was his boss' voice on the film track. He hurried on.

¶ Architects who work on multiple-dwelling designs might, in this period of extreme tensions, snatch an idea that is working out pretty well in the city's La Guardia Houses project on the lower East Side. One unit there has a built-in psychiatric and mental-hygiene clinic in its basement. The Henry Street Settlement staff suggested that part of the basement, ordinarily a garage for tenants' go-carts, be made over into the clinic. The City Fathers appropriated extra money for clinic facilities—interview booths, playroom for children, consultation rooms. Henry Street Settlement's psychiatric staff runs the establishment.

¶ All seats at tomorrow night's preview of "All My Friends," staged by sightless Lighthouse Players at 119 East Fifty-ninth Street, will be held by blind folk, led to their seats by sighted kinsmen or by Seeing-Eye dogs. Later performances will be open to the general public.

¶ Barbers, it seems, don't do all their cutting with shears. In one barber shop in Nostrand Avenue off Flatbush Avenue in Brooklyn a window sign offers: "Haircuts, 60 cents." Downstreet a sneering sign in a competitor's shop counters with: "Sixty-cent haircuts repaired here. 75 cents."

¶ Yasha Lisenco of Teachers College faculty, the director of arts and crafts at the New York Guild for the Jewish Blind on Broadway, has worked out an ingenious device to enable the sightless to paint. With wire, clay, or string, the blind painters outline their subjects on canvas, then apply the colors of their choice inside the outlines. The technique has produced some excellent primitives. A former professional artist, a woman whose sight has gone, is using the same technique. It has lifted her heart.

November 19, 1958

¶ Sometimes the Whimsey Gods work amusing patterns into the looms of human history.

A little over 325 years ago, white men edged the Indian out of the primitive jungles and the green hills in the wilderness where New York's skyscrapers stand now. They buried his artifacts and his middens under their farm acres, then covered them with building sites and with hard paving. They all but ploughed him into oblivion.

Last week the Whimsey Gods reversed the pattern. By some mystically subtle suggestion they inspired the Iroquois Tribe of the Improved Order of Red Men at New Dorp on Staten Island, a white men's fraternal organization, to dream up the notion of digging on Staten Island for Indian relics. The Iroquois Tribe's rolls bear the names of some seventy men of many races and many nationalities, but of none linked by blood to the red men.

The Improved Red Men perpetuate in their rituals the ceremonies, the legends and somewhat the same dress worn by the original owners of the island. The island tribes were mostly Raritans and Delawares of the Leni Lenape family. The Staten Island Historical Society, working on short budget as many such institutions do, has accepted the white Indians' bid for the right to dig for buried villages and campsites.

Loring McMillen of the historical society thinks important finds might be made in Richmondtown. The white Indians will probably start archaelogical work there in the spring.

Patrolman Dan Iatauro of the Old Slip police station in Manhattan, sachem of the Iroquois of the I.O.O.R., doesn't think that his white braves should stop with the search for Indian relics. He has offered the historical society their services for restoring and painting seventeenth-century and eighteenth-century houses on Staten Island. Professional carpenters, metalworkers and painters in the tribe would make this contribution of weekends.

If the program comes off, the sachem says, it may set the pattern for similar aid to historical societies all over the United States.

¶ Complete commercial candor speaks from a shop sign in Fourteenth Street:

"Keep Fourteenth Street Green. Bring Money."

¶ The City Planning Commission's monthly bulletin, out the other day, said that the five hills on Staten Island, including 410-foot Todt Hill, were "the Alps" of the Atlantic seacoast, and that Todt Hill was "reputed to be the highest point" along the seaboard.

Actually it is nowhere near the highest. Cadillac Mountain on Mount Desert Island in Frenchman's Bay, forty miles south of Bangor in Maine, holds the distinction. It is 1,532 feet high. Nothing else along the East Coast comes even close.

Yet the commission's bulletin deserves a reading. It tells New Yorkers—and visitors, too—about vantage spots near the city, where unusual views of the harbor may be had.

The Staten Island ridge, of which Todt Hill is part, includes Fort Hill, a few hundred feet from the ferry terminal at St. George; Ward Hill, Emerson Hill and Todt Hill. They represent a violent volcanic upthrust in prehistoric time.

The same commission publication tells of another ridge in the city—a strip of glacial terminal moraine that shows the stopping place of an Ice Age glacier. It reaches from Nassau County on Long Island to the Narrows in Brooklyn. This ridge cuts between Brooklyn and Queens, whose southern shores are made of silt carried by glacial melt.

High point of the Brooklyn-Queens ridge is in Little Neck and Douglaston, northeast of Cross Island Parkway and Grand Central Parkway. The altitude there is about 240 feet. The ridge runs west from the high point through Alley Pond Park, Cunningham Park, Jamaica, Kew Gardens and Forest Park. It then crosses into Brooklyn at Cypress Hill and drops to Bushwick, Crown Heights, Prospect Park, Park Slope, Sunset Park and Bay Ridge before it wets its feet in Upper Bay.

Manhattan Island once had many hills. A ridge overlooked the Hudson west of lower Broadway. You see part of it back of Trinity Churchyard. A fairly high ridge ran north and south, west of Foley Square, but it was leveled and dumped into Collect Pond, on which the Foley Square buildings stand.

Washington Heights is Manhattan's top eminence just north of George Washington Bridge. It comes to 240 feet. In the Bronx the hills are still clear in Riverdale, Van Cortlandt Park, Kingsbridge Heights, Woodlawn, and University Heights.

⁋ The New York Convention and Visitors Bureau at 90 East Forty-second Street offers 100 tours in its "Educational Tours in New York" pamphlet. The pamphlet is free. It tells teachers and other group guides where and how to reach people whose plants or institutions are open for public inspection.

November 21, 1958

⁋ The Mergenthaler Linotype Company has sold the block-square manufacturing plant it started in Ryerson Street in Brooklyn, across the way from the Navy Yard, almost seventy years ago. It is setting up new plants in Wellsboro in Pennsylvania and in Plainview in Nassau County on Long Island.

In the old building stand eleven cumbersome typesetting machines of one manufacture or another, representing steps in mechanical typesetter development, from 1872 to 1911. Before the old building comes down, the Mergenthaler people want to find homes for these printing-trade relics.

The Ford Museum at Dearborn has offered to take all the units, but Mergenthaler officials seem to think it might be fairer to spread the collection to different museums, colleges and newspapers. They are ready to accept and consider bids. They offer the units as gifts.

There was a twelfth historic machine in the collection, the James Paige Compositor, in which Mark Twain sank his fortune in the Eighties. The Paige worked, but it had 18,000 parts and a multitude of weaknesses. Yale University will have the Paige set up in the Mark Twain House in Hartford, Conn., before National Printing Week in January.

Men have toiled over mechanical typesetting devices for about 140 years. When the first Mergenthaler Linotype went into commercial production in 1886 it was counted the greatest advance in printing after Gutenberg. The service now provides machines for more than 1,000 languages.

Models in the factory museum include the Empire Composing Machine of 1872, which dropped type at keyboard touch but called for manual line adjustment; an early (1884) Mergenthaler Band Machine, and an 1885 version. The first had a metal pot for type casting, the second did not.

Other units are the John Rogers Typograph (1888); the Lee-LeBrun, the Dow Composing Machine, J. Thorne's Unitype, the Mergenthaler Round Base (1898), the Logotype Casting and Composing Machine, the Dow Typesetting Machine, which didn't set type at all, but simply ejected it for hand set, and the Polytype (1911), which looked efficient but never got into production.

The Mergenthaler Company will keep the prototype of the 1886 model, which, except for refinements including a more modern power source, works pretty much as new ones do, seventy-two years later. This unit is kept under Ottmar Mergenthaler's portrait in the company offices at 29 Ryerson Street.

¶ Fifty street-corner Santa Clauses in full holiday kit—scarlet garb, snowy beards—will have breakfast together at 10 o'clock this morning in Cavanagh's, at 260 West Twenty-third Street. Then they will scatter throughout the five city boroughs to collect Christmas money for the Volunteers of America.

The morning feast marks the day, a half-century ago, when the Volunteers sent out the first street-corner Santa Clauses. Each Santa Claus will have been through a fortnight's intensive study of his role. Each will carry to his post the rules laid down for the part:

"Ring your bell, but don't be a nuisance," "Give special attention to your mouth and whiskers," "Keep your breath clean, no garlic," "Don't smoke, eat or drink while on duty" and "Don't lean on your chimney."

November 24, 1958

¶ Yukon 3 is a New York telephone exchange that has only one function this month and next. It is a direct line to Santa Claus at the North Pole. Children have been using it at the rate of 75,000 calls every day since Nov. 7.

They dial YUkon 3-2121. Santa Claus comes on with a booming laugh. He says: "Hello there! This is your friend, Santa Claus, at the North Pole. I'm busy making toys for you for Christmas." He runs off broad categories of things in his workshop, goes into a subtle commercial and hangs up with the rain-barrel laugh.

Macy's arranged the North Pole

hook-up. It will be available through most of December. The lines tend to jam a bit just before bedtime and the children are apt to get a busy signal for a while, but they seem to understand. Santa Claus is creeping up on deadline now.

Actually, YUkon 3 doesn't exist as a telephone exchange. It is a dark chamber in the New York Telephone Company at 104 Broad Street. The laughing Santa Claus is a recording made up for a Philadelphia advertising company that offers what the telephone people call "mass service," the use of telephones for recorded advertising. Gimbels used it in early fall with the Marquis of Zorro talking on the back-to-school theme, with a sly line about school supplies and school garb available at the store. Because Zorro is a dashing television character, the calls on that were astonishingly heavy, too.

The telephone company's midtown sales office on the sixteenth floor at 165 West Forty-sixth Street has the Santa Claus greeting on demonstration in its mass-call exhibit there.

Company salesmen tell visitors of other uses for the device. Five churches in the city have twenty-four-hour dial-a-prayer service for the heartsick and the weary. The recorded prayers are changed almost every day, in some cases several times a day.

The Agricultural Department of the Nassau County Extension Service, a nonprofit state unit, uses the mass-call to dispense information on care of lawns, trees, flower beds; on how to put down garden insect pests. It is robot adviser to all manner of husbandmen.

It answers to the dialing of PIoneer 6-6555 all day, all through the night. The Home Demonstration Service of the same state body has PIoneer 6-8340 for news on food-buying, meal-planning, keeping foods fresh. It gives counsel on food bargains—tells what fruits, meats or vegetables are in good supply and reasonably priced.

A sporting goods store in Manhattan uses the recorded telephone message to give tips on where salt, or fresh-water, fish are running best. Fresh-water anglers call one number; deep-water men call another. The shop owner has not made this a general service. He gives the numbers only to his own customers.

Two bright young men up in White Plains in Westchester are working right now on another mass-call set-up. They will offer free information on "best buys" in various local establishments. This will be bait to lure shoppers into stores that subscribe to the young men's service.

The telephone people seem a bit bewildered by the spread of the mass-call. They won't attempt to predict its future. We could be headed into the robot era faster than most think.

¶ A gentleman from South Africa, in town for a week's visit last week, found that his hosts—a different one each day—had worked up for him the best entertainment schedule they could think of. On Friday, he met his fifth host. This man told him: "We'd like you to come out to the house tonight, have dinner and then just sit around, if you think you'd like that." The man from South Africa was almost pitifully grateful. His eyes misted. He breathed a fervent, "Thank God." The fifth host wondered at the visitor's obvious emotional reaction to a simple evening-at-home invitation. The South African explained: "I have been four nights in New York. I went to 'My Fair Lady' on Monday evening. I went to 'My Fair Lady' on Tuesday, on Wednesday, on Thursday. I could not refuse. My hosts had gone to great expense to give me the best. If you had bought me seats for 'My Fair Lady' I would have gone, but I am afraid I would have cracked up." He had a quiet meal, a bit of family chit-chat, a few heartening glasses of spirits; went back to his hotel restored and glowingly mellow.

¶ The cultural note in modern banking keeps taking odd directions. The Manhattan Savings Bank at Madison Avenue and Forty-seventh Street is offering in its lobby this week authentically garbed Puritan choristers against a seventeenth-century New England setting, singing Thanksgiving music. The soloist, a pretty contralto in Indian maiden garb is Hoté-Mawe, a Cherokee. Her name, appropriately, means Mocking Bird. She sings ancient traditional dawn and sunset songs, the butterfly dance, the happy song of her tribe and a moving invocation

to the sun god, all against the background clink of coins going into, and out of, the tellers' cages.

November 28, 1958

¶ In the great ballroom in the Waldorf-Astoria Hotel come Monday evening, 1,200 Scottish gentlemen will sit down to cockaleekie, to haggis and to salmon. Scotch whisky will run as in spring freshet. Wild pipe music will shrill and whimper in the deep chamber. Much of the food will have been flown from the Scottish Highlands.

It is always so when the kilted members of the Saint Andrews Society come to the board. The Monday spread will be their 202d. The society is the oldest group of its kind in the States. It had met for two decades before the American Revolution. In the beginning most of its members were Scottish officers serving in His Majesty's forces in the Colonies.

The earliest meetings—rousers all—were in Scotch Johnny's Crown and Thistle near Whitehall Slip, later called the Kings Head. Scots then, as now, could hold their liquor better than most. Daily journals of the period reported, "The Company was very numerous, everything was conducted with the greatest decorum and the whole made a most brilliant and elegant appearance."

When men of the Royal Highlanders died in battle, or at gentler sweep of the scythe, George Burns, who took over from Scotch Johnny, would sell their personal effects at public vendue in the inn. The dinners and the auction were held in what was called Burns' Long Room. By and by the place was called the King's Arms. The tavern went up in smoke in the Great Fire of 1776, which wiped out a good part of the city.

In the past fifty-two years the society has held all its feasts in the Waldorf-Astoria.

Tradition calls for only four toasts at the feast, so that a man may get on with his drinking. This year one will be, as always since the Revolution, to the President of the United States. Another will be to Her Majesty the Queen.

The toast "To the Land of Cakes" (Scotland) is almost always uttered by someone born among the heather. The final toast is "To the Land We Live in," a response to "Land of Cakes." It is always led by an American citizen.

The society's ancient charter, binding its members to charitable purpose, limits benevolent disbursements only to Scotsmen and to their descendants. A full-time almoner keeps busy handling the funds.

In 1794, though, a doughty member felt called upon to say: "If the application of this charity is confined, so is the manner of collecting it; neither will it in the least prevent their acting up to the principles of universal charity on other occasions." It has worked out that way, down the years.

Society members have given of their substance generously to scotch, so to speak, the libel that Scotsmen were ever slow to open their own purses. Alexander Hamilton, Rob-

ert Livingston and Lewis Morris, all of them society members, gave liberally to all in want in their day.

So, in later years, did John S. Kennedy, who donated the building that houses the United Charities; Andrew Carnegie, who endowed libraries, colleges and universities and left millions for universal peace. John Taylor Johnston, another member, supported the art gallery that developed, eventually, into the Metropolitan Museum of Art.

Aye, the Scotch will flow in the great hall at the Waldorf on Monday evening, and men will quaff deeply, but Lawrence Beattie, chairman of the banquet committee, said last night: "On Tuesday morn, the almoner's office will be open as usual."

MARGINALIA: ❡ Washington Square, Harold Klein reports in "Pleasures of Learning," a New York University events calendar, got that name on Dec. 23, 1858. The greensward was dedicated as a public park on July 4, 1828, at a feast for which two whole oxen were roasted, more than 200 hams gobbled, and a quarter-mile of barreled beer put away. When it was renamed thirty years later there was no hullabaloo at all, and no feasting. . . .

December 3, 1958

❡ Human moles, now seen all over town digging under roadways, started to multiply during the Eighties, mostly after, and because of, the Great Blizzard of 1888. The first burrowers worked for the telegraph, telephone, gas and water services.

One of the oldest corporate mole groups is the Empire City Subway Company, Ltd. organized in 1891; known before that as the Consolidated Telephone and Electrical Subway Company. It was started in 1884 by the Metropolitan Telephone and Telegraph Company.

The corporation never operated a rapid transit service. Its "subways" are bricked and tiled conduits under the streets, rivers and creeks of Manhattan Island and the Bronx; burrows that carry communication lines. It used the term "subways" twenty years before underground transit was ready.

Back in the Eighties all large cities were made unsightly by telephone and telegraph poles and their great wire webs. The wires carried power, too, and were a menace to firemen. It was difficult to run fire ladders past them without shocking firemen.

Sometimes, in storm, the wires were blown down. The power lines carried lethal voltage and amperage. Horace Grant, chief engineer for the Empire City Subway Company, owns records that tell how fallen power lines killed cartmen and their horses. In the Great Blizzard snow-laden lines came down in thousands.

Four years before that the State Legislature had passed a bill ordering the wire networks underground. Nobody paid any attention to that until after the great storm. Then the city's newly formed Board of Electrical Control got

tough, and the moles were organized.

In 1891, the Empire City Subway Company had men all over town, burrowing two to four feet under cobblestones and asphalt, building tiled runways for telephone lines, for burglar-alarm systems, for ticket services to Wall Street. At peak it used up to 1,200 human moles. Now it uses 178.

When the transit subways were dug, provision was made beside them to carry the communication lines conduits, but Empire City Subway Company moles usually ended their construction at the point where the transit tunnels dropped under rivers and let the transit people pick it up from there.

The corporation doesn't have its own divers for telephone cable beds. It hires them from the New York Submarine Contracting Company. It has no part in the actual laying of cable. Its parent company, the New York Telephone Company, uses its own men for that. For general marine cable jobs, the Telephone Company operates its one-ship navy, the cable-layer Cable Queen.

The Empire City Subway Company, under its contract with the city, always builds extra tiled space in its underground passageways for the municipal signal and alarm services—for the Fire Department, the Police Department, and for Western Union.

Close to 9,000 manholes cover the company's tiled underground conduit passageways. These bear the company name. Consolidated

Edison and its subsidiaries like the New York Steam Company have distinctive marking on their manhole plates. The city uses its individual marking for its installations. So does the Transit Authority.

The Empire City Subway moles run into only a few disasters. Most of these are traceable to inadequate mapping of the city's networks of underground ganglia. A few years ago, one of the men drove the point of a pavement breaker—a pneumatic drill—into a 13,000-volt power cable on Thirty-eighth Street between Second and Third Avenues and was killed.

The empire moles run into Colonial and Indian relics in their burrowing, but only now and then, because they do not dig more than four to six feet under street level. They found a Revolutionary War musket on a Canal Street job a few years ago. They've run into tree-stump mains used in the city's first water systems in the early part of the nineteenth century.

Consolidated Edison moles frequently encounter rats, as sewer-working moles do; the Empire City men but rarely do because they seal their tile subways more tightly against damp, dirt and debris. Their manhole set-ups are mostly double-rig—a top cover and a foot or so under that a tight rubber-sealed plate. When inspectors find rattling covers, crews are rushed right over to change them, or do a grinding job.

Empire moles rarely encounter insect life under the pavement, but once they did. A single termite managed, not long ago, to gnaw through the covering on some telephone cable at Broadway and Thirty-third Street and water seeped in and damaged a few telephone lines.

Bell Laboratory engineers were fascinated over the discovery of under-pavement termites. They figured the insects might have gone after old wooden supports left over by subway construction workers, so they baited the spot with wood that would seem tasty to termites. The bait, Mr. Grant confides, is still there, but so far no other termites have showed up.

December 29, 1958

❡ The little white stone building at 70 Broad Street off old Petticoat Lane is headquarters for a corporation that makes more money than any other single enterprise in New York, if not more than any one establishment in the whole world.

The American Bank Note Company designs and prints paper currency for sixty-two nations and does most of their postage and revenue stamps, too. It is the official printer for the United Nations.

Money printers got into full swing in the United States during the American Revolution. Paul Revere was one of the busy engravers in that period. After the Revolution most of the business was done by seven independent engraving-printing concerns.

These seven were merged 100

years ago into the American Bank Note Company. At that time it printed all United States currency and stamps, but the Government set up its own money-printing plant in 1879; started doing its own stamps in 1894.

It is impossible even for executives of the corporation to figure out the total face value of what it prints each twelve-month. Its output includes, besides the currency, all kinds of official stamps, including postage stamps, bonds, stock certificates, travel checks, dividend checks, voucher checks.

The company designs and builds its own special presses. It grinds and manufactures its own printing inks to secret formula. It makes its own rag paper of special fiber beaten and bonded in its own plant up in Hunts Point in the Bronx; even cuts and assembles the boxes in which it ships finished work.

American Bank Note has been, since its beginnings in 1795, sternly conservative, shy—almost horrified —of publicity, mainly because the nature of the business demands every possible safeguard against prying eyes and the criminal mind.

It has large affiliates with great printing plants in Britain and in Canada. Its land, buildings and machinery in this country alone are valued at $8,602,600.

The company has 249 policemen, mostly former marines and retired city detectives and patrolmen. These guard every phase of manufacture and of delivery. There have been almost no robberies in the concern's long history.

One shipment did get lost fourteen years ago, but American Bank Note officials don't like to talk about it. It was war time then and the Dutch Government in Exile ordered 300,000 guilders for pay for its troops and for underground work in Java and in Sumatra.

All company shipments are done in tight bundles wrapped in tough brown paper. They are fitted into soldered metal containers against possible water damage. The containers then fit snugly into the special boxes made by the company.

The guilders were delivered to Pier 46, Hudson River, in five boxes but there someone, not a company man, nodded. The shipment, then worth about $100,000 in United States Currency, vanished. Five years later, in August, 1949, detectives traced part of it to a West End Avenue apartment in town.

Guilders then were worth about 37 cents. The West End Avenue man was offering them at four cents. The police nabbed him and the money, but they never told who stole the shipment, or how, and still won't.

The company's engravers are probably the world's best. They serve at least ten years' apprenticeship. Some represent the third or fourth generation in the trade, with the corporation. Will Ford is chief engraver now. He has forty-six years in the job.

William F. Ford, Will's father, was official counterfeiter for American Bank Note. He sat for years in a locked tower in the Bronx plant trying to duplicate, to the last detail, work turned out by company engravers. If he succeeded, which he sometimes did, the design was rejected.

The company employs 3,500 men and women. Of these eighty have served a half-century or more. Every sheet of paper that goes through their hands is counted at every one of the thirty-eight stages of processing. When counts do not tally the whole operation stops dead until everything checks out as it should.

All manner of electronic gadgets check the work—numbers, imperfections, differences in margin width, printing "slywipes." Every bit of rejected material goes into an incinerator and the burning is carefully recorded. Billions in scrip, printed when American banks closed in the depression, went into the company fires when the Government, in sudden switch, decided not to use it.

The company does a certain amount of emergency work; makes new plates when governments change, or new finance ministers take over. W. Frederic Colclough, the corporation's president now, remembers that when he was an Air Force officer in China during World War II China's demands for new money in ever greater denominations kept the Bronx plant presses hot.

Money wears out with handling, even with the tough paper used by the United States Government and by American Bank Note. It accumulates dirt and grit that eventually abrades the fast-dye print. One-dollar notes wear out, generally, in about twelve months because they're used more than notes of higher denomination.

American Bank Note Company researchers use melamine, a wet-strength resin, in their currency printing. They developed it sixteen years ago. It prolongs the life of their output.

Annual company reports are mildly amusing. In 1957, for example, the accounting showed "sales" of more than $21,000,000; "cost of goods," $14,938,257. A good part of the goods, of course, was money. The outfit, incidentally, does best in times when there are stock splits all over the world, corporate mergers and new stock issues. These keep the presses humming.

The corporation has always had one inflexible policy; it insists on payments for "goods" in United States dollars.

December 31, 1958

❡ There was a lively underworld in New York City before the first criminal gangs, made up mostly of the light-fingered and the violent banished by court order from Britain, began to swarm to the Five Points and around East River waterfront groggeries in the Eighteen Thirties.

This underworld flourished, in all likelihood, millions of years before even the Indians showed up. It still carries on under the skyscrapers, to sidewalks and the subways, making remarkable adjustments to endless city change. It will probably survive the darkest possible disasters that might befall a modern city.

The eternal underground society is populated by termites. They do best, these days, below Fourteenth Street, where the oldest buildings are, and in outlying boroughs where there are still fair amounts of frame dwellings, decayed trees and other vegetation that are the termites' favorite diet.

Manhattan dwellers rarely see these creatures of the ancient underworld, except in the spring—usually in March or early April—when some primal instinct urges them to nuptial fight for a few brief hours. That time of year commercial establishments in pest control get telephone calls in volume.

Calls are just as likely to come from skyscraper office workers as from dwellers in Flatbush, Hunts Point, Flushing or Richmondtown —not that termites dig into the newest steel, stone and glass structures (though sometimes they even establish beachhead in such places), but because they swarm somewhere near by and get through cracks and open windows.

Termite-control people never let on who their clients are, because clients react violently to publicity, but they tell you, slyly, for example, that "a certain university in town" lost great mounds of examination papers and old records stored in an earth-floored basement.

A whole library of valuable music scores basement-stored by a great music school became termite fodder right in midtown and so did a chemist's oldest books. A big railroad company found hundreds of thousands of commuters' tickets gone to termite feed.

A chain grocery in town figured its canned goods were safe in a damp cellar, but when it went to draw on this reserve, it couldn't tell one can from another; the termites had used the labels for dessert. The unlabeled stock went to hospitals and orphanages for hit-or-miss menus.

The astonishing society under city pavement—it has workers, soldiers, a king and a queen in each colony—keeps going in Manhattan, the control people tell you, because lazy or penurious contractors won't treat wooden concrete molds with creosote (termites can't abide the stuff) or mix their concrete thin. Then it cracks and the pale things of the underworld get through.

The control people are especially careful when they're called to examine ancient Greenwich Village houses or old warehouses at the island's tip. J. J. Hess, an expert who supervises termite crews for a West Twenty-ninth Street establishment, fell to the armpits through a dining room floor in a lovely old brick house off Washington Square not long ago. The underworld nippers, which can't stand direct sunlight, had left only the thinnest bit of wood in the floor covering. The termite man was lassoed and hauled out by rope, just as if he'd broken through ice.

Ogden Nash must know about termites. He wrote the verse:

*Some primal termite knocked
 on wood
And tasted it and found it
 good
And that is why your Cousin
 May
Fell through the parlor floor
 today.*

Mr. Hess' associates took unholy delight in mailing him copies of the verse after his Washington Square slip-through. He had used that very stanza on a card mailed by his company to prospective clients.

1959

January 5, 1959

MARGINALIA: ¶ Rockefeller Center people get floods of letters and poems every year when they set up their giant Christmas tree. The other day they got their first cable. It came from Wiesbaden in Germany. It was addressed: "The Christmas Tree, Rockefeller Plaza, New York." It said: "Best wishes for Christmas and the New Year. You are more than ever in my thoughts at this time. God be with you till we meet again—A Soldier Overseas."

January 7, 1959

¶ Superstition doesn't die. Even in the Time of the Atom, even in an age when men shoot robot talkers and measuring agents far beyond the moon, there's still lively demand for love philters, for conjure medicines, for oils, herbs and stones to attract reluctant affection or to repel all manner of evils.

There's a little drugstore—Kiehl's Pharmacy—at 109 Third Avenue just north of Thirteenth Street that has passed from owner to owner the last 107 years. Until last week it always stood just at the corner, but that building is coming down in Third Avenue's rebirth. The new address is two doors up.

When the shop opened in 1851 much of its shelf space was given over to herbs, unguents and roots mixed or boiled to family recipe generation after generation, time out of mind. And there were primitive, voodooistic charms and philters for sale, too, alongside standard items in the conventional pharmacopoeia.

In the beginning the little corner apothecary was the Brunswick Apotheke, owned by a German whose name has been lost with the first store records. After thirty years or so the shop was owned by two men named Englehardt and Huber, then by John Kiehl who worked for them. Forty years ago Irving A. Morse took it over.

Mr. Morse has kept some of the old relics—the Eastman Capsule Roller, battered wrought-iron pestles and mortars, the old Seth Thomas clock with the authoritative tick. He still owns some of the hollow wooden balls, which, filled with hot water, were used for hot body massage and as hot-water bottles. You couldn't buy one today.

But the fascination now lies in the conjure herbs. A big seller, openly displayed, is High John the Conqueror, which is merely jalap, a dark, warty root intended as purgative. Superstitious folk carry it in a bag around the neck or in a pocket as a love charm.

Adam-and-Eve root is another love drug carried on the person. Actually it is only Aplectrum Hyemale, a specific for bronchial trouble. Low John the Conqueror, curiously, is a root intended for the same general use as High John, except that women prefer Low John and men go for High John.

The shop sells a lot of Attraction Oil and Attraction Powder. Both are made of calamus. You drop the powder form on the man or woman you yearn for. You rub the oil behind your ears or on secret places and that's supposed to make you irresistible.

Dragon's Blood is an ancient flower exudation that dries into a stick and comes cased like sausage. It is used in printing, but the customers who buy at Mr. Morse's carry it to excite them to great love feats. In medicine it is an antiasthmatic, Draconis Sanguis. Mr. Morse gets his supply from British Malaya.

Among the 3,000-odd items in the shop's listings are Life Everlasting, Holy Oil, Purity Oil, Commanding Oil (supposed to make the meek strong), Wife Oil. An important item is the common lodestone, sold at $2 a pound or 35 cents an ounce. It has magnetic properties. The superstitious believe it attracts affection.

Most of the oils are simply perfumes. Love oil, for example, is merely a mixture of rose and bergamot, but superstitious folk ascribe great magic to it, even as they do to Charm Oil which is a mixture of jasmine and heliotrope. Lovage, or Snake Charm Root, is a stimulant aromatic. Swains swear by it.

Ginseng is bought mostly by Chinese customers for all kinds of healing and as a charm, too. They simply walk in and ask for "Make Happy Flower" and Mr. Morse or one of his assistants knows what to serve.

The shop sells a lot of licorice twig these days. Men and women chew it in effort to break the smoking habit. Others chew galango, another root. There's big demand among older folks for Sioux Indian Herb Powder and Sioux Herb Tea. Mr. Morse is clear out of eye stones —flat beach pebbles for clearing foreign particles from the eye—but customers buy "eye seed"—that's flaxseed—to serve the same purpose.

The shop isn't too far from Gramercy and Stuyvesant Parks. Through generations it has served wealthy families in the district and still does. Its books carry the names of Tammany Leader Charles Murphy, of famous jurists, and barristers and Wall Street brokers, but much of that clientele has fallen away.

Mr. Morse says you'd be astonished, though, how many old families still secretly send for raw herbs —for Pale Rose Buds for sachets, for Iceland moss to replace salt in the diet, for powdered kelp, which is salty, too, but free of sodium. There is still heavy sale of lavender flower, of quince seed for hand lotion, of frankincense and myrrh.

Mr. Morse goes to a jar filled with yellowish crystallized powder. He says, "Taste this," and you do and it's wondrous sweet. "That's manna," the apothecary confides. "Old as time. People sugar laxative with it—manna and senna and prunes. It's the manna of Scriptures. Still a good seller."

You stand in Third Avenue again. A jet whistles high overhead, invisible against a starry night. Manna and Luniks. It's a bit bewildering.

January 12, 1959

¶ On weekdays from dawn through early afternoon Piers 27, 28 and 29 on the Hudson River are heavily citrus-scented. Stacked crates of oranges, lemons, grapefruit, tangerines are set out in endless rows in the dark sheds—all that a city of 8,000,000 souls eats.

Every weekday the produce goes under the hammer to chain-store men, hotel buyers, purveyors, brokers and independent dealers. Only they seem to understand the oral outpour as auctioneers' voices, tremendously amplified, call the offerings and ask for bids.

The syllables echo in the rafters, flee down the long corridors, ricochet off the concrete and glass walls. When you get multitudinous echo mixed with auctioneer doubletalk at 450 words a minute, it is pure Babel. You wonder how the buyers get any of it, but they do.

Bidders' gestures are almost as puzzling. Unless you are trained for it as auctioneers are, you don't see it. A finger is lifted, an eye winks, a head nods—but rarely—and the clerks ranged either side of the auctioneer's microphone scribble like fury. How they unscramble it all in the uproar even they don't seem to know. They shrug. They say, "You just get used to it."

Buyers' garb is widely varied. The hotel men seem to be the neatest and most formally dressed, though even that isn't always true. Sometimes a hotel bid goes through a fellow dressed like a waterfront larrikin, sweatered against the cold with a battered hat at rakish tilt and scowling behind a frayed cigar end.

Sometimes buyers rush out of the bare, harsh-walled auction chambers in panting flight. You follow down the corridor and into another cavernous room, much like the auction shed. The twenty-five telephones set along the walls are leased by Vincent Varvaro. He rents them by the month to buyers.

They use the lines to check orders, to relay price trends of the day, to ask around town how much stock customers might take on when the quotations are favorable. It is all clamorous and confusing. You wander through it as through a nightmare. There is system and order in it, but you'd never think so just from sight and sound.

Around 6 o'clock in the morning the buyers start entering the frigid sheds. The crated fruit is stacked by brand and by grade. The buyers scatter, reading from catalogues printed only a few hours before, as newspapers are. Some of the largest fruit auctioneers, like Brown & Seccomb, maintain their own catalogue printing plants.

Brown & Seccomb, incidentally, is the oldest firm in the fruit auctioneering trade. Its first office, opened in 1798, stood next door to the Tontine Coffee House at Pearl and Wall Streets. The men who started the firm were keen Yankees who came down from New Bedford, originally to sell sperm oil and candles for New England whalers.

Pretty soon the Yankee traders were deep in the shipping business. They paid sharp-eyed young men to stand-to with telescopes on waterfront State Street's rooftops to give the earliest possible reports on homing vessels, so they could spread notice of auction. The spotters were called "the Daybreak Boys." In that time, cargoes were auctioned right on ships' decks.

When British blockades kept out cargoes from overseas they ran raw cotton up from the South and auctioned that. When the Erie Canal opened in 1825 their ships raced down the Hudson with fruits from the north and the west to be in first for top auction prices.

In the Eighteen Thirties almost all citrus came from Mediterranean ports. Brown & Seccomb got on the edge on that trade. It sold the first oranges from Sicily in 1832. Thirty years later it handled a tremendous inpouring of domestic fruits, mainly peaches and apples.

Sixty years ago the firm rented seven acres on the three Hudson River piers to handle produce floated across the river from New Jersey rail terminals. Much of it still comes in that way, but refrigerated trucks, ships and fast planes run the cargo, too, in the new age.

It wasn't until thirty-five years ago that Brown & Seccomb started to bring green tomatoes up from Mexico and Florida to ripen in Manhattan. They built a special tomato auction theatre at 206 Franklin Street just for tomato sales. They don't own it any more; another tomato man does, but off-Broadway producers may get it eventually.

Rumors that 206 Franklin might become a real theatre seem to amuse the burly fruit people along the waterfront. They say, "Actors and tomatoes—boy, that's asking for trouble."

January 14, 1959

⁋ A dark, brown-shingled Dutch cottage broods in a little hollow hemmed by winter-blackened trees, bushes and tall weeds at Clarendon Road and East Fifty-ninth Street in Brooklyn's Flatlands district. It lies just off an ancient Canarsie Indian trail that even now is deeply rutted and gemmed with ice pockets.

James A. Kelly, deputy Kings County Clerk and borough historian, is certain that the cottage is the oldest inhabited dwelling in the United States. He says it was the first house built on Long Island by white men; that from the outside it looks today pretty much as it must have looked when it was assembled of oaken timbers in 1637.

The land on which the house stands was the Canarsies' maize region. They called it Kekschauge. Director General of New Netherland (Manhattan) Wouter Van Twiller bought it for himself, as he had Governors Island and Wards Island. Later, the West India Company, his bosses, took all three places from him.

Van Twiller put two husbandmen on the place—Elbert Elbertson and a peasant named Spicer. Jamaica Bay inlets surrounded the place and there were great deposits of shellfish. The Canarsies used it as their chief mint. They produced the best wampum on the East Coast there; wampum that even the Dutch used in trading.

For many generations, though, the old cottage has been called the Wyckoff House. It got that name from Pieter Claesen van Nordingen. He was bouwerie (farm) superintendent and Keeper of the Kine there for Director General Peter Stuyvesant, who owned the acreage and the cottage after the West India Company took it from land-greedy Van Twiller.

Pieter came out of Nordingen to Fort Orange (Albany) when he was only 12 years old. For seven years he was a laborer on the Fort Orange farm of Killian van Rensselaer, the patroon. When his time was up in 1644 he took to wife Grietje Van Ness, a brewer's daughter at Fort Orange. They raised six sons and four daughters in the cottage.

As grumpy Petrus Stuyvesant's man on the farm, Pieter swung a lot of weight. He was the local wyk-hof—town magistrate—for several terms and, after Stuyvesant's time, took over the acreage for himself. He founded the Flatlands Reformed Church; was the original patentee when Flatlands (which had been Amersfoort under the Dutch) became an English settlement in 1667.

The British wanted Dutch subjects to take English surnames and Pieter obliged. When he died on June 30, 1694, he was Peter Wyckoff. He had merely changed his old Dutch title, magistrate (or wyk-hof), for the purpose, with modified spelling. He left the house to his widow and his sons and Wyckoffs held title to it for 260 years, down to 1901, when they sold it.

Thirty-three years ago it was still farmland. Then William and Stella Aliferis, both originally of Sparta in Greece, took title. Street and sewer improvement projects threatened the place several times but Mr. Kelly and the Wyckoff Family Association persuaded the City Fathers to save it.

Flatlands farmers were using it as a barn when the Aliferis bought it, but the new owners emptied it of rubbish, closed up the giant stone fireplaces and Dutch ovens; papered the old oak timber walls and a few years ago stuck a television aerial on the roof. They put in heat, too.

William Aliferis, incidentally, thinks he was the first man to bake an ice-cream cone. That was his business fifty years ago. He raised two sons and three daughters in the old house. He had to cut down a giant walnut tree when it was blighted, but he planted apple and pear trees and grape vines that still flourish.

The Wyckoff Family Association pays the old house an annual visit, coming sometimes in a full two busloads. The widow of the late Robert Young, head of the New York Central Railroad, came calling, too, and tried to buy the cottage but the Aliferis wouldn't sell. Mrs. Young, they say, was a Wyckoff. Groups of Brooklyn schoolchildren come to stare and take pictures.

One time, Father Aliferis remembers, a little white-haired lady tapped timidly at the door. She told him she was 92 years old. When she was born in the cottage a bay inlet came right to the door. "The old lady has tears down her cheeks," Mr. Aliferis recalls. "She looks on everything, and she cries. She says, 'Be good to this old house.

It has much history,' and we are good to it. We keep it nice."

January 16, 1959

¶ Young matrons of the Junior League of Stamford in Connecticut have put together, after more than a full year's toil, a guidebook of day trips for children in the New York-Connecticut-New Jersey area.

They took the data from two sources—from Mrs. Ruth McAneny Loud's "New York, New York: Knickerbocker Holiday," printed in 1945, and from a work produced a few years ago by the Junior League in Evanston, Ill. Both suggest to parents one-day journeys with children.

The Stamford Junior Leaguers divided the work. They sent mothers out along suggested routes with orders to study child reaction, to take notes on time spent, on prices, on available eating spots and homely facilities of one kind or another.

The mother-reporters worked on various kinds of trips—nature studies, the arts, sports, foreign flavor, business and industry tours, hobby shops and on historic sites. No trip got into the book if it took more than a full day.

Special trips were arranged for groups that included toddlers. Sharp eye was kept for journeys that yielded "treasure" in the form of free booklets, postcards, free samples or other souvenirs. Special holiday junkets were worked out. So were behind-the-scenes visits to local industries and to municipal departments.

Specialty stores—butterfly shops, shell and shore establishments, mineralogical stores and the like—were listed. So were exhibition halls, broadcasting stations, ocean liners, airports, candy factories, bakeries, ice cream plants, dairy farms. Free trips are in the listing. So are places that charge admission.

The book sells for $1. The mail-order address is: Junior League of Stamford, 35 Scofieldtown Road, Stamford, Conn.

MARGINALIA: ¶ A painted sign of the Gold Dust Twins, five stories high, holds out bravely against sun and storm on a house wall in Eighteenth Street between First and Second Avenues. The twins' grins stay wide and infectious; their ballet skirts are still faintly pink. Sight of the sign carries the middle-aged back to the early Nineteen Hundreds. . . .

January 19, 1959

¶ It occurred the other day to Harry W. Levy, a retired city engineer, that the city's millions know little or nothing about the ground on which they tread all their lives.

He said: "They know street backdrops—building façades, light poles, traffic signs—but hardly ever seem conscious of pavement, curbs and sidewalks."

Mr. Levy got to thinking about this, it seems, when he heard that John Godfrey, who had charge of street repair for the Manhattan Borough President's office for thirty years, had just retired.

Mr. Godfrey, his associates knew, was a dedicated man; he loved Manhattan's pavement and sidewalks. He always preached a kind of sidewalk gospel; kept pleading that American cities should put greater stress on the esthetics of paving and on uniform sidewalks. However, he didn't make much headway with indoctrinating city officials and property owners.

Under municipal law, property owners are supposed to keep their sidewalks safe for pedestrians. Nothing in the law says they have to keep them neat and uniform. A good inspector can go out any day and write up thousands of violations, but in most cases when property owners get repair notices they just do botchy repair jobs.

When owners plead that they can't arrange for repair and have no skill at it themselves the city makes up charts of areas where work has accumulated and lets it out, by bid, to contractors. The city pays these bills but collects by assessment against the properties involved.

Mr. Godfrey and the Borough President of Manhattan got out a pocket-sized gospel on sidewalks twenty years ago, telling all about sidewalks and how to maintain them and keep them uniform and neat. It helped a little but not enough, and sidewalk care languished.

Mr. Levy can, and sometimes does, get lyrical about the sidewalks of New York. He likes to tell people that the old type of sidewalk of Hudson River bluestone, a pleasant blue-gray material, was laid down by nature millions of years ago. It was guaranteed to withstand centuries of pedestrian hurry and scurry.

When Portland cement started to replace the bluestone because it was easier to transport and lay (bluestone called for hand-cutting) the city's walks lost their uniform look. Different property owners mixed different coloring into the new cement types; they didn't all use the same sand and that brought variations in texture. Patching made matters worse.

Mr. Levy thinks that architects should give more attention to sidewalks, if only to add to the attractiveness of the buildings they design. He has suggested that awards be offered for better-looking sidewalks. He has suggested the same thing to the New York Chapter of the American Association of Architects.

Modern city children probably don't do it any more, but fifty or sixty years ago the New York urchin, heading down or upstreet in no particular hurry, was careful to step on every sidewalk crack. The belief was that to step on a crack was to break the devil's dishes.

January 21, 1959

❡ For more than forty years the gentlemen of the Amateur Comedy Club, Inc., have rehearsed their shows in two century-old brick stables in Sniffen Court, off East Thirty-sixth Street.

They are at work these January nights on "Small War on Murray Hill," a neighborhood piece. It will be their 857th offering since

the club was started in April, 1884. The play will be presented to a private audience, as all the club's performances are. Club tradition calls for formal garb.

The Sniffen Court players are the second oldest group of amateur actors in the United States. Only the Footlights Club, started in Boston in 1877, is older.

Seventy-five years ago, the best-known amateur troupe in town was Mrs. James Brown Potter's Madison Square Dramatic Organization. It drew its membership from the so-called "400" and was inclined to excessive eye-rolling and hand-wringing in almost all its shows. That characteristic might have been attributed more or less to its professional director, a young man imbalanced on the side of bathos. He was David Belasco.

A small group of young blades in Mrs. Potter's troupe, sickened by endless weepers, broke away in mid-April in 1884 and started the Amateur Comedy Club. They swore to give only comedies, to limit membership to thirty males and to perform only for charities. All were of prominent families— Alexander T. Mason, Robert Sturgis, James B. Ludlow, S. B. P. Trowbridge, Edward McI. Whitney, Hoffman Miller. No women were to be admitted.

The group had no theatre of its own as Mrs. Potter had. It gave its first performance, "One Too Many for Him," in the German Club Rooms in Stapleton, S. I. Sometimes they permitted recitations and sometimes they staged banjo concerts. It was not until 1896 that the troupe appeared in a real theatre. It rented Carnegie Lyceum that year for its shows.

It has gone to other cities, but only rarely—to Pittsburgh, Utica, towns in New Jersey, to Veterans Hospitals in wartime and to the Military Academy at West Point.

Most of the shows in the beginning were one-act bits and many still are. The first full-length performance, "A Scrap of Paper," was staged in Berkeley Lyceum in 1888. The curtain was held a full half-hour for that one because some zealous policeman decided the club's license permitted only charity exhibitions. A member galloped by hansom to the Police Commissioner's home, wrote a check "to any charity" for $100, and the show went on.

The Sniffen Court stables, two of ten built by Old Knickerbocker families of Murray Hill, were bought by the club in 1918. They were done over, but heavy rafter beams still show and the gray-painted brick outside still betrays stable lines and stable doors, which are now fire exits. The place has its own kitchens, a luxurious Green Room, rare prints and books on the theatre and a wide work space in which the members make their own stage sets, props and lighting boards. They hire costumes.

Young women from old New York families have always been brought in for female roles. Some have gone on, eventually, to the professional theatre—Hope Williams, Kay Emery, Mildred Dunnock, Elsie De Wolf, Julie Harris, Clare Booth Luce. Club membership, still all male, is up to 100 now, with annual dues $100. There are 250 associate members.

Distaff kin of the Sniffen Court players formed the Snarks fifty years ago. When they had their fiftieth anniversary dinner in the Plaza last week the Sniffen Court troupe were guests.

The oldest living member is Norman F. Cushman of Lower Fifth Avenue. He joined sixty years ago. Steinways of the piano-building family have been in it almost from the start. The late Theodore Steinway met his bride, Miss Ruth Davis of Murray Hill, at one of the group's shows.

The club has performed a lot of firsts—Lord Dunsany's "Gods of the Mountain," with Lord Dunsany as guest; Robert Sherwood's "Acropolis" with sets, props and costumes shipped over from London. Otis Skinner brought over Pirandello's "Legal Title" in 1924. The club's first serious play, incidentally, was "The Ghost of Jerry Bundler," staged in 1908.

The blue-stocking players delight in manual chores incidental to their shows. They slave as stage hands, toil at carpentry, climb about painting their sets. After each show, the players drive back to Sniffen Court to watch a burlesque of the night's performance, written and rehearsed by the stage hands. That's tradition, too.

January 23, 1959

❡ Last Friday a welfare worker led a slender, pale old man into the old Straus mansion at 9 East Seventy-first Street. Franciscan nuns run the Eye, Ear, Nose and Throat Division of St. Clare's Hospital there.

The old man was blind. His clothes were shabby. His sunken cheeks were stubble-covered. He tried to sit on the elevator floor as it lifted to the second floor. In dimly lighted Room 203, to which he was assigned, he tried to sit on the floor again.

The welfare woman said: "He has lived a long time in Bowery flophouses. When there are no seats in flophouses, the men sit on the floor."

The old man was shaved, bathed and put into pajamas. He gave his history as though through a veil. His memory failed now and then. He said he was Laurence Stroetz, born in Fifth Street between Avenues A and B on Aug. 10, 1877, when the lower East Side was mainly German.

His father was Frank Stroetz, who played cornet for Squadron A of the old National Guard in the Seventies. The family had a grocer's shop at 165 Second Street. He could remember some of his brothers and sisters—Frank, Hannah, Barbara, Madeline, Annie, Mary.

"All gone, now?" he was asked, and he nodded. The listeners were conscious of mental groping behind the sightless, cataract-covered eyes that might once have been blue. He said, "My wife was Maud Baker." He repeated, "Maud Baker."

"She gone?" He nodded.

"No children?" He said, "No children."

By last Monday the old man had mellowed under the kindly treatment of the dark-clad Franciscan sisters and the white-clad nuns who are nurses. He told of life on the East Side in his boyhood, of how he had taken violin lessons there and of playing in his twenties with professional orchestras.

He said he had been two years with Victor Herbert in the Pittsburgh Symphony Orchestra; with the orchestra in the old Academy of Music in Fourteenth Street next to Tony Pastor's. He told of playing in the Savoy and in the Lyceum when Billie Burke was in "Mrs. Dot," long, long ago. He snatched each memory from the past with difficulty.

He kept talking about Charlie, who had been his guide and companion in one Bowery flophouse or another the last thirty years. He said: "When my eyes began to go, Charlie was my boss in a restaurant in Radio City. I had a broom and a pan. I picked up cigarette butts and napkins. Charlie had his own office."

It took a long time before the old man could better identify Charlie: "He slept in the Majestic, same as me, and in the Alabama." Those are Bowery lodging houses. "He brought my coffee. Charlie was good to me." Then he remembered Charlie's last name:

"Charlie was a Frenchman. He pawned my old violin for me. I used to play in the Hotel Oriental in Coney Island. I played in Beethoven Hall and in the Liederkranz. Charlie Messier—he was a good pianist. He led the boys' choir in the old Mariners' Temple when

Dr. Hubbell was there. I played in the Church of The Land and Sea. Mrs. Morris was organist."

The mental scraps had to be snatched before they fled. At 82 they don't stay put, the old man said. A few times he fell asleep. His head fell to his chest and his white lion's mane—he looks like Franz Liszt—caught feeble light that came through the hospital window.

Nurse Josephine Wynne spoke with Sister Pauline Marie. They remembered that Sister Francis Marie had in her room the old Biotte violin that had belonged to her sister, the nun Sister Anthony Marie. Sister Anthony Marie died in St. Clare's three years ago. Cardinal Spellman had found the instrument for her in Rome more than thirty years ago.

The staff talked with Sister Mary Fintan, who has charge of the hospital. With her consent they brought the old violin to Room 203. It had not been played for years, but Laurence Stroetz groped for it. His long white fingers stroked it. He tuned it, with some effort, and tightened the old bow. He lifted it to his chin and the lion's mane came down.

It was 8 o'clock. Dinner was over. Room 203 was all but dark. Only diffused light filtered in from the silent corridor through the partly open door. The old man had told the nuns he had not played since Charlie had pawned his violin, but the pale fingers rippled up and down the strings as he sought touch.

He played "Sidewalks of New York," true, but quavery. The fingering was stronger in Handel's "Largo," in "Humoresque" and "The Blue Danube." Before each number the old man mumbled the composer's name and hummed opening bars to recapture lost melody. The nuns, the patients and the nurses were silent.

An audience assembled in the tiled corridor as the strains quivered and hung in the quiet, as they fled in thin echo. Laurence Stroetz murmured another tune, barely heard by the nuns and the nurses. Then he played it, clear and steady. It was Gounod's "Ave Maria."

Black-clad and white-clad nuns moved lips in silent prayer. They choked up. The long years on the Bowery had not stolen Laurence Stroetz's touch. Blindness made his fingers stumble down to the violin bridge, but they recovered. The music died and the audience pattered applause. The old violinist bowed and his sunken cheeks creased in a smile.

Next week eye surgeons at St. Clare's will try to remove the cataracts. If they do, the Welfare Department will try to place the old violinist in a nursing home to get him off the Bowery. If someone would offer a violin that he could call his own again, he would know ecstasy.

"It would make me feel good," he told the sisters. "It would be wonderful."

January 26, 1959

¶ Eight violins were offered the other day to Laurence Stroetz, the

82-year-old, cataract-blinded violinist who was taken to St. Clare's Hospital in East Seventy-first Street from a Bowery flophouse. The offers came from men and women who had read that though he had once played with the Pittsburgh Symphony Orchestra, he had been without a violin for more than thirty years.

The first instrument to reach the hospital was a gift from the Light-house, the institution for the sightless. It was delivered by a blind man. A nun took it to the octogenarian.

He played it a while, tenderly and softly, then gave it back. He said: "This is a fine old violin. Tell the owner to take good care of it." The white-clad nun said: "It is your violin, Mr. Stroetz. It is a gift." The old man bent his head over it. He wept.

ABOUT THE AUTHOR

MEYER BERGER, for thirty years a reporter and columnist for the New York *Times*, was born on Manhattan's Lower East Side on September 1, 1898. He knew bitter poverty in his early years; at thirteen he left school for a job with the New York *World*. In 1917, rejected for military service because of bad eyesight, he memorized the eye chart, passed the examination, and went to France as an Infantry sergeant, where he earned the Purple Heart and the Silver Star.

On his return, Mike Berger became a police reporter for the *World*, then top rewrite man for the old Standard News Association in Brooklyn. In March, 1928, he came to the *Times*, where he remained, except for one year spent as a writer on *The New Yorker*, until his death on February 8, 1959. During World War II, again he tried to be part of the big show; this time ill health forced his return from London after two months as a war correspondent, although in 1945 he went overseas again, touring Europe and North Africa.

His stories of the trial of Al Capone in Chicago for income-tax evasion were nominated for a Pulitzer Prize in 1932. Eighteen years later, he won a Pulitzer Prize for his reporting of the shooting of thirteen persons by an insane veteran in Camden, New Jersey. His account of the first soldier dead to be brought back from Europe after World War II is a classic. All of his work had the touch of a great human being and a great reporter that made him one of the best-loved newspapermen of his day.

Above all, Mike Berger was an incurable New Yorker who spent even his days off roaming the city, collecting anecdotes. Thus, his column, "About New York," which appeared in the *Times* for a time in 1939-40, and was reinstituted in April, 1953. Thus, his official *The Story of The New York Times, 1851-1951*, published in 1951, was told, in the Berger manner, in anecdotes of the people who get out the paper. His other books include *The Eight Million; City on Many Waters;* and *Men of Maryknoll*, written with the Reverend James Keller.